More praise for
The Task of Criticism

"The rediscovery of American pragmatism is followed, at last, by the recovery of American idealism. Miller and his teacher Hocking are original thinkers whom we neglect at our peril. This book offers a marvelously rich introduction to Miller's life work, providing all the evidence needed to demonstrate that he is a philosophical figure of great distinction and direct contemporary relevance."
—John Lachs, Centennial Professor of Philosophy, Vanderbilt University, and author of *The Relevance of Philosophy for Life*

"*The Task of Criticism* is a work of major significance that combines the insights of three excellent scholars with the philosophical corpus of a philosopher whose originality and importance have long been overlooked."
—Herman J. Saatkamp Jr., president of Richard Stockton State College, founding and senior consulting editor of *The Works of George Santayana*

"This book is a valuable introduction to the philosophy of John William Miller and should also interest people who are already familiar with his work. A number of the selections have not previously appeared in print, and, in addition to expanding on ideas dealt with in earlier publications, some of them cover topics Miller did not discuss elsewhere. Of special importance is his treatment of the nature and function of philosophy. The editors' introductions to the volume and to the individual essays clarify and provide new insights into Miller's complex, subtle, and highly original thought."
—Beth J. Singer, professor of philosophy emeritus, Brooklyn College, and author of *Pragmatism, Rights, and Democracy*

The Task of
CRITICISM

Also by John William Miller

The Paradox of Cause and Other Essays

The Definition of the Thing with Some Notes on Language

The Philosophy of History with Reflections and Aphorisms

The Midworld of Symbols and Functioning Objects

In Defense of the Psychological

The Task of
CRITICISM

ESSAYS ON PHILOSOPHY,
HISTORY, AND COMMUNITY

John William Miller

*Edited, with an Introduction
to Miller's Philosophy, by*

Joseph P. Fell
Vincent Colapietro
Michael J. McGandy

 W. W. Norton & Company
New York   London

For information about permission to reproduce selections from this book, write to
Permissions, W. W. Norton & Company, Inc., 500 Fifth Avenue, New York, NY 10110

Manufacturing by The Haddon Craftsmen, Inc.
Book design by Anna Oler
Production manager: Amanda Morrison

Library of Congress Cataloging-in-Publication Data

Miller, John William.
The task of criticism : essays on philosophy, history, and community /
by John William Miller ; cditcd, with an introduction to Miller's philosophy,
by Joseph P. Fell, Vincent Colapietro, and Michael J. McGandy.—1st ed.
p. cm.
Includes bibliographical references (p.   ) and index.
ISBN 0-393-32733-7 (pbk.)
1. Philosophy. I. Fell, Joseph P. II. Colapietro, Vincent Michael, 1950–
III. McGandy, Michael J. IV. Title.
B945.M4761F45 2005
191—dc22
2005005616

W. W. Norton & Company, Inc., 500 Fifth Avenue, New York, N.Y. 10110
www.wwnorton.com

W. W. Norton & Company Ltd., Castle House, 75/76 Wells Street, London W1T 3QT

1 2 3 4 5 6 7 8 9 0

Contents

Preface

We have joined forces to design an introduction to the thought of John William Miller (1895–1978), an American philosopher whose importance we regard as out of all proportion to present awareness of him. We are, in effect, three generations of his students. Joseph P. Fell was a student of Miller's at Williams College from 1950 to 1953 and subsequently a professor of philosophy at Bucknell University from 1963 to 1993. He edited *The Philosophy of John William Miller* (1990) and has since 1995 been chairman of the John William Miller Fellowship Fund at Williams College. Vincent Colapietro, presently Professor of Philosophy at The Pennsylvania State University, was the recipient of a Miller Fellowship and is the author of *Fateful Shapes of Human Freedom: John William Miller and the Crises of Modernity* (2003). Michael J. McGandy, an independent scholar, also received a Miller Fellowship and wrote his doctoral dissertation on Miller under the direction of Professor Colapietro at Fordham University. He has a book drawn from his dissertation, *The Active Life: Miller's Metaphysics of Democracy* (2005).

All three of us are indebted to an earlier, fourth, generation student of Miller's, George P. Brockway. Brockway studied with Miller at Williams College from 1933 to 1936, and was founder in 1984 and first chairman of the Miller Fellowship Fund. As executor of Miller's literary estate, Brockway organized and deposited the extensive papers of Miller in the archives of the Williams College Library and edited five volumes of Miller's papers published by W. W. Norton & Company. The first of these volumes appeared only months prior to Miller's death in 1978, while the remaining four volumes were posthumously published from 1979 to 1983. Brockway was an editor, then CEO, of Norton, as well as an economist whose chief publications were *Economics: What Went Wrong and Why, and Some Things to Do About It* (1985) and *The End of Economic Man* (1991), which is now in its fourth edition.

In editing Miller's writings it was never Brockway's intention to produce an *introduction* to Miller's philosophy. Brockway sought to produce topical volumes in each of which Miller's essays cluster around a principal concern, such as the philosophy of history. Brockway provided no background for the essays, taking the view that it was best to let Miller speak entirely for himself. His own understanding of Miller's philosophy stood on the firm ground of over forty years of discussion and correspondence with Miller. In the years since the publication of the five volumes of Miller's essays, both we and Brockway came to a fuller realization that the combination of the revolutionary challenge of Miller's central ideas and the unusually simple, even charming, style in which Miller sought to convey these novel ideas made him less than easy to understand.

In assembling a new, sixth volume of Miller's writings, we therefore decided to design it specifically as an introduction to his philosophy. We asked ourselves what sort of volume would best help the reader approaching Miller for the first time. Such a volume would begin with a general introduction to Miller's philosophy. Further, unlike the preceding five volumes, it would feature essays by Miller representing the whole of his philosophy rather than just one or more specific aspects of that philosophy. Our volume would also depart from the earlier volumes in not limiting itself to the publication of hitherto-unpublished writings. Rather, it would present a number of the very best of Miller's essays, which Brockway had earlier selected and published as optimally representing the particular aspects of Miller's philosophy covered by those volumes, or which Brockway or one of the younger scholars working in the Miller archives had picked out for publication in journals, or, in one case, which appeared as the afterword in a Norton edition of José Ortega y Gasset's *History as a System*. On the other hand, our volume could not be simply a "best of" reproduction of already-published essays, for even all of the already-published essays taken together do not cover everything essential in Miller's philosophy. With the exception of Miller's Harvard dissertation *The Definition of the Thing* (1922), Brockway did not publish much of Miller's early work. In particular, he did not include writings specifically devoted to working out a basic conception of philosophy itself—its genealogical character, its supplanting of both dogmatism and skepticism, and its conception of criticism as *the* philosophical function.

Part 1 of our volume is thus devoted to Miller's conception of philosophy, and it is mainly this part of the book that offers a number of hitherto-unpublished essays. As in Parts 2 and 3, each essay in Part 1 is preceded by a brief introduction. These introductions can be seen as supplementing the volume's general introduction by alerting the reader to specific features of the essay at hand and to the relation of this essay to others in this volume, in the preceding five volumes, or in the Miller archives. The Part 1 introductions are by Joseph Fell, who also wrote the general introduction; those of Part 2 are by Vincent Colapietro; and those of Part 3 are by Michael McGandy.

Part 2 centers on Miller's primary achievement—his own striking contribution to the genealogical and critical process of revision he finds formative of history as such and of the history of philosophy. This contribution is his discovery and description of a *midworld* that is disclosive of both oneself and one's world, and can be disclosive of both only because it is a functional *union* of self and environment. Because this is where Miller critically revises his philosophical inheritance, where his attempt at reorientation is at a maximum, there is perhaps here the maximum danger of the reader's disorientation. So in Part 2 the need for and potential help of introductions and notes to Miller's essays is at a maximum.

Part 3 brings to the fore a vital descriptive and prescriptive implication of Miller's historical, genealogical, and critical emphases, together with his claim for the constitutive role of inherited and shared language in human acts. This implication is the *essentially* communitarian character of human experience and action. In its deepest sense, community is not something individuals enter into or withdraw from. There is no simple precedence of individual agents over community, or of community over individual agents. The relation between the individual and the community is dialectical or correlative. It is on the basis of this critically revised description of an interdependence of self and community that Miller is able to make sense of moral experience and argue for a democratic political philosophy.

Notes on Miller's essays will be found immediately following the essays. Miller was very sparing in his resort to notes. Unless a note is specifically identified as Miller's own, it is the work of the editor who wrote the introductions for the essays in that part of the volume.

Works by Miller or about him can be found in a bibliography at the end of the volume. Bibliographical information on other works cited is given either in the notes for chapters or in the final, "source" paragraphs of our introductions.

Citations from and references to Miller's manuscripts locate them by box and folder numbers in "Miller Papers," the central repository of Miller's writings in the Williamsiana Collection of the College Archives in Stetson Hall, Williams College.

In addition to our indebtedness to George Brockway, we have learned from other students of Miller—above all Robert Elias, Robert Gahringer, Edward A. Hoyt, Gary Stahl, and Cushing Strout—as well as from Miller's sons Eugene and Paul, from Miller's one-time colleague Henry Johnstone, and from the pioneering work of the first Miller Fellow, Stephen Tyman. We also want to acknowledge the gracious help on many occasions of Sylvia Kennick Brown, Archivist of Williams College.

Joseph P. Fell
Vincent Colapietro
Michael J. McGandy

The Task of
CRITICISM

Introduction

This volume is designed as an introduction to the philosophy of John William Miller (1895–1978), primarily through a representative selection of his own essays. For reasons outlined below, Miller's philosophy has been slow in gaining recognition. We shall try here to give a sense of what is there to be recognized.

For the moment, by way of forecast, we can say that Miller wrote an original and sorely needed new chapter in the history of modern philosophy and thereby in American philosophy. Most broadly, it has the character of a philosophy of history. More specifically, it is premised on Miller's addition of two new categories to traditional lists of categories, and its greatest achievement is what Miller calls the *midworld* of symbols and functioning objects, a powerful but difficult revision in both ontology and epistemology. It needs to be said straight out: Miller is difficult, and he is powerful *because* he is difficult. He sees that a successful assault on the long-standing, long-challenged, yet never resolved dualism of modern philosophy requires a drastic revision. Drastic revisions challenge inherited habits of thought and so demand rehabituation. Immanuel Kant demands such rehabituation when he calls his epistemological shift *Copernican*. Miller can be said to have affirmed that Copernican revolution while insisting that Kant did not push it far enough. That revolution made Kant difficult, and pushing it further makes Miller difficult.

We cannot gauge the importance of philosophies by the speed with which they become recognized. Recognition that comes quickly is likely to recede quickly. A new work that is easy to understand is not likely to be of major significance, for such significance belongs to works that transcend what has already been understood. We might almost say that the initial fate of a great contribution to philosophy is that it be ignored or misunderstood. Kant certainly realized this. In the year in which he published his *Critique of Pure Reason*, whose initial reception was poor, he wrote to his friend Marcus Herz: "One cannot expect a way of thinking to be suddenly led off the beaten track into one that has heretofore been totally unused. That requires time, to stay that style of thinking little by little in its previous path and, finally, to turn it into the opposite direction by means of gradual impressions."[1]

I

John William Miller taught philosophy in Williams College from 1924 to 1960. For the last fifteen of those years, he was Mark Hopkins Professor of Intellectual and Moral Philosophy, a chair he inherited from his distinguished predecessor James Bissett Pratt. Miller had a deep influence on generations of students. A vivid and accurate account of Miller's teaching, offered by George P. Brockway, can be found in *Masters: Portraits of Great Teachers*.[2]

Miller's career was amply justified by his classroom teaching. Prior to the last year of his long life, he had published only four essays. It seemed an evident case of a man whose wholehearted devotion to teaching had precluded reams of publications, even if his teaching gave evidence of a great learning and a striking originality that warranted publication. Over the years he had in fact written a large number of essays on a variety of interrelated topics. Toward the close of Miller's life, Brockway persuaded him to release some of this material for publication, and the initial volume, *The Paradox of Cause*, appeared in 1978, only months before Miller's death. The second volume, *The Definition of the Thing*, consisting of Miller's 1922 Harvard dissertation plus some later notes on language, appeared in 1980, to be followed by *The Philosophy of History* (1981), *The Midworld of Symbols and Functioning Objects* (1982), and *In Defense of the Psychological* (1983). Brockway served as editor of all these volumes, in some cases able to work from indications left by Miller for ordering the essays, in some cases faced by the sort of difficult organizational decisions that confronted the editors of the papers of Charles Sanders Peirce. The result is an intelligently organized thematic selection. The five volumes comprise a complementary set of variations on a single broad and philosophically basic theme. This theme, the epistemological and ontological unity of persons and things, occupied Miller from first to last. It is no exaggeration to say that Miller's tracing of this unity has profound and pervasive implications not only for epistemology and ontology but for metaphysics, ethics, politics, aesthetics, and virtually every other dimension of human existence.

Why had Miller withheld the bulk of his work from publication? The self-imposed demands of his teaching cannot account for this, for Miller was convinced that he was making an important contribution to post-Hegelian philosophy in general and to American philosophy in particular, and he knew that he had to make his peers aware of that contribution. But, when he did publish or privately share some of his work with his peers, he felt his work largely met with either misunderstanding or indifference. His style of writing may have had something to do with this; his essays were fashioned in a deceptively simple, almost colloquial prose—sometimes reminiscent of Lincoln's and Emerson's, though harder to understand. But the primary reason was that Miller's thinking was even more unfashionable than his prose, and could thus appear as idiosyncratic and estranging. This contrasted with his senior colleague Pratt, who published a good deal and was a member of a movement, Critical Realism. Miller stood alone, and the misunderstanding of him started at home, for Pratt did not understand what Miller was attempting to say.[3]

Miller was in certain respects like his older contemporary, the American composer Charles Ives—a craggy, independent spirit who, while working out of an inherited tradition, significantly departed from his contemporaries' way of building on that tradition. Both were loners whose colloquial yet original efforts are late in gaining recognition. As the premieres of many of Ives's works have occurred since his death, so has the publication of many of Miller's works occurred since his death. Both of them wanted to evoke the American spirit, yet neither of them was mainstream, and each had the strength of will to persevere in his own direction despite its incongruence with the prevailing winds of the times. While recognition of Miller is growing, it is not yet clear whether it will become as widespread as has the recognition of Ives.

How was Miller alone? At a time when others were abandoning philosophical idealism, he sought to revise it. And his revision was drastic, because he saw that the price of conserving idealism had to be steep. Most of Part 1 of this volume is devoted to the early stages of this revision. Though he worked for the whole of his career at fleshing out the revision, its first steps had already been taken in his daringly original dissertation, where he labels his revision "naturalistic idealism"—an apparent oxymoron that suggests the sharp readjustment in mind-set that is going to be required to make sense of the revision. Part of the complication Miller faces is methodological. The revision requires dialectical logic, but to make dialectic a procedure his readers can take seriously requires that Miller overcome not one but three enemies: Karl Marx's materialist reduction of G. W. F. Hegel's dialectic, Søren Kierkegaard's caricature of Hegelian dialectic, and Hegel's own hypostatizing of human logic into a transcendental logic of divinity.

In the course of Miller's career, a fourth enemy, Friedrich Nietzsche, gained prominence. Nietzsche's self-confessed alliance with the Greek Sophists in the skeptical dismantling of the claims of reason undercuts not only Hegel but the entire tradition of *logos* and *scientia* from Plato and Aristotle forward. Nietzsche's claim is not that *he* can destroy this grand tradition, but rather that it is destroying *itself.* Miller himself might seem to confirm this. He was acutely aware that the environment in which he was teaching and writing did not appear to be an intelligible environment—that is, an environment meeting the epistemological conditions for ontological disclosure. (More simply put: It was not an environment in which *knowledge* of entities as they *really* are, as they really relate to each other, seemed possible.) Instead, the environment appeared nihilistically. In a sense, Miller lived in a Nietzschean century, and it can help us to begin to understand and situate Miller to see how his position relates to Nietzsche's.

II

About seven years before Miller was born, Nietzsche wrote: "What I relate is the history of the next two centuries. I describe what is coming, what can no longer come differently: *the advent of nihilism.*"[4] Miller's life thus occupied most of the first of the two centuries that Nietzsche forecast as the era of nihilism, and Miller indeed in a number of places characterized the thought of his time as nihilistic.[5] But this by no means makes Miller a Nietzschean.

Nietzsche defines nihilism as a condition in which "'everything lacks meaning' (the untenability of one interpretation of the world, upon which a tremendous amount of energy has been lavished, awakens the suspicion that all interpretations of the world are false)."[6] Nihilism is, for both Nietzsche and Miller, a condition of radical skepticism in which the grounds for intelligibility and valuation are regarded as unattainable. Nietzsche wrote that "the overall character of existence may not be interpreted by means of the concept of 'aim,' the concept of 'unity,' or the concept of 'truth.' . . . The faith in [these] categories of reason is the cause of nihilism. We have measured the value of the world according to categories *that refer to a purely fictitious world*."[7] In taking this position, Nietzsche (unlike Miller) sides epistemologically with the skepticism of the Greek Sophists and ontologically with the Heraclitean vision of the world as sheer becoming. What Nietzsche does (again unlike Miller) is to reject the entire tradition of reason, being, and truth in Parmenides, Plato, Aristotle, Descartes, Kant, and Hegel as in effect a massive metaphysical escapism directed at deliverance from becoming and finitude; it has been, in Nietzsche's words, a "revenge . . . against time and its 'it was.'"[8]

Here we need to be careful, lest we miss two very important similarities between Nietzsche and Miller. (1) In holding that the philosophical tradition has been "ahistoric," and that it has failed to take *accident* or contingency as a category, Miller joins Nietzsche in calling for an honest, if difficult, embracing of finitude and a rejection of transcendental flights. But Miller takes this as a *revision* of Plato and later proponents of reason, a consequence of a balanced *critical* evaluation that does not dismiss wholesale, but that looks as much for what survives criticism as for what succumbs to it. He saves the aforementioned concepts of *aim, unity,* and *truth* by finding their sole locale to be historical. (2) Nietzsche, like Miller, seeks to get beyond nihilism. Nietzsche sees nihilism as "a pathological transitional stage" in which "we are losing the center of gravity by virtue of which we have lived; we are lost for a while. Abruptly we plunge into the opposite valuations, with all the energy that such an extreme overvaluation of man has generated in man."[9]

What Nietzsche does is to *welcome* nihilism as the occasion for a wholesale rejection not only of Christian theology but of the categories of Platonic philosophy—the categories that govern the operation of *logos* and, in its Latin rendering, *ratio*. These are categories that formally define and guide the basic discourses of philosophy and science all the way into the twentieth century, and that essentially remain at work in the pragmatism of Peirce and Dewey. It is not that they have never been subjected to criticism; it is rather that they have for the most part survived criticism because observance of them is a condition of criticism. This will have to mean, if Miller is right, that these categories are surreptitiously relied on by Nietzsche himself in his massive *criticism* of that very tradition.

While Nietzsche's philosophy is massively critical, in not subscribing to the conditions of criticism it exposes itself to the charge of dogmatism. Nietzsche proposes to supplant nihilism not by a nonabsolutist, strictly *historical* justification of reason but by an allegedly pan-*natural* "will to power." Some of the essays in Part 1 of the present volume show Miller forcefully arguing for the conditions of criticism as the only alternative to a demoralizing skepticism and a polemical dogmatism, both of which are the enemy of truth, of responsible and effective freedom, and of democracy. It is worth noting here that while Miller never suggests that conflict is eliminable from human life, it appears that the resolution of conflicts by arbitration was the original and central moral motivation of Miller's philosophy. The personal trigger of his decision to devote his life to philosophy was his battlefield experience of the First World War in France as a member of an American ambulance corps, Base Hospital 44. (Here one might be reminded of the service of another champion of American democracy, Walt Whitman, as a field nurse during the Civil War.) Miller approached philosophy as an arena devoted to the peaceful resolution of conflict—in contrast to Nietzsche's early attraction to the Heraclitean notion of a cosmic *polemos*. The moral aspect of Miller's thinking, and his philosophy of democratic community, are treated primarily in Part 3 of the present volume.

Nietzsche's thought has had widespread influence, since Miller's death, in poststructuralist French philosophy and beyond, and it can be argued that Miller's philosophy is in this environment more needed than ever. (For a recent critique, within France, of this influence, see the essays in *Why We Are Not Nietzscheans*, edited by Luc Ferry and Alain Renaut.)[10] But Miller's philosophy is also needed on the American scene. As sympathetic as Miller was to the philosophy of pragmatism, he found pragmatism lacking the "new Metaphysics . . . of the American Democracy" that

Walt Whitman had rightly called for.[11] Miller himself speaks of "a meta-physics of democracy."[12] Miller was, like Charles Ives, an "American original," deeply sympathetic with his country but decidedly out of step with recent developments in his chosen field. It is not surprising, then, that Miller's philosophy tended to be greeted with either incomprehension or indifference from his colleagues, to the point where he largely abstained from publication.

Miller stuck to his guns as wave after wave of anti- or post-idealist positions swept the American philosophical scene: critical realism, behaviorism, instrumentalism, logical positivism, linguistic analysis, existentialism, phenomenology. Characteristically, he found reasons for taking all of these stances seriously, yet in the last analysis he found most of them "ahistorical" in orientation, and he found none of them capable of coordinating the human and the natural in a manner that did justice to both. On these points he was insistent.

III

Miller will say, at certain critical junctures, "I don't like" such-and-such an idea. This isn't an intrusion of arbitrary preference into his argument. It's rather a recognition that arguments are made by persons who are themselves at stake in their arguments, and Miller displays an uncanny ability to isolate the often-unspoken personal premises (acts of will) behind the arguments of a number of philosophers and psychologists. He frequently reminds the reader that the objective or natural, an impersonal order, occurs in consequence of a human will or demand or it doesn't occur at all. The "paradox of cause" is that in a world that comprised only natural causation, natural causation could not be disclosed. Subjective purpose and objective nature are mutually implicative; their relation is *dialectical*. To attempt to understand the personal entirely in terms of the impersonal is to rule out of court the very will and understanding that demand a stable and independent environment, thus launching the idea of an impersonal order in the first place. Those, such as B. F. Skinner, who wish to have an ordered environment but discredit free human agency fail to recognize their own inevitable role in disclosing that environment. It is a lapse common even in otherwise-brilliant scientists.

Miller characteristically reaches his own conclusions about the interrelation of human beings and nature by means of probing examinations—both sympathetic and critical—of the major interpretations of the self–world relation that have been generated in the history of philosophy. His two-semester introductory philosophy course was the study of a logical sequence of basic types of philosophy. Miller encouraged his students first to *identify* with the type being studied by seeing what demand it met; you earned the right to *criticize* a type only by first espousing it, living it from the inside out. Each type arises as a *revision* of its immediate predecessor, and the revision marks an indebtedness to that predecessor as well as a progression beyond it. Miller sees each of these types as an essay in "control"—a proposal of a general order (an *infinity* or *form*) in terms of which humans have tried to disclose the nature and interrelation of the particulars (content) of their world. It is only by this will to control (to know, to utilize) our environment that we are able to gain real control (self-knowledge and personal efficacy) over ourselves. Thus, spiritualist and voluntarist philosophies arise out of the demand for a world in which the human act makes a difference (can be regarded as *ontological* or *constitutive*). Naturalisms arise out of the need for an environment independent of all purposes, one of ascertainable causes and predictable effects. Subjectivist and objectivist philosophies each arise from a demand that must be met, yet each destroys the other if it takes itself to be the whole story. The recognition that one needs *both* "purpose control" *and* "cause control" (or "data control") is the strong suit of the philosophy of dualism, which refuses to sacrifice cause to purpose or purpose to cause. But dualism fails in its inability to show how an originative human will and a natural order can coexist or interact. Postdualistic (post-Cartesian) positions such as empiricism, idealism, and pragmatism are shown to be efforts to interrelate the order of will and the order of natural causation.

Thus far, Miller's tracing of the development of types of philosophy is reminiscent of, and frankly indebted to, the thought of Hegel and of Miller's teacher William Ernest Hocking.[13] The history of philosophy exhibits philosophy's revision of itself by a dialectical development in which each successive type of philosophy satisfies a demand hitherto unmet, yet remains only part of the story of the human will to order itself and its world. Philosophical revision thus has the form of a process of both persistence and change, in which the legitimate demand of each philosophy is inherited and preserved, while the claim of each philosophy to be the whole story is cancelled.

Although Miller's philosophy—essentially a philosophy of history—is in these respects indebted to Hegel, he cannot accept Hegel's claim that this odyssey of self-revision culminates in "the absolute"—a final knowledge in which human beings have collectively risen to the standpoint of God. Fond of Abraham Lincoln's assertion that "we cannot escape history," Miller remains humanistic and accordingly skeptical of all claims to theological finality. He was, he told his students, wary of "mountain-top experiences." His temper is Kantian, with some affinity to American pragmatism in that he argues that knowledge does not depend on completeness and absolute certainty. Insist in advance that truth be final and incorrigible and you doom yourself to skepticism. Philosophy must come to terms with finitude, contingency, the accidental. Therefore he added "the accidental" to the lists of categories he inherited.[14] He wanted, he said, to "affirm the moment," to "give ontological status to finitude."

But how to do this? While Miller apprentices himself to the history of philosophy and finds it far more than a record of naïve errors, he is an original thinker. He refuses, in fact, to see apprenticeship and originality as anything but complementary—another sign of the dialectical cast of his thinking. Originality lies in revising an inheritance, and Miller sees a moral urgency in this. He maintains that the sole possible locus of defensible order and lawfulness is human history, but finds most of his contemporaries guilty of discounting it—suspicious of the precarious, all-too-human sort of order that history exhibits. Miller's response: If you want an order that owes nothing to human beings, you'll end up with no order at all. The quest for the safety and security of an ahistoric finality overlooks our own collective responsibility for maintaining an ordered environment. But recognition of the failure of the quest for absolute finality has, in Nietzsche and his epigones, resulted in the *antithesis* of that quest: nihilism. Miller's entire career can be seen as his urgent exploration of a middle ground between absolutism and nihilism: "If we want reverence, anything sacred and so imperative, we must advance now to history. . . . There is the common world, the actual one."[15]

History is the region of human originality, of those human *res gestae* or "utterances" that "declare a world." No extrahistorical or extraphilosophical conditions can account for these originative utterances, for it is these utterances *themselves* that first propose or "project" the formal orders (e.g., mathematics, logic, causation) that are the prerequisites for finding causal conditions. Without human history, no natural history; without this projection of the formal conditions necessary for knowledge (e.g., identity, difference, antecedent, and consequent), no sciences. Such acts of will, or "utterances," propose the "norms" or "rules" presupposed by any particular disclosures. Anything that presents itself as real, fact, or datum can do so only within a formal order that determines what is to count as real, fact, or datum. In arguing for such free and "constitutive" formal ordering, Miller clearly sides with one particular part of his inheritance, philosophical idealism.

The basic and formative historical crises, whether in science or in society, are philosophical—not conflicts in detail, but those in which one conception of the order of the whole is pitted against another. Here originality comes into play. Such *constitutional* disputes are "the loci of radical disagreement." Philosophy is the history of these conflicts, a fate that thought must undergo once it has committed itself to the search for intelligibility and lawfulness.

Hence the central problem posed by Miller's philosophy, and by post-Kantian thinking in general. If human proposals of an ideal order are prerequisite for the disclosure of real particulars, and if such proposals conflict with each other and none has any ahistoric or absolute guarantee, then must we not conclude that these proposals are simply competing human fictions? Miller allows that this is the historical juncture we seem to have reached, but holds that "the chaos of today [nihilism and skeptical relativism] is the historical consequence of a metaphysical lapse . . . a consequence of the account of the world that the learned propagate. For them the actual has no authority and rates no reverence because it is not recognized."[16] Miller's bold and original crusade is for "the as yet unacknowledged actuality of the midworld."[17] So, to inherited lists of categories, Miller adds not only the aforementioned category of "the accidental," but the category of "the midworld."

IV

Miller rightly regards his treatment of the midworld as his primary accomplishment (though he finds it prefigured in Hegel and in Josiah Royce).[18] The notion of the midworld, or region of the actual, challenges *at its roots* the inherently dualistic presumption that the sphere of human formal utterances is simply a sphere of "subjective" fictions or simplifications that has nothing in common with the region of natural reality from which these utterances allegedly cut us off.

The essays in Part 1 will prepare the way for and primarily in Part 2 will exhibit Miller's conception of a midworld. For a start, it is important to recognize that Miller doesn't pull the notion of the midworld out of thin air; he finds it illustrated again and again in the history of science and technology, but more widely in all human communication and all ordinary experience. Thus the midworld is already present. The task is to recognize it and so take it into account philosophically. That it is difficult to recognize, and that philosophical talk about it sounds so strange, is owing to an "intellectualism" that has strayed from the nature of human action and its objects, chiefly because it has been felt that if you wanted an ordered world you had best keep the potentially unruly human element out of it. It has not been well understood that the conditions that permit disorder and error are the very same conditions that make possible avoidance of error and genuine knowledge of the real. These conditions are "constitutive" human acts.

The midworld is to be understood as a historical process, to be identified by an analysis that goes back from the subjective and the objective, the ideal and the real, to their *common genesis* in concrete human activities of grappling with nature: "A genetically [historically] produced end [such as a science of nature] must not scorn the base degrees by which it has risen."[19] Miller warns the reader that his account of the origin and justification of the categories on which knowledge depends will be thoroughly "earthy." Either these categories originate in common human action and also find their justification there, or else they will be said to have a "transcendental" origin (as in Plato or Kant) that renders their application to the here-and-now experience of nature problematic—a kind of imposition from above. In other words, if thought and reality are not intrinsically conjoined from the beginning, there is no possibility of ending up with a thought that truly discloses reality. Formal thought and reality emerge together, in the *act*. The only possible basis, or orienting point, for any philosophical analysis is human action—in the aforementioned sense—in history. It would thus not be amiss to call Miller's position a Philosophy of the Act, or of Actuality. Action is "original," "immediate," or "unenvironed" in that it is human action that itself first establishes or uncovers any definite, ordered, and hence intelligible environment. We find this action, in the first instance, in primitive spiritualism, and the subsequent naturalistic critique of spirit is not a rejection but a new, a *critical*, instance of that action. Miller thus sees something fundamental and lasting occurring in the Ice Age cave paintings.

Miller defines the human act broadly, so that it is coextensive with what he calls "utterance." In so doing, he intends to recognize that distinctively human action not only sees and uses but names (gives form or identity to) what it uses. Language is not a kit of tools that one might or might not use, but is rather the proposal of an order that organizes things *as* things in the first place—no language, no intelligible world. In saying that this act of uttering is "original," Miller is claiming that it neither precedes nor follows the disclosure of things (contrary to most of the usual accounts of the relation of language, and action, to things). Absolute idealism or rationalism, holding that thought generates universal categories independent of experience, is wrong. Absolute empiricism, holding that experience of data occurs independent of thought and will, is equally wrong. The act or utterance, then, is the *simultaneous* disclosure of form and content, of universal and particular, of idea and datum. They are *strictly correlative.* That is the price of making the accidental a category: form, universal, idea, are not pure and free-floating; they are correlates of accidental (contingent) content, particulars, data. And vice-versa.

For this to make sense or have any plausibility, examples are needed. Miller generously supplies them. Many of them are drawn from mathematics—but not from pure mathematics, for Miller holds that mathematics begins as, and has its final justification in, the disclosure of things. These examples are thus concrete illustrations of a primary Millerian thesis: that the pure/applied and form/content *distinctions* are also dialectical *relations*. Utterances, including the utterances of mathematics and logic, are in their origins *at once* pure and applied. Form (universality, the systematic), if it is to be justifiable, occurs first of all *in* an action that discloses content (particularity, the contingent). Example: One who so much as counts one's toes has disclosed both the number of toes one has (a particular, finite content) and the order of mathematics (an ideal or formal order, infinitely applicable). Example (a favorite of Miller's): the use of a yardstick to measure the distance between two points. Thereby the real puts in an appearance ("these trees five yards apart") and an ideal order is warranted (a system of mensuration).

Miller asks us to attend closely to the "ontological status" of the yardstick as a typical example of the actual. One cannot choose between regarding it as ideal and regarding it as real, as subjective or objective, as human or natural, as form or content, as universal or particular, as mathematical or material. No traditional "dyadic" account of it can tell us what it is; it challenges our usual habits of thought. It is, in Miller's terms, "triadic" or "actual."[20] What is still missing in Kant is the story of the genesis of forms and categories in the actual, in historical utterances, and it is here alone that their validation can be found. The actual is, as Miller's use of the term indicates, the correlate of an act in this case, the act of mathematical measurement. *What is ontologically and epistemologically primary is actuality*. The actual is neither a mere personal function nor a mere impersonal object; it is a "functioning object" or an "embodied utterance" or an "incarnate word" or a "unit of account." While it is the embodiment of a human will to order, it is at the same time a *critic* of the merely subjective: The tree I thought to be fifty yards from my house turns out to be seventy five. The act not only launches purposes but controls them. The world of words, numbers, time and space; of volts, atoms, and miles; of microscopes, telescopes, and clocks is a midworld—the midworld as a whole encompasses them all. The primary functioning object is the human body: the mouth's words, the eye's and the ear's identifications, the hand's and foot's movements, are constitutive and disclosive of a world.

The crucial point is that the actual isn't an adding of the ideal to the real, or of thought to matter, as if we had prior separate experiences of the ideal and the real and somehow subsequently brought them into relation with each other. Miller's claim, on which his entire position stands or falls, is that both the ideal and the real appear thanks to the actual. "Both assured form and assured content derive from actuality."[21] In an important sense, as Miller himself saw, this isn't idealism—as opposed to realism—at all. It is a way *behind* the idealist–realist controversy. (Thus critical realism could not last as a rejection of or substitute for philosophical idealism. The legitimate claims of both could be recognized and interrelated only in a situation comprising both—namely, the actual.) The functioning object is the common "vehicle" of the ideal and the real—it is *both*, and it "enforces the distinction" between them. This is what Miller was driving at with his strange notion of a "naturalistic idealism," and there is no way to make it an easy notion to grasp. It is frankly difficult, like Albert Einstein's conception of relativity, and it takes time and hard thought to understand it. It critically modifies our inherited, and so habitual or intuitive, sense of the "self–world" relation.

Through a complex series of arguments, Miller is able to show how functioning objects or actuality enables us to generate, to distinguish between, and properly to interrelate appearance and reality, error and fact, contingency and formal order, purpose and cause, mind and body, even the humanities and the sciences. These arguments arguably comprise the genuine resolution of the still-vexing problems posed by Cartesian dualism. Cartesian dualism cannot simply be fled or forgotten in an alleged "postmodern" world. It has to be *revised*. If it is at all true, as is often suggested, that the philosophical dilemmas of the last three centuries are primarily the consequences of Cartesian formulations, Miller's concept of the midworld of functioning objects deserves an important place in the history of modern philosophy. One index of a fruitful philosophical concept lies in its enabling us to see a whole range of other notions in a new light, and in the course of Miller's essays such light is shed on many problematic notions, such as stimulus and response, freedom, fate, the moral, democracy, law, the accidental, sign and symbol, myth, quality, organism, and intersubjectivity.

V

For those steeped in the problems of the post-Kantian philosophical situation and faced by the specter of nihilism—which may be all of us—Miller offers a response that is original and positive without being idiosyncratic or uncritical. We find in Miller's thought a compelling answer to the question of what remains of philosophical idealism once it is freed of its rationalistic excesses, its claims to absoluteness—excessive claims that still haunt Husserl's transcendental idealism. After Miller, it is necessary to say that Marx, Nietzsche, and the existentialists have only tempered the claims of idealism, not destroyed them. Miller has demonstrated the original and ineliminable role of freely proposed categories in the constitution of human experience, but as *actual* conditions of objectivity rather than as subjective, as idiosyncratic, or as fictive bars to knowledge. The manner in which Miller has reconciled the claims of mind and its ideality with the claims of nature and its reality makes him one of the more provocative successors of Kant and Hegel. If his way of talking takes some getting used to, what he says is thoroughly contemporary. If he rejects all metaphysical claims of transcending history and its contingency, he nonetheless shows science to be possible. There may be no saner *via media* between skeptical relativism and metaphysical certitude. His arguments will by turns remind the reader of Plato, Aristotle, Kant, Hegel, the early (but not the later) Martin Heidegger, Maurice Merleau-Ponty, Charles S. Peirce, John Dewey, and Thomas Kuhn. He arbitrates convincingly between the ancients and the moderns, and between the continentals and the Americans.

Looking over the entirety of Miller's philosophy, it would not be amiss to title it, in Walt Whitman's terms, a metaphysics of democracy. Miller's constant subject is human *acts*, and what he has in mind are the acts of *all* human beings. More specifically, he is attending not just to the instrumental but to the *constitutional* function of these acts. They disclose an environment as a complex order of kinds of things and interrelations of kinds of things. All agents, all utterers or declarers, share in the constitution of this common environment. The most general present record of this complex order is the dictionary, whose words must be understood primarily not as inert names but as constitutive utterances of the human community. As utterers, all contribute to, are subject to, and are beneficiaries of this order. As a humanly constituted order, it is an order that is found only insofar as it is made—and remade—by ongoing human efforts to maintain it in the face of change and in response to criticism. It is, in other words, a *historical* order—the constitutive work of the human community across the ages. It is an order continually threatened by disorder and continually capable of reordering or amendment.

That the premises or grounds—the metaphysics—of democracy must be human and historical is indicated by the very word *democracy*. It is the active power of the people. Miller strenuously rejects any appeal to ahistoric or transcendent premises, and that rejection is where Miller departs from the invocation of a theological premise by Plato, Aristotle, Thomas Aquinas, Descartes, and Hegel. Alleged hotlines to the Absolute have been and remain dogmatic and divisive premises for gross human conflicts. Philosophy can never be assured, and can surely never be global, until it is premised in *the common*, in two senses of that word: the ordinary/everyday and the shared. Socrates offers the clue to it. It is found by looking to no authority, to nothing and no one external to oneself (it is in Miller's terms "unenvironed"); it is found in self-examination. The occasion of its being found is most likely to be one's finding oneself blindsided by dogmatism or rendered powerless by skepticism. As a last resort, perhaps, one encounters *one's own critical agency*. It is an encounter with one's own constantly exercised power to direct and redirect oneself via a conceptual and categorical ordering that, as a historical legacy, one has in the first instance had to learn but is from thenceforth one's own ideation— intelligible to oneself and the source of one's own self-control and one's effectiveness in a natural and social environment.

What can be expected of this metaphysics? It is relative rather than absolute, temporal rather than eternal, historical rather than ahistoric, corrigible rather than final. In an era of nihilism it may seem a poor sub- stitute for the lost absolute metaphysics. But the old metaphysics is laps- ing because it cannot produce its own credentials. In contrast, Miller can claim that a "merely" human and "merely" historical metaphysics is to be found in each of us, has been and remains disclosive of an actual world, and—of great importance—is *revisable* under the critical scrutiny that is the power and the responsibility of the free human being. It may only be this metaphysics of democracy that offers a credible way out of the absolute skepticism of nihilism without recourse to a new dogmatism.

NOTES

1. Immanuel Kant, *Philosophical Correspondence 1759–99*, Arnulf Zweig, ed. (Chicago: University of Chicago Press, 1967), p. 95.
2. Edited by Joseph Epstein (New York: Basic Books, 1981), pp. 155–64.
3. "The Pratt-Miller Correspondence," in *Papers and Letters of John William Miller* (edited and transcribed by Eugene R. Miller), Miller Papers 55:2, pp. 332–53.
4. Friedrich Nietzsche, *The Will to Power*, Walter Kaufman, ed. (New York Random House, 1967), p. 3. The emphasis is Nietzsche's own.
5. E.g., *The Midworld of Symbols and Functioning Objects*, pp. 125, 138; *In Defense of the Psychological*, p. 69.
6. *The Will to Power*, p. 7.
7. Ibid., p. 13.
8. Nietzsche, "Thus Spoke Zarathustra," in Walter Kaufmann, ed., *The Portable Niet- zsche* (New York: The Viking Press, 1954), p. 252.
9. *The Will to Power*, pp. 14 and 20.
10. Chicago: University of Chicago Press, 1997.
11. Walt Whitman, "Democratic Vistas," in Whitman, *Poetry and Prose*, Justin Kaplan, ed. (New York: Library of America, 1982), p. 984.
12. *The Paradox of Cause*, p. 74.
13. See especially Hocking's *Types of Philosophy* (New York: Charles Scribner's Sons, 1929).
14. *In Defense of the Psychological*, p. 160.

15. Ibid., p. 151.
16. Ibid., p. 105.
17. Ibid.
18. *The Midworld of Symbols and Functioning Objects*, p. 34.
19. Ibid., p. 8.
20. Ibid., p. 34.
21. Ibid., p. 178.

PART 1

The Conduct of Philosophy
Genealogy and Criticism

I like civility and so I have to fall back on common sense and its validation and not pose as a seer. While the actual, the midworld, the functioning object, the utterance, the accidental as constitutional, the world as incomplete, the world as philosophically defined—while all that may seem very esoteric, it derives from counting my fingers and going to the post office. Intellectuals have no verbs; the common man does. I am joining that common man. And if this is a free country, we'd better get ourselves a metaphysic that has respect for the man on Elm Street.

—*The Midworld*, p. 191

INTRODUCTION

Part 1 consists of essays by Miller that, taken together, show how he understands philosophical activity. It will be seen to be a conduct that is devoted to self-definition and world-definition. Miller finds that neither can be properly understood unless the *relation* between self and world has been subjected to a strenuous *historical* analysis. The essays in Part 1 will exhibit two basic features of this historical analysis of philosophical conduct.

The analysis will be what might be called *genealogical*, for it holds that what we have done and where we have done it are the sole sources for grasping who and where we are, can be, and ought to be. An essential place we have been is the history of philosophy, and Miller in his teaching and writing was ever and again establishing who *he* was—what he stood for—by relating himself to other philosophers past and present. Thus, to help the reader gain a sense of what Miller stood for, the introductions to Miller's essays in Part 1 repeatedly situate him relative to other philosophers.

The other basic feature of Miller's analysis is its stress on criticism. By *criticism* Miller means the process of responsible definition—in other words, the maintenance of an articulation of the complex order or structure of one's world. Lest this sound excessively abstract or vague, Miller points to the unabridged dictionary as the record of this complex structure. The dictionary was, he said, his bible. Miller can be seen as having conducted a moral crusade on behalf of the recognition and affirmation of the conditions that have made this order possible and against anything that threatens the maintenance of this order.

Part 1 will point to the critical role of Immanuel Kant in Miller's personal genealogy and, if Miller is right, the vitally needed recognition of Kant's legacy in our common genealogy. The whole of Miller's work suggests that we are still in the process of coming to terms with Kant's call for the maintenance of criticism as the sole alternative—personally, nationally, and globally—to the destructive forces of dogmatism and skepticism.

Style in Philosophy

This brief essay makes an excellent preface to the essays on the nature of philosophical inquiry that follow. Here Miller boldly proclaims the inherently public and democratic character of philosophical inquiry. One may be reminded of C. S. Peirce's rejection of "the method of authority" and of John Dewey's attention to "the public and its problems." But it is in the dialogues of Plato that Miller finds both the necessarily dialectical *style* of philosophical inquiry and the personal conversion that is the proper *outcome* of that inquiry. The communal style of philosophy is for Miller inseparable from the subject matter of philosophy, which can be provisionally denominated as either "the common" or "the universal and necessary." What this is will become clearer as one reads further. Here it is only hinted at in a few phrases such as "necessary axioms," "basic words and concepts," and "what is essential in us."

This essay was written in 1933 or 1934 (Miller Papers 19:11).

The content of a philosophy is not unrelated to its style. For the content, being concerned only with reflection, devoid of specific or sensory features, can be revealed to one only through the discovery of one's own mind. And to give another person philosophic information is, therefore, to win him to a cooperative effort in reflection. It is to lead him from his own opinions to their correction, for only in that criticism of his own opinion can he discover his necessary axioms.

Philosophy is genial and not argumentative. No one can win a philosophic argument and no one can lose. Both gain in the renewed or discovered perception of their own ideals. One cannot force philosophy. One must appeal to a man's willingness to be accountable to himself for his basic words and concepts.

Plato is the great example of philosophic style. He does not contradict; he does not, as a rule, launch into his own point of view. He seeks to make his point of view and his conclusions emerge from the statements of others. His questioning of others, giving opportunity for their thought to clarify itself, stands as philosophy's greatest achievement in technique. The Socratic irony has deep justification, for only by refraining from his own opinion could Plato make his opinion persuasive. He knows he can make no impression except as others freely discover the implications of their own thought.

Philosophy is, then, the chief example of the achievement of influence by a complete yielding to the point of view of others. The student of philosophy is always right. The teacher of philosophy is always futile when he develops his own ideas without first assuring himself that his starting point, his questions, and his presumptions are those of the student.

Philosophic style can never be strident, never insistent, never hortatory. It must be couched in the language of self-abnegation. Its success is always and necessarily common. It is an aristocratic enterprise because it seeks the best in men, their essential humanity and freedom. It is democratic in that it is never based on authority but on the cooperation of equals. Men differ in all details, but as men, as seekers after their essential excellence, they are alike. Philosophy itself is loved by only a few; but within its own domain there can occur no personal eccentricity and no superiority. Whoever pursues it faithfully has acknowledged his community with all others similarly engaged. The philosopher must assume that what he can understand, others can understand. They will understand him only as they understand themselves. For a philosopher, every problem is another's as well as his own, and every solution must make good in terms of the opinions and questions of another. Were it to fail to achieve this neutrality to the personal and psychological, it would become dogmatic.

Philosophy is a school of sympathy and of understanding. To sympathize with the problems of others is its goal. For those problems are always one's own. The cultivation of philosophy is the cultivation of a deep respect for the questions and difficulties of every man. Here men meet, not as doctors, lawyers, or economists, but as men.

In contrast with this geniality, sympathy, and impersonality is the fact of the *persistence* of the philosophic question and teacher. A philosophic conversation cannot be lax or casual. Since philosophy has to do with what is essential in us, it requires sternness of attitude as well as of thought. One must be held to the mood of self-understanding, and to the difficult progress of an idea. Nothing is done in philosophy until one is changed as a person. This Plato clearly saw. Philosophy requires self-reformation, because its story concerns the self and its world in their most fundamental relations. The answers of a philosophy are never indifferent to one's character. Hence philosophy often seems impolitely pressing, insistent, and intrusive. One must only remember that in philosophic matters there is no privacy, for these problems refer to the impersonal in us. Privacy is for the psychological and historical, for our special experiences and purposes. But every man shares his essential nature with every other and philosophy can save no man from facing himself. It cannot leave one alone, offering a merely intellectual acquisition. One does not have philosophy at all until one engages upon a process of self-scrutiny. The self-satisfied man can never be a philosopher. No one has so complete an understanding of himself that he need no longer modify his outlook and his deeds.

Philosophy presses on the student with insistence. Problems must be seen through, they must be understood; they must be made one's own. One cannot study philosophy without accepting the burden of its issues as one's own.

The combination of persistence with sympathy Plato illustrates. This union is possible only as the persistence is not that of an alien mind, but of one's own. What Plato does is to perform his midwifery on the ideas, questions, and doubts of the student. It is impossible to be provoked with such a procedure since one is harassed not by another but by one's own ignorance and blindness. Philosophy has no meaning save as it deals with one's own questions, and mercilessly requires an answer.[1]

NOTES

1. The "genial" style Miller here describes was consistently exemplified in his own teaching. Thus a student of his writes of him: "If you were eighteen years old, what might be the impact on you of a man who appears to know something about nearly everything, and nearly everything about a few things, and who is willing to reason with you in your deepest ignorance and unreason? Imagine this man treats you with dignity, never tries to overcome you, that he leads you onward without deceit,

clearly trying also not to fool himself, until your thinking might acquire some rudi-
ments of form and a spark of initiative. Imagine further that by the age of twenty-
one you are confident that this man does not merely appear that way. He *is* that
way" (Theodore Friend, "Infinity and Limit: A Teacher's Eye," *The Yale Review* 73
[3] [1984]: pp 446–47).

The Genesis of Philosophical Study

This essay will serve to introduce a central Millerian category, the act. Miller holds the human act, not contemplation and not intellect, to be the occasion of philosophy. The genesis of philosophy, both historically and individually, is not abstract and is not for Miller just one interesting question among others. Unless philosophy begins *in medias res*, in what one has already done and in what others have already done, it is baseless and loses its authority. Philosophy's thoroughly ordinary locus is the quest for control and order in the common conduct of life. The serious study of philosophy is provoked by the frustration of one's will, a breakdown in one's natural or habitual manner of maintaining order and control. While this seems reminiscent of American pragmatism, Miller is going to find the act "constitutive" and "revelatory" of a universal order, "structure," or "world" that he finds presupposed rather than identified and justified by pragmatism.

It is possible that the centrality of will and the relation of will to community and to universal order in the philosophy of Josiah Royce may have influenced Miller, who in his senior year at Harvard College studied with Royce. But Miller gives no sign whatsoever of accepting Royce's belief that the human will shares in a divine will. Rather, he offers a philosophy of finitude and limit—that is, a philosophy whose sole locale, subject matter, and basis are historical. Similarly, Miller's interest in Ralph Waldo Emerson's version of a universal community of thought and will, the Over-Soul, is tempered by his rejection of Emerson's association of this community with the eternal and the divine. Universality and community are for Miller strictly historical in origin, and their maintenance and revision are entirely a function of human acts of will—primarily the acts of constitution and criticism, roughly, the acts of "projecting" an order and of "revising" that order. This sets Miller's "historical idealism" apart not only from Emerson's and Royce's idealism but from all the inherited forms of philosophical idealism.

Miller in a number of places characterized his philosophy as "earthy." The present essay gives several signs of that earthiness: Philosophy is continuous with the activity of prior ordinary experience; it is an exercise not in disengaged intellectuality but in the maintenance of an egoistic self-identity via willful (but not arbitrary) projections in the interest of personal control; its concern is the description not of a static and abstract order, but the order or "form" located in what is "immediate" or directly present to us.

These pages were originally part of an undated letter, circa 1970, to the University of Minnesota philosopher Alburey Castell (Miller Papers 21:1). On Miller's conception of the relation of the act to a universal order, see his essay "Action and Order" in The Midworld of Symbols and Functioning Objects *(pp. 48–58).*

Philosophy is not another "natural" sort of learning. It *ensues upon* natural learning. This is the characteristic origin of all philosophical interests. This origin is plain and clear in the case of logic, for example, where one must have spoken, addressed others, attempted to persuade others, before logic has either material or occasion. Ethical study is similarly *ex post facto*: It requires that one *shall have acted* and shall have been regardful of others in action. What one is to change in one's doing because there are others is somehow to be a resultant of the recognition of others, just as in logic what one may say in order to make sense is the resultant of *any* saying about *particulars*. In both cases, and in *all* cases of philosophy, the philosophical interest occurs in a context of action and in the interests of more effective action. What the philosopher "contemplates" is not a state of affairs but an *activity*. There has been a view, a mistaken view, that, whereas most persons act, the philosopher contemplates, that he contemplates the same scene that leads others to act or invites their acts. While others *do*, he *contemplates*. Actually what the philosopher observes is not a factual scene, but an active one. He notes what is being done. This is not the case in natural science, where one *never* notes an act but notes an appearance to which no action can be ascribed. Natural science makes a point of this exclusion of action from its own explanations. Only the act, in contrast, furnishes the occasion of philosophy.

In these prior activities there lies the presumption of a *control*. Indeed, the center and essence of an act is in that presumption. A man speaks and takes it for granted that his utterance makes sense. He deals with another person and does not doubt that the transaction is really between persons. But it may be that in these natural and naive activities he finds himself ineffective and so confused. You do not believe what I say, yet I spoke in innocence. You allege that my act disregarded or offended you, yet I had no intention of such disregard or offense. On the contrary, I took you to be there, took your presence into account. But I discover that my own natural saying or doing fails *in the intent that controlled it*. The activity prior to philosophy is not random. Children speak and act with some control. That there be such action, and that it be taken for granted as control, assumed so, is the setting for any philosophical concern—as logic, for example.

It is curious to consider that to have become a philosopher one must have been a child. This, I think, is often forgotten, and not least by philosophers themselves. And so they lose the occasion and the authority of their own discourse.[1]

Philosophy is the locus of the control that natural learning had merely assumed. But, as natural, such learning had never raised questions about its order, which is also its control. To control better what comes naturally is the occasion of any philosophical study. The control that one had assumed turns out to be a source of confusion and frustration. You do not believe what I innocently say. What am I to do to establish control so that my word can be understood and effective? My act is disregarded or arrested and so brings no control. What do I do to restore the control I had never questioned?

Well, then, I am told to mind my grammar, to put a plural verb with a plural subject; to mind my *p*'s and *q*'s, and not to try eating my cake and having it too; to remember to do as I would be done by, if I am not to find my acts rejected as so ineffective. Then one pauses to ask, "Is that really what I have let myself in for in acting as a speaker, a maker of inferences, a member of the team, family, or state?" At that point many recoil. The natural mode of action is good enough for them. In any society the unquestioned act has enough scope to permit one's getting on without being disabled. Jobs and occupations are to be had in the line of natural learning and skill. One speaks well enough for the purpose. One pays one's bills according to custom or evades payment when opportunity offers. One speaks and acts but one has not *defined oneself* as a speaker.

There is the watershed. For suppose one feels a need not only to speak and act but to *be* a speaker and an agent. Suppose that one's acts, even when natural and unforced, have a bit of egoism in them so that to appear as a speaker and a doer has been a vague accompaniment of play, reading, study, membership. Someone has charged that one had made a "mistake," that one did it "wrong," that one had been "naughty." Words like "You made a mistake" are heard. If so, one gets a bit self-conscious about the act. One can speak naturally and be said to fail, and the failure is in one's power to correct. One *need* not make that mistake. So, one pays attention to such arrest because one had been wanting to get results and to be effective. Correction has no hold on the indifferent.

Logic, to revert to that example, seems about as far removed from egoism as anything that could interest a person. But not so if one is on the debating team; *p*'s and *q*'s and fallacies become the very stuff of effectiveness, so that one focuses on esoteric lore like the rules of the syllogism and hasty induction—even with excitement—while to another for whom speech and argument lack *personal* value the technicalities of logic are indifferent or repulsive.

Philosophy, then, is the *absorption* of "natural" learning to the *will*. Its force is not intellectual but egoistic. For the student the turn to philosophy comes at the point where a natural activity must either seek alliance with the egoistic will or else fade away into a mere possibility of more skill and knowledge.

Philosophy is the egoistic appropriation of a prior competence. It is not for children. It is not for those who have felt no need of active identity, nor for the indifferent and slack. Ethics, for example, is for those who require a social identity and a social effectiveness.

The will is not something philosophers talk "about." It is the philosophic temper itself. The will is the actual, the equation of person and his act, that is to say, his control. If the genesis of philosophical study is in a natural activity, it can move from such activity only when the nonphilosophical has some hold on the individual as a power that must be sustained. This need has to be vaguely felt by the student. What one cannot say to him from the outside is that he "ought" to study logic, ethics, metaphysics. One can try to meet his puzzles, if he has any. One can never disqualify his natural learning. Nor can one say that in addition to such learning there is another subject, philosophy. Philosophy is not "in addition." It is the continuum of the assumed controls felt by the person who already has natural learning. It is a continuum not of learning, but of the control assumed in learning. It is the will, not the intellect.

Philosophy is the locus of will. In a climate recognizing no will, how is the philosopher to find credit? It seems fair to say that one needs to acknowledge one's limits. Some things one cannot do. Well, the philosopher, too, needs to discover his limits, that is, the limits of his powers. One finds oneself in limit, but in a self-identifying limit. No one except the philosopher can do so. For all others, limit is frustration. Hence many have sought alliance with the unlimited, as in *Vedanta*, or in the related ecstasy of drugs or other intoxications, including a violent self-assertion.

When philosophers have found limits, it has driven them to skepticism, a radical and annihilative limitation, but a proper result. For a philosopher can deal only in the *constitutional*, and skepticism is a constitutional incapacity, not a *particular* inability. Others have tried to rescue limit by making it a participant in the absolute, where, in a *"totum simul,"* all limit is abolished. But to make limit constitutional has rarely been attempted. But what business has philosophy with limit if it is *not* constitutional? Is limit a fact? No, it is a factor of structure.

If philosophy be the self-limiting it must expect difficulty from those to whom limit is an obstacle to the self and from those who admit to no self. Most people say, "Remove my limits, my incapacity." Others, notably the psychologists of all varieties, admit to no self, or person, or will, which has either limit or no limit.

So not to have found the limits of power as a philosopher is not to have seen the self-defining process and the arrest of natural activity in a formal confusion. If the above story of the genesis of philosophy is the account of one's own experience, then one has admitted to limits of philosophic access. This limit is personal and in terms of the self-conscious as a control and authorization of natural activity.

An immediacy that has *form* is a revelation; an immediacy without form is an intoxication. When natural activity demands a form for its own effectiveness, then one has mathematics and logic and history and these become revelations, projectors of a world and of an infinite order. The pragmatic is a halfway house—rather a ship without a compass, steered not by a will but by an accidental purpose, which may lapse. Anyone who sees history as constitutional also sees the limits of present powers. We are now in a historical movement rid pretty much of dogma, but not self-possessed in the liberty that has rejected dogma. Liberty now is dissent. It is not yet affirmation. It is not yet revelation.

NOTES

1. This passage is akin to several places where Miller calls attention to "the base degrees by which we have risen" (see note 3 for "The Absolute Authority of Criticism," below). Miller's genealogical inquiry pushes one back to origins not suffi-

ciently attended to—origins enacted in the primitive history of the human race that are reenacted in the childhood of each individual—where one first freely wills control over oneself and one's world. What is at stake in remembering these origins? At the end of the present essay, Miller claims we are not yet "self-possessed" in our liberty: "It is not yet affirmation. It is not yet revelation." In other words, we are not yet self-consciously taking charge of and responsibility for the *constitutive acts* that disclose and critically maintain an intelligible world. One might compare this with Martin Heidegger's outlining of an "authentic repetition" of a mostly inauthentic (i.e., not owned up to) human "thrown projective making-present" in *Being and Time* (especially sections 72–74).

The Quality of Philosophy
Is Not Strained

Miller could emphatically second René Descartes's assertion in *The Search after Truth* that "we cannot take too many precautions in the establishment of our bases." But for Miller, always thinking historically and contextually, consideration of what might be called the *genealogy* of philosophy—the story of its origin and descent—provides the crucial clues to the nature and the viability of the philosophical enterprise. This historical consideration cuts decisively behind Descartes's allegedly reflective and solitary grounding of philosophy and science, placing Miller in agreement with Charles S. Peirce's vigorous rejection of the Cartesian beginning in "Some Consequences of Four Incapacities." In a 1958 letter, Miller writes: "Descartes's ego was reached in the *absence* of an order, not *because* of some mode of order in which his powers and rational being were already manifest." By contrast, Aristotle wrote, in a passage that could serve as an epigraph to the present essay, that "by starting from what is inadequately known, but familiar to us, we can learn to know what is intrinsically intelligible, using what we do know . . . to guide us." This amounts to a common beginning and, for Miller, a historical beginning. Something that Jean Hyppolite said of G. W. F. Hegel is also apropos here: "Spirit is a 'we': we must begin not with the *cogito* but with the *cogitamus*." But Miller is intensely concerned not just with a prior community but with the present maintenance and revision of that community—in particular, the liberal democratic community, where dispute and critical discussion are encouraged but violence is constrained with the aim of its elimination. This will be especially evident in some of the essays of Part 3.

As in "Style in Philosophy," Miller calls attention to what he finds to be the necessary manner, style, and attitude with which philosophy must be conducted. If the manner is not "genial," if it does not acknowledge the common ground on which philosophical inquirers and disputants already stand, then the very *mode of inquiry* and the very *subject matter* of philosophy will be missed. That mode of inquiry is at heart a recognition and reappropriation of the common human power to identify entities and to discriminate between truth and error. That subject matter is the formal structure of all human experience. Not given to us from on high, this formal structure has been both proposed and revised by human acts—that is, historically.

This essay was written in 1933 (Miller Papers 9:5). The Miller letter of 1958 cited above was written to Robert E. Gahringer (Miller Papers 22:14). The Aristotle citation is from Metaphysics *1029b10–12. The Hyppolite citation is from* Genesis and Structure of Hegel's Phenomenology of Spirit *(Evanston: Northwestern University Press, 1974), p. 322. For further discussion of the teaching of philosophy, see "The Scholar as Man of the World" (below, Part 3), Miller's letters to Robert E. Gahringer (Miller Papers 22:14), and George P. Brockway's "John William Miller" in Joseph Epstein (ed.),* Masters: Portraits of Great Teachers *(New York: Basic Books, 1981).*

No one can be forced to a philosophical conclusion, or to become a philosopher.[1]

A man's philosophy always expresses what he finally holds valid, the beliefs that most basically direct his acts, his judgments of books, persons, education, and politics. To attack a man's philosophy from a point of view alien to it is to attack the man, and what is more, it is to attack him in his most intimate quality. No man can accept such an attack leveled from an alien source without admitting his complete and radical error. One gladly admits error of detail, but one *cannot admit complete error*. Above all one cannot admit that there is not present in oneself the agencies or means of *correcting one's errors*. But if one already possesses the means of correcting one's errors, one must possess the essence of truth, its deepest quality. No one ignorant of the truth can be brought to it; no one quite out of touch with reality could ever be brought to recognize it were it presented to him.

Consequently the method of philosophy must always be directed to the elucidation of agreements *already present* in the minds of supposed antagonists. Were there no such basic agreement, no argument would *avail*, and every argument *besides being futile* would also be a *menacing danger*. For it would imply a way of life and a course of action that in its prolongation would destroy the values and institutions congenial to the other view.

In a philosophical discussion there must be peace without victory, for the victory must be mutual. The "right" claim in a given argument must finally show its necessity in the mind that has opposed it, and it must do this by revealing the basic agreement and fellowship of both contending minds in their fundamental attitudes and axioms. Basic disagreement in philosophies could only lead robust and earnest men *to violence and to despotism*, for in the measure that one traces out the implications of divergent systems one discovers the changes they would require in personal values and in institutions.[2] A convinced transcendentalist would tolerate or perhaps welcome authoritarian government, whereas a believer in human capacities and responsible self-direction leans toward free government. Naturalism destroys religion and values, while a belief in the spirit in asserting the whole as superior to the parts would produce its characteristic society, art, and education. And so the earnest man, careful of his future, could meet absolute opposition only with absolute antagonism. On the stage of affairs this is *revolution*. No reason can be given for tolerating hopeless opposition, hopeless because irreconcilable and irreconcilable because at no point sharing common standards of truth and value. And a man who values his life, and who wishes to see perpetuated the friendships, institutions, and values he now enjoys and in which he carries out his action, must seize violent means of preserving or establishing them when nothing better offers. *To a basic opposition there can be no basic reconciliation.*

But reconciliation, if possible, implies that there can be no basic opposition. It implies that a failure to understand *oneself* has occasioned disagreement. Now this understanding of oneself requires discipline, the laying aside of vanity and pride, the conquest of everything arbitrary and personal. It implies the labor of overcoming one's sense of difference and antagonism, the rejection of self-satisfaction in such differences from others, the acceptance of conciliatory attitudes. For the truth that one has discovered about oneself cannot be disclosed in opposition and antagonism, cannot be conveyed through dominance, but only by the exhibition of identity of basic meaning, through the revelation to another that he also means to assert the same truth. Thus, the appeal is not to one's own argument, but to the other's free acceptance of a truth. And there can be here no question of authoritative or accidental dominance. One accepts the result not because a famous, rich, well-born, or learned person proposes it, but because one perceives its presence in one's own mind and so makes oneself *the essential equal* of the mistakenly supposed antagonist. He can win me only as he first assumes that I am quite as authoritative as he is, quite as genuinely in possession of the criteria of value, of the meaning of truth. His thought has anticipated mine and has led it, but *it has no better authority*.

Thus, the teacher succeeds only in his humility and the learner only by the establishment of his own essential dignity. To have become the teacher of conciliation is first to have undergone the humbling but not humiliating experience of self-correction. The teacher has nothing to gain, no point to make, no triumph to record, *except the achievement of the freedom and equality of another*, an equality always in principle present, and only as an accident of history not previously perceived. But the slightest sign of opposition, of self-congratulation over the superiority of one's insight, of the pharisaical gratification over one's distinction from the rest of men, creates a fatal bar to conciliation because it implies that victory humiliates the antagonist and that one's own insight has left room for pride.

The very nature of philosophical truth, if it be possible to assert it, destroys every vestige of egoism, because it can be won only by the conquest of egoism, only by the hard labor of self-discipline in which every accidental prejudice is brought under the impersonal law of a self-declared truth common to all. And if it is not common to all, one reverts to arbitrary violence in order to safeguard those arbitrary values that express one's own chance for satisfaction. Indeed, *our prejudices are merely the loci of vagrancy from the common truth and reality open to all.* And we must either accept them as final and accept war, or else one must search diligently for the factors of community and identity in all. And if such factors exist, they must express a common ideal, self-declared by each man, not imposed arbitrarily by nature or by another person. They express the fact that only where we are free and autonomous can we be at one. *But there is no victory over a free man, except his victory over himself*; the contrary course destroys liberty and expresses a plain contradiction.

Truth is as much in manner as in substance. There is no truth to be won from antagonism and unfriendliness, from exhortation, contention, or declaration. The manner of truth is both genial and persistent; it is essentially conversational and social. What breaks down conversation breaks down truth; what keeps the intercourse of thought alive promotes truth. Thus there is an inseparable connection between truth and virtue. It is a mistake to suppose that truth is for the intellect and virtue for the sentiments; the intellectual conquest of truth, the escape from dogmatism, is possible only as the expression of the attitude of goodwill. Nor is goodwill of any significance in the abstract; it can become actual only in the common pursuit of solutions to problems.

NOTES

1. Hence Miller's title, a paraphrase of Shakespeare, *The Merchant of Venice*, Act IV, scene i, line 184: "The quality of mercy is not strain'd [i.e., constrained, forced]."

2. It is worth stressing here that Miller's career in philosophy was motivated by his direct encounter with violence on the battlefields of the First World War in France (personal communication, Katherine Miller, February 26, 1989). It is not an accident that war is mentioned in the course of this essay. The question of *a philosophical arbitration of radical disagreement* stands in the insistent background of his thinking. Therefore the reader probing and testing the viability of Miller's thought (which he himself calls "earthy") has every reason to try to bring it to bear on whatever vehement disputes are on the world stage at the time of one's reading.

Dogmatism, Skepticism, and Criticism

This essay prepares the way for the next essay, "The Absolute Authority of Criticism," which in turn prepares the way for the essay "The Dialectic." The very titles of these essays evoke central themes of Immanuel Kant's *Critique of Pure Reason*, for which the title of the present essay could serve as a subtitle. In that work, Kant justified the authority of *criticism* through the critical demonstration of rationalism's *dogmatic* failure, empiricism's *skeptical* failure, and the necessity of a *dialectical* union of the rational and the empirical. Kant maintained, as the outcome of his enquiry, that "the *critical* path alone is still open."

But if the present essay is centrally concerned with dogmatism, skepticism, and criticism, it is Plato rather than Kant who stands in the foreground. The essay was written in the mid-thirties when Miller drafted no fewer than six essays on the problem, or paradox, of Meno in Plato's dialogue *Meno*. The essay mentions Meno but once, in passing, but Meno is very much on Miller's mind. Meno encounters Socrates after having been influenced by the dogmatism and skepticism of the Sophists. He cannot see how to establish contact with a real world, as is evident in his famous paradox, which Socrates restated as follows: "You argue that a man cannot enquire either about that which he knows, or about that which he does not know; for if he knows, he has no need to enquire; and if not, he cannot; for he does not know the very subject about which he is to enquire." In the present essay Miller seeks to formulate the basic thrust of Plato's response to the Sophists, and it is probably fair to say that Miller regards this response as the central and (with revisions) permanent contribution of Plato to the history of philosophy. As had Miller in "The Genesis of Philosophical Study," Plato called on the human act. And as had Miller in "The Quality of Philosophy Is Not Strained," Plato paired the human act with a common beginning or prior community. That is, Plato was calling attention to the relation of the human act to its common context. Miller holds in *The Definition of the Thing* that if philosophy does not begin in community it will never arrive at it and so will not be able to revise or improve any human community. It is clear from Miller's argument that neither dogmatism nor skepticism can reach any community behind our differences. Meno appears to be isolated: As dogmatist he can propose *anything*, because he sees no environment that could limit his assertions, that his assertions would have to accord with or abide by; as skeptic, however, Meno can propose *nothing*, because he sees himself as having no access to a real world. In either case the consequence is solipsism; there is an unbridgeable "epistemological gulf" between the self and a real world. There is nothing evidential to confirm what one says or to challenge what one says. That is, there can be no effective *critical judgment*: a judging that is both a free (and ideally impartial) act and a judging that is empowered and limited by universal and necessary categories. What Meno, skeptical of any real and common world, must be brought to recognize is that access to the real world is already *present in his own thinking and speaking.*

In the present essay, Miller expresses his debt to Plato's answer to the Sophists by invoking G. W. F. Hegel, the only philosopher to have fully appreciated a crucial insight reached by Plato in his *Parmenides* and *Sophist*. Miller here directly and concisely formulates that insight: "The definition of reality is the structure of criticism." But it is not easy to understand this and to see how it answers the problem raised by Meno. What Meno has to be brought to see is that the terms used in his own skeptical questioning are the same terms that disclose the real. These terms name what Miller calls "concepts of universal incidence." These are nothing other than the "structure" of organizing ideas already embodied in the ordered world "defined" and so disclosed by common, ordinary human action. In Platonic terms, they are *forms* that have already made possible the disclosure of the discriminable and interrelatable *content* the world happens to present to us.

The particular contents of the world are contingent, but the form is the universal categorizing or organizing principles that have been necessary for that content to be intelligible or articulatable. The crucial recognition here is that categorial or universal thought is first present as the self-effacing formal *structure* of experienced reality before it is ever separated out and regarded by itself in reflection. Forms, or concepts of universal incidence (e.g., ideal/real, universal/particular, mental/physical, present/absent, the number system), empower the process of discrimination that has disclosed the real. Only after the fact—subsequent to the disclosure of a real world—does the *explicit* reflective distinction between the ideal and the real get made. According to Plato, this distinction is made by "recollection" of forms that are eternal. Miller can make no such appeal to the atemporal or the ahistoric. But, with his characteristic dialectic of geniality and criticism, he revises rather than rejects the Platonic conception of recollection. In Miller's thought, recollection means spotting in reflection the *human* and historically generated universal and necessary conceptual acts already at work in our thinking and speaking. And so Meno (or the present-day skeptic) must come to see that the system of his own critical thinking has already given him the definition of reality he has been seeking.

This undated essay comes from the unpublished Papers and Letters of John William Miller, *edited by Eugene R. Miller (Miller Papers 55:2, pp. 326–31). The assertion of Kant, above, is from the* Critique of Pure Reason *(1787), A856/B884. Socrates' restatement of Meno's paradox, above, is found in* Meno, *80e. For more on universality and necessity and concepts of universal incidence, see the essay "The Dialectic," below. Meno's problem is discussed directly and at length by Miller in "The Problem of Meno" (Miller Papers 55:2, pp. 375–402), an important but very difficult essay.*

W ere we to characterize the real or virtuous apart from the questions about them, apart from the process that discovers them and the implicit but unclear intention they fulfill, it would be necessary to adopt dogmatism. It would be necessary, in short, to be uncritical. The history of philosophy discloses an inevitable return to criticism after every dogmatic or empirical venture, for empiricism in philosophy is only a disguised dogmatism. This is itself instructive, for critical philosophy registers the unsatisfactoriness and meaninglessness of assertions that will not submit to justification or examination. Without criticism, assertions become irre sponsible, untrustworthy, and, in fact, unintelligible. The Platonic philos- ophy is best understood as a polemic against the irresponsible dogmatic relativism of the Sophists, but the concern of Plato was not in an ungra- cious fault-finding but with his own need for an orderly, free, and hence critically oriented personality. The structure of criticism became the defi- nition of reality, especially in the *Parmenides* and the *Sophist*, which almost no commentator has understood and no philosopher but Hegel fully appreciated.[1]

The definition of reality is the structure of criticism. Criticism has no basis except itself. One may as well acknowledge at the outset that to go beyond this, to introduce a single specific fact into one's conception of real- ity, be that fact one's own self or scientific data or God, is to accept dogma- tism in principle. But philosophy deals with nothing in particular. It deals with the structure that creates particulars and accepts them as facts, the structure of criticism.

Criticism has no background. It is underived. It is absolute. The attempt to develop it from a historically prior environment or from a more funda- mental region of existence assumes the whole work of the critical process in order to establish it. Common sense and scientific practice are both averse to unsupported assertion of specific fact. They acknowledge that the process by which facts are accepted is more fundamental than any one such fact, and hence it is absolutely necessary to define that process with- out recourse to assumed specific fact. This is very difficult to do, but it is the part of honesty and of hope to face a problem and accept the conse- quences for better or for worse. The critical process will not, then, be definable as a historical or mechanical event supervening on already assumed conditions, whether empirical or transcendental. For the basic objection to transcendentalism is not that it violates empiricism but that, like empiricism, it avoids criticism.

But if criticism and reality are one, the *question* about it is part of its definition.

What, indeed, could more surely defeat metaphysics than the divorce of its answers from the essential meaning of its questions? Negatively, the result would be an inarticulate agnosticism, and positively, an equally inapplicable and silent mysticism. But in neither case would discursive, intelligible, and practical philosophy be possible. What I wish, accordingly, to emphasize is that this point of view about the origin of philosophy represents not an advocacy of a specially formulated outcome, but the prolegomena to any possible philosophic solution. For it seems obvious that before philosophers can agree on a special solution, they must first agree on its general character. It seems plain that no two philosophers can ever hope to engage in fruitful and cooperative discussion if they initially differ on the method of attack or on the type of answer that would prove satisfactory. The sad and barren controversy between realism and idealism is due in essence to divergent theories of what philosophy is about, although there seems to have existed no realist and few idealists with an understanding of the radical difference between absolute and relative philosophic *origins*. Absolutistic *conclusions* are common enough, and are ineffectively opposed or defended on the ground of their absoluteness, whereas the basic and radical objection to them lies in their being conclusions. For what is absolute will always occur in the origin and not in the result, in the meaning of the question about reality and never in an answer or conclusions achieved as a logical sequent. Since all relative origins divorce the question and answer, they are equally worthless, whether they lead to absolutism or to relativism. They are worthless because they do not answer the question of Meno.[2] A nonpartisan statement of what it pursues, of what would be acceptable as an answer, the materials with which it can work, and the methods appropriate to those materials form the indispensable preliminaries of any hopeful philosophic study and discussion.

It often appears that philosophers rebel at this initial restriction. Yet every honest game has its rules. Why should the scientist not welcome the predetermination of the type of question he can raise, of the sort of answer he can give? Indeed, science has acquired prestige largely because of a growing clarity as to its task and limits rather than because of the unalterable necessity of its theories. It seems agreed that science is essentially a method and not a set of conclusions. Without the guidance of those restrictions and rules inherent in its purposes, it would wander off once more—as it sometimes still does—to magical forces or substances. But it need not chafe under these restrictions, for they are indigenous to its motive and hence vehicles of freedom. Why, then, should not the general type of answer in philosophy be also forecast by its own peculiar concern? And if the reader hesitates, he need only consult once more the charming insight of the lucid Meno. That philosophy must answer its question in terms of itself does indeed rule out a good deal of highly intricate, undeniably learned and scholarly work; yet every man must lay himself open to defeat if he is to achieve strength, and a traveler without a specified destination remains a vagabond. Hence every maxim of good sense, every desire for a hopeful, genial, and cooperative philosophy, recommends the search for this restricting rule as the locus of its freedom and assurance. Philosophy can humbly endure the charge of being subversive in its conclusions and, like science, look forward to their general acceptance; but no more than science could it long survive the conviction, shared by its own devotees, that it possessed no confident direction, fruitful procedure, and progressive development. It ought not to be a device for the elaborate concealment of human futility. But to establish itself, it must understand itself, that is, the question that defines its meaning and its task.

Dogmatism, the unsupported assertion that a proposition is true or an object real, offers no alternative to the definition of standards. Such assertions could never make headway against their own contradictories, which, accordingly, acquire all the plausibility of their rivals. And dogmatism fails to give any meaning to its own assertion, since it will not pause to define what features of its propositions or facts make them trustworthy. Avoiding the definition of reality, it cloaks its poverty in the bright garments of assurance. In not submitting to possible refutation, it deprives itself of possible truth. It is harassed by the inner confusion of its position, which asserts a reality it cannot define.

The history of philosophy, with its strife of systems and its winds of doctrine, makes plain that dogmatisms pass over into skepticism. Unfounded assurance invites the claim that no assurance is possible. In this rejoinder, the skeptic is, of course, as self-contradictory as the dogmatist, since he, too, borrows the axiom or the feeling of reality in order to deny it. In view of this historic vacillation, many have proposed that we need to fall back on faith. We have faith in the reality of purpose, in the moral order, in the processes of logic or of intuition. The advocate of faith acknowledges with the dogmatist and the skeptic that starting points cannot be proved, and in this he is correct. Avoiding the unsocial egotism of dogma, he employs the more genial term and draws from the region of feeling a buoyant assurance that the frowning intellect withholds.

But many advocates of faith insist that what they believe is not nonsense; it is, rather, one of the intelligible alternatives. In the Christian theology, it is a matter of faith to hold that the world was created in time, whereas Aristotle had urged the eternity of creation. Thomas Aquinas here calls the decision a matter of faith, since reason is incapable of arbitrating, and the church has its preference and so must be followed.

Faith as so understood does not, however, define reality. It only chooses within the real those logical possibilities it prefers. In this way, one may have faith in the future of democracy or of fascism, not because one perceives the inevitability of its triumph but because in the absence of precise knowledge one holds to the general validity of a direction and of a hope. Where there is necessity there is no call for faith. The mystic who experiences the divine reality does not say that he believes in God. He knows God. When faith passes over to complete and placid assurance, it becomes a mystical intuition and hence unnecessary and even subversive.

NOTES

1. See Hegel, *Lectures on the History of Philosophy* (1805–1806. London: Routledge and Kegan Paul, 1955), II, pp. 52–71.
2. The question, as posed by Meno, is: ". . . how will you enquire, Socrates, into that which you do not know? What will you put forth as the subject of enquiry? And if you find what you want, how will you ever know that this is the thing which you did not know?" (*Meno*, 80d).

The Absolute Authority of Criticism

In "Dogmatism, Skepticism, and Criticism" Miller had asserted that "The definition of reality is the structure of criticism." This is evidently of great importance for Miller—at the very heart of his thinking—and yet its meaning and its force are by no means obvious. What, specifically, is this assertion claiming about the relation of criticism to reality? The present essay claims that the relation to reality is one in which criticism has "absolute authority." But how and why? It helps that Miller here invokes the relation between criticism and *idealism*, an association explored at length by Immanuel Kant. What is at stake is the relation of the real to the ideal; the definition of reality is the structure of *ideation* and *ideality*. Yet the final relation bequeathed by Kant to his successors was that between the ideal and the *phenomenal*, so that Miller's task is to challenge or qualify Kant's distinction between the phenomenon and the thing-in-itself with the help of G. W. F. Hegel's critique of Kant's ahistoricism and with the further help of Miller's own critique of Hegel's theological absolute. In other words, Miller has to dispose of a residue of skepticism in Kant and a residue of dogmatism in Hegel. In so doing, Miller is himself exhibiting the task of criticism in maintaining the disclosure of the real. The positive outcome of Miller's both genial and critical reception of his philosophical inheritance is that between the extremes of dogmatism's absolute assertion and skepticism's absolute denial stands what both of them miss: "the order of contingency."

One might suppose that the critical alternative is *realism*, and Roy Wood Sellars, James Bissett Pratt, and others did indeed work out a "critical realism" in the early decades of the twentieth century. But Miller here carefully differentiates his position from realism, and the "idealism" he espouses is far from being idealism in the forms he inherited (whether the "subjective idealism" of George Berkeley or the "absolute" or "objective" idealism of J. G. Fichte, Hegel, or Josiah Royce). Not a "transcendental" idealism, it is rather a *finite* idealism, which Miller first, in 1922, dramatically called a "naturalistic idealism" and later called "historical idealism." It maintains that only "the order of contingency" is absolute, and even this order is absolute only because it provides for its own critical revision.

When, at the end of Section II, Miller claims that realism "repudiate[s] the base degrees by which it has risen," he is referring to a situation, at once human and natural, that is *prior to* that envisaged by either realism or idealism. That situation, "the actual," generates the very distinction between the real and the ideal. The adjectives *naturalistic* and *historical* so heavily qualify the usual meaning of "idealism" that Miller could write in a 1974 letter: "So, I am neither realist or idealist. At [Harvard] University it was assumed, or argued, that . . . you had to be one or the other. . . . The debate was futile (so I felt) because neither party could define the basis of the distinction. There was no middle ground which could account for the genesis of the different." It is not only interesting but probably important for assessing the need for mediation in the course of twentieth-century American philosophy to observe that while Miller found it necessary to "naturalize" idealism, Justus Buchler found it necessary to "idealize" naturalism by working out a categorial metaphysics for naturalism. It is also worth noting that, like Peirce, both Miller and Buchler found it necessary to situate the pragmatic aspect of their philosophies in the context of a general order, "world," or "domain."

This essay (Miller Papers 1:10) was probably written in the early 1940s. It was published under the title "For Idealism" (in The Journal of Speculative Philosophy, *I [1987]: pp. 4, 260–69). The Miller letter cited above was written in late 1974 to Robert E. Gahringer (Miller Papers 22:14). Part 2 of this volume elaborates Miller's understanding of the actual, which is "neither subjective nor objective but the basis of that distinction and of all other constitutional distinctions." (letter to George P. Brockway, November 1970 [Miller Papers 17:15]). See also "The Portrait of Man," below. For a more extensive treatment of Miller's dialectical correlation of cause and purpose in Section IV of the present essay, the reader may wish to consult the title essay in* The Paradox of Cause and Other Essays *(pp. 13–18). Miller's essay "Constitutional Utterance: Its Archaic Form and Abiding Force," in Part 2, sheds further light on what he means by his frequent expression "the base degrees by which we have risen." "Are There Two Kinds of Categories?" (below) elaborates Miller's claim that "the order of contingency" is the same order as "the structure of criticism." For Buchler's revision of naturalism, see his* Metaphysics of Natural Complexes *(New York: Columbia University Press, 1966).*

I

Idealism is the answer to the opposition between skepticism and dogmatism. It has no peculiar relation to realism except as the latter is a form of dogmatism.

Between dogmatism and skepticism there is no conciliation. Both are absolutisms, because both deny the sway of criticism. Dogmatism, by making unconditioned assertions, entails an unconditional denial of alternative assertions. Skepticism, recognizing the contingency of assertion and denial, will do neither, since it can find no standard of criticism in terms of which either can be made. Both, then, repudiate criticism; but dogmatism makes assertions in spite of criticism, and skepticism will make none because of the rejection of criticism. And since each is arbitrary, neither can be reconciled to the other by means of its own standpoint.

In other terms, dogmatism asserts specific being as absolute, while skepticism asserts the absolute nonbeing of all specific assertions and denials. Neither recognizes the necessity of limitation and contingency in being. Dogmatism does not restrict assertion, skepticism does not restrict denial. Yet every assertion of content must be restricted by some other possible content to give the assertion distinction and meaning.

But dogmatism, since it makes specific assertions, asserts what might be otherwise, and consequently draws its meaning from what it rejects. What it asserts is limited; yet, as dogmatic, it repudiates the conditions of limitation. It makes limitation specific, and consequently asserts as absolute what can secure significance only through contingency and relativity. There is its inherent weakness. It has no provision for negation, although it absolutely negates. To make a responsible assertion is also to make a responsible negation. Dogmatism does neither.

Skepticism, in turn, places no restriction on denial, and for the same reason, namely the repudiation of the absolute authority of criticism and of the point of view of criticism. It has no principle for restricting denials, and consequently neither for assertion.

Thus both repudiate limitation, and both are abstract absolutions wavering between being and nonbeing. They cannot understand each other, nor overcome each other.

Since dogma denies nonbeing, that is, since it does not provide for negation in what it affirms, *it can never generate a negative* within its own system. Dogma can use only dogmatic negatives, namely all those it posits at the outset as external to what it asserts. Yet what it asserts has no meaning apart from its dogmatic denial. Hence, in principle, no dogmatism can define its terms, and thus it wavers between the exclusion of nonbeing from reality and its inclusion in its own system. Nor can dogmatism employ logic, for logic requires disjunction, but no absolute disjunction. All logical disjunctions determine a unity with respect to which they are affirmed: for example, a unity of genus, species, or cause. Without such a unity to which the disjunction appeals, thereby becoming in principle relative, there is no force in the alternatives and both may be true. Apart from the unity that conditions a disjunction, no occasion for making it could occur. Atomism offers no occasion for logical disjunction. Thus, dogma, stripped of the possibility of negation, becomes finally inarticulate, sterile, static, and meaningless.

Skepticism, analogously, also denies disjunction, but arbitrarily rejects affirmation instead of denial. It denies being. But as between the sterility of dogmatic assertion and dogmatic denial there is no difference and no choice. Skepticism can generate no affirmations. This is generally recognized by skeptics themselves, but dogmatists sometimes erroneously suppose that they can make denials, that is, introduce the idea of negation. Dogmatists enjoy an exhibition of logic, but there is no logic without negation, and dogmatists can show no meaning in negation.

Skepticism is more sophisticated than dogmatism in one respect; its historical occasion presumes the occurrence of conflicting dogmas and the failure to reconcile them. This situation is, of course, necessary, since dogmas are mutually exclusive, or only accidentally similar in content. But systematically considered, the skeptic is not the superior of the dogmatist, but only his complement. The impossibility of making progress with either the dogmatist or the skeptic is well known. The former judges all proposals in the light of his own arbitrary premises, so that no other proposal can get a hearing, being rejected in advance; the latter hears all proposals only to refuse judgment upon them, thereby equally removing the possibility of compulsion of thought. The former is all compulsion, but he is arbitrary about it; the latter is all indifference, and equally arbitrary. Neither submits to judgment in his abstract position. The former brings philosophy into disrepute by neglecting any method of disposing of his opponents, the latter by his neutrality to all opposition.

Dogmas do not really conflict. Would that they might! They merely negate each other. *What cannot be reconciled in thought offers no conflict of thought.* Dogmas have no common ground except their exclusiveness; but no dogma can recognize any other, since each system has no vocabulary for its alternatives any more than it has significance in itself. Nor do dogmatism and skepticism, taken abstractly as they intend to be, make for either conflict or conciliation. If there be conciliation it will be through a perception of the necessity of this abstract diversity, and hence through the point of view that can define both. For they cannot, within their own limits, reach out to each other for so much as an acknowledgment. Yet they are nothing without each other. Actual skeptics and dogmatists may object to such a statement because, in fact, they *do* see the other point of view. But they see it only as they depart from the strict confines of their own. Thus, neither dogmatism nor skepticism is a self-conscious philosophical type, and to make them so is to invoke a more radical point of view that, by seeing their abstract necessity, establishes a conception of the real, inclusive of both affirmation and denial, of being and nonbeing, of absoluteness and contingency.

II

The point of view capable of conciliating dogmatism and skepticism will be neither an assertion nor a denial. Yet, apart from thcm, no discourse is possible since no restriction, limitation, or specification would be possible. They are unavoidable. So much is true of the claim that one must somehow "get started," that is, assert some content.

But while discourse requires content, it does not require any given content as absolute. That would be a reversion to dogmatism and to skepticism. But if assertion and negation oppose each other when absolute, they imply each other when they are responsible and restricted. A responsible assertion of content is a restricted assertion. This restriction equally marks the assertion and the content. Indeed, there is no restriction of assertion except as the content is itself responsibly limited. Knowledge is the responsible restriction of content.

A restricted content is finite, and expresses *a finite point of view*. It expresses the incomplete and the contingent. To assert responsibility is to do so in view of alternatives, and those alternatives are not absolutely, but only conditionally, excluded. An absolute exclusion has no ground and reduces to dogmatism, since the alternative may be asserted with an equal right, where neither can show any right. Thus, to escape dogmatism, all specific assertion must become contingent, and no such assertion offers either original or eventual finality.

The situation so defined is the process of securing meaning by progressive limitation. It defines no absolute content, nor can it ever win such content. The restriction of content is the symbol and the actuality of a *finite point of view*, and hence implies a code of criticism as the necessary condition of responsible assertion. Dogmatisms always try at some point to escape from that code.

For example, the attempt to treat realism as a hypothesis that is well grounded but concerned with an existent physical realm which has a structure of its own independent of what we think of it is a contradiction in terms. Here we have an attempt to use logic on materials that escape the contingency of the finite point of view that logic defines. There can be no logical "hypothesis" nor any "well grounded" assertion about any situation or event that escapes the order of the standpoint that asserts it. Not by logic can one reach any independent region. For logic is the order of assertion and of negation in a context of eternally incomplete, accidental, and actually finite content; and whatever it touches must be part of the region of contingent finitude, and not some transcendental region independent of the finite point of view. Nor can one say that by logical hypothesis one has made such a region "probable." It is neither probable nor improbable, but simply outside the scope of any logical procedure. No realist, interested in asserting an "epistemological gulf,"[1] or in crossing that gulf, ought to borrow authority from logic. There are some features about realism that merit the concern of all students, but the attempt to make it logical is not one of them. Realism is a form of dogmatism, since its essence is the denial of the ontological status of criticism, that is, of the finite point of view. It must escape from that finitude in order to establish a region related to it, perhaps "causally." But to do so is to make assertions that, by avoiding the restrictions by which finitude is defined and generated, become unrestricted and dogmatic. Consequently, the line between realism and skepticism is purely temperamental. Santayana declares that "there is no first principle of criticism"; but from that alone one could not read off whether he was a skeptic or a realist.[2] Curiously, he seems to stand in both camps. But such a result is no accident, since the acceptance of criticism as definitive of all possible assertions of content is repugnant to both. Realism must somewhere become dogmatic. The alternative is to grant criticism an ontological status, and that is not realism, but idealism.

This issue seems fairly straightforward; to prove that one could avoid dogmatism and skepticism by repudiating the ontological force of criticism, of the finite point of view.

One reason why realism has had so much success is that so-called idealisms have also set up some "epistemological gulf," only they tell a different story of what lies over it. They call it God or spirit, or many spirits. That is all the same. It doesn't matter what form dogmatism takes; what matters is that somewhere assertions of specific content are made that claim to escape from the relativity of a critical process. Josiah Royce's Absolute is an essentially realistic device. It is the completion of a finite point of view, although that point of view defines the impossibility of completion in every one of its categories and processes.

Final, completed, and independent content is impossible by definition. Content, as limited, necessarily invites restriction, and hence the order of contingency. Consequently, Absolutes shade off into mysticism. They become indefinable in any terms through which meaning is won, that is, through the categories. Categories are rules for limitation. To be sure, they also define direction and movement, but never a *fait accompli*. It does not matter whether such Absolutes are realistic or "idealistic"; they are equally nonsense, because they have removed themselves from the region where sense occurs.

Consequently, all Absolutes beyond the gulf are meaningless, whether they be realistic or "idealistic." Realists seem often to be more generous than idealists in claiming only probability for their view. But one may fear the Greeks bearing gifts. To argue with realism on the basis of probability is to have granted its position in principle. And so-called idealists who urge the greater likelihood of their own view of what lies over the gulf, by admitting the gulf, admit realism. Consequently, the issue is, once more, the possibility of escaping the restriction of limited assertions responsibly made, and of defining the order of criticism as the order of the real. If the order of criticism is not the order of the real, then all rules are off; and if it is, then it seems necessary to forgo all claims to what is not illustrative of the absolute order of contingency.

To avoid dogmatism is not the same as avoiding assurance, although the two are frequently identified. It is responsibility—criticism—that avoids dogmatism. The alternative to an authoritative code is dogmatism and skepticism. Indeed, dogmatism can be avoided, not by avoiding assurance, but by placing that assurance in the code of criticism. No assurance at all is skepticism; uncritical assurance is dogmatism; criticism as assurance is idealism.

It is fair to recognize that realism has no conscious wish to be dogmatic. Indeed, the contrary is the case, as its emphasis on logic, analysis, and tentativeness so clearly shows. Nor yet does it avow skepticism. It attempts to avoid them both. But the manner of the avoidance accepts the standpoint of contingency, only to repudiate the base degrees by which it has risen and to overleap itself as it falls into the epistemological gulf.[3] It urges tentativeness over conclusions that, most assuredly, are not certain, but that by its own logical methods cannot claim even the color of probability. It gives reasons for what reason repudiates—the unconditioned, yet related, region of absolute objectivity. Thus realism helps to set more clearly the problem of avoiding the unconditioned by developing impossible probabilities "pinnacled dim in the intense inane."[4]

III

It is characteristic of realism that it deals with the content rather than with the order of experience. For that reason, it produces hypotheses, that is, logical solutions. The content of experience, as accidental, might be otherwise. Data that are assumed, but are essentially accidental, *require* hypotheses to explain them. Consequently, realists insist on doing more than describing the real; they reach it as the consequence of a theory.

There is no theory as an answer to necessary problems, but only to accidental problems. Where there is theory the data might be otherwise, and the explanation of them might also be false. If the data cannot be otherwise, their understanding invokes no condition, that is, no theory. What cannot be otherwise, that is, the absolutely necessary, is contradicted by any attempt to explain it, since to explain is to destroy its necessity and to render it contingent. Thus, when realism deals with the body-mind problem, it cannot regard either body or mind as necessary, but only as contents of experience. For if either or both are necessary to the possibility of experience, if they are not accidental content, then any attempt to explain their occurrence or their relations must be question-begging.

Theory can deal only with the accidental, and for that reason is for science and not for philosophy. For any theory is no more than the exemplification of the real in a special case. The validity of a theory derives from its faithfulness to good form—that is, to its power to force accidental content into the pattern of the real. Consequently, as the real is defined as causal, spatial, changing, coherent, the scientist can force a theory on his data. His data may be wrong, or his theory false, but the power of theory lies in this unification of diversity in accordance with the form of being. To suppose, for example, that not every event has a cause, or that contradictions are permissible, is to rob scientific theory of its authority and compulsion. In detail a theory is tentative, and that seems to win our hearts;

but in principle it must be necessary if it is to win our heads. Consequently, what any theory precisely misses is a definition of the real. The real is what tests; it is not something tested. The real is the order that permits theories, but it is not itself a theory nor derived from theory. A theory of reality is a contradiction.

Realism has no necessary problems. It cannot account for the occurrence of its problems. They merely happen. Contrast this with even so simple a situation as that with which the Milesians dealt. The real, they said, must have some sort of unity. There lies a necessary problem for thought. But it was a problem not about accidental content, but about the possibility of intelligible content. Their answers were dogmatic because they asserted a specific content as absolute. But their problem was not dogmatic. Or again, Kant faced the atomism of Hume and found no unity. Yet unity seemed necessary; to secure it he made some dogmatic assumptions, but in the interests of a necessary problem. But realism, stressing its logical, empirical, and accidental content, can give no explanation for its own endeavors. Why project hypotheses? What requires them? To answer such questions is to go beyond hypotheses and to assert necessary order as the character of the real, leaving hypotheses to do the work that they so plainly are fitted to do—namely, to apply that order to accidental content. Realism can give no warrant for its own endeavors. Traditional dogmatism at least possesses a necessary problem and so regards it; realism is a curious variant in that it makes even the problem dogmatic. But because it announces its devotion to logic and to theory it often succeeds in an appearance of cautious scrutiny. And, of course, the merely hypothetical or probable status of its *answers* is only the necessary reflection of the accidental status of its *problem*. They go together.

IV

Idealism, if it is to be more than another form of realism, can be no doctrine of content. It must be a doctrine of form, order, structure. It must deny that body, mind, cause, universals, and so forth, are materials for logical play. Take, for example, the fortunes of space from John Locke onward. So long as space was regarded as a quality it was content, and because it seemed so invariable it was given a status outside the mind. It was not subjectively variable. Nowadays it has come to be regarded as one of the factors definitive of the finite point of view, a category of orientation for any axis of reference. It has lost its objectivity but it has not become subjective, that is, psychological. Rather it defines the psychological. Books on psychology show an amusing tortuousness over space, because they cannot make it content nor derive it from content. But if the independent physical realm is to be robbed of space, it becomes nothing that any physicist could recognize as his domain.

It is, of course, impossible in a short essay to do more than assert that, for idealism, the alleged content for which realisms invent so many theories and so much cosmic machinery is not content at all. Psychology and physics, for example, deal with different but necessary aspects of the same content, ordering it as purposive and as causal. Both orders are necessary to its meaning, for without cause purpose can neither formulate nor execute itself, and without purpose no cause can be investigated in its specific conditions. Both cause and purpose imply the dynamic teleology of a finite point of view. All the categories represent codes for the restriction of the content of finite points of view. Every category describes at once an infinite order and a finite content that seeks to enlarge itself. Categories are not transcendental, nor are they psychological and accidental. They are the structure of criticism, the dynamic of expanding meanings according to law. Thus, idealism asserts no Absolute, but rather denies the possibility of any assertion immune from the order of contingency. It is that order which is absolute.

Idealism cannot claim to be another philosophy. It must claim to be philosophy, because it has grappled with the problem of how philosophic assertions can occur without dogmatism and skepticism. All its problems and, accordingly, all its answers are necessary. *There is no necessary answer except to a necessary problem.* Very rightly, realism claims no necessary answers. For illustration consider the antithesis presented above. Dogmatism and skepticism challenge by their opposition the possibility of responsible assertion, and how to make such assertions is an unavoidable question if questions are to occur. The great genius of Plato defined this problem in the *Meno*, where it is clearly brought out that the definition of virtue (or reality) lays a challenge as to how specific assertions are to be made; "for if one knows one has no need to inquire, and if not, one cannot; for one does not know the very subject about which one is to inquire."[5] All necessary problems refer to this possibility of making any assertion.

Accordingly, the program for idealism prescribes the very arduous analysis of the finite point of view. Just what is included in that view no one fully knows. But bit by bit the history of philosophy has been revealing its features. The alleged Aristotelian correction of Plato, that matter as well as form is necessary for the assertion of any content, is thoroughly Platonic in its emphasis, namely, in the further exploration of the conditions of meaning. More recently, the arguments of J. G. Fichte, Friedrich Schelling, O. H. Howison, Royce, and William Ernest Hocking have elaborated the dialectical union of self, other, and nature. They have shown that objectivity occurs only as social contrast, and that the communal status of nature, so often invoked by realists, expresses the union of minds and has no meaning apart from them, nor they from nature. In short, the moral imperative is imperative only as a phase of the absolute assertion of being, one of its laws or categories. Detailed expositions of such problems are difficult, but few have attempted them.

Finally, it seems fair to ask what the history of philosophy is about. Idealism answers that it is the progressive exploration of the structure of criticism, of the possibility of assertion, of the finite point of view. And if that history is more than a collection of variant theories, those theories must be aiming at something. What a theory says is of small importance; what it is aiming at is very important. But what it aims at is the real, and it can never test the success of its purposes in terms of its theoretical result. What, then, enables one to arbitrate among theories? Idealism answers that there is no arbitration except in the rejection of theory as the instrument of defining the real. If one knew how to arbitrate one would not need hypotheses, for they are the very assertions to be judged. Thus, the history of philosophy is the objectification of the endeavor to reach the conditions of assertion. There will be no bar to new inventions until philosophers focus on the conditions that make even error possible.

The true philosophy, it seems fair to say without partisan bias, must be capable of reconciling opposed philosophies. It can do this only as it finds all of them in a measure correct. But no one can assert correctness save as the necessary. And that is the ontological force of the critical structure. To explore that is the task for idealism.

NOTES

1. The term "epistemological gulf" was used by Miller's Williams College philosophy colleague Professor James Bissett Pratt.
2. See George Santayana, *Scepticism and Animal Faith*, chapter 1, which bears the title "There is no First Principle of Criticism."
3. For other occurrences of the expression "the base degrees by which it [or "we" or "one"] has risen, see *The Paradox of Cause* (p. 86), *The Philosophy of History* (p. 64), *The Midworld of Symbols and Functioning Objects* (p. 8), and *In Defense of the Psychological* (p. 83). The several uses of this expression, and of Miller's references to primitive animism, are indications of what Miller sometimes calls the "earthy" character of his philosophy, and point to early stages in the history of the human acts that have constituted a "midworld," or "the actual." For the earliest occurrence of the themes of the earthy and the primitive in Miller's writings, see *The Definition of the Thing*, pp. 11, 143, and 152–53.
4. Percy Bysshe Shelley, *Prometheus Unbound*, III, iii, 193.
5. Plato, *Meno*, 80e.

The Dialectic

This essay offers one of Miller's best discussions of his critically important concepts of universality and necessity. It might be supposed that his thoroughly historical philosophy—among whose categories are finitude, contingency, relativity, and revision—would and could have no place for the notions of universality and necessity. But, writing in an era whose chief mode of skepticism he sometimes calls "nihilistic," Miller defends a conception of "the universal and necessary" that not only challenges the nihilistic outlook but equally challenges the rationalist and theocentric philosophies with which the notions of the universal and the necessary have largely been associated. Miller locates universality and necessity not in any alleged timeless truth but in concrete acts that are the dialectically interdependent categorial preconditions for the achievement of any disclosure, any truth, at all. It is the "constitutional" that is universal and necessary. Frankly indebted to Immanuel Kant's tempering of rationalism by limitation of the categories to the spatio-temporal and the contingent, Miller embraces G. W. F. Hegel's historicizing of the categories while rejecting Hegel's absolutist conception of history as "the march of God through the world." He can be seen as both tempering Kant by Hegel and tempering Hegel by Kant.

This is one of the many applications of Miller's strategy of dialectical mediation, a *critical* procedure for the resolution of philosophical differences, while also a *genial* procedure seeking the sympathetic reconciliation of philosophical antitheses that might otherwise appear to be contradictories. As such, it is obviously indebted to Hegel's dialectical procedure. But it is also indebted to Socratic dialectic, a matter of *talk* between inquirers where the talk is motivated by the quest for a common wisdom. Yet again, it is indebted to a more specifically Platonic sense of dialectic, where the syntactical uniting and differentiating of talk is itself the bearer and sign of *logos*—that is, speech as thoughtful ordering. The universality and necessity Miller evokes in the present essay are resident in the formal order of human thought and speech, a specifically *historical* order of human acts. They are a matter of a thoughtful speech that declares and so defines, that conceives order and thereby discloses both order and disorder, and is subject to the very order it discloses.

In the present essay, Miller claims that what bars the way to a genial and critical resolution of philosophical disputes is a skepticism that has resulted from the assumption
that "a condition of the validity of philosophy is the satisfactoriness of some one philosophy" that allegedly "can give an unambiguous and complete argument on all philosophical issues." Miller claims, to the contrary, that "all systems have some truth," or, as
he sometimes said, "nobody is just plain wrong." The great problem for community,
whether philosophical or political, is not wholesale ignorance, blindness, or confusion;
it is rather partial truth that has not recognized its partiality, its need for dialectical
interrelation with other views within a structured, syntactical "whole" or "world" of necessarily interdependent features. This is in accord with Miller's conception of a philosophical beginning: It can only be historical. It cannot begin at all unless it has a basis
in a degree of truth already resident in ordinary experience and action, and it is needed
because this prior truth *is* partial and partializing: There is a "discord of running experience." Ordinary life is thus for Miller both a locale of truth and a locale of discord. In
the former lies the justification for geniality, while in the latter is found the justification
for criticism. Miller here offers a number of examples of discordant antitheses that,
when dialectically reconceived, are found to require each other.

Appended to the three sections of Miller's essay as a fourth section is a brief note in
which he succinctly characterizes dialectic relative to the logical operations of analysis and synthesis. He holds that dialectic is the functional interrelation of analysis and
synthesis.

"The Dialectic," written in the middle 1930s, is found in Papers & Letters of John William
Miller, *edited by Eugene R. Miller (Miller Papers 55:2, pp. 256–71). The note here appended
to it is a May 9, 1933, entry in a notebook located in Miller Papers 9:5, bearing the title
"Analysis and Synthesis as Philosophical Ideals." On talk as constitutive and disclosive, see
"Philosophy Is Just Talk," below, and the chapter "'Explaining' Language" in* The Mid-
world of Symbols and Functioning Objects *(pp. 66–75).*

I. THREE SORTS OF PHILOSOPHIC CONCLUSIONS

The chief obstacle to a confident study of philosophy is the common
belief that its problems are insoluble, that the utmost to be hoped for
is an acquaintance with the typical formulations of world views and with
the more persistent issues concerned in the disputes between world
views. Indeed, skepticism has always played a large part in the history of
philosophy and appears among its very earliest solutions. This tendency
has eloquent contemporary defenders. George Santayana, writing in 1915,
has given voice to a profound skepticism. "How should a complete chart
of the universe descend into the twilight of an animal mind, served by

quite special senses, swayed by profound passions, subject to the epidemic delusions of the race, and lost in the perhaps infinite world that bred it?"[1] He is prepared to respect philosophers for their sincerity and humanity while rejecting their thought as "personal, temperamental, accidental and premature." Philosophies, he says, are "human heresies." And the student of philosophy not uncommonly feels that he cannot hope to acquire impersonal information but only the individual view of an author approved by tradition or by fashion, or else the vagrant and unsanctioned opinions of an instructor blindly unaware of his own absurd inconclusiveness.

Skepticism, examining the various systems of philosophy and finding no one of them adequate, concludes that no system can be adequate. Since no formulation is or can be final, any system is merely personal heresy. Apparently the skeptic assumes that a condition of the validity of philosophy is the satisfactoriness of some one philosophy. There ought to be one correct system if confidence is to be restored. A definite final system and no final system are the alternatives.

It seems unnecessary to argue that if the alternatives are adequately stated in that way, the game is up. No one can possess all the answers to all the questions; no one can give an unambiguous and complete argument on all philosophic issues. Any system that fails to find a place for every fact and every question must abate its claim to completeness and to inclusive validity. It will not be a world view, but a partial view. Consequently, a rival formula in which the neglected interest secures respectful treatment is bound to appear.

There is, however, a third way of approaching philosophy, which rejects both skepticism and its usually suppressed assumption that some one system should be the right one. This third approach finds its chief historical exemplification in Plato (427–347 B.C.), Aristotle (384–322 B.C.), and G. W. F. Hegel (1770–1831). In reviewing the speculations of his predecessors, Aristotle finds much in them to admire and to adopt. He does not reject even fantastic solutions as wholly wrong, finding in them sound insights that somewhere went astray. He writes in his *Metaphysics*: "For the earliest system of philosophy concerning all things was like unto one articulating with a stammer."[2] No one can deny either that stammering speech lacks clarity or that it makes some sense. He thanks his predecessors: "But not only is it just to return thanks to those with whose opinions one may have fellowship, but also to those who have enunciated their sentiments more superficially."[3] Apparently, then, he finds both truth and error in what has gone before. No one system has all the truth; all systems have some truth.

The climax of this third view of philosophy, that all systems contribute to the truth, is found in Hegel. He regards "the diversity of philosophical systems as the progressive evolution of truth."[4] A false philosophical formula must be its own physician, finding in its own unrecognized assumptions the corrective of its blindness or of its exaggeration. The true philosophy is no special or exclusive result; it is rather to be found in the understanding of the motives that produce varied and apparently conflicting answers. Those answers are never contradictory; they are supplementary. The task of a sympathetic, urbane, and undogmatic philosophy lies in the patient discovery of the way in which the truth includes seeming antitheses.

Of this tendency to reject some part of the truth there are many examples. We are likely to say that Suez is east of New York, but some people reach Suez by proceeding to the west. From an abstract point of view, a point to the east lies in a direction opposite to west, but clearly that is not the whole truth. One needs both ideas for the full story of how to get about. In politics, there has occurred for many centuries a struggle for personal freedom, climaxed in Europe by the French Revolution. Yet it took but a few years to exhibit the brutality of extreme liberty, the need for concessions to one's neighbors and a sovereign authority to enforce on the individual those very limitations without which his freedom could satisfy not even himself. The Bible contains a great example of such paradoxes in the claim that to find oneself is to lose oneself. Thomas Carlyle, searching for the recipe for contentment, found that it could be won only by reducing one's demands on the universe, although, in a sense, one could never have too much. We find ourselves dealing with a lawful, causal, and mechanical nature, irked by its apparent prohibition of freedom and independence; we thereupon assert that necessity must give way in order that freedom can find its opportunity, only to discover that a lawless nature would quite prevent the very control we so desperately covet. We like to command others, to be served by them in order to be free from heavy labor and detailed planning; but we find that disintegration, feebleness, and uncertainty follow fast upon the authority that seeks to escape the labor of mastering its materials. "In the very temple of delight, veiled melancholy has her sovereign shrine."[5] And the psalmist declares that it was from the depths that he cried unto the Lord.

What philosophy has done, according to Hegel, is to emphasize what is only partially true, and, by neglecting other elements in the picture, to make false and unsatisfactory essential features of the whole. Consequently, there arise quarrelsome schools, each asserting an exclusiveness it does not possess. These schools and systems see contradictions where there is only paradox; they refuse conciliation because they do not understand their own need to complete themselves by embracing necessary supplements to their own partiality. Liberty is not achieved without law, but through law; command can be won only through discipline; effectiveness of will is possible only through natural order.

It would, however, be a great mistake to suppose that this third and conciliatory view of philosophy is an eclecticism. It would be a mistake to regard it as a patchwork composition of many systems. An organic mutuality must govern the union of elements. In making a map one does not arbitrarily mix a bit of east with a bit of west in order to include both; rather, one perceives the mutual necessity of each factor, its abstractness and meaninglessness without the other. Indeed, no necessary reconciliation of systems could be possible unless the incompleteness of each were self-confessed. The union of space and time as presented in the modern theory of relativity is not an arbitrary and mechanical compound but an organic integrity of meaning. No one can tell time apart from the changes that objects undergo in space, and no one can declare what he means by space without using the concept of the simultaneous. It is an accurate, though incomplete, definition of space to call it the theory of the simultaneous. If space and time could obtain independent demonstration, if it were possible to tell the story of one without invoking the other, the theory of relativity would collapse.

This union of concepts is what philosophy calls the dialectic. The reason special systems are partial, inaccurate, and dogmatic is very simple: They have failed to carry out the dialectic extension of their own partially accurate claims. For example, to assert duty is to assert freedom, as Kant pointed out in one of the great arguments in the history of philosophy. Obviously one cannot rest there; one must go on to a further examination of the character of a world in which one could be free. Certainly such a world would entail mind, will, and purpose. But shall one define mind apart from nature and its laws? Some insist that such a separation is required; others that it is impossible. What is here important is not a solution of the problem but rather the fact that, in terms of this third and dialectical view of philosophy, the answer can be found only in a careful analysis of the factors that enter our definitions of mind and of nature. If in defining mind one cannot omit nature, and vice versa, a unity of these two troublesome ideas will have been achieved, a union dialectical and organic rather than externally mechanical. And surely, were the externally mechanical account of the relation of mind and nature correct, it would be only decent to make good on the claim that the definition or meaning of each could be given in complete independence of the other.

Indeed, it seems historically accurate to say that there are only two kinds of philosophies: on the one hand, those that treat the world as an association of independently definable elements; on the other hand, those that claim that in the necessary union of all basic factors a world becomes intelligible. The separation of factors into independent regions, things, or concepts necessarily breeds skepticism, for one can never be assured that all the factors are known, or, what is much more important, that there is any way of finding them out. A world broken into disconnected pieces, a world without an inner, organic, and dialectical unity, offers no sure way of approach. What one finds remains an accident; what one finds may even quite pass away so far as one could tell. To tell the story of the world in its larger outlines requires a mode of approach to it that fits the facts to be discovered. But a broken, separated, and unconnected world cannot be systematically investigated because it offers no law, rule, or organization. A systematic study requires a systematic object, an object that expresses and embodies the sort of order through which the investigation proceeds. It is possible to discover and assign a date in history only because the order of time in which we investigate sequences fits the facts to be discovered. It would be useless to look for temporal sequences among events having no time relations; it would be useless to investigate causes if events happened without mutual influence; it would similarly be useless to attempt a picture of the world as a whole were there no path along which we could proceed, no rule of procedure, no clues to the next factor, and no way of being sure that our discoveries were more than a subjective revelation, a personal heresy, an accidental experience that might pass with the day and never be capable of universal acceptance. What the dialectical view of philosophy claims is that from any philosophical idea all philosophical ideas necessarily flow; that no matter where one begins, whether with space, time, mind, cause, nature, truth, error, or illusion, all the rest will inevitably follow in the completed meaning of the starting point itself. And furthermore, it is the claim of this organic and dialectical view that it not only defines the road to conciliation between systems but also defines philosophy itself.

II. THE NECESSARY

Philosophy may be defined as the study of necessary questions. Questions are necessary when they are implied in any experience and action regardless of its special content. Science and history concern themselves with the details of the world. What they have to say deals with local truth and the evidence for it. Local truth depends on local evidence. To decide what was settled at the Treaty of Versailles in 1919 requires examination of documents irrelevant to the decisions of the Council of Nicaea in 325. Science and history study parts by examining parts. One may know a good deal about space and time without knowing places and dates, a good deal about arithmetic without knowing the population of New York or the amount of gold in the Federal Reserve banks. Any object or group of objects has numerical properties neutral to its specific colors, weight, or length. What one means by counting is, accordingly, a question that appears regardless of what one may count in detail. In a similar manner, what one means by a true proposition has nothing to do with the specific denotation of subject and predicate; all sorts of content may enter true or false propositions. One may study geometry and be none the wiser as an astronomer, since no theorem in Euclid demonstrates the diameter of the earth or the distance between earth and sun. Again, one may be armed with sound moral principles without understanding their interpretation in the family or in the state. Men of good will may differ over details of action because of difference in their knowledge of fact. There may be agreement on the universal sway of causal order but no end of dispute over the specific cause of a specific event. There are, accordingly, two types of questions and two corresponding types of answers: The one refers to the local, specific, and relatively accidental; the other to the universal, general, and necessary. Philosophy studies only necessary questions.

Not everyone asks these necessary questions. Most of our daily tasks concern special questions, and consequently it is difficult to effect the orientation of thought required by philosophy. We habitually deal with parts of the world, not with its general character. And yet that general character pervades all parts and makes possible their organization. To count dollars or planets seems to most men more real and concrete than a knowledge of counting generally. To investigate the benefits or harm of direct primaries seems more useful, direct, and concrete than an investigation of justice and the basis of political association. As a matter of fact, many have held that mathematics is more concrete than its applications, and that a knowledge of justice is concerned with a deeper, because more inclusive, value than direct primaries. In any case, it is stupid to suppose that the laws of numbers or morals can be separated from their applications, or that the applications make sense without the laws. We sometimes fail to ask necessary questions because the difficulties and contradictions of theory and of practice have not yet caught our attention. It is only when we get into trouble that we summon physician, priest, or philosopher, or that we consult the road map. Necessary questions, like local questions, occur in a context of uncertainty and contradiction.

Our normal world is full of such apparent contradictions, and there are many philosophers who see no way of resolving them. Some such paradoxes have been mentioned above. We commonly treat nature as a causal order; yet we commonly act as if we were free, as if our bodies and their environment responded to will. We are much impressed by the influence of heredity and environment; yet we treat criminals as if they were responsible for wrong. We say of space that it is infinitely divisible, that between any two points lies a third; yet we suppose that from a given point some other can be reached. We ascribe a predicate, or many predicates, to a subject, treating each term as an independent variable; yet we would be at a loss to denote the subject stripped of its predicates, or the predicates wandering in disembodied irrelevance to their subjects. Such examples could be extensively multiplied. They all present a challenge to the integrity of our experience. When we perceive that challenge, we have asked a philosophic question, and when we perceive the necessity of the challenge, we understand the difference between a local and an inevitable problem. Philosophic questions do not represent the clever invention of idle minds that have cut away from special facts or deeds. On the contrary, all the problems of philosophy spring from the blindness, incoherence, and suffering of daily living. They engage any mind that looks for power, control, and orientation, that wishes to understand itself and its world. Order is said to be heaven's first law; it is also the law of philosophy. Necessary questions, although not always asked, are always waiting to be asked because they lurk in every bit of our experience.

III. NECESSARY QUESTIONS AND STRUCTURE

The third or organic view of philosophic systems deals with skepticism by denying its argument. It does not follow from the partiality of many systems that no system is possible. No system is wholly false; all contain an element of validity. What is valid in them is their discovery of inevitable problems concealed in running experience and only occasionally so deeply disturbing as to bring about an attempt to deal with them. Those problems are concerned not with the local details but with very general features of the world.

Those general features concern order, form, or structure. No problem of detail is inevitable; every problem of structure is inevitable. One may prefer to tell the truths of physics rather than of psychology, but the meaning of truth will be found in both. One may prefer the counting of money to the counting of years, but counting remains. One may choose to walk over wood-paths or over concrete, but one cannot choose to deal with space and time. For these concepts denote not things but the order of things. Necessary concepts are concepts of order.

In the second place, they are *concepts of universal incidence*. No necessary concept can fail to strike everywhere. It seems obvious that what must strike every fact cannot be found in one place, time or condition; it must be involved in every fact or event, and under all conditions. And, what is more, a concept of universal incidence cannot be restricted to some part of a given fact; it must permeate every part of every fact. It will not be possible to cut off one end of a board that contains, say, space, leaving no space at all in the remainder. Nor will such an operation be possible with any truly universal and inevitable idea. Every universal idea must be found wherever any other is found. The reason there are many philosophies is largely explained by the failure to investigate the full story of any one universal concept.

Now it must be immediately apparent that where *many* concepts are universal, they must be related in an organic way. They must be organic or dialectical; otherwise their complete universality collapses, since their incidence would be local. They would not spread throughout the whole; they would not be completely neutral to what is peculiar and local.

Thus, a concept of universal incidence is dialectical *because* it is universal. Whatever aspect of experience could claim to be universal must necessarily be organic with every other universal concept. This relation is itself an illustration of a *dialectical pair* of concepts. Absolute universality requires organic or dialectical unity. Consequently, the demand that philosophy tell a story about the whole of the world is *equivalent* to the requirement that it deal only in structure, organism, and dialectic.

Organism can be roughly defined as the self-sustaining and the self-explanatory. There occurs among biologists and certain psychologists a bewildering confusion in the use of the terms *organism* and *mechanism*. On one page, the body is an organism; on the next, it turns out that all the explanations of its activities and changes follow the pattern of mechanism. Mechanism may be defined as the lawful or conditional interaction of *parts*. Consequently, whenever one deals with the human body as a thing among things, determined by its environing objects, one gives a mechanical description. As a matter of fact, no *separate* object can be an organism because its dependence on the order of all finite objects will abolish its self-containment. Only the whole is organic. It is organic because of its dialectical form and for no other reason.

If, then, we are to find necessary concepts, they must be structural, dialectical, and organic. In no other context can one find necessary questions and necessary answers. What makes questions necessary is the incompleteness of any dialectical concept taken in itself. To tell time is to encounter space. Subjects become meaningless when not qualified by predicates. The recipe for truth is also the prescription for avoiding error. In psychology, a very dramatic interdependence of concepts discloses the inevitable progress from one to all, from perception to memory, imagination, purpose, attention, and emotion. And one should make it quite clear that apart from this structural whole there is no whole and no philosophy, that there are no necessary conclusions to be drawn from accidents and that without necessary conclusions, skepticism—or its twin, dogmatism—is reinstated.

Concepts of universal incidence are not analogous to class names, that is, to logical universals. A class name denotes a finite and particular type of object in terms of content; a concept of universal incidence denotes a property of all objects in terms of structure. "Table" is a class name—all the tables can be put on one pile; space is a structural concept—not all spaces can be put on one pile leaving a remainder. A concept of universal incidence is not at all the same as a finite universal, or class name, which gets its whole meaning from its explicit difference and partiality. Class names are variables, accidental, and fall within the structure of experience; philosophical concepts are constant, necessary, and descriptive of structure as such.[6]

No one will understand the world as a whole except through its form. Within the world there are many objects with all sorts of qualities, but the world as a whole is not an object and has no qualities. It is not an object of sense, for the eye is within it; it makes no sound to an alien ear of flesh and blood; it does not move in relation to another object, for there is no place external to it from which it can be viewed and that it does not include. In short, "You cannot stand on a platform outside the universe and snipe at it."[7] It is not even an object of imagination. Imaginary objects contain all the difficulties of real objects. One may in imagination tell a truth or a falsity, but what one means by truth is quite as vague in the imaginary as in the "real" world.

One often hears talk about the "physical universe," an expression designed to denote the whole; but that expression is a contradiction in terms. Physics as a science can study only the relative and only the qualified. It must use clocks, balances, and yardsticks, its actual findings often reducing to the reading of a pointer on a scale. Consequently, it studies lawful relations between special facts, and were it to relinquish that procedure, it would cease to be experimental or scientific. The sort of features that a world as a whole possesses will *in no case* be physical, where by physical is meant such properties of experience as can be studied by scientific method, by experiment, measurement, and the statement of lawful conditions for specific sorts of events.

Because the world as a whole quite lacks all the properties of specific events, it is often supposed that a knowledge of it is impossible. "Whatever we know must be specific" is the axiom of that agnosticism. Consequently, the aim of philosophy could be accomplished only in an ineffable transcendentalism where discursive thought and speech lost all application.

The basic answer to this obscurantism is a denial of its assumption that parts may be known and understood, while the whole cannot be grasped by thought. That assumption is false, provided that the whole is the *order* of its parts, an order without which the parts themselves cannot be known. Could one know parts without, in principle, sketching out the law of the whole, every philosophy would necessarily be an irresponsible transcendentalism. One ought, then, to gaze into a crystal or pass into a swoon in order to become ineffably enraptured. But to a person with questions about the paradoxes of partial features of experiences—such paradoxes as have been illustrated above—it is no comfort to be informed that his question about the order of parts can have no reply, and that it is answered by means of an escape to a region in which it doesn't occur! No, if one asks a fair question about the discord of running experience, one is entitled to an answer in terms of the question. For otherwise there is no answer, because there would no longer be a question. Indeed, if the questions of philosophy spring from inevitable paradoxes of experience, as the third and organic view holds, then one could abolish the question only by abolishing the total region of relative experience, the total region of specific fact and conditional events that science studies. For in that region alone can philosophic questions occur.

Here we face one of the most stimulating and decisive issues of the history of philosophy. All the questions about the world as a whole are prompted by the paradoxes of relative facts and finite purposes. Subject and predicate, body and mind, causation and freedom, truth and error—all these arise in the context of the relative. And yet, there seems to be no answer either in the world of specific facts, which only multiplies and perpetuates these difficulties, or in a transcendental region where there is not even a question. In terms of this apparent impasse, one could trace the motivation of agnosticism and mysticism. But the alternatives are false; they are false because the parts of the world do not make sense even as parts until they fall into an order. At this point it is, of course, dogmatic to declare what that order involves; but it may be indicated that it is the order of space, time, cause, truth, error, body, mind, and so forth. To order those concepts is the detailed business of philosophy, and a difficult business it is. But what is here important is the impossibility of talking about parts unless one has more than parts, unless, indeed, those parts express and embody the very relations that define an ideal whole. The structure of parts is the structure of the whole, and wholeness has no other meaning. To try to give it any other meaning is to lose the parts, the questions about them, and the answers to the questions.

IV. ANALYSIS AND SYNTHESIS AS PHILOSOPHIC IDEALS

Dialectic achieves both analysis and synthesis at once. Its analysis is simultaneously a synthesis. No philosophy should be one or the other abstractly. To manufacture a whole out of parts is to miss the law of totality, which has no parts, but only order. But order demands variety and hence also analysis.

Philosophy is the exhibition of dialectic synthesis by the analytic process of investigating the full meaning of its concepts. To analyze is to organize, when one deals with philosophic universals. On the other hand, to show the organic whole is to make it discursive and articulate. One needs a principle of "unlimited generality" as Ralph Barton Perry says, but it must not be an empty principle.[8] Without such a principle of unlimited generality there can be no ultimate unity. But unless that principle be the organic *order* of reality, it cannot be useful as an agent of intelligibility.

NOTES

1. George Santayana, "Philosophical Heresy," in *Obiter Scripta: Lectures, Essays and Reviews*, Justus Buchler and Benjamin Schwartz, eds. (New York and London: Charles Scribner's Sons, 1936), p. 102.
2. Aristotle, *Metaphysics*, I, 993a15.
3. Aristotle, *Metaphysics*, II, 993b12.
4. Hegel, *The Phenomenology of Mind*, trans. J. B. Baillie (1807. London: George Allen & Unwin, 1949), p. 68.
5. John Keats, *Ode on Melancholy*. Miller has updated Keats's spelling and capitalization.
6. On Miller's relating of the "structural" (or "universal," or "constitutive") to "the unique" (or "content," or the "special" or "specific," or "accidental"), see Stephen Tyman, *Descrying the Ideal: The Philosophy of John William Miller*, pp. 39–40.
7. Miller credited this assertion to a Williams College colleague, Romance Languages Professor Asa Henry Morton.
8. Ralph Barton Perry (1876–1957) taught philosophy at Harvard University from 1902 to 1946. Miller took a seminar given by Perry in 1920 (personal communication, Katherine Miller, August 1988). Now Perry is chiefly remembered as the author of *The Thought and Character of William James* (Boston: Little, Brown, 1935). In his early years Perry was best known as one of several proponents of a "new realism,"

and Miller's revision of idealism in his Harvard dissertation *The Definition of the Thing* (1922) was probably worked out in part by his reading of and discussions with Perry. One can see Miller arguing with Perry in several places in the dissertation. Miller's general agreement with what Perry called the principle of "unlimited generality" is evident in all of Miller's writing on universality, infinity, and order. But all of this work is an attempt to show that this is not an *empty* principle. A case in point is what Miller says of the unlimited generality of mathematics or physics: "Mathematics and physics develop within their own orbits. Whatever seems to be happened upon in those steadily powerful modes of discourse has grown from their own requirements. They are not pensioners of circumstance; rather, they declare the universal form of all circumstance. They haunt whatever we may say in particular" (*The Midworld of Symbols*, p. 107).

Are There Two Kinds of Categories?

This selection sheds considerable light on Miller's genealogy of philosophy. It helps one see why Miller looks to what he calls "the base degrees by which we have risen." Miller finds the basic grounds (the "constitutive" structures) of both philosophy and science not primarily in a historically recent dispassionate rational reflection but in an age-old, even primitive, human action in the world.

One might at first assume that reflective thinking generates categories that were absent in prereflective and precritical experience of the world. Miller explicitly denies this. What reflection does is to bring to explicit awareness the categorial order already lurking at the heart of human action. This is reminiscent of an abrupt realization reached by Socrates in Plato's *Republic* after he and Glaucon have been struggling in perplexity for a definition of justice: "Here! Here! Glaucon. . . . As men holding something in their hand sometimes seek what they're holding, we too didn't look at it but turned our gaze somewhere far off, which is perhaps just the reason it escaped our notice . . . we have been saying and hearing it all along without learning from ourselves that we were in a way saying it." Or, as Miller observes here, "Truth is told long before truth is defined; virtue occurs in conduct long before its meaning is understood." Philosophical reflection discloses that "ideals are always operative"—that the familiar world is already shot through with an ideality, or lawfulness, or normativeness that has articulated both a natural and a moral or teleological order; and that same process of articulation governs reflection on its prior unreflective functioning. What accounts for this is that human experience is inherently active—thoughtful, linguistic-categorial, and syntactical. This helps to explain what Miller had meant by his claim in "Dogmatism, Skepticism, and Criticism" that "the definition of reality is the structure of criticism": The same conceptual ordering already self-effacingly present in our ordinary experience of reality structures critical reflection on that reality and on our relation to it.

Thus philosophical reflection in principle cannot understand itself as shifting from the temporal to the eternal, from the historical to the ahistoric, or from data and facts to metaphysical speculation. It must understand itself as still historical, as made possible by the very same prereflective experience of an articulated reality that it might otherwise aspire to supplant or transcend. Thus it will find the most basic task of critical reflection to be that of taking its place within history—recognizing, affirming, revising, and so maintaining the ideational order already inherent in every disclosure of reality, no matter how unreflective, pedestrian, or base. It is not that this order is not subject to revision; history is the story of that revision. It is rather that it is universal in its incidence and a necessary condition for all disclosure and all truth. So there can be no question of suspending it wholesale, only of revising it in one or another specific respect, one step at a time, insofar as changing historical conditions demand a revision. It is a matter of dealing with what is "constitutional." The situation is analogous to operating within a political constitution that anticipates maintaining itself in changing historical circumstances by providing for its own amendment.

These pages are found in running notes Miller made during a course he taught in the spring of 1933 (Miller Papers 19:11). It should be noted that Miller's use of the expression "will to power" derives not from Friedrich Nietzsche but from Miller's Harvard mentor William Ernest Hocking (see Man and the State, *passim [New Haven, Conn.: Yale University Press, 1926]). The passage from Plato's* Republic *(432d–e) cited above is translated by Allan Bloom (*The Republic of Plato, *New York: Basic Books, 1968). For Miller's detailed and systematic exposition of the linguistic-categorial ordering mentioned above, see* The Definition of the Thing. *On what Miller finds of philosophical relevance in "base" primitive thought, see in Part 2, "Constitutional Utterance: Its Archaic Form and Abiding Force." On the relation of metaphysical constitution to political constitution, see Part 3 of this volume and Michael J. McGandy's "John William Miller's Metaphysics of Democracy,"* Transactions of the Charles S. Peirce Society, *31 (1995): pp. 598–630.*

T he question whether there are two sorts of categories is suggested by the peculiarity of reflection.

For reflection discloses standards and ideals: truth, beauty, and goodness. These seem to get meaning only as they are appreciated, as they are perceived as the locus of standards, as the meaning of standards. Yet unreflective knowledge *contains all the categories* necessary for a world of experience. Are there, therefore, peculiar categories applicable to reflection?

Reflection does not change either the content or the form of a world of experience. What reflection does is to reveal the order as *order*, the whole as *whole*, but in so doing it does not yield another principle of organization.[1]

Truth is told long before truth is defined; virtue occurs in conduct long before its meaning is understood. Beauty is created unconsciously. Reflection only intuits the order of such norms. When that order is disclosed, the work of reflection is finished.

Immediate knowledge could not add further categories, for then the need of directly appreciating *their* dialectical unity would arise. Reflection halts the regressus, because it is the means of absolute understanding. It deals not in the relative, but in the status of the relative order as a whole.

The categories are not understood by the aid of categories. They are merely known for what they are, namely, the rules of an orderly universe; ideals, always incomplete but dynamic and living.

Without the reflective appreciation of the categories, these ideals remain merely unconscious and impulsive. Not until one understands the truth, or virtue, can one defend the claim that one has really told the truth. For such a claim requires the ability to define what that truth is, and to *know that one knows* what one means by it.

So too with virtue. One may have excellent standards, but until one can show their absoluteness, their independence of accident, their freedom, one cannot prove one's virtue. And any standard not approved by reflection may be challenged and so overthrown, or at least doubted. Until the reflective appreciation of truth has been won, an attack on one's standards is always possible, leaving them arbitrary if unshaken, or else weakened and unsure. Of a good man whose standards are unreflective, another and reflective man may say that he is good; but the good and unreflective man cannot defend his virtue to himself or to another.

Thus reflection and reflection alone leaves one invulnerable. The invulnerable man is the reflectively assured man. Yet reflection *does not alter the law of the will*; it only perceives that law. This is the only law that is not capable of evasion by being understood (i.e., no law of empirical psychology can stand once it is known—thus in advertising). The law of freedom cannot be circumvented, but any law based on special and accidental features may be.

Reflective knowledge strengthens the will, but does not change its essence or direction. It can only report and appreciate that direction. But such a report and appreciative understanding prevents vacillation and vagrancy because it removes hesitation. It also permits a survey of a process to test its conformity with the law. To be sure, we always *intend* to realize that law, but our intention, unconscious of its own laws, can misinterpret itself. Thus, ethics is a form of the will to be, of the will to power; yet to know the general law of that power is to be able to avoid in principle a self-defeating self-assertion.

Thus these fundamental teleological and ideal intentions never cease to operate even in error and evil. But although operating, they miss the knowledge of the conditions on which they could be fulfilled.

Natural laws never fail. They always operate and do so successfully, or rather they *merely* operate, and there is no question of their failure. Teleological laws always operate but they may not achieve their inner intention. Ideality of purpose is persistence of operation of tendencies. No purpose, that is, no ideal purpose, can know itself in full detail at any stage. It cannot *cease* to operate *and still be an ideal tendency.* Its ideality is inseparable from its persistence.

Such ideal tendencies can get discovered to themselves only as they are first unconscious. For in no other way could their ideality be discovered. They need opposition, and failure, yet they must be revealed in their failure as truly as in their success. Their failures indeed stamp them as ever-present. Only for that reason can failure be asserted. The triumph of freedom is in its acquisition, that is, in reflective appreciation. The freedom of the self is a *free discovery of the self.* This discovery requires a question, an initial error and hesitation. To know what one wants requires the ability to indicate what one does *not* want, and that is possible only as ignorance of one's true want is one's initial situation.

To restate: The ideality of purpose must be discovered and cannot be known in advance. One must ask what one's purpose is, and make good on one's answer. But neither the question nor the answer could occur except in limitation and ignorance, in error, vice, or conflict. The question and the answer must occur together. Each implies the other.

The answer to the question of ideals, of direction, of freedom, is an absolute answer, and describes an absolute fact. But if so, then the *process* by which both question and answer occur must also be absolute, for both question and answer occur only in that process.

Thus, natural laws operate indifferently whether they are understood or not. They do not operate more surely when understood. But teleological laws, although always operative, seek an understanding of themselves as part of their operation and then they operate with greater sureness, with less self-defeat.

For it is remarkable that the defeats of life are brought about by the laws of life, that is, the defeat of mind is an inner defeat worked through its own ideal tendencies. This alone makes tragedy possible. Moral and spiritual death also comes through the law. Moral error has the same motive as moral victory, namely power, freedom, strength. Thus it is *because ideals are always operative*, but can also operate to their destruction, that their reflective recognition gives them force and firmness. Could they *cease* to operate, a knowledge of them would be useless and without guarantee of freedom; could they not be *liberated* and *augmented* by being known, the knowledge of them would again be unnecessary. In these ways, then, the laws of the spirit differ from laws of nature.

NOTES

1. Miller finds this inherence of form in the ordinarily, commonly experienced environment to be a sine qua non for an intelligible world. See *The Midworld of Symbols and Functioning Objects*, p. 163: "*Form has no application to a situation that is formless.* No test of 'fitness' of a form to the formless could be devised or imagined."

Categories as Historical and Existential

The two selections in this chapter from Miller's extensive philosophical correspondence were written after he had arrived at what is surely his greatest achievement, the notion of the "actuality" of a "midworld." The brief first selection summarizes what Miller takes to be the major problem bequeathed by Immanuel Kant to his successors: "universality without actuality," the absence of the historical act as the union in practice of form or concept and material content. This union affords "local control" through certain artifacts, as for example the clock or the yardstick, which can function to disclose particular times and spaces inasmuch as "clock" and "yardstick" are *embodied universality*, the system of mathematics present in material things. Miller first called them "artifacts" and later, more specifically, called them "functioning objects."

In "The Dialectic," Miller held philosophical concepts, such as space and time, to be "necessary and descriptive of structure as such," and it is amply clear in Miller's writings that he found Kant, whatever his limitations, to have made critical contributions to the establishment of that claim. But "The Dialectic" had identified G. W. F. Hegel as another important predecessor. The second selection presented here again invokes Hegel, and Hegel's revision of Kant, on behalf of the notion that universal and necessary concepts, far from being "a priori deliverances," emerge only from the historical process of the human "struggle for coherence." This supplies the motive for the shift to reflection discussed in "Are There Two Kinds of Categories?" Philosophical reflection has risen out of confusion regarding one's own identity and one's relation to one's natural and historical origins. A striking feature of this selection is its implication that philosophical categories are not "truths," but rather are processes that make possible any and all disclosures of truth or of fact. Categories, concepts of universal incidence, are "constitutional" acts. But they come to the fore in constitutional *crises*, when the entire relation of the self to others and to nature is in question; these are *personal* crises in which one's thought is forced back on the problem of its own authority, power, and freedom to criticize and revise itself. In Miller's view, as in Hegel's, such a crisis is not accidental. Rather, it is a precondition for exercising genuine and wise control as an individual and as a member of any community. That is why the personal crisis of skepticism is for Miller an uncircumventable prelude to becoming a self-critical and thus a responsible agent. One might perhaps compare this with William James's more psychological characterization of the "twice-born" individual in *The Varieties of Religious Experience.*

It is worth noting that in the late 1940s and the 1950s Miller responded, characteristically, both positively and critically to his students' fascination with existentialism. Alongside his teaching of the Americans Peirce, James, and Dewey, he was teaching the continentals Jean-Paul Sartre and José Ortega y Gasset, and he was reading, but not teaching, Martin Heidegger. He thought that important elements of existentialism were already present in Hegel. He identified with existentialism's vision of free self- and world-defining acts in finite historical circumstances and with its critique of ahistoric metaphysics. But he was critical of existentialism's tendency to celebrate the irrational and of its inability to credit common and constitutional formal order; it had not yet accomplished a dialectical coordination of the subjective and the objective, of existence and order, of freedom and community. In these respects, Hegel had already surpassed the existentialists.

The first selection is from a letter dated March 12, 1962, to Robert E. Gahringer (Miller Papers 22:14). The second selection is from a letter, ca. 1950, to Miller's son Paul (Miller Papers 21:8).

I

A characteristic of Immanuel Kant is a lack of concreteness and limitation. In the *Critique of Pure Reason* he has "space" as a category but no yardstick, "time" but no clocks, "cause" but no local controls. In the *Critique of Practical Reason* he has nobody living in Königsberg. So, he gives us a "phenomenal" order and a morality that draws on transcendent realities.

Universality without actuality leads to an abstract formalism or else to the [transcendent, noumenal] reality that is discontinuous with the immediate as articulated.

A formal actuality is functioning. It is the order of limitation. Beyond Kant one can come only to the actual. And so to the artifact, not to the concept, nor yet to content.[1] Kant left their presence, and their union, a mystery. These modes of actuality set up our conflicts.

II

In G. W. F. Hegel, philosophy becomes the dialectical order of constitutional concepts. But this order is genetically history; statically it is what Hegel calls "logic."

Genetically, the process starts anywhere. But, as genesis, it always starts with existence, with an actual puzzle or threat. Thus Hegel's intellectualism has a dynamic origin. It operates on emotion and desperation. This is not the emotion of psychology but more like that of religion. It is not cold reason. There is nothing to reason about except one's predicament, the baffling division of the self, of nature, or of a point of view as it asserts itself against its negation. Thus, self asserts itself against others. It is *not* others. They are external, casual, accidental. Yet without them it is incomplete, can't quite give shape to itself. Others can't quite be ignored without invading the self. The self is a puzzle to itself. So too with nature when one excludes that, makes it object, irrelevant, unessential. So with "cause"—when one asserts it one stands for it, and against purpose, or vice versa.

Outside this process of self-clarification there is no point of view. Hence philosophy is the same as history, that is, as the actual development in time of the categories.

This philosophy is, therefore, an "existence" philosophy. Dealing only in concepts, it finds those concepts demanded only in the concrete, applicable only to the life that is unorganized. They have no other locus or meaning.

Compare this with Kant. He too found the concept empty without content. But his categories have no genesis. They are a priori deliverances.

Hence, in Hegel, the categories, as in Kant, are related to experience. But they also grow from experience. They do not grow from induction of particulars. They grow from another dimension of experience, namely its struggle for coherence. Experience in Kant had no dimension in time. Hence, for Kant, time was phenomenal only, part of appearance. In Hegel time is lived, and Kant's abstract time is a generated result of experience when it considers itself, not objects. There has been this problem in philosophy: how to apply the maxim of experience to the categories. This is impossible, as Kant and others have shown, if one means psychological or inductive experience. But in Hegel experience becomes evolutionary, that is, historical. Time has lessons. These are not lessons of psychology, nor of natural science, but those of history, namely the revision of an outlook, not the verification of truths within an outlook.

All this is set out in a general way in the preface to *The Phenomenology of Spirit*. There Hegel makes it plain that he is dealing with the process of pure thought. Pure thought has itself as object. But thought makes itself object only in some concrete guise, as the thought of someone, or of some period, as asserting comprehension of some state of affairs. Thought is object to itself only when limited; but the limit, the source of confusion, is also imposed by thought, as when the self seeks to deny its involvement in the limiting selves of others, or in the limiting object called nature. Actuality, that is, existence, is this limited self.

The consequences of actuality are actuality. Yet this actuality is known only as the existence of pure thought, for example, of "self" in principle, or as "object" in principle, as "this," "now," "here," and so forth. This is the ideality of the actual. All categories are factors of life and experience. They are not general properties of the content of experience, but the operational modes of a life, its method of construing itself.

It seems worth pointing out that in Hegel philosophy becomes like art, "life disporting with itself."[2] Truth is no longer in question. What there may be in heaven or earth is irrelevant. I believe that philosophy must come to this. Freedom is nonsense in any other context than free activity, self-contained, enjoyed for its own sake. Thus the mystery of Hegel in a time when work must be useful and thought "truthful." That thought is its own object and *for that reason alone* discriminates between subject and object, self and nature, is the mystery. But it is a mystery that makes philosophies of "truth" taste like dishwater.

NOTES

1. That is, not to the bare concept or to bare content, but to the artifact (or functioning object) as what "enforces the distinction," as Miller sometimes says, between concept and content. Alternatively put, reflection shows the concept and content to be already present, and already *interdependent*, in entities as *actually* encountered, where, as Miller writes in "Philosophy Is Just Talk" (below), "Utterance is the actual." See especially *The Midworld of Symbols and Functioning Objects*, pp. 34 and 186.
2. See Hegel, Preface to *The Phenomenology of Mind*, trans. J. B. Baillie (1807. London: George Allen & Unwin, 1949), p. 81: "The life of God and divine intelligence . . . can, if we like, be spoken of as love disporting with itself. . . ." Miller has intentionally or inadvertently changed "love" to "life," and the "life" he is writing about is clearly not divine life but human life.

Philosophy Is Just Talk

In a letter of 1974, directly linking the genealogical and the critical aspects of philosophy, Miller writes: "I have to join Plato or Kant and go on from there. The great imperfections reveal also the great necessities. Why else bother with them?" But how Miller goes on from there, and how far he gets, is by no means fully evident in his early essays. Only with his conception of the "midworld" and its "actuality" as "utterance" in the essays of the 1940s and beyond does Miller reach his most decisive and original contribution to the understanding of concrete experience and its environment. In the same 1974 letter Miller says: "People want a 'real' world, not an actual world. But the verb has been a philosophical orphan. The great Kant gave no constitutional role to clocks and yardsticks nor to utterance, to the word which is spoken in various ways, to the syntactic as actuality." The "actual" world is the domain of the "verbal" taken in two interdependent senses: as "acts" and as "utterances." In "Philosophy Is Just Talk," Miller argues that concrete experience is informed by what has been called a real or an objective world if and only if that same experience has actively informed that world—only if acts of utterance are constitutional. But they are not actual or constitutional apart from their *embodiment*: the conceptual ordering *in* speech, and thus, for example, the mathematics *in* the yardstick, the clock, the thermometer, or the entasis of the Parthenon's columns.

Philosophy is just talk, but the talk is systematic articulation in and of a physical world, starting with one's body and extending out infinitely from there. This gives a specifically formal and constitutional twist to William James's assertion that "the trail of the human serpent is . . . over everything." Miller's own way of putting this is to say in the present essay that "object is a status within a discourse," or, as he says in *The Definition of the Thing*, "talk has no environment. It is the medium in which environment occurs." This is the common and the constitutional medium. The third from the last paragraph of the present essay, in which Miller criticizes James, shows Miller rejecting the usual understanding of universals as abstract inert ideas. They are *deeds* disclosing the entire realm of fact and practice. "Utterance is the actual. Every universal is a form of actuality, of doing." That is how Miller joined Plato and Immanuel Kant—and the

Jamesian *pragma*—and went on from there, both genealogically and critically.

Miller thought James's term *radical empiricism* better described his own position than it did the position of James. In "What Pragmatism Means," James said the pragmatic method means "the attitude of looking away from first things, principles, 'categories,' supposed necessities; and of looking towards last things, fruits, consequences, facts." The present and several of the foregoing essays in Part 1 show what Miller's response to James must be: One must attend to both. To look away from categories is to look away from pervasive structures organizing experience itself; empiricism becomes genuinely radical only when it recognizes these structures. Where does one encounter these structures? In the shared universals ordering the most common human talk. "Language of all sorts is not the *means* of communication," Miller writes in *The Definition of the Thing*, "but the *actuality* of communion." It is the shared reenactment of the inherited but revisable conditions constituting a common world.

"Philosophy Is Just Talk" previously appeared as Chapter 5 of The Midworld of Symbols and Functioning Objects *(pp. 59–65).* It originated as a letter to Alburey Castell, probably written in 1971 (Miller Papers 21:1). The letter cited above is to Robert E. Gahringer, dated November 8, 1974 (Miller Papers 22:14). The first James citation is from his *Pragmatism: A New Name for Some Old Ways of Thinking *(1907. New York: Longmans, Green, 1949), p. 64. The second is from his* Essays in Pragmatism *(New York: Hafner Publishing Company, 1951), p. 146. The quotations, above, from* The Definition of the Thing *are found on pages 179 and 189.*

Philosophy is just talk; its distinctive words and their order have *no denotation*. Critics have succeeded in removing philosophical terms from the "control of consciousness"—soul, mind, matter, necessity, and so on. George Berkeley's denial of "matter" is not peculiar, only more arresting, and its lack of acceptance by common sense shows that common sense has a deep attachment to talking "about" something to which talk is directed. Matter seems to make talk "about" possible. But what one talks about need not be "matter"; it could be a spirit—the soul, ghosts, a deity. Such objects have also been attacked as no content of consciousness.

What we talk "about" is not, it seems, defined by the talk. We could talk or not without changing or affecting what we refer to in our talk. This has seemed an essential feature of talk "about." Anything talked about goes its own way, talk or no talk.

Even the content of consciousness gets talked about, as if its being noted by speech had nothing to do with its occurrence. But "content of consciousness" has met the same critical fate as Berkeley's "matter."

"Consciousness" is not itself in the stream of consciousness, any more than is matter or the soul, or causality.

The result has been that the commonsense insistence that talk be "about" something not defined in the talk, with a status unaffected by talk—that this insistence has been discredited. Nothing talked "about" can be captured in the talk. No one can exhibit *in talk* what he is talking about, not matter, mind, soul, or the moon. We can give no account of what it is that we talk about. A man cannot say "I know what I am talking about" and expect to be credited insofar as what he claims to *know* has that separation from whatever he may say about it that talking "about" it requires.

The statement "I know what I am talking about" is met with skeptical reserve. Someone else may say that he does *not* know what I am talking about. Berkeley said that, as for himself, he did not know what others were talking about when they spoke of matter or of cause. Hume, of course, made a more explicit denial of cause and of those "necessary connections" that so many had been talking "about."

Some access to what one is talking about is required. What is that mode of access? Who admits that I have it? Can I expect an audience if I say "You may not like my words, but just the same I know what I am talking about"? I would get set down as a dogmatist or as an unreasonable fellow. I would be claiming that whatever sense you could find in my words I know what I am talking about. I would not, of course, blame you for not knowing what I know. Each would be "entitled" to his own knowledge and his own talk about it. You might, of course, soon tire of my talk since you were not yourself directly acquainted with what I was talking about. But you could not allege that my talk was foolish. Your not knowing what I was talking about would disqualify you from alleging any lack of sense or truth in what I was saying. No hard feelings either way.

It seems worth noting that we often associate for just talk, enjoying remarks and stories, talk for its own sake. There is something of this in mathematics, where we go on talking in mathematical terms, not raising questions about the numbers, zero, infinity, not asking what in the world a man thinks he is talking "about" when he speaks of negative numbers or irrationals. What was Homer talking about? About Zeus or the grey-eyed Athena? But you can't talk about such persons as if they and their ways had a status quite apart from the talk. They are myths, unrealities, not possibly independent of anything said about them. Nobody "knows" anything about Zeus. One cannot talk about Zeus. Sober and emancipated people patronize such talk. In history it is not evident what one is talking about where, as on the premises, one is to have knowledge of or acquaintance with Plato, the polis, or the French Revolution as things, or objects, or realities quite apart from anything said "about" them. It would be hard to say "Let's talk about logic," where nothing said now or ever before exhibited or defined what one claimed to be talking about. And it has been claimed that logical talk is *not* about that nonlinguistic thing, object, or region "about" which we talk. In fact, it is claimed that logical talk is *bad* talk. William James and B. F. Skinner want no part of it. The real is not logical.

It appears, then, that much talk is not "about" a prior state of affairs known quite apart from a saying. It appears that such mere talk is enjoyed, valued, and, in the case of math, given great authority. Chartres and the Parthenon are just talk, utterances that are enjoyed, sometimes viewed as revelatory, as John Keats said of Chapman's Homer.

We face a condition where it has become hazardous to claim that one talks "about" anything at all. One is laughed at for venturing to say what one is talking about. The tables are turned. So, now we have lots of talking where anyone who claims to "know" what he is talking about is denounced as a dogmatist or a metaphysician. Nobody can "know" what that may be which he then proposes to talk about. It is a curious reversal of common sense. But it was in the cards. The demand that we talk "about" what is in no way defined by talk, what goes its own way *whatever* we say, or *whether* we say anything at all, has backfired and left it impossible to give any account of what we talk about.

What, then, is the status of talk? On the premise that what we talk about is not defined by its being talked about, we would have to find talk itself as another alleged *object*. This object, or state of affairs, or reality, or thing—I don't know what to call it—would be as separate from talk as any other when it happened to be talked about. And since criticism has alleged that many such things talked about were not real—matter, cause, soul, and so on—it is not to be taken for granted that we could talk *about talk*. Indeed, what we ordinarily call talk has kept bad company. It is associated with persons, minds, souls, truth, falsity, other minds, usually with a purpose, a seeking for an end, a value. All that is very bad. For those are *precisely* the associations that have been most severely attacked as illusion. So it is not at all plain and clear that talk is something to be talked about.

It may fade away like Berkeley's "matter" or David Hume's "necessary connections" or "innate ideas" in John Locke.

One must consider, too, that talk as commonly imagined has peculiar properties. For example, there are exclamations and questions, and these seem rather unlike ordinary objects, like swans or the moon. There are moods and tenses. In what way is one to come upon the subjunctive or imperative mood as an object about which we then talk? The usual properties of objects—color, odor, place, size, velocity—seem not to disclose a mood, let alone a subjunctive. The classic "categories" name properties that do not apply to a sentence containing "not" or "if," or to a sentence involving a past or future tense. But where else is one to look for a past or future, a negation, a hypothesis? How am I to talk about so elusive an object, or reality, as the past? Yet, if one is to talk "about" talk there must be, on the premises, a state of affairs in no way affected by its being talked about. Whatever a question may be it is not to be found in what we say, no more than we suppose that the maple tree in my yard requires talk in order to be the occasion of talk.

A sensible man who talks about ordinary objects—sticks, stones, the color of the moon when just appearing over the top of the hills—would, I believe, have some difficulty talking about the subjunctive mood on the same basis of observation or perception. Nor does the scientist peering through microscope or telescope come upon such items about which he then talks.

It very much looks as if talk were an illusion, in the same way as Berkeley's matter or Hume's necessary connections. As something to talk about in the usual way, talk seems elusive or even an absurdity.

Common sense does not treat talk as similar to objects talked about. The response to what someone says is made in the same medium as the provoking word. One *word* leads to another *word*, but the moon does not provoke another satellite of earth. One does say "Speak louder, please" and in that request one treats talk as an object to be perceived. Or, one might draw a chair closer to the speaker, or closer to a person hard of hearing. But in responding to what is said, the objective properties of a voice or a visual medium are not operative. One notices that a speaker lisps or is hoarse or has a local accent, qualities that are ignored in a reply. It seems no part of common sense to deal with utterances as one does with a downpour of rain. The reply to what one takes to be an object is not a word, as Canute discovered.[1] Nor can one reply to a word as if it were another object, making an appearance in the order of objects, accounted for in that order.

But the view that in terms of objects talk is an illusion seems entirely proper. This, I take it, is the conclusion reached by the scientific operator. Why not join him? There is then no such event as talk "about" objects. For the objects go their own way whether or not there is talk. Confining one's attention to objects, one comes upon no talk in the region of objects, among rocks or stars or protoplasm, in test tubes or telescopes. Talk is one of those illusions, a nonentity, nowhere observable, like matter, soul, or necessary connections.

For my part I agree with this claim that talk is not to be found. I join in it. Talk is not another item of common experience, like maple trees and oak trees, like red or some other color. It is not an empirically discovered event. In this it is analogous to matter or the soul or necessary connection, or plain connection. Give the behaviorist this point, and welcome. He is not to be refuted by the claim that one *does* find talk as well as pigeons or trees. One does not. I join in that insistence. I find no talk among objects.

Here is, then, the radical issue, for the claim that one does not find talk among objects seems to assume that one finds objects without talk. This I deny.

The reason one does not find talk among objects is the *same* as the reason one does not find cause, persons, space, time, or logic among objects. Nothing pervasive, constitutional, structural, or universal is found among objects.

Unless utterance be present in the discovery of objects, no objection to the behaviorist is possible. Unless utterance is a universal, it is an illusion.

Ask any man to show you a universal—cause, "this," "the," personal pronoun—and you embarrass him. He keeps talking in such ways, but has no defense. And should one not have a defense? Is one not to account for one's utterance of a personal pronoun, the definite article, matter, mind, value, fallacy? Must not the "intellectual" be prepared to account for what he says, the words he uses?

We resist the unconditioned. It seems obscurantist not to require an accounting for any word used, for speech itself insofar as it is an item come upon. But I am rejecting the assumption that I come upon utterance. I say it is *unconditioned*. It is rather the self-conditioning. No object is identified without a name. The word *object* is itself a word. Without the word no one perceives an object. Object is a status within a discourse. It is itself one of those baffling words and has given rise to a radical mistrust or radical confusion, as when one alleges a difference between subject and object, or between object and illusion, between a real and a fictitious object. People balk. They say one is dealing in "metaphysics," raising dust, dealing only in words.

I grasp the nettle. Yes, one is dealing only in words. But I am not allowing *any* object without the word *object*. Nor do I allow "I see a maple tree" where there is no word, including the word "not"–oak.

I want an *unconditional surrender*. But this surrender is to the presumption of conditioning, to that immediacy within which, and out of which, all conditional statements appear. "Where" has surrendered to the order of space. This order is in utterance, ultimately in a yardstick, which is *not* a perceived object nor so identified, not a content of consciousness, but a functioning object, like a word or *the* body, never found, but a premise of all findings, of all data, which are not discrete miracles.

Utterance is constitutional. I am not open to the claim that I have stumbled on utterance when I might not have done so had I lived in Ireland or Israel.

Utterance is the actual. Every universal is a form of actuality, of doing, as space is of using a yardstick, or time of telling it by a clock, or cause by producing or preventing—present active participles. The present active participle has been overlooked by philosophers. In terms of *nouns*, all organization words, all universals, have fallen into disrepute. Why should James deny logic? But why not, if utterance be only a phenomenon.[2] On that premise there is no basis for any authority in logic. Civilization means utterance and its formal order.

To see utterance as unconditioned and constitutional is to make *all* action constitutional. Act apart from utterance has proved elusive. It does not turn up among the "facts." The categories are the basic acts. They are verbal. They require present active participles.

Nature itself is then a consequence of formal action. This is essential if the behaviorist is to be met. Give him objects or nature *without* action, without utterance, without *presence*, without present active participles, and then no way of escaping from his staccato account of behavior is available. Let speech or action be an empirically discovered event and one can say good-bye to logic and to ethics, to history and civilization, to energy and its inherent discipline.

NOTES

1.   Canute, Danish King of England from 1016 to 1035, once sat in his royal chair at the water's edge and commanded the incoming tide to come no farther. Some claimed that, when the tide failed to obey, he took off his crown and never wore it again (see William J. Bennett, *The Book of Virtues* [New York: Simon & Schuster, 1993], pp. 67–68).

2.   Justus Buchler observed that James identified with nominalism, while quoting Peirce as asserting that " 'the most important consequence of pragmatism' is that by its adoption 'we must abandon nominalism' " (Buchler, *Charles Peirce's Empiricism* [New York: Octagon Books, 1966], p. 168). Here, as often, Miller is much closer to Peirce than to James. "Philosophy Is Just Talk" is effectively a refutation of nominalism.

The Portrait of Man

The chief themes of the foregoing essays all contribute to the mature formulation of Miller's philosophy in "The Portrait of Man," written in 1968. In this essay he applies his conception of a midworld to the question of the true interrelation of the humanities and the sciences, which he finds to be one of dialectical interdependence.

For most of Miller's career, the humanities were on the defensive. The paradigm for the pursuit of knowledge lay in the natural sciences, and social inquiry sought, as "social science," to model itself on the "objective" inquiry of the natural sciences, as did psychology, reconceived as "behaviorism." In this academic climate, the humanities suffered the fate of being defined by negation, as the *non*objective modes of inquiry, meaning the (merely) subjective modes of study. Philosophy, religion, literature, art, music, were modes of human feeling, preference, aspiration, acculturation. It was a story of two worlds, defined antithetically, one the world of objects, order, cause, control; the other the world of subjects, conflict, purpose, the arbitrary. It was a rank dualism, but it appeared so obviously correct that Miller's critical challenge to it was met with incomprehension. Yet the argument of the present essay is clear, direct, forceful.

Summarizing his conception of the conduct of philosophy, Miller asserts that "the discrimination of modes of utterance and their interrelation is the philosophical job," and he notes that "every control word in science is an action word." The scientist is reminded that the conduct of science consists of human utterances—acts, not natural events. But the humanist is reminded that the act has no object without natural events. "The antithesis of scientism is not humanism but historicism," and both the scientist and the humanist must embrace historicism. "The central category" in history is "the utterance, the artifact [or functioning object] as expression, the symbol, which is not a representation but an interpretation." This is the embodied word, the *actual* as the incarnate act.

Such is the midworld—a world at once formal and bodily. Whether as humanists or as scientists, we are *there* in that world, and so it is articulate and speaks to us, disclosing itself. There is intelligible order, but it is the order of the contingent, the order of becoming, of change. Claiming his place in that historical order, Miller says: "To lists of categories I have proposed two additions: (1) the accidental, and (2) the midworld of utterance." And it was this revision, these two new categories, that justified Miller's dramatic claim, toward the end of his life: "I feel that I have solved the 'problem of universals.' " This may seem a highly dubious claim, given the historical persistence of the problem, which is that of establishing the warrant for apparently abstract and merely verbal concepts (the "nominal," "conceptual," or "ideal") to organize a concrete physical environment that is in itself entirely nonconceptual (the "real"). Miller's response to this problem, the midworld, is a site neither "nominal" nor "real" but the source of the very distinction between them. Insisting on the midworld as a site that would not exist apart from the accidental, Miller finds the warrant for universals not in reflective isolation but in historical commitments; not in a theoretical seeing or "pure thought" but in practical engagement; not in a Cartesian or Husserlian suspension of judgment but in the mundane act and its will to control; not in innate ideas but in bodily, material "actualities"; not in "being" but in "functioning"; and not in bare perception but in utterance, embodied speech, "the incarnate word" that has to prove itself in disclosure and, as historical, is always subject to critical revision. The incarnate word is *an immediate unity* of universal and particular, of the infinite and the finite, of the ideal and the real. It is the task of Miller's genealogical reflection to call us back to this midworld. If universal thought and contingent reality are not from the beginning *correlative*, there is no possibility of a thought that truly discloses reality. Formal thought and reality emerge together in the act. As Miller writes in *The Midworld*, "Both assured form and assured content derive from actuality."

"The Portrait of Man" originated as a letter of October 29, 1968, to Alburey Castell (Miller Papers 20:7). It was published in In Defense of the Psychological *(pp.152–62). For a good outline of the long-standing problem of universals and its recalcitrance to solution, see A. C. Ewing,* The Fundamental Questions of Philosophy *(New York: Collier Books, 1962), Chapter 10. Miller's claim to have solved the problem of universals is found in a letter of October 29, 1974, to George P. Brockway (Miller Papers 31:3). For a further characterization of the midworld of actuality, including its specifically symbolic nature, see Part 2.*

Does psychology draw the portrait of man?[1] Well, in a painting one can compare the representation with the original. Newspapers sometimes print a portrait, attach a wrong name, and have to make a correction the next day. But in telling what "man" may be, there is no original to which the account may be referred for accuracy. The president always has his portrait painted. He "sits" for the artist. Anyone can tell whether the painter has put more hair on his head than the facts warrant, or whether he has omitted a blemish or shortened his nose. But who sits for the portrait of man? Is it Greek or barbarian, Jew or Gentile, child or adult, male or female?

Not only that, but it seems that the subject never sits long enough for the artist to catch him in one attitude. A moving *object* can be represented in an equation—$S = 1/2gt^2$. What equation accurately includes all conditions of even one man, let alone "humanity"? And, anyhow, the changes seem not those of an object, like a stone carried to the top of the tower at Pisa and then sent on its accelerated way.

Of course one can make difficulties apropos of the claim that the artist is no neutral observer. What one of them sees is not what another sees and reports. This variation does not, however, apply to reports of objects. Everybody agrees with Galileo. I have seen students dropping stones from the roof of the physics building. All tell the same story. Why is that? Because all such observation is mediated by instruments, in their case yardsticks and clocks. The object is not observed directly. Treat a man as an object, and similar agreement would result as in measuring the length of his nose, or the rate of his falling from the roof of the physics building. But what is there analogous to yardsticks and clocks with which one tells the story of a man or of humanity? Of course, as I have been saying, the yardstick is not an object. Take away the yardstick, and you have Bishop George Berkeley, not Sir Isaac Newton. To know objects you need yardsticks, and yardsticks are not objects analogous to stones dropped from the roof. In short, if no nonobjects, then no observation of objects and no physics.

Now a natural science has to proceed through a medium of these artifacts as controls and warrants of observation. I go further and say that these controls *define* an object. What one cannot say is, "There is a stone, let's weigh it," as if the stone appeared as an object quite apart from any account of it in terms of place, size, or weight and then was subsequently examined in those respects. A specific stone can be inspected after it has been noticed, but the region of stones appears only as the correlative of the artifactual nonobject. Berkeley wasn't having any stones because he had no midworld of artifacts. He had only "the divine visual language" and no actual eye with which to apprehend it. He argued that on his terms one lost nothing. True, color and other properties were undisturbed, and what more could one ask? Well, one can ask for objects, for that status. But the price is the nonobject, which is also not discovered in Berkeley's "perceptions." The artifactual is not "perceived." What color is a yardstick?

Well, this is rather a long way around the barn, but it helps to explain the *scientific* psychologist's nonhumanism. Science needs objects and—*therefore*—it needs instruments to enable it to count and to measure. The

absence of instruments with which to describe man then leads to the conclusion that there is no man there to describe. To be an *object* of study one
must have those instruments. The two go together. If the portrait of man
is to be drawn with the instruments of science, the representation *must* be
in centimeters, grams, seconds, and numbers. So if a so-called man moves
his arm, or wags his tongue, and if these events are treated as objects,
then there is nothing for it but to track them down through nerves and
muscles and so to chemistry and physics. Only an obscurantist would deny
it. We have an enormous stake in *maintaining* the region of objects. We
maintain it by confining our statements to those controls that are the correlative of objects, that is, to the artifactual determinants.

So, where are the humanities? Following the scientist, it is alleged that
there are objects, or events among objects, that elude the scientist. There
is a soul, or a mind, or an act; an error, virtue, or crime; a good and evil,
quite as much as a ten-pound stone. This gets more difficult to defend. On
what terms characteristic of objects is one to give an account of the object
called a "mind," or of the event called an "act"? The catch is that *science is
not a peculiar way of describing certain objects and events, but is the very
form of objects.* If the account is not scientific, it is not about objects at all.
That has come to be a pretty general feeling. Soul, mind, act, even cause,
have come to be viewed not as possible objects that happen not to exist,
but as nonsense and "pseudo-concepts." This is more than a prejudice or
fashion; it is a consequence of a deep feeling that objects are to be maintained and that the emergence of this object-region is precisely an enormous triumph, the very place where we are at last in some control of
statements and outlook. It is getting harder to surrender that hard-won
authority. Though it slay us, yet will we trust in it or, at least, mistrust its
repudiation.

The attempt to make another object of the subject has failed. Man is not
to be portrayed in any way suitable for objects of actual or possible experience. The humanist may then ask, "Well, who wants to draw the portrait
as if it were an account, a reproduction, of any object? No," he says, "we
deal in subjects, minds, persons—not in things, which are objects." If the
humanist speaks in that way, he lacks the basis for claiming any general
acceptance. Perhaps he does encounter subjects, minds, egos, but the scientist is not prohibited from turning away, saying that he has never
encountered a subject. Let those who say they have talk among themselves but not to him. The scientist has the advantage that even the

humanist admits there is talk about objects, and very disciplined and splendid talk, too. And what is more, the humanist is at a loss to propose his own preference *unless* there are objects and scientific lore. Without the region of orderly objects, the very sense of individual selfhood grows indistinct. It was so during the long ages of primitive man.

So the scientist has an advantage. His position is safe, accepted by all, and, ironically, necessary for the humanist himself.

The scientist has another advantage. It is that he has defined an inquiry that permits error. And this capacity for error is inherent in his own statements. He makes mistakes, he can correct them; he can accept a charge of error, he can make such a charge. Consequently he discloses a common world, in that way a decent and disciplined world. He is likely to feel, too, that if it is "mind" that is wanted, why then one need only look at the starry heaven of Copernicus, Galileo, and Newton. What is the poetic portrait of Dante's world without Ptolemy?

The humanist can hardly disparage such claims and sentiments. What more does he want? I think that he wants to appear to himself and to others as an *agent*. When he looks at the starry heavens, he sees no act, nor does he find one in a test tube. So he thinks he must look elsewhere for his act. Insofar as we learn *via* machine, we become machinelike in our responses. There is, then, the suggestion that we avoid machinery in order to act. But is not that suicide? How is one to formulate or execute purposes except in terms of regularity in objects? If you want a soft-boiled egg, you need to watch the clock.

The one move we cannot make is to propose a humanism as a foreign addition to science and to the world it has disclosed. Yet such has been a strong tendency. Action, agency, is dependent on the very area in which it seems not to find itself.

Now, instead of attempting to stake out a separate claim for the humanities, why not look for them in science itself? Instead of dreading science, why not embrace it? Because science sees the humanities as incapable of defining scientific purposes and their results, the humanist need not initiate that rejection and allege that science is also outside his interests, or that if he has an interest in science, it is subordinate to his interest in agency.

What I have been proposing is that science is itself a resultant of action. This is not the pragmatism of William James or the instrumentalism of John Dewey. Their views are psychologically derived. They say that the "true" is found in the success of a purpose. Now, "purpose" is one of those "subjective" forces that the scientist cannot define. Nothing that he says is so illustrates purpose-control. He has swept away such explanations. The starry heavens and the test tube reveal no purposes and no purpose-control of events. But what if one reminds the scientist that his own operations entail not purposes but action?[2] What if one says that the vehicle of action is the yardstick, clock, balance, voltmeter, number, and calculation? To use a yardstick for a purpose is to violate its office. One treasures it and does not use it to prop a window. Liars and sophists use words for a purpose. Embezzlers use numbers in a ledger, or abuse them. Thieves abuse property. Rioters abuse the civic order that has provided their commodities. It is action that establishes the environment in which purposes become possible. And this action occurs through the artifact.

The yardstick, and so forth, is no object. It is not of a color, material, genus, or species. It has no length. It is, rather, the determiner of length. It is not psychological, a content of consciousness, along with all sorts of miscellaneous content. Well, to be more brief: no yardstick, then no physics; no artifact, no physics; no functioning object, no physics; no utterance, no numbers and no anything. If what the humanist wants is the "act," then he has it in the functioning object—and nowhere else. The humanist is not settling for purposes. The most ordinary man has them, and they are a mess, volatile, without command. He wants criticism of purposes. Well, the critic of purpose is the act. It, that critic, is the environment in which purposes are formulated and executed. And that environment is the implication of the artifactual, as space is of the yardstick, time of clocks, logic of the negative word. Psychology must be rewritten. There is no "perception" of the maple tree unless it is *not* an oak tree, and *not* is a word. Without words—artifacts—psychology loses perception and becomes the reaction of rats and pigeons, an event among alleged objects, where no object can be defined, no object-status can be discovered. For that status requires the word.

The humanist should, then, embrace science as a primary locus of action, of functioning. But he needs to see that action operates not from some hidden sanctuary in the ego, but in the public domain, which is not objects but the functioning object. We become skeptics if we see the common and public domain in the unmediated object. There have been many stories. That, in fact, is the root cause of skepticism, as well as of dogma.

Both are antihumanist, and for the same reason; neither recognizes the midworld, the artifactual precondition of its own formulation.

The yardstick is an utterance. It is a control. It commands. It projects an infinity, one sort of infinity. But so does logic, for which one must have words. The same applies to numbers. Wherever purposes are arrested by the conditions of formulating and executing them, one has an artifact. Speak a number, and you have to go on to say that there is no last prime number. Say a word, and you must have other words and a dictionary, which is a history book, not a teaching machine. Like a yardstick, the Constitution expresses no purposes and is violated when used for a purpose. It, too, projects a world of action. It aims to state the *form* of action. No more than a yardstick does it serve an ulterior purpose. It launches purposes; it controls them.

When not seen in this way, humanism becomes anarchy. And some supposed humanists sound like anarchists, as a supposed privacy rejects the establishment and so prefers drugs to decimals and to the world projected by constitutional artifacts. It is fair enough to suspect the humanists and humanitarians of vagrancies. Where is their law? It had better not be merely "inner." And if it is outer, it is not so among objects. Where then? Why, in the utterance, in the midworld, in the functioning artifact and its inherent control, which is also the projection of a world.

The antithesis of scientism is not humanism but historicism. Indeed, science is notably our own and has to fight to win recognition. But the artifacts of science extend the static. They show clock-time, not dated-time. The actual requires a date, as does the individual. The world is as much historic as static and physical. And even physics has a past, that is, controls that were inadequate to its own operations. History is constitutional revision, not addition of new information or the correction of errors from an assumed base. It is wholly and entirely concerned with actions, not with objects, not with purposes. It is the revision of outlook in the enlargement or defeat of artifactual controls.

Plato is no part of the humanities if one sees him speaking "truths," as some do. Those truths are not scientific and cannot be so verified. But as a figure whom we must consider but overpass, he belongs to the historic. We owe him our controls because our own emerge from his, although very different.

The humanist must embrace both the scientific and the historic. The question I have tried to answer—sketchily—requires a common factor. It is the functioning object, the locus of action and autonomy. Given the yardstick, what must I then do and say? Vast things, of course. Given the Constitution, what ensues? And so with the Parthenon or Plato or Shakespeare.

The discrimination of modes of utterance and their relation is the philosophical job: What is the structure required by any distinctive utterance, a number, a poem? So I suggest that the humanist can exploit what the scientist is doing, provided he recognizes that every control word in science is an action word and not the name of any object under the broad blue canopy of heaven.

The portrait of man or of humanity lacks analogy with any representation. An object, and only an object, can be *re*presented. Only an object can be *presented*, that is, put into some relation with other objects. One may see a "model" of a ship, of a building, or of a battlefield. In the exhibition of clothes one hears of "models," where a dress represents what others would see if the spectator were to wear it.

There is no model, no representation of the individual, or of man, or of humanity. One cannot say, "Please point out to me the object that you call an 'individual.' " The soul, mind, spirit, is no object either, and so has been regarded as an illusion or worse, namely, nonsense. Such an illusion cannot even be represented as a *possible* object that happens not to exist.

To say "You would do well to become interested in the humanities" is to suggest a possible interest, such as golf, tennis, or aviation. But then the exhortation stumbles because there is no analogy with any specific interest. Advocates of the humanities labor under that grave difficulty. One cannot exhibit as object something called the individual, or man, or the humanities "about" which one then gives an account.

One cannot find *an* individual as one would find *an* apple, that is, an example of a species. If an apple comes to be regarded as anything more than a *specimen* of apple, it becomes a fetish. An apple is merely *an* apple, but an individual or mankind is not merely an instance of a genus of species. One might prefer pears to apples, or one prefers a Baldwin to a Northern Spy and so takes one of that sort from a basket. But an individual person loses that quality so soon as one treats him as a sample.

I think myself that in our time we are quite lost here. I notice, for example, that college students hear talks in sex hygiene where they are informed what to do about *a* man or *a* woman and what to avoid, in view of health and the police. Some like apples, others pears; some Baldwins, others Spies. Pears are juicier than apples, also preferable if one's teeth are sensitive. So select one of those fruits that best meet one's purposes, remembering, too, that apples keep better than pears and can be used in pies when they lose their perfection. The learner is here addressed as *a* male, or as *a* female, as a sample. So, of course, he can only encounter other samples. Suppose you resist being treated as a sample; then you come under suspicion as a vagrant, or else as an obscurantist if you make a point of your dislike of being a sample.

If there is to be no portrait of man, or of the individual, what does one do as evidence that one has recognized man and individuals? To modify Plato, what is it that is always becoming and never is the same? I answer that it is utterance. The English language is always becoming. The Constitution is always reinterpreted. History is always being rewritten. Any historic individual needs a new biography, and what he said, as contained in an authorized edition, is restated in every new epoch. The central category here is the utterance, the artifact as expression, the symbol, which is not a representation but an interpretation. Humanistic studies require the vehicle, the actual word—the poem, song, building, ceremony, ritual, discourse. The seven liberal arts are all discursive, and all are based on the sort of control enforced by some utterance. In those arts you do not "react" erroneously; you *say* it incoherently.

To lists of categories I have proposed two additions: (1) the accidental, and (2) the midworld of utterance. That is why I look for the humanities in discourse itself. The real, the apparent, the ideal, the useful, are the categories of the nonhumanist. Humanism deals in the actual, in the present as formal utterance, and so joins the career of utterance in history. So, I am mentioning the actual not as a smart idea but as an ontological factor. There is no portrait of the actual, no model, no representation, no talk "about" it, as if it were a peculiar object or content of consciousness.

The acknowledgment of the actual is also the recognition of the individual. He is *re*cognized, not cognized. He produces a *re*vision, not a vision. Treat a man as an object, and he arouses no question of one's own identity. See him as a person, and one's own acts and utterances undergo change of control. This man speaks like a scientist, and I do not; what would I have to change in myself to deal with him? And why deal with him at all unless I were somehow vaguely allied with his ways? Another is a poet, a queer fellow too, and what he has to say is not what I can say. Yet, if I so much as say " 'Twas the night before Christmas," I have some alliance and have on my hands the question of what there is about me that finds a vague attraction in a poem or a song. What would I have to become in order to write a poem? Here is a well-ordered room, a kitchen, perhaps; one is alerted to one's own qualities, or lack of them. I had that experience in a farmer's kitchen years ago and I had to be very careful.

The humanities are the authority of the moment, of the here-and-now, of the actual. Today that authority is not felt in colleges. Teachers are truth-tellers, or moralizers, or propagandists, or utilitarians. One does not go to class just to hear a discourse. Students want it to be "relevant." To what? To their purposes and desires. Even in literature the teacher "explains" a poet psychologically. He is an object, a resultant of a world not poetically *constituted*. Who says today that the world is as surely historical in form as it is physical? And who says that the physical world is the projection of an artifactual immediacy, of a functioning object, which is never a "real" object nor yet a psychological "appearance"?

This moving scene in which we participate has no representation, no portrait made of a sitter, no model. It is the actual, not the real or the apparent or the ideal. It is not phenomenon, not noumenon. Those words are also words and live only in their career.

Ordinarily we use words for a purpose, and that, too, is essential. But the humanities are just talk and *for that reason* are the controls of any world treated as object.

The word must be its own warrant, and that is hard to bring off. So, rather crudely, I grow insistent on the ontological status of the articulate immediacy. Where one has it, one has the humanities. I can see the attraction of song for the poet and why Homer is a sort of magician. But so was Plato, as events prove, only Plato never gave his own utterance an ontological force. His very discussion of the "right" word is a humanistic utterance, in spite of his uncertainty.

The business of a philosopher is to revise the constitution. Well, I propose some constitutional revision. That is not the same as proposing errors. We control the immediate, not the supposed objective world. Cicero has an interesting expansion of the importance of the "appropriate" *occasio* in *De Officiis*. Why would he have fussed with the importance of the moment? Perhaps it was because he was an orator and a rhetorician. He felt some authority in utterance.

NOTES

1. It is worth noting that Miller is here raising this question of the province of psychology with Alburey Castell, a colleague of B. F. Skinner's at the University of Minnesota—and a colleague of Miller's during the year (1938–39) Miller spent teaching philosophy at Minnesota. Alburey Castell was caricatured as "Augustine Castle" in Skinner's *Walden Two* (New York: Macmillan, 1948).

2. Miller is of course not denying that there is purposive behavior. He is, as the end of this paragraph and the next paragraph state, trying to show that purposes presuppose an "environment" of action within which particular purposes are possible. The sense of action meant here is given by Miller in *In Defense of the Psychological*: "Any act is the voice of a design, of a general and universal order" (p. 148). Acts are utterances of will, and are "constitutional."

PART 2

The Actuality of History

My affirmation is the midworld.

—*In Defense of the Psychological*, p. 72

INTRODUCTION

The essays in Part 2 trace out the trajectory of those in Part 1 by developing in greater detail and specificity the conception of philosophy as a self-
consciously genealogical and critical activity. But they do so by bringing
into sharp focus the way such activity is preoccupied with the *media* of
human utterance and artifacts of human contrivance. That is, they show
how inextricably philosophy is bound up with what Miller in his mature
thought called *the midworld*. The midworld is the totality of artifacts, but
especially functioning objects such as words, laws, and instruments of
measurement (for instance, yardsticks, clocks, and calendars); in addition,
it is what is disclosed through the use of such artifacts and objects. This
world is a vast, complex inheritance. It is also an inescapable personal
task. Philosophy, precisely as the conduct devoted simultaneously to self-
definition and world-definition, becomes for Miller an *apologia*—a defense
of the irreducible status and importance of the historical domain in which
we live and move and (without exaggeration) truly have our being. The
actual world is neither an immutable order of physical objects and events
nor a publicly inaccessible stream of mental states and occurrences. It is
rather the historical world, one generated, maintained, and revised by
human actors implicated in their complex inheritances. It is also an artifactual and, thus, fabricated world, though in a sense quite different from
what is often meant by "social constructivists." Consider here a simple
example. What the dictionary clearly shows is that words mean what they

have come to mean. What language in use manifestly reveals, however, is that words are ongoing processes of coming to mean something other than was previously meant.

A dialectic of appropriation and alteration is discernible here. We did not invent, for example, the language(s) on which we rely. We actually carry community (linguistic and otherwise) "within" us: It is part of the constitution of our selves. In making something other than our selves our own, however, we ineluctably made our selves other than they were. But the only way of securing any inheritance, of meeting its demands and addressing its exigencies, is by being willing, in moments of crisis, to revise it. The significance of such seemingly disparate "events" as the Protestant Reformation, the Civil War in the United States, evolutionary theory, and quantum physics shows how the task of remaining faithful to one's inheritance can demand a radical revision of the defining contours of one's actual world. Thus, what the essays in Part 2 make clear is that, given our inescapable histories, the intertwined tasks of self-definition and world-definition become, at certain critical junctures, those of self-revision and world-revision.

Alliance with Time

This is one of many texts in which Miller not only underscores the need to forge an alliance with time but also makes important substantive suggestions for how such a radical revision of our inherited mistrust is to be realized. The deceptively simple example with which this piece opens bears the most careful attention: "If one uses words one is allied with time and with the past." Any word "means now what it has come to mean." Thus, to utter the simplest word is, quite apart from consciousness or intention, to ally ourselves with those from whom we have inherited this word. Language serves here as one of the paradigms of our inescapable though ordinarily unacknowledged alliance with time and history. The need to forge a self-conscious, self-chosen relationship to the actual histories in which we are implicated, and by which we are defined, is brought into sharp focus in this short essay. Moreover, the relationship between reason and history implied in "The Mistrust of Time," "The Ahistoric and the Historic," and other selections in this section is revisited here. So too is this mistrust itself: The disparagement of time is a persistent theme in Western culture and, thus, Western philosophy. Miller's objective is not so much to disparage this disparagement (much less to ridicule it) as it is to encompass this deep-rooted tendency in a historical narrative in which the noble character no less than the debilitating consequences of this fateful outlook is made manifest. Miller's affirmation of the midworld entails an alliance with time; in turn his alliance with time entails a thoroughgoing identification with the finite actualities, in their constitutional incompleteness and fateful entanglements, exemplified in such historical practices as religious worship, artistic innovation, experimental inquiry, and philosophical reflection as well as such historical institutions as governments, families, schools, and markets.

Written in 1960 (Miller Papers 4:25), this essay was originally published in a slightly different form in The Philosophy of History *(pp. 61–65). For texts dealing with the same themes and topics as this one, see the suggestions offered at the end of the editorial introduction to "The Ahistoric and the Historic."*

If one uses words one is allied with time and with the past. No word makes sense in the present tense. It means now what it has come to mean, so the unabridged dictionary can run to many volumes. We live, too, in a legal order where a rule of law contains earlier interpretations now modified or sharpened. Lawyers cite cases that once were the specific occasions of disputed meanings. When not arbitrary, the law takes time. The affections, too, need time for the disclosure of their solidity and power as well as for their impulsiveness or mutability. A nation takes time to establish its unity, its character and its aims, its capacities and its frailties. In all these instances the past appears as the necessary condition of a present action. No man can tell what he is doing or what he is saying if he has not already acted and spoken. Nor can that be discovered by another where act and word are no part of a continuum reaching into the past.

While involved in the processes of time, we are, and have been, reluctant to grant them authority. The past has often been felt as a bondage. "The wisdom and the folly of ages speak constantly in us," says Johan Huizinga.[1] "Time and again there are those to whom it seems as if history is suffocating us all." Feeling may seem inhibited by established custom. To use the right word entails the delay and, perhaps, the clogging confusion of deliberation. We long for Arcady—"a shepherd I, a shepherd he."[2] It is a difficult matter to attend the university and not lose simplicity in the learned proprieties. François Rabelais presents a version of the ahistoric ideal in his remarkable pleasure dome, the Abbey of Thélème, where everyone walked in elegant refinement and no one was quickened by those risky energies that generate problems and uncertainties. There a gallant and a lady might fall in love, but once married they lived elsewhere, as François Rabelais blandly relates.[3] One still reads occasionally about a person who, like Henry David Thoreau, refuses to pay taxes, mistrusting the institutions and purposes for which public money is spent or, perhaps, agreeing with certain statesmen that expenditure is more wise and efficient when the self-reliant man does his own shopping around for schools and drinking water. In many ways the processes and institutions that take time have appeared as a threat to the autonomy of the moment. Nor would one be able to deny that the past can shackle the present, although when the sense of constraint is strong, it is because some particular aspect of life has changed from what it was, and so has come into conflict with another and static element of politics or thought.

A chronological past that is throughout no more than an earlier version of the present furnishes no suggestion of constraint.[4] And a novelty that can pretend to nothing but difference with an arbitrary heritage has no better claim to acceptance. The past, if it has become repressive in some aspects, must furnish its own grounds of reform if the change is to have the articulate sanction.[5] Saint Paul drew quotations from the older prophets, even though he also said, "But now we are discharged from the law, dead to that which held us captive, so that we serve not under the old written code but in the new life of the Spirit."[6] Except for anarchists, time retains a hesitant prestige. Education struggles with this problem, especially in the humanities, where concern with the past is unavoidable.

Using the current idiom one might say that attitudes toward the past are "ambiguous." But what we confront here is no verbal slipperiness or uncertainty of particular purposes. We face rather a fateful conflict in the interpretation of our world. The disparagement of time is no fitful impulse. It draws its strength from the orthodox and traditional background of our most systematic thought. This ahistoric ideal José Ortega y Gasset calls Eleatic, from the city of Elea, in southern Italy, where there appeared a number of men who argued with originality and brilliance that change was illusion and not reality. To Elea there came from Colophon, in Asia Minor, the philosopher Xenophanes about 540 B.C. He was a monotheist who rejected the current anthropomorphic view of the gods. "But mortals suppose that the gods are born (as they themselves are) and that they wear men's clothing and have human voice and body."[7] Anticipating Plato, he says further, "Homer and Hesiod attributed to the gods all things which are disreputable and worthy of blame when done by men."[8] A second and more celebrated figure was Parmenides. He says of the One Being, "It is unmoved, in the hold of great chains, without beginning or end since generation and destruction have completely disappeared, and true belief has rejected them. It lies the same, abiding in the same state, and by itself . . . but it is lacking in nothing."[9] As everyone knows, it was Zeno the Eleatic who contended that Achilles, the swift-footed, the goddess-born, could not really overtake the slow-coach tortoise once the plodding reptile had, incautiously, been allowed a start in a foot race. It stood to reason, argued Zeno, that one could not additively exhaust the infinite. And, since the real is the rational, motion, which entails infinity even in its briefest extent, could only be the illusion of appearance, and no reality. In our day, Henri Bergson and Bertrand Russell have not thought it anachronistic to address themselves to this annoying problem, although for very different reasons and with dissimilar results—Russell, like a good Eleatic, still trying to be rational, and Bergson associating motion with vitalism and its immediacies.[10]

Reason unifies; so it was believed. To be quite rational was, then, to propose in one form or another a single substance, being, or process in which all plurality is dissolved. No literate man in the Western world lacks acquaintance with this way of interpreting experience. Philosophy began as the cult of rationality. There is a story about Thales of Miletus, in Asia Minor, which tells that when he had at last brought a problem in geometry to a solution he went to the altar of his house and made grateful sacrifice to the god. Why should he not, indeed, as a majestic universality loomed about him? This was no longer Miletus; it was a world, and he himself the individual whose pure and formal thought had penetrated to universality and so to infinity. Mathematicians from Thales and Protagoras to our own day have felt this emancipation from time and change. "Euclid alone has looked on beauty bare.[11] The logicians, or some of them, also claim that their order holds sway in all possible worlds, and owes nothing to this one: quite a large saying, if one stops to think of it, rather breath-taking in fact, since breathing, a biological accident, has nothing to do with it and never appears as a postulate on page one. "There be two men of all mankind / That I'm forever thinking on," sang Edwin Arlington Robinson in "Children of the Night." "They chase me everywhere I go— / Melchizedek, Ucalegon."[12] Like these two, mathematics and logic are sometimes said to lack mortal ancestors and to be without legitimate progeny. And this is considered creditable. The rest is an accidental and psychological multiplicity upon which it is necessary to impose an alien logical structure.

The knowledge that is also power discloses the nature of things. Hammers drive nails, and petrol drives pistons, as practical control demonstrates. Purposes can be neither formulated nor executed without reliable sequences in nature. If, as Ralph Waldo Emerson says, nature is what I may do, then accomplishment reflects regularity among objects while objects gain precision through purposed control. In the end, when naturalism has become absolute, having forgotten the base degrees by which it has risen, it may seem, and it has seemed, that purpose must vanish into the uniformities that first found discovery and recommendation through its own activity. To know the causes of things may be to lose the name of

action when the absolute order is no longer a function of the finite energies without which its particular ways get no exploration and convey no
value. The idea that power lies in knowledge becomes "demonic" when
knowledge engulfs all that we are and do. Man becomes an object and his
ways can be formulated.

It is only a question of the scope of our information. John Stuart Mill
finds oddities and irregularities in conduct, such as were formerly found
in an undeveloped astronomy or in the description of tides. Much of what
is known about man remains statistical although "it is evidently possible
to make predictions which will *almost* always be verified."[13] For a proper
"science of Human Nature" he wants something more. "But in order to
give a genuinely scientific character to the study it is indispensable that
these approximate generalizations, which in themselves would amount
only to the lowest kind of empirical laws, should be connected deductively
with the laws from which they result; should be resolved into the properties on which the phenomena depend." This is Eleaticism in the guise of
empiricism, stalking through the world seeking what it can devour.[14]

There must be few men educated in the past fifty years who have not
encountered the hope that knowledge might attain a sweep in which all
but a few odds and ends had been included. This seductive vision is not to
be scorned. It is the application of ancient rationalism to empirical multiplicity and to the quest of man for power. Except for miracles, nature is
now acknowledged by all as an intelligible order. The strength of this conviction rests not on inductive generalization but on the concepts and symbols of quantitative order.

NOTES

1. Johan Huizinga (1872–1945), historian and author of *The Waning of the Middle Ages*
   and *Homo Ludens*. The first part of the quotation ("The wisdom and the folly of the
   ages speaks constantly in us") identifies what is central to Miller's project. "We
   are," as Miller puts it, "the heirs not only of past wealth, but also of past debts" (*The
   Philosophy of History*, p. 188). If he was not influenced by Huizinga's efforts in
   Homo Ludens to bring the element of play to the attention of philosophers and other
   theorists, Miller was at least in sympathy with these efforts. "To be human is,"
   Miller contends, "to be playful. "To be human is, thus, to live in a world of one's
   own creations, for one's own sake" (*In Defense of the Psychological*, p. 132).
2. W. S. Gilbert and Arthur Sullivan, *Iolanthe*, Act 1.

3. The French author François Rabelais (1483–1553) and the American transcenden-
    talist Henry David Thoreau (1817–1862) represented in different ways what Miller
    identified as an evasion of the actual. The resolve to form an alliance with time is
    one with that of confronting actuality. All of the selections in Part 2 bear upon this
    resolve or task. For Miller's complex relationship to Thoreau and Emerson, see
    Vincent Colapietro's *Fateful Shapes of Human Freedom.*

4. One of the most important distinctions in Miller's lexicon is that between clock time
    (what he calls here "chronological time") and dated time (or "historical time"). The
    alliance with time he is forging in this and other pivotal texts is primarily with
    dated (or historical) time. The meaning of this mode of temporality, and at least by
    implication, its difference from the more fully accredited mode (chronological
    time) are clarified in the essays especially in Part 2.

5. The past must provide its own grounds for reform or revision if the transformation
    of our inheritance is to have an articulate and effective warrant. Hence, immanent
    critique of our historical past is both imposed by the confusions and conflicts inher-
    ent in that past *and* warranted by various parts of this complex inheritance. The
    theme of inescapability and bases of immanent critique is one of the most central
    themes of Miller's writings.

6. Romans 7:6.

7. Xenophanes, Fragment 14. See G. S. Kirk, J. E. Raven, and M. Schofield, *The Preso-
    cratic Philosophers*, 2nd edition (New York: Cambridge University Press, 1983), p. 119.

8. Ibid., p. 168.

9. Parmenides, Fragment 8. See G. S. Kirk, J. E. Raven, and M. Schofield, *The Presocratic
    Philosophers,* 2nd edition (New York: Cambridge University Press, 1983), p. 251.

10. In "The Ahistoric and the Historic," below, Miller develops these points in greater
    detail. He took Bertrand Russell, an enormously influential philosopher during the
    earliest decades of Miller's academic career, to be a representative of the dominant
    tradition in Western philosophy, one in which preoccupation with static, atemporal
    forms is allowed to discredit alterable, historical patterns of genesis, maintenance,
    and revision. Thus Miller identifies Russell as "a good Eleatic."

11. "Euclid alone has looked on beauty bare" is the first line from an untitled sonnet by
    Edna St. Vincent Millay. *Collected Sonnets of Edna St. Vincent Millay* (New York:
    Harper & Row, 1988), p. 45.

12. Melchizedek is a priest from Hebrew and Christian scripture who is solicitous of
    the ways and will of God, whereas Ucalegon is a figure from Greek literature who
    is indifferent to the gods.

13. *A System of Logic* (1843. Toronto: University of Toronto Press, 1943), Book 6, chap-
    ter 3.

14. Like Immanuel Kant and G. W. F. Hegel, Miller took with utmost seriousness the
    necessity to appeal to experience in our efforts to know anything whatsoever. But,
    also like these predecessors, he thought that the most influential forms of empiri-
    cism have offered fatally flawed accounts of human experience. Experience must
    be something other than what empiricists have claimed regarding it. The constitu-
    tional or structural element of experience must be given its due.

History and Case History

A case history such as a doctor or a psychiatrist pieces together is not, properly speaking, a history. The main reason is that a case history reduces the individual to an instance of a type or a case (e.g., you have a case of the flu, this being a type of disease), whereas histories disclose individuals in their irreducible individuality and thus uniqueness. In countless circumstances, it is of course legitimate and often desirable to reduce what an individual is undergoing or exhibiting to an instance of a type or a case. "When it comes to one's disease," Miller notes, "one hopes not to be original; one prefers to be a 'case' so that the doctor will have some idea about treatment."

The dramatic successes of nomothetic explanation have, however, tended to eclipse the power and importance of another way of rendering intelligible the actualities of our lives and undertakings. This bears on our understanding of rationality. The view of reason derived from the astonishing developments in physical science needs to be corrected by consideration of the distinctive character of our efforts to exhibit the meaning of human history. The form of rationality exhibited in the natural sciences is neither the sole nor necessarily the most important form. Indeed, insofar as our understanding of science demands recourse to the histories in and through which experimental inquiry into physical reality acquired its unique prestige and authority, this form of rationality is hardly self-explanatory. For an understanding of science, a study of history is necessary; and the form of rationality exhibited in such a study is markedly different from the form being investigated. "The philosophy of history is," as Miller suggests in "The Sense of Time," "an essay in the rationality that does not exclude the *unique*—that is, the act—and the moment." But it is precisely uniqueness that one loses in compiling case "histories" and proffering nomothetic explanations. "History and Case History" is one of the texts in which he underscores the necessity of recognizing this alternative form of human rationality.

Moreover, in this essay Miller draws a crucial distinction between clock time and dated time. Time is *told* and, as something only disclosed in an act of telling, it depends in various ways on artifacts. The objective time told by means of clocks is not to be contrasted with subjective time (as though the sequence of historical events were reducible to the stream of a private consciousness); rather it is to be contrasted with the personal time told by means of the monumental utterances of human agents, especially where these utterances enable us to identify a world (e.g., a medieval cathedral) or mark a transition from one world to another (e.g., the literary works of the Renaissance humanists). The Gothic cathedral marks a transition from one world to another, just as do literary genres and innovations of Renaissance authors. Our ability to tell historical time is one with our ability to discern the continuity and ruptures between, say, Gothic architecture and the style of building before roughly the second half of the twelfth century or, say, between Renaissance and late medieval authors. We live in a Darwinian and Einsteinian world, quite different from that of Aristotle and even that of Isaac Newton. Indeed, Charles Darwin's *Origin of Species* (1859) and Albert Einstein's four papers in *Annalen der Physik* (1905) are intellectual events of such transformative significance that they are indispensable for telling historical time. Such time is, in contrast to physical (or clock) time, not a homogenous but a punctuated continuum. Time of either form is told, but the symbolic means by which historical (or dated) time is told are quite different from those by which physical (or clock) time is told. Thus, narration of a history is essentially different from the assemblage of materials for a case history.

Miller's insistence on actuality, in contrast to reality and appearance, is closely connected with these points. Thus, Miller in this essay stresses: "History deals in acts. Any act is the voice of a design, of a general and universal order. It is only the act that makes history possible, and only history that makes the act possible." The *actual* world is the one generated, sustained, and revised by human actions. It is more primordial than either the real or the phenomenal world, though our more or less desperate espousal of reality is understandable, if not justifiable on its own terms. "No one is to blame for clinging to the 'real' world instead of the *actual* world of which [both] the real and the apparent are derivatives." Even though such tenacity is understandable and, in a way, not blameworthy, Miller worked strenuously to show how our appeals to reality are consequent on the actualities of our inheritance. To affirm the actual world in its finitude yet authority is to recognize the dated sequences of historical time for what each one of these sequences is—a matrix of humanity. To subordinate actuality to either reality or appearance is to reduce the historic to what is presumed to exist outside the actuality of history. The reduction of the historic to the ahistoric effectively effaces—or eradicates—the historical in the sense being advocated by Miller. The reduction of history to a case "history" is an example of this.

Written as a letter in 1970 (Miller Papers 30:5), an abbreviated version of this piece was first published in The American Scholar *49 (1987): pp. 241–43. The full version of the essay, which appears here in a slightly different form, was published in* In Defense of the Psychological *(pp. 144–51). The quotation from "The Sense of Time" appears in* The Philosophy of History *(p. 73). It is illuminating to read this essay in conjunction with "The Portrait of Man" (*In Defense of the Psychological, *pp. 152–62), "The Sense of History" (*The Philosophy of History, *pp. 80–86), "The Role of the Actual" (*The Philosophy of History, *pp. 165–67), and "Action and Order" (*The Midworld of Symbols and Functioning Objects, *pp. 48–58). On the topic of how the study of history bears on the study of science see "The Constitutionally Incomplete" (*The Midworld of Symbols, *pp. 118–26). Since this essay is one of Miller's numerous attempts to elevate history to the status of a category,* *to show how history is both self-explanatory and explanatory of other actualities, a large number of other texts bear directly on its central concerns.*

Physicians talk of "case history," as do psychiatrists. I hold that case *history* is a confusion.

A medical man keeps a *record*. Neither the patient nor the physician is making history. I go to a medical doctor because I expect him to identify the sort of ailment I happen to have and then to know what remedy to apply to my sort of disease, in this *case* an application of ice; in that, of heat.

Diagnosis is identification of a sort of object or state of affairs. We discover what peculiar condition accounts for an equally peculiar effect. Say your car's engine lacks smoothness; you may think a spark plug fouled, but the mechanic says it's the carburetor. He makes a test to verify his diagnosis. The physician operates in a similar way—takes temperature, pulse, respiration; perhaps sends a specimen to the laboratory or takes an X ray, all to say in the end that he finds symptoms of appendicitis. Your condition is that of a case. You are not unique. Others have had that ailment, and you hope that the doctor has had plenty of experience with that *sort* of disease. When it comes to one's disease one hopes not to be original; one prefers to be a "case" so that the doctor will have some idea about treatment. That is not the way to egotism, but it is the way to medical cure.

You damn a man when you can classify him as a mere sort of thing. No sort of thing is unique. We wish to be unique. If so, one had better not have a medically curable disease. It is humiliating to have the dentist say "Take two aspirin." He says that to others, to anyone, to people of whom I have a low opinion. He shows me no respect at all. I am a case.

You take some satisfaction in your auto. As is said, it is an "extension" of your personality. All the advertising encourages that attitude. But the garage man tells you that what your car needs is a new spark plug, and he takes one from a box, one of several. You drive out with no more personal distinction than I could command in the old days with my Model A Ford. Not a bit. Of course, the mechanic also has his bedside manner; but actions speak louder than words, and he put a plug into my Ford just as he did in another's Imperial. As Burke observed, "Calamity is a mighty leveler."

Now, what are we to do about this relegation to a mere case? The fact is that we have prided ourselves on scientific achievements, and science has no place for the ego, for egotism, for the original. To satisfy purposes you have to understand what *sort* of object you have to deal with. You get down to cases, as we say. Insofar as science is also technology, it is "know-how" in specific cases. Our common detergents contain phosphates; these cause pollution in lakes and rivers. What cleaning agent can avoid the specific effects of such a chemical? What *sort* of thing can wash clothes and not promote the growth of weeds in Lake Erie, monopolizing oxygen and killing off the fish? We deal in cases. Be vaccinated and avoid a case of smallpox, but for measles some other antitoxin is required. Knowledge of cases brings control. It gets results or avoids them.

It seems not too much to say that the rise of such power appears as a chapter in history. It gave us a turn. There was a *Novum Organum*, a new method.[1] The very earth was a case of a gravitational body, to many a shocking disclosure. Science seeks the uniformities that permit us to say that the earth is a case of gravitational order. Mere "data" are absolute. A case never is. It assumes a regularity. That is why I take aspirin for my toothache and get a new spark plug for my car. I do not put an aspirin tablet in the gas tank to cure a sputtering engine: I am not a radical empiricist. I hold with law and order, a very much assailed temper nowadays. Yes, I will have cases. I insist on it. I pay money to doctors because they understand my case and do not prescribe aspirin when my peculiar ailment requires nux vomica.

An early factor in the environment of cases was the atom. The atom has a history. There was, for example, the hypothesis of Amedeo Avogadro that made a distinction between the atom and the molecule.[2] That a molecule could be composed of several atoms is said to have led to the development of chemistry in the nineteenth century. It opened up procedure. It gave new definition to oxygen and hydrogen. That an element could be diatomic permitted an understanding of many chemical substances and their changes.

Discoveries that modify procedure are historic: Everyone who, like me, has had only one course in chemistry has heard of Avogadro. Now the question: Is Avogadro a case? Is chemistry itself a case? I say not. The atom is not a case within any inclusive genus. It does not "happen," as I happen to catch the grippe. I cannot go to Arizona to avoid atoms or indeed any constitutional factor of experience, any historical factor. Nor can environmental engineers arrange a healthier climate, more convenient or pleasing circumstances, by eliminating atoms, genera and species, yardsticks, clocks, balances, voltmeters, and dictionaries.[3] There is one way out:

You can take drugs. If you survive, you are back in the same demanding environment. Having expanded consciousness, you will be wanting your supper.

I should have trouble telling of what the history of chemistry or of America is a case, something that "happens" and could, perhaps, have been avoided. We take steps not to become a case of grippe. We stay out of crowds or keep the children from school. Cigarette smoking may bring on a case of cancer; one quits the habit. It seems awkward to say that geometry or chemistry "happened" to us. A world without bridge is not impossible, and I hazard that even tennis is more of a diversion than a necessity. The Russians play chess, not bridge. But in all such cases one has to do a bit of counting. Any tennis player can count as high as forty.

A world without smallpox seems not impossible. Why not, then, a world without mathematics, physics, or history? We take pains to perpetuate mathematics and other sciences—an odd thing to do if they were accidental events falling within an environment, like measles or a bad spark plug. Alas, there seems no cure for mathematics, no specific remedy for ridding us of all of this harassing obsession.

You may say that math is a case of learning. If so, you must, I believe, be able to show "learning" in the absence of math, just as you show health in the absence of measles, or even sickness without that malady. Be learned, but omit all numbers, as for example that you eat three times a day or have one wife and live nearer to one neighbor than to the other, who lives twice as far away, fortunately. Even to say one had two eyes and one nose would beg the question. Math and history are not cases of something called learning but rather are learning itself. I do meet people who say that math is a "tool" and language a handy utility—as if they could live without numbers and words as their grandfathers lived without autos, not so well, maybe, although one could argue the point on the premises.

Where I get into really deep trouble is in saying that psychology is not a case of anything but, like math and logic, is a constitutional factor, that it has a history but does not define history any more than it defines physics. There is no more a history in terms of psychological hysteria than in terms of physiological measles. There is no case of which it is an aberration. No difficulty that makes history is psychological. Any such difficulty, like that faced by Avogadro, is posed in terms of structure and procedure.

Psychiatry can tell what you have become (say hysterical, elated, depressed, fantastic) in terms of what you are, or are taken to be, as a matter of fact. The libido, for example, is a fact.[4] Certain modes of satisfying it are facts, a sexual mode perhaps. Of course I consider it odd that anything that "is so" could generate conflict; but passing that by, I would say that in history there are no original "facts" at all. When you first meet the idea that no historian ever tells you what is so you may well be surprised. But how can he? If you want to know what is so about the stars, you ask an astronomer; for the composition of aspirin, you ask a chemist; for the medical virtue of aspirin, you ask the physician; and so on. And you certainly do not ask a historian about your auto, what kind of gas to use, or where to get a good trade-in. The historian does not tell you what is so.

Well, what has he to say, then? What he says is only that at some dated-time—not clock-time—such-and-such stories were told about nature, God, and man. Then he notes a change in the way stories were told. He speaks of what was done, but not of every sort of doing—not of walking over a field, boiling a cabbage, spanking a child, smoking a pipe. On such terms we should all be mentioned in History 1–2 and should charge prejudice if our own acts were passed over. The doing that he reports is a critical doing, one that changed outlook, redirected energies, made men conscious of themselves in a new way. Isaac Newton, Avogadro, Charles Darwin, did such things.[5] The deeds of history are the critical deeds, those that give a new shape to action itself. Attempt to describe such deeds in terms of theology, physics, or psychology, and they are no longer historical. They become "cases" of some ahistoric and static order. All "theories" of history try to do just that. They want to stand outside of history and view it as an episode, a happening, like measles or a spell of rainy weather.

History deals in acts. Any act is the voice of a design, of a general and universal order. It is only the act that makes history possible, and only history that makes the act possible. It is act itself that has provided the very terms that have called it into question—physical and psychological terms. Those very terms have been hammered out of serious and constitutional difficulties, not accidental discomforts in an otherwise quiet world, not specific discomforts calling for specific remedies while normal life goes on and all our troubles get ascribed to a vague fortune. The historical act shows the difficulty as the very man. He is the same as the difficulty. The historical act declares a world in a constitutional aspect. It is a revelation, a disclosure, a declaration. Psychology describes no act, no originality, no constitutional novelty, no composition.

I am not attacking psychology. On the contrary, I am defending it. To defend it one has to put the psychological in its place among other constitutional and self-defining factors. One has to see its necessity. One has to say that the psychological is no more a "case" of something or other than is mathematics, physics, logic, or the dictionary.

When you see a supposed historian treating the Renaissance or the Reformation as a phenomenon to be "explained" on other than purely historical grounds, you can spot the psychologist or sociologist or perhaps the theologian. He makes a "case" of it. Action is not a case of anything. Cases derive from action, not action from cases. The authority of psychology rests on its historical emergence.

One has to remember, too, that history can be discovered only by itself. What else could possibly do so? You do not come on it by chance or contract a case of it because you did not drink your orange juice regularly.

I have woeful feelings and some indignation when I see that the world and the person may not be historically defined. Well, the indignation is a mistake. No one is to blame for clinging to the "real" world instead of the *actual* world of which the real and the apparent are derivatives.[6] History is secular destiny, and that is a hard idea to present. A good and honest psychiatrist remarked to me that he wished his patients could acquire an "ethical" sense. Apparently "adjustment" is not enough. There is no energy in it, no continuum with the past, a historical and eloquent past.

Of course I can hardly venture in personal safety to say that without the history of philosophy—or philosophy as history—there would be no history at all. Philosophy is pure history and never tells what is so. Nor does one say what is so in terms of philosophic controls. You say what is so in terms of mathematical and physical controls. It is so that Mount Greylock is 3491 feet high or, perhaps, some other amount. Find out on what terms you would call it "false" that Greylock is 3491 feet high and you will have named the special science to which appeal was made in telling what was so, in this case math and physics.

If philosophy were anything other than pure history, its failure to tell anyone what was so would justify the contempt in which it has so often been held. All its words would become nonsense in terms of what is so. In fact, that such is the case has been claimed. "What is it about?" people ask, and there is no answer. But history is not about something else. It is the self-revelatory. There were men not long ago who repeated the old tune about "pseudo-concepts"; A. J. Ayer was one. Bertrand Russell had a good deal to do with that temper. It is plain that they found the constitutional universal a pseudo-concept because they were pseudo-philosophers. They were not historians. The act, which is the basic historical word, made no appearance in the stream of consciousness or in a postulate set. The success of these men shows the depth of our ahistoric temper. They were all "intellectuals." The intellectual is the outsider not immediately present in his own act. This is the basis of the mistrust of intellectuals on the part of those for whom a past is even vaguely self-identifying. In any past there is something sacred. It is the barbarian who lays his hand on monuments. These intellectuals did not burn the books, but it amounted to that. They were personally annihilative. Russell could not make room for a proper name. What have I done to the past if I treat it as a phenomenon rather than as an actuality continuous with my own?

The pure continuum of history is philosophy, where one never says what is so, but where one develops the ways of telling what is so. Russell wrote a book titled *Scientific Method in Philosophy*—a plain absurdity, a nullification of history and the self-declarative at one stroke. On that basis there is no present to be maintained, the actuality that generates history.

So, I grasp the nettle and say that the very authority of those who tell us what is so is historical and philosophical. The modes of telling what is so are all historically generated. The physicist and the psychologist look around on their terms and find no actuality, and so no history and no philosophy. In consequence the special sciences do not even find themselves. They are not self-conscious, not aware that their very terms make no sense and have no authority apart from the process that forced their discovery. Yes, forced. Any imperative rests on its historical origin, on the self-maintaining actuality that clarifies itself in asserting causes, atoms, and the psychological itself.

If we want reverence, anything sacred and so imperative, we must advance now to history and—I cannot avoid it!—to pure history, which is philosophy. There is the common world, the actual one.

Well, then, a "case" is always described in terms of abstractions, which do not define the present, or, of course, the past. The physician takes your temperature. He takes mine. I have a thermometer in this room. You describe a case in terms that are general, abstract, nonindividual. That is why a "case history" describes a *sort* of event, not a unique one. But history itself is not a case; it is self-declarative and includes the very modes of abstraction by which a case history is recorded. Without philosophy, no history.

NOTES

1. Francis Bacon's *Novum Organon*, written to replace Aristotle's *Organon* or collection of treatises on logic. Along with René Descartes's *Discourse on Method*, Bacon's work symbolizes a central feature of the early modern revolt against classical philosophy, especially its scholastic (or medieval) form.

2. Amedeo Avogadro (1776–1856) published his article proposing the idea in the *Journal de Physique* in 1811.

3. Though Miller thought John Dewey's instrumentalism and, more generally, pragmatism lacked an adequate conception of the structural or constitutional dimension of human activity and experience, Dewey's definition of history (or the historic) is quite close to Miller's claim here: "From a humane standpoint our study of history is all too primitive. It is possible to study a multitude of histories, and yet permit history, the record of the transitions and transformations of human activities, to escape us (*Human Nature & Conduct* [Carbondale: Southern Illinois University Press, 1988], p. 1922).

4. The crucial distinction between *facts* and *acts* is drawn in this and other selections in Part 2. According to Miller, facts are derivatives from acts and, in turn, acts occur in and through artifacts. Thus, he contends: "*There is no fact without an artifact*" (*The Paradox of Cause*, p. 113). The following selection ("Functioning Objects, Facts, and Artifacts") is important for seeing the connection among these three topics.

5. "In the end," Miller asserts in *The Midworld of Symbols*, "authority is in the person who reveals an environment" (p. 89). The authority of Newton, Avogadro, and Darwin must be appreciated in this light.

6. One of Miller's most important distinctions is that between the real and the actual. He grants primacy to actuality. Part of the reason for doing so is that the distinction between appearance and reality is drawn in terms of actuality: "The 'real' is the content generated by the actual" (*The Midworld of Symbols*, p. 115).

Functioning Objects, Facts, and Artifacts

The actual world is (as already noted in other introductions to selections in this section) the world insofar as it is generated, sustained, and revised by human action. This is nothing other than the midworld, but with the emphasis falling on action rather than the media in and through which action takes shape and exerts its authority. But our action is always embodied, either directly in the somatic agency of historical actors or indirectly in the various means on which such actors rely to define their complex purposes. This implies that the human body is itself what Miller calls a functioning object (see *The Midworld of Symbols and Functioning Objects*). It further implies that the symbolic extensions of our somatic agency are also functioning objects. Such objects are not mere tools designed to assist us in accomplishing purely adventitious aims; they are rather definitive of vast, enveloping regions of always incomplete, fateful engagements.

The constitution of a nation defines such a fateful region, as do the historically effective strategies of experimental investigation. A nation, at least one such as ours, is such by virtue of its constitution and the institutions authorized by the inaugural act embodied in this founding document. In an analogous way, the specific means of quantitative measurement such as yardsticks, clocks, and more sophisticated "instruments" effectively define spatial and temporal regions wherein ongoing investigations into specific phenomena can be conducted. In a quite different yet related way, the temples built in ancient Greece or the cathedrals erected in medieval Christendom define a distinctive region of human engagement in which the corporate purposes of a historical community assume palpable shape. For this reason, Miller insists here: "History is not chronicle but rather the quest for the energies that found utterance in Chartres or the Magna Carta. In history we both exhibit and discover our energies and thereby ourselves." Our political, scientific, and religious histories (to name but three) are vast, encompassing regions in which historical identities are forged in intimate conjunction with functioning objects such as laws, measurements, places of worship, and (at a more rudimentary level) words, numerals, and prayers.

The present active participle exemplified by speaking, counting, measuring, legislating, praying, and countless other activities is neither a purely objective occurrence nor an inherently subjective act. It occurs apropos the midworld, the corporate actuality of such functioning objects as words, numerals, yardsticks, clocks, and other media of disclosure. Such corporate actualities allow us to distinguish in a responsible manner the subjective from the objective, the apparent from the real, and indeed to draw other crucial distinctions. Insofar as functioning objects define (or project) a region of human engagement, they "are legislative." Yet they are also revelatory. Hence, the ineliminable role of the mind is recognized along with the genuine discovery of what is not merely of the mind's own making or imagining. This is Miller's way of trying to do justice to both the constructive, creative role of the mind and the obdurate, forceful character of whatever we disclose as real.

Originally titled "Functioning Object, Tool, and Artifact," this piece was composed as a letter dated November 16, 1977 (Miller Papers 31:5), and first published in a slightly different form in The Paradox of Cause *(pp. 127–43). The general topics of the midworld and the specific role of functioning objects within this actual order are also addressed in "Facts and Artifacts" in* The Midworld of Symbols and Functioning Objects *(pp. 127–43).*

A rrowheads rate as artifacts; they are not found in nature. They are tools, instrumental aids. They serve a purpose. Any tool serves a special need, facilitates a desired result. For certain purposes a crosscut saw serves less well than a ripsaw, a screwdriver than a hammer. *Artifact* is a term more restrictive than *tool*. A stone may be a tool but is not an artifact designed for a purpose, not exhibiting design, art, craft, or skill. The anthropologist does not come upon man until he discovers the artifact, a revelation of *local control*, that is, something done at a specific place and time. Man is an artisan; he makes artifacts. Find an artifact and you encounter a man; find a stone and you do not. The artifact is an awesome revelation. At hazard—it is an incorporate psyche. An absurd contradiction? Better not to say so if one speaks of artifacts.

Facts and artifacts differ. We are supposed to have had no hand in the facts. The iron law of knowledge commands that we Keep Out. But someone has not kept out of revelatory artifacts. They betray a purpose; the facts do not. The artifact is an actuality, the fact a passivity. The fact is impersonal; the artifact individuates the maker, his tribe, his intelligence, his "culture." The artifact leads to history and to dated-time; the fact invokes an undated order as the price of not being rejected as an illusion. The artifact reveals an agent and the tribal range of skill; the fact derives its status and authority from its immunity to interference or control by any individual at a place or time. The fact is anonymous. No purpose can improve the facts, but it can improve the efficiency of a stone arrowhead or of a steam engine. The incorporate mind is the only mind ever discovered. It eludes the passive psychology of "data." To speak at great hazard: The only word is the incarnate word.

Nature has always been characterized in the terms of action. Animistic nature reflected the abruptness of agency. A magical object had the same uncomposed efficacy as the act that struck fire from flint. All things were full of gods. Primitive man was not a fumbling intellectual entertaining a detective theory. Order in nature waited on the order of deed and utterance. Pythagoras did geometry, and nature loomed in the mode of space. But nature is not the "great apparition"; it never was an apparition—an instant appearance.[1] Indeed, an enduring frustration has marked the many attempts to reach "reality" from a basis of appearances. Nature is *ex post facto*. It vanishes in the abstract present tense. Magical objects are the reflection of the magical act. The order of nature, similarly, reflects the order of the *actual*. Any continuum resides in the actual, in the verb, in the *midworld*, never in passivity and its discrete and miraculous data.

The long disrepute of the universal is the consequence of the failure to have recognized universals as the shape, order, form, continuum, of the incorporate actuality. The universal then seemed "pure thought," mental, ideal, psychic, divorced from *the* body, from the organism, from local control, from self-maintenance. Even today what we call the "organism" has remained mysterious. In scientific terms there is no organizing object, that is, no local control. Biology has been an irritant to physics, and physics to biology. Physics does not speak of "adjustment" or of "adaptation" to an "environment" by stars, stones, or electrons. Biology retains a spooky quality. But nothing is more spooky than nature itself when regarded as a datum or apparition. As merely "there" and unaccountable, it has the status of an apparition without connection with any control, very like a spook. To put the matter in blunt terms: I am proposing to rescue nature from that spooky status which it still occupies insofar as it is treated as an apparition, uncontrolled within itself and without generation. Short of an incorporate actuality of which nature is the material and formal continuum, nature has remained a spooky apparition, a phenomenon. It may be added that short of local control there is no history of physics because no evolution of its order.

Going to the post office, telling time, counting fingers, and in all ways

identified in a verb, I have found old problems made plausible because
their basis was passivity. I have felt respect for George Berkeley because
of his decent appeal to say what one could possibly mean by "matter."
Berkeley found no matter as a psychological datum. Radical empiricism
has never found any. I will say briefly that if one has any strong penchant
for a material world one had better settle for the *functioning object* as its
locus, for the organism, for yardsticks, clocks, balances, numerical nota-
tion, and for the word, for the eloquent utterance of any sort, and for their
revelation. If matter be not constitutional then the philosopher has no
business with it. Similarly, the denial of connections in David Hume
becomes a consequence of empirical passivity. Necessary connection is a
tautology.

But such notable problems are not to be dismissed. They have had cur-
rency and authority. And then there was Immanuel Kant, proposing to
restore order to natural science but without yardsticks or clocks or other
functioning objects as the source of projected order. What is the resulting
"phenomenal" world if not a spooky apparition? Still, it was an ordered
apparition as against the discrete unconnectedness of all alleged psychological data. Where all is empirical, no empirical inquiry has any basis,
necessity, restraint, enforcement. Again, there has been a long-standing
"problem of universals," a source of controversy in medieval times.[2] One
cannot shrug it off or get around it by argument. As the form of the actual,
the universal becomes resident in the verb and so in the functioning
object and its continuum. Philosophy has no necessary answers apart from
necessary problems. But the equation of the present person with his intimate, necessary, and identifying problems has rarely been made or written.

But I have promises to keep and cannot keep them all. Perhaps others
will elaborate the consequences of the actual in many other constitutional
ways. I propose the actual as the neglected source of order and selfhood.
It is a risk. But

> He either fears his fate too much,
> Or his deserts are small,
> That dares not put it to the touch
> To gain or lose it all.[3]

Nevertheless and for all that, we are not likely to abandon the facts
although admitting artifacts. Thoreau picks up an arrowhead at a place

and time, at Concord, say. And that artifact is made from stone. Stones are among the facts, items in nature. On that basis we are required to accept them, as if nature imposed a control on the accreditation of any alleged fact. The familiar question "Is that a fact?" suggests criteria and so restraint, guardedness, responsibility, accountability. Strange that we should be accountable where we could exercise no personal control and may not do so. Whatever the facts may be has been regarded as quite out of our power to originate or modify. This has been a powerful persuasion. Had we such power over the region of facts, "would we not shatter it to bits and then remold it nearer to the heart's desire?" But desire has given hostages to the facts. In both its formulation and its execution it assumed nature and then has sought to evade that dependency. The result, both East and West, has been a suspicion of desire itself, as in Stoicism, Buddhism. All is vanity. Abandon desire or patronize it as a deluded privacy.

The tenacity of the persuasion that the facts do concern us in utterance and other acts suggests that we have not been disposed to settle for their irrelevance, we proceeding on our untrammeled way. We take satisfaction in recognizing the facts, chide those who will not, and pity those who cannot. We do, we should, allow them some control. Responsible actions take them into account. But unless the facts are also constitutional to our deeds, our disregard entails no criticism, no charge of failure, nor censure of oneself by oneself. Ought one to take them into account although not a party to their authority? Admittedly we can be held responsible only for what we do. Unless the facts in their status and authority reflect and embody our doings, they lose their command and tenacity. I am responsible for what I do only if the doing be itself the source and cause of my responsibility.

Certainly a sticky point, this alliance of command and action—that we cannot be *responsible to* when we are not also *a party to* what would command and control. This being "a party to" the facts and to nature suggests what I have been calling the *functioning object*, not a functional object, not a tool, not an instrument, nor a means to a specific and terminating satisfaction.

The functioning object is that immediacy which embodies the verb—organism, yardstick, clock, balance, number, word. Functioning objects are legislative. They are revelatory. They are not perceived. In the midworld projected by functioning objects we behold ourselves. "For the eye does not see itself but by reflection in other things," as Brutus says to Cassius.[4] The Parthenon reveals the mind of Athens, its glory and its failure, as the Republic does for Rome. Primitive art reveals the primitive mind. History is not chronicle but rather the quest for the energies that found utterance in Chartres or the Magna Carta. In history we both exhibit and discover our energies and thereby ourselves. History is no spectator sport. If I rather drum on this point—on functioning objects and on the mid-world—it is because in the opposition of appearance and reality I could find neither. Each cancels the other. Neither allows that local control of which the distinction between them is a consequence. Short of counting fingers or marbles I cannot make a mistake; short of going to the post office I cannot lose my way. Our common sense—the common and the universal—derives from the verb and the actual. A common sense has long been sought. The universal was a distinctive discovery of classical Greece. But it was divorced from any doing and so obliterated the agent and the individual. No one was authoritatively present, nor was any functioning object, *the* body, or the utterance. There was no midworld.

Berkeley had no eye for the reception of "the divine visual language"; Kant had no legislative yardstick or clock; Ralph Waldo Emerson was not "looking"—a verb—with his "transparent eyeball." The psychologist measures reaction time; he refers to a stopwatch; there is no clock nor any other legislative actuality in the stream of consciousness. In the absence of local control no one ever found a cause or an effect. Why seek the living within the alleged appearances or else in some reality that may not be among the appearances? Any negative advertises local control, and a threat to self-maintaining actuality. Why not "lose the name of action" if the actual be not the revelation of both world and individual?

NOTES

1. In denying nature is the "great apparition," Miller is likely carrying on his quarrel with Ralph Waldo Emerson, for whom nature is also described as "a divine dream, from which we may presently awake to the glories and the certainties of day" (*Ralph Waldo Emerson: Selected Essays*, Larzer Ziff, ed. [New York: Penguin, 1922], p. 72). But his disagreements with this towering figure in American literature should not be allowed to obscure a deep kinship. Indeed, there is to be found in "Nature" (1836), one of the texts in which Emerson seems to reduce the natural world to a "great apparition," a passage that Miller was fond of quoting: " 'Every scripture is to be interpreted by the same spirit which gave it forth'—is the fundamental law of criticism" (p. 54).

2. In another context, Miller goes as far as to assert: "Sorry, but I feel that I have solved the 'problem of universals' " (*The Midworld of Symbols*, p. 110). His solution is summed up in his assertion that *the universal is the form of the actual*, an assertion making explicit the link between actuality and universality and, by implication, the intrinsic connection between universals and their careers in history.

3. These lines are from "My Dear and Only Love" by James Graham (1612–1650). The third and fourth lines were incorrectly quoted in the version of the text appearing in *The Paradox of Cause and Other Essays* (p. 127).

4. Shakespeare, *Julius Caesar*, Act 1, scene ii,

Constitutional Utterance: Its Archaic Form and Abiding Force

In teaching (especially his introductory course to philosophy), Miller often used William Ernest Hocking's *Types of Philosophy* as a text. Here Hocking defined animism as "the belief in mental agencies as the explanation of striking natural phenomena." To use Miller's own examples, the sound of thunder is the bellowing of Zeus, as the movement of the waves betokens the exertions of Poseidon. Of course we suppose animism to be thoroughly discredited; but our manner of understanding knowledge, truth, and error tends to make animism completely incomprehensible, for it makes action completely irrelevant to this understanding. "The philosophy of knowledge is," as Miller suggests in *The Midworld of Symbols*, "the problem of *how to tell* that one has made a mistake, or *not* made one." But is it possible or intelligible that some individual or some outlook is totally erroneous? Accordingly, Miller asks in the present essay: "What would be more mysterious—and more arbitrary—than to allege that someone [e.g., the animist] was *all wrong?*" (emphasis added). We might add here: What would be more erroneous than to suppose that error could be committed on this scale? At any rate, Miller insists that our errors make sense, even the most wild and egregious ones: There is not only method in our madness but also logic in our mistakes. So also in the errors of others, even the seemingly fantastic ones of our most primitive ancestors.

The point is not to ridicule the silliness or stupidity of others, but to discern the basis on which our judgments are actually made and, *then*, to connect our own basis of judgment with that of those whom we judge to be mistaken. That basis cannot be anything other than exertions vulnerable to frustration and modification consequent upon their own momentum or continuance. In brief, that basis must be action. So Miller wonders whether he is permitted to count the animists among his ancestors and, moreover, wonders about the conceptual cost of identifying with these historically remote figures. He suggests that: "The price is that I now recognize them *as agents*" (emphasis added). This makes of history a locus wherein we identify with (rather than judge) others: "History is" as Miller asserts in "The Sense of History," "the place where one goes when one gives up passing judgments and accepts identifications. It is the alternative to seeing all things *sub specie aeternitatis*. They are to be seen *sub specie temporis*. This is the heresy of history. But it is also the condition of all humanistic concerns." This includes our various adventures in human knowing. This essay is one place where Miller himself explicitly identifies with animists. Implicit in his identification is the judgment that they were erroneous; however, the demand to exhibit his kinship to them requires us to see beyond their mistake to its basis in action. Not only does Miller take the animists to be agents but also he insists they "felt themselves to be. They could make a fire and even draw and paint on the walls of a cave."

But what is the price to be paid for recognizing our intellectual kinship with our animistic ancestors? This recognition requires nothing less than the revision of the constitution—that is, the concepts legislating our understanding of knowledge, truth, and error, including some of the most fundamental parts of the very framework from which our concepts derive their authority, must be revised. Above all else, this revision concerns action and thus actuality: It demands making action, understood as a somatic and artifactual affair, integral to knowing. Apart from action so understood, knowledge becomes utterly mysterious; coupled with action, it becomes readily intelligible, for there is, as Miller writes in "In Sum," "no difficulty in locating error apropos of the artifactual, in the yardstick in use, or in words [or in countless other modes of human symbolization]. . . . You have to *make* a mistake. It needs a vehicle." Once you grant embodied agents and the artifactual enhancement of such agency their full weight, and acknowledge the hazards typically confronting such agents, nothing is easier to understand than how mistakes are made and why they occur so frequently.

This manuscript offers an excellent example of Miller's explicitly genealogical approach to what he calls "constitutional words." Its opening sentences make it clear that an adequate understanding of our constitutional words (e.g., space, time, causality, agency, nature, or history) must be historical and thus genealogical. Both the form and the focus of this account are important. Genealogy is the appropriate form of historical understanding (e.g., "The Ahistoric and the Historic"); words and utterances declarative of a world, not denotative of items in a world already declared or constituted, deserve more critical attention than they have been given thus far. This chapter is one of the many texts in which Miller articulates his important conception of constitutional utterance, with the emphasis on the *act* of such utterance.

Miller notes in "The Midworld" that his concern was to "consider the price to be paid for enfranchising discourse." The price to be paid here is to grant discourse an authority and status that many would find fantastic. In "Explaining Language," Miller was nonetheless "unwilling to say . . . 'There is the world, and here are the signs.' " Words are not simply names arbitrarily attached to antecedently (or independently) identifiable objects, nor is language in its totality primarily a nomenclature. Words and other symbols are nothing less than modes of revelation: they are the means by which a region of experience is originally delimited and inevitably redefined. Think here of a yardstick or other means of measuring spatial relationships. The yardstick defines a region in which points and areas might be related to one another, just as a clock in one way and a calendar in a quite different manner enable us to define moments and durations of time relative to one another. The categories are, for Miller, verbs, present active participles such as measuring, timing, dating, speaking, and narrating. These actions are embodied always in the sense of somatically embodied actions (they inescapably involve our embodied agency) and characteristically in the sense of artifactually embodied processes. The act of measuring is a paradigm of what Miller means by a constitutional utterance, for it is an act by which a region of experience is constituted or defined. The hand wielding the yardstick defines thereby a domain in which infinitely complex relationships among spatial points and areas can be established. But the most primitive forms of mythic narration no less than our most sophisticated instruments of spatial measurement are to be counted as constitutional utterances. The hands that now wield yardsticks and use more sophisticated implements are ones related to those that long ago made fire and painted caves; and the *acts* of making fire out of dry twigs and images using pigments themselves made for just this purpose are of a piece with the acts of mythic narration and thus animistic consciousness.

One word leads to another, and it does so in a manner intelligible only in reference to how certain words have historically (i.e., actually) led to certain other ones (e.g., how φύσις has led to *natura* and, in turn, how *natura* has led to our own word *nature;* how animistic explanations of observable events have given way to mechanistic explanations). The world is actual insofar as it is generated, maintained, and revised by our actions. But action is inherently a mode of articulation, as articulation is an instance of action. One does not argue about constitutional words, as though the propriety or efficacy of such terms could be determined in the same way that one could show the propriety or efficacy of denotational words. Their function is revelatory, not referential. Thus, one must tell a story about the genesis and transformations of the universals or categories by which historical individuals have actually defined themselves and their world ("that is," as Miller writes in "Management," "an infinity of order where even accidents are constitutional").

How Miller stands *in* the present is, for him, dependent upon how he stands *to* the past — not to any past, certainly not to an abstract, amorphous past, but to his own actual, confusing past. So the problem, as he writes in this essay, turns out to be: "May I say, or not, that I had animistic ancestors?" Most of his contemporaries dismissed their animistic predecessors as superstitious thinkers who illicitly and misleadingly clothed natural phenomena in anthropomorphic garb. In contrast, Miller claimed the animists as *his* ancestors. But the price for this identification is, as we have noted, to grant the animists agency. "They could make a fire and even draw and paint on the walls of a cave. They had their *Being* as a local control. They were effective. The rest of the world . . . was a blur. Only in so far as they acted was there any clue to the proportions of objects, indeed to objects themselves." The world is actual only insofar as it is generated, sustained, and revised by the historical acts of finite agents. The distinction between appearance and reality, on which philosophers and others have been so fixated, is dependent on an identification with actuality. In his later years, Miller's growing preoccupation with the actuality of history was connected to his explicit acknowledgment of his intellectual ancestors. The animists were the first among these ancestors, for in their artifacts we can observe the most archaic shape of human *agency*. In acknowledging or recognizing them as our ancestors, we are in effect joining a career.

What Miller wrote of the Eleatics (those who denied the reality or, to use his own word, actuality of time and history) might with equal force be said of the animists: If they too are in history, then as Miller writes in *The Philosophy of History*, "they spoke for their time, thereby creating a past and purchasing their own historicity at the price of their modification." We ought to speak of these historical actors in a truly historical temper.

But, again from *The Philosophy of History*, if we speak about the animists in this manner, "it is not to overthrow or to excommunicate, but to bring them into the continuum of our living heritage." Indeed, the "great seduction of philosophy is to pass judgment and so to be right." Miller turns to history not for the purpose of passing judgment, let alone ridiculing others, but with the hope of solidifying his identity as a citizen and also a philosopher.

He knows and even celebrates in "Portrait of Man" in Part 2 that "History is always being rewritten." The revisions pertain far more to the form of action than to this or that specific deed or event. One of his most profound insights is found in "The Environment is Actual": "Revision is the conversation of functioning. That is the premise of history." The effective conservation of, say, political authority at some decisive moment in an actual history might require radical revision (e.g., the shattering realization that such authority derives not from a divine ruler but from the human subjects themselves, or the equally shattering realization that even the most secure polity at bottom rests on nothing more than a revisable consensus of highly fallible citizens).

The most archaic form of human utterance with which we are familiar is the animistic utterance of our most distant ancestors. These utterances and thus these predecessors are hardly intelligible to us. But the paintings on the walls of caves long unknown compel us to recognize that our own drawings and inscriptions are somehow linked to these images. These artists were either themselves human or akin to us in some hidden way. Theirs is a human eloquence echoing across a vast stretch of human history. Our ability to hear them as *our* forebears requires "an attitude of piety." Such an attitude prompts, as Miller writes in "Action is Inherently Historical," "our reconciliation with the conditions of our own endeavors. It is the story not only of acts—*res gestae*—but of their condition." Our agency is of a piece with theirs. "In so far as I have another man's problems of form, I am not analogous but actually identical. It is this identity of actuality that is our only community," Miller states in "Order and Disorder."

One vital link between this selection and the theme of actuality can be seen if we recall that the immediate present needs to be extended both backwards and forwards. It needs to be seen as part of a continuum, Miller writes in "Documentation," for the purpose of intensity as well as that of intelligibility: "it is as if the life of the present would lose much of its vigor and tenacity if it were to be deprived of its continuity with those who have gone before, finding no evidence [in the present] of their presence." The clarification of our defining purposes along with the intensification of our sustaining energies seem to require forging and renewing our kinship with agents who must appear to us as remote and baffling, but also eloquent and admirable. Such agents include the animists for whom thunder was the sound of Zeus bellowing.

This essay was originally penned in 1973, as a postscript to a letter (Miller Papers, 20:4). The first edition of Hocking's Types of Philosophy *was published in 1929 (New York: Scribners). The numerous references to Miller's other published works are, in order of appearance:* The Midworld of Symbols *(p. 176), "The Sense of History" in* The Philosophy of History *(p. 85), "In Sum" in* The Midworld of Symbols *(p. 189), "Explaining Language" in* The Midworld of Symbols *(p. 75),* The Philosophy of History *(p. 186), "The Environment is Actual" in* The Midworld of Symbols *(p. 85), "Action is Inherently Historical" in* The Philosophy of History *(p. 149), "Order and Disorder" in* The Philosophy of History *(p. 129), and "Documentation" in* The Philosophy of History *(p. 110).*

It is always essential in dealing with constitutional words to show their origin or genesis. Otherwise they seem like bolts from the blue and not to lie in the public domain. A constitutional change is radical and the radical needs to be *genetic* if it is not to seem ungoverned or even incomprehensible. That reality is a consequence of actuality is a radical revision of knowledge. I studied epistemology. It is so said on my diploma. But knowledge was to appear where I kept myself out of it. The "known" had no presence. What one took for presence was only appearance. "The trail of the human serpent is over everything."[1]

It seems not denied that our ancestors were animists. Events showed a power. Why did it thunder? Zeus made thunder and Poseidon stirred the waves. In Genesis Jehovah made the world and Adam too. He laid "the foundations" of the world, as in Job. All that was local control. The real world was the consequence of an act. But God, or Jehovah, was not real; he was pure act. One was not to make another object of God. His actuality did not fall within knowledge. "And Job laid his hand upon his mouth."

In animism every act, or power, was a miracle or a catastrophe. This came to be regarded as unsatisfactory. "Order is Heaven's first law,"[2] as we say. Virgil said, "Happy is he who is able to know the causes of events." This direction was away from catastrophe to an order, from miracle to the total absence of astonishing novelty.

Or was it a direction? How could one say so unless animism was more than a passive appearance? Why did we not go on with animism? What was to arrest it? In terms of passivity, of "data," there are no illusions, no errors, no failures, no deed. We say that animistic explanations are unsatisfactory; the puzzle is how to account for their having ever occurred.

The modern temper declares animism an illusion. It does not deny that our ancestors were animists. But, on premises of empiricism, animism is not an illusion at all; it is *incomprehensible*. Nobody can tell how the illusion occurred, while we claim that it did occur.

This is a consideration that I have not seen raised. It is well enough to call a person in error provided one can explain how he went wrong. He had not read a book; he miscalculated. But the error has a basis. Where an error is denied *any* basis, what entitles us to allege that it has been made? On what basis, then, are we to say that there *ever were* animists? What could be more mysterious—and more arbitrary—than to allege that someone was all wrong? Who is arbitrary now? To claim that animism is an absolute delusion is to make its recognition impossible. Yet this is the consequence of the view of knowledge that allows no verb, and no present active participle.

The story of the breakdown of animism was told in terms of universals—for example, that every event had a cause, that quantity and space were modes of universal order. Many "categories" were proposed, and all are universals, as in "The real is the rational." It is questionable whether animism was completely abandoned even by Epicureans, by Lucretius, say. But universalism did tend to discredit the here-and-now, the authority of the individual. Nor was it historical. Time, and *dated*-time, which is the time of history, was not of the essence.

We entered a third stage. There has been an attack on universals as timeless essences. They could not be found within experience. There were no "necessary connections," a claim going back to the cynics and reappearing in David Hume. The rejection of animism on the grounds proposed by most of the philosophers, and by some who were considered among the great—Plato and Aristotle—was now declared to have been invalid. You don't get rid of animism by insisting on an ordered world— that was the claim. The alleged order was itself an illusion in terms of a passively empirical cognition. But this rejection of universal order was not intended to reinstate animism. Now there was no control at all, neither local control nor universal control.

In order to make sense of this result it was necessary to give our animistic ancestors some credit if we were to allege that they had emerged from their errors. They must have had some way of going right as well as of going wrong. They pulled out of their ignorance and error. The alternative would leave both universalism and empiricism as a pair of miracles. The later views, if they were to avoid being miraculous, had to ascribe to animists some way of working their way out of it, out of their illusions.

Now this could not be done if the animist was nothing but an animist. The claim is then made that he was also an explainer of events, that when it thundered he hazarded a "theory." Zeus thundered. In time he came to see that the explanation was defective. He became a physicist, never attributing events to an act, purpose, or will. Animism then stands as a theory of events, mistaken, but creditable insofar as it ventured into explanation, into a broader world.

This is very fetching, but it does not answer the question of why an explanation did take—or *could take*—an animistic form. What would suggest such a solution to thunder? The critics of animism deny that anything in experience could give a clue to an act. They insist on this. They don't say "*We* find no act, but we must suppose that *Homer* did." They deny that he did. Nobody ever did. Nobody could possibly do so. I am to believe that my ancestors spun a "theory" about an entity or force or power that neither they nor I had ever experienced and that neither they nor I *could* experience. That seems a bit thick, even hilariously absurd. But this is what the best people say.

Our ancestors appear to have had the view that the earth was flat, a view that has persisted to my day. A man named Voliva had that view.[3] As a theory it is considered false. Yet it is not incomprehensible as an interpretation of actual experience. We can still think it odd that people in Australia are standing upside down. It is a consideration that arrests children. But this theory, this interpretation, rests on solid ground, so to say. The earth is no illusion, and "it" looks flat. But then there are other appearances that induce doubt. What about that ship on the horizon? You see the masts, but not the hull. How do you account for that? It was a point made when I was in school. The flat earth turned out to be an inadequate theory, false, but not based on an illusion for which there was no evidence in experience. Nobody says that one cannot have a theory about the shape of the earth because earth and shape are illusions or myths. Yet that is what is said about the act, mind, soul, the individual, universals, efficacy, power.

So, in order to avoid an abrupt break with our ancestors, we say that they were just like ourselves in that they had theories, even though we *also* deny that anyone could, or did, experience the entities or forces on which such a theory as animism could be based. They had a theory that—unlike the flat earth—could not be proved false. Illusion or false theory—which is it to be? So, not to break with them entirely, and to show that we "know" better, we say that they theorized, just as we do also.

Did they, though? The evidence is negative. Certainly the apparatus of theory appeared much later. Grammar, logic, dialectic, geometry, arithmetic, are late. And yet we see our ancestors as animists. They did not see themselves so. They did not say "We are aware of purposes and of causes too, and we opt for purpose-control." In fact, our earliest scraps of documents are themselves vague on that distinction. It was an evolution, not an a priori frame of reference. It was historical, not scientific.

The problem is this: May I say, or not, that I had animistic ancestors? If so, I want the price.

The price is that I now recognize them as agents. So they felt themselves to be. They could make a fire and even draw and paint on the walls of a cave. They had their *being* as a local control. They were effective. The rest of the world—so to say—was a blur. Only insofar as they acted was there any clue to the proportions of objects, indeed to objects themselves. How, then, was one to "understand" the shape of change? Why, as the consequence of agency and power. No other *basis* of order was known or felt. Well, of course, if it thundered a mighty man or a god brought it about. How did anything come about? Efficacy was not an impersonal "theory"; it was actuality. It was *via* the act that objects themselves were distinguished—what one could eat, drink, throw, wear, and manage.

I note that as we have lost the act we have also lost the order of objects and this in the most radical way. Apart from act, nothing is necessary. "Data" are miracles. We cannot even make good on the term "datum." *Given*, to what? We cannot say. On our premises we may not speak of "data." The abstract intellect is hoist by its own petard.

A technical note: It has been observed that when George Berkeley found some order it was in mathematics. There one statement *followed* from another. I cannot deny that this discovery sets me roaring or into depression. What on earth had Pythagoras been doing? Was he an observer of phenomena or did he draw lines, angles, figures, and from that *doing* announce a universal order and the music of the spheres?

I don't use fancy words. I say, "The universal is the form of the actual," and I get stared at.

For centuries we wrestled with "the problem of universals." Why so? Because they eluded cognition, but still they were supposed to be cognitive or else just wind in the ears. That they are the form of the actual was not considered.

History is the evolution of the order of action. Animism was the immediacy of the act. That is why I say, and claim, that my ancestors were animists. No radical empiricist has ancestors. Albert Einstein has no ancestors. Physics—within its own statements—has no past, no history.

And so Einstein declares that past, present, and future are "illusions," although "tenacious."

I behold on this campus a course on the history of science. Is science to be reduced to a historical illusion? "Oh God! Oh Montreal!"[4]

Back to the beginning. The *manifestation* of act is the midworld. It is utterance. It is words, monuments, constitutions, a triangle drawn in sand and so proclaiming a world. Tell me what is the classic or medieval world, leaving out the voices, leaving out Parthenon and Chartres. What we call "knowledge" has not recognized a midworld, *therefore* has no manifestation of act. But God spoke to the prophets and so was made manifest. Any word is a revelation, or else wind in the ears.

Our orthodox world is a silent world. No voice is heard.

Please excuse. One word leads to another. What else *leads* at all?

NOTES

1. William James used this expression in a philosophical context in *Pragmatism* (1911. New York: Longman, Green, 1949), p. 64.
2. "Order is Heaven's first law" is a line from Alexander Pope's "Essay on Man" (Ep. iv, l. 49).
3. The Reverend Wilbur Glen Voliva was an individual associated with the Flat Earth Society.
4. "O God! O Montreal!" is taken from "Psalm of Montreal" by Samuel Butler (1835–1902).

History and Humanism

In this essay, Miller articulates in a detailed, systematic manner his distinctive conception of history and, closely allied to this, his historicist conception of philosophy. Philosophical reflection is, at bottom, a historical enterprise in which the implications of historicity demand fuller explication and formal recognition. "One does not stand outside the issues of philosophy and judge them," as Miller asserts in this selection; rather one is implicated in the intellectual and, more broadly, cultural history in which these issues have taken shape and acquired significance. For those who unblinkingly acknowledge their definitive locus in an actual though ongoing history, the issues of philosophy (as he writes here) "are judged by history alone, that is, by any successor who has embraced prior commitments, made them his own, and suffered their bewilderment." This means, the "philosopher, like the artist or statesman, must settle with some actual and self-defining difficulty and speak to its demands." It also means we ought to be deeply suspicious of "those reformers who see in the past the record of errors and confusions that might have been avoided in a fuller possession of ahistoric truth." Not only in philosophy but also in every other significant region of human engagement, "all history displays this equation between actuality and selfhood." Yet, part of the task of the philosopher is, at this juncture, to illuminate just this equation in its various guises.

The history of philosophy demands of this enterprise that it become in explicit, systematic form the philosophy of history. The "function of the philosophy of history" is nothing less than "to bridge the gulf between essence and existence, and it can do this only insofar as essence becomes historical and existence ideal." Historically defined essences and ideally envisioned existents are not likely to satisfy the desires of the Eleatic temper. But Miller slyly points out that this temper is recognizable only as a historically instituted and consolidated position (in other words, as a historically defined essence).

Some of Miller's most memorable assertions about his most fundamental concerns (including several assertions already quoted) occur in this essay. For example, in a paraphrase of Abraham Lincoln (highlighted in our Introduction to "Mistrust of Time"), he insists in this essay: "We cannot escape history, and we cannot escape the study of history." History, as Miller continues, "avoids finality, establishes finitude, emerges from commitment and conflict, allies us with evil, and presents the universal [not as something statically given but] as self-revision in terms of the necessary." In his sense, then, history "is the most concrete of all categories, and one of the latest to emerge."

Moreover, it is the work of our own hands and the portrait of our unique selves. "Neither God nor nature can make history, for they are infinite." Human agents are, in contrast, finite actualities whose lives are caught up not only with one another (including their ancestors) but also with other such actualities (not the least of which are their laws, languages, and other modes of symbolization). This means that we are in a position to make history; indeed, we cannot avoid doing so, however unwittingly or ineptly. The adventure of striving to be spectators of all time and all existence, while undeniably noble, needs in our own time to be seen for what it is—a historical undertaking of fateful significance, one in which finite, mortal beings desperately seek an immutable, transcendent warrant for their definitive practices.

Presented initially to the Harvard Philosophy Club in 1948 (Miller Papers 2:6), this essay was initially published in a slightly different form in The Paradox of Cause *(pp. 75–96).*

The idea of a philosophy of history may, at first sight, seem contradictory. History is of all subjects the most earthbound and timebound, not venturing beyond the records and documents that set forth what has happened in a particular place and time. Philosophy has, from the first, been concerned with eternal objects rather than with events in time. Philosophers will often consider a proposal as if it possessed meaning anywhere, and at any time. One may seriously debate the problem of mind-body dualism, as if it were a question of general concern, touching all men everywhere. Not uncommonly, the doctrines of the great figures in the history of philosophy are presented in this way. Such treatment of men and issues creates an atmosphere to which time and accident seem irrelevant.

Furthermore, there are in fact many philosophies that set out to proclaim a doctrine of salvation, which is to be found precisely in the measure that one can identify oneself with truths and values that rust and moths cannot corrupt. Perhaps those attempts may be regarded by some as poor doctrine, but they cannot be disavowed. And they represent that quest for imperturbability, for stoutness in the face of fortune, which is commonly associated with the name of philosophy.

If one seeks eternal truth one may perhaps inquire of the philosopher, but hardly of the historian. Historians deal in the transitory and corruptible. They have no interest in any event or statement except so far as it falls within time and is accounted for by other quite temporal events in accordance with methods of interpretation that are themselves but changing fashions. Of this strange involution of his work the historian is often subtly or even explicitly aware. He works in a field that has its own infinity, but it seems a shapeless one. Everything that gets done by an act is grist for his mill. There seems no solid ground under his feet. He cannot even indulge in the luxury of philosophic skepticism, for that position registers defeat in the quest of an ideal that the historian does not seek, and that he must treat like all else as another hope or expression of belief.

Looked at this way, history is a study that appears to dissolve the solidity of nature into opinions about nature, and to treat the most elaborate scientific studies of objective reality as no more than human documents. For traditional philosophy, that is, for philosophy that is itself ahistoric, such a study can have no form because it has no controls. It is a Humean essay where the data include the tentative organizations that are acts, and the symbols that acts leave as their residue. But if one asks for the fixed frame of reference in which this discourse operates, there appears to be none, and none seems possible. For were one proposed, the acts, events, and symbols that history studies would fall into that ahistoric frame of reference and time would be lost in the static.

For this reason history seems to be a study without form. And if it has a form it must be a new one, construed out of the elements of change, time, and finitude. Time and history can have no form except that of time itself. To see whether that is possible is one way of posing the idea of a philosophy of history.

The idea of a "philosophy of" does not fall in too readily with this situation. To undertake a "philosophy of" some special science is to seek to identify, analyze, and relate the categories in which it operates. For example, minimal elements in mathematics are the factors of identify and difference, pure and abstract, and without qualification of space, time, or sense property. These factors are universals and they are taken to hold sway anywhere and at all times. They are concepts of universal incidence, organization words, not denotation words. They seem general conditions of all discourse. And they are therefore treated as being timeless. They are eternal essences. So, too, when in physics the list of categories expands to include space, time, and body there is no suggestion of any local event, of anything that happens in a particular place and time. Such a pattern for the idea of history is inappropriate. A philosophy of history must be a story in terms of time, and of events in time. In history there is no static truth antecedent to its own investigations.

It may be felt that tentativeness and insecurity mark all sciences, including philosophy, and that all beliefs suffer change. This may very well be the case but for all that it does not make for clarity in defining this issue to obscure the aim of a study. It seems most likely that all persons feel the attraction of history's absolute empiricism, but this does not imply that philosophy has usually regarded itself as nothing but history, or its quest confined to events in time. On the contrary, I believe, philosophy has not widely announced that finitude is a category, that is, a constituent factor of the real. On the whole, philosophy has sought the ahistoric, with realities and forces that deny efficacy to time, and leave it in a region of shadow.

Time has been a cosmic stepchild of dubious parentage, and always a problem child. It is commonly represented as moving in bad company with ignorance, impulse, and vice. It is the scene of our fall from the true and the good, our alienation from the ideals of knowledge and virtue. The problems of error and of evil are among the most common in philosophy.

Philosophy has proposed that we become the spectators of all time and all existence.[1] All things are to be viewed under the aspect of eternity where if one must love God, it is to be done intellectually, and not from a passionate heart. There have been first causes, prime movers, unmoved movers, substances both one and many and of every description, atoms and their prolific progeny, or laws through which the bewildering changes of time might be arranged in patterns of unvarying constancy. But everywhere time is a doom, an exclusion from the ideal. It is finitude, a region in which philosophy has not characteristically found rest and sufficiency of being.

It may be felt that time is quite an acceptable concept since it occurs in physics. But the time of physics differs in important ways from the time of history. In physics time has no efficacy. There, no event is understood because of yesterday, but only because it illustrates the dateless law. For this reason it deals in the repeatable and therefore permits experiment and observation, neither of which procedures operates in history. The experiment has a date, but not the order of nature that it is designed to reveal. The laws of moving bodies hold no less today than yesterday, and as surely in Poonah as in Pisa. Physics has become a very paragon of knowledge and enjoys enormous prestige. But it purchases this sublimity at the price of a radical impersonality and at least an apparent irrelevance to action and values, a feature of impersonal knowledge that has proved disturbing to humanists. Physics defines a region without blemish, a seamless garment of nature. It contains no error, no passion, no evil, and no conflict. Facing it, men may abandon hate, but will not, as some seem to suppose, find love. It remains ahistoric in all its immensity, and somberly threatens to disqualify limitation and all those areas of experience that must give to limit a central and controlling function.

In survey: To deny ontological status to finitude is to disqualify historical time, and yet to give time the status of a category appears to bar access to that totality of object and integrity of person which philosophy purports to offer.

There is about the concept of time the flavor of empiricism, that is, the rejection of the complete. It is not to be assumed, however, that a defense of the systematic status of time and limit will win the approval of all empiricists. Indeed, the idea of history, since it carries us into the past, which is irrevocable, is less agreeable to the usual versions of empirical knowledge than is the idea of the eternally contemporary. For there tests can be made, and the common and public world established. It seems possible to suppose that empiricism owes its continuing, as well as its original appeal, to its promise to unveil the impersonal and objective truth, the truth about nature that can be useful to men. Francis Bacon took knowledge to be a kind of power, and our contemporary instrumentalists still inveigh against any concepts of truth that do not accrue to the execution of particular purposes.

Scientific empiricism has sometimes become positivism, which, in extreme form, involves the repudiation of criticism. An outcome of this tendency has been logical positivism, where the form of finitude is lost in the description of a peculiar datum, namely language. The general position of incompleteness is threatened by empiricism with loss of form, and so with a loss of the necessary, that is, metaphysics. It becomes difficult to avoid reduction of all beliefs and statements to psychology. This is the historic and characteristic charge made against empiricism.

The difficulties that occur in the study of a philosophy of history center on the disposition one makes of the element of limit. It seems plain that the problem of historical order would be most seriously affected by the assumption of antecedent determinism. It is a question of one's frame of reference, of how one would tell the story. One would certainly need to be very cautious about allowing history to vanish into some ahistoric background of which it would become only a phenomenal derivative. Nor would it in the least matter whether such a background turned out to be mundane or celestial. One can abandon all ontology, but what one cannot do is to define the ontological in some ahistoric way and then propose a philosophy of history. Physics, psychology, or theology may well take over, but one should then raise no fundamental puzzles about the order of events in historical time.

There is a proper reluctance in the acceptance of any compulsive idea. And ontology is compulsive. The overall quality of experience or of nature is not disclosed in any event that could be some other way. It goes without saying that one does not want to make an *argument* for finality. Whatever is proved is unsure, and whatever happens is without constitutional force. To represent history as a category is to offer it as compulsive. One needs to discover how that can be done.

There is a sentence in René Descartes' *Discourse on Method* that may serve as an indication for dealing with this problem of compulsion as it relates to finitude. Descartes wrote: "For it occurred to me that I should find more truth in the reasonings of each individual *with reference to the affairs in which he is personally interested*, and the issues of which *must presently punish him if he judged amiss*, than in those conducted by a man of letters in his study, regarding speculative matters that are of no practical moment, and followed by no consequences to himself, farther, perhaps, than that they foster his vanity the better the more remote they are from the common sense; requiring, as they must in that case, the exercise of greater ingenuity and art to render them probable."[2] What is here, I suggest, the important phrase is this: *"the issues of which must presently punish him if he judged amiss."* This penalty, Descartes points out, is not found among speculative matters. And yet Descartes was not a pragmatist either, trying to find ways and means of satisfying an accidental or instinctual want. His problem of discovering a true method of knowledge will seem to most persons speculative enough, yet it was apropos of such a quest, deliberately remote from accidental particulars, that he spoke of being visited by some penalty for his failure. Philosophy is viewed by many as a study without consequences, that is, as a study that cannot specify the punishment for failure. The real difficulty, however, occurs apropos of showing how failure could occur among the universals, even a failure of reason; for there is no logic among the essences. A practical failure, touching us in our finitude and partiality, would hardly seem to make sense in eternity.

One may well hold that any belief has consequences because it gives shape to personality and character and therefore controls action. This is often claimed. William James thought that "over-beliefs" bore on one's hopes and fears, and so on one's undertakings, and he identified rationalist and empiricist as men of differing stamp. "See the exquisite contrast of temperaments," he exclaims.[3] Johann Gottlieb Fichte in *The Vocation of Man* admits himself stopped in persuasion by the character of materialists and idealists; and Plato in describing the career of various political types speaks of the democratic man or the timocratic man as responsible for the parallel forms of government. In his *Types of Philosophy*, William Ernest Hocking quotes a remark of G. K. Chesterton's that "the most practical and important thing about a man is his view of the universe."[4] Perhaps we can do nothing about the universe, but our view of the universe seems to do things to us and to others.

Descartes is not clear on the meaning of the punishment that follows error. But it seems fair to believe that he did not mean that one became ill, or lost one's money, or laid oneself open to a suit at law. The punishment was not, it seems, of the sort visited on imprudence or ignorance of the ways of the world. In general, if the consequences of a philosophy are to be construed as practical, the controlling concern of the individual would then fall into the particular satisfactions of life and not in the intrinsic fulfillment of philosophy itself. Somewhere, great satisfactions must be shadowed by a great threat. But what threat, what punishment, what nemesis, is there among the categories and the eternal essences? They seem remote from consequences and have been traditionally courted for that very reason. And when they do have consequences they lose their priority and stand under the smiles and frowns of common pleasures.

Yet failure to discover punishment of a fundamental sort is likewise failure in the quest for the necessary ingredients of experience. So far as I can tell, the instrumentalist party in pragmatism cannot define radical failure, and consequently must repudiate all necessities. A view of truth based on purpose, that is, on psychology, would not, of course, be able to name any fundamental threat.

The punishment of which Descartes speaks conveys the flavor of an inescapable consequence, as if there were something more operative than intelligence and circumspection. There is here a suggestion of darkness, of forces to which one must bow, of something restless and inescapable, while at the same time made operative and manifest *in time* and to finite endeavor. And it seems well to say again that the penalty in question does not frustrate an aim that is itself avoidable, an aim that one might relinquish without any sense of radical defeat or defect. College students sometimes consult psychologists who purport to tell them the occupation in which they might best hope to succeed. Should it turn out that a penchant for medicine gets no support through such an analysis, the young man may turn to law or business with no sense of defeat, and sometimes with a sense of satisfaction over the discovery that he can be more successful, or useful, in those endeavors. But here defeat is not fundamental. One turns to something else. There are other fish in the ocean. But a radical frustration presumes a radical aim. How are we to be punished in time for our metaphysical defects? Yet how else can punishment be administered? Were one to say that one cannot escape nature one would, I believe, find a broad tendency to agree. There has also been uttered the statement that we cannot escape history. This was said at a time of great emergency in the American career. Something was at stake, and this was declared to be the last best hope of earth. There was in prospect a new birth of freedom and the more secure establishment of the institutions that expressed and guarded the endeavor of men to achieve their befitting excellence. There was here a threat and a promise, the prospect of consequences of a grave and controlling sort.

There were many who *did* want to escape history, to exclude the inexorable from time. For while time is a doom from the point of view of eternity, it is an opportunity for those who mistrust responsibility and hope to elude nemesis. With this attitude, the attempt to escape from the shocks of necessity, one may have the deepest sympathy. George Santayana makes much of the shock of data, and of the confusion and instability visited on the soul in the entire region of action, the region of animal faith.

Others have sought to avoid the issues of essence by dwelling only in time and so making the best of circumstances. History, however, is satisfied with neither solution. Its peculiar flavor is found in the union of form and finitude, in the acceptance of time as a region from which one cannot escape because it is the condition of the disclosure of all necessities.

The residual heresy of the idea of history as it is of the idea of action and of morals is that we can very easily escape history by renouncing all egoism. So can we, on that basis, escape nature. For nature, I venture to say, is no datum. It is, perhaps, environment, but even as environment the extension of will. Nature, as order, is pure act. Physics is a study of the general conditions of action, and it is a science that has obtained scope and articulation only as egoism has sought out the general conditions for all particular purposes. It is this that bestows on physics its nonpsychological quality while at the same time drawing it into the orbit of the humanities. We can escape nature, and we can escape history, and we will always try to do both insofar as we would shrink from that punishment of which Descartes spoke.

The terror that has been spread abroad by the atom bomb is the disclosure that many do shrink from nature and the awful power it bestows on those who know its ways. But it also marks the point where physics enters history, not as an accumulation of knowledge, or the removal of ignorance, or the extension of means for the accomplishment of psychological purposes, but as an enterprise shrouded in fate and sustained by the dark forces of will. In the Old Testament there was an avoidance of the true name of the deity, and we confront a parallel reluctance to use the name of nature. How different this is from the optimism of Bacon collecting "instances" the better to extend his power. Knowledge is not power; it is rather fate and the disclosure of the systematic relation of limit to essence. Knowledge is not the way to eternity; it is the way to history. Until knowledge discloses its systematic penalty, it dwells in its ivory tower or else becomes the ignoble servant of arbitrary and subjective aims. The Baconian aim has failed. It has become a nightmare and a menace. This is, I believe, the reason for the bewildered and sincere cries that demand that nature study be now bent to human and to humane purposes. This effort, too, will fail. There is nothing we can do to escape from the perils that attend our discovery of the necessary. For these perils are our fate, and they alone give to fate any meaning. The fault may not be in our stars, but in ourselves. But this does not make us underlings. Nor does it make us masters. It leaves us caught in a destiny of our own making, where every inexorable force represents one of the conditions of our own finitude. *The absolute is the form of finitude.* This, so far as I can see, is the simplest way of formulating the meaning of a philosophy of history. The punishment of which Descartes spoke is the consequence in time of the unwillingness to treat time as a category. There is not, so far as I can tell, any other way of bringing home to any man the experiential equivalent of necessity.

No man will accept necessity until something happens to him to make him do so. Yet this seems absurd, since what happens is regarded as never necessary. We are not dogmatists, nor do we usually allege that we have stood on Pisgah and seen the promised land. We must settle for experience, yet experience being finite and fragmentary seems a most unlikely source of the inescapable. It discloses no meaning to punishment. Even the civic punishment of wrongdoers, so-called, illustrates this hesitation. Ignorance of the good, as Socrates urged, calls for instruction. There seems no ground of punishment until the wrongdoer has fitted himself for it by accepting the equation between himself and finitude. History is the maintenance of finitude, and more closely, its self-maintenance. I suggest, in passing, that this is the reason why Plato kept returning to the problem of virtue, baffled by an inability to discover the locus of evil, and of good, in limitation itself.

In broad summary: Philosophy has difficulty in including history where the past exerts efficacy and the static laws themselves dissolve into the fluidity of experience. But among the essences there is no necessity because no penalty. Descartes proposed such a penalty. How is one to interpret it as falling within experience? How is limit to contain anything unconditioned? Time confronts us at last with the constraints generated by egoism, that is, by any assertion of the conditions of finite existence. These include nature and all knowledge. History is disclosed when any attempt whatsoever at assertion, whether theoretical or practical, forces on us the sense of inherent fatality and compels attention to the self-maintaining process. It is apropos of this process alone that all necessity is disclosed and definable.

Against this background we can now move to name and briefly characterize some concepts and theories that are involved in a philosophy of history.

A remarkable and, I think, defining element in the generation of the historical process is the need of commitment. This is the mark of limit, and of self-identification with limit. In the more intellectual sort of historical development, skepticism may serve as an example. Skepticism is not an original position, but is always derivative. One may be born great, but one must achieve skepticism. It does not matter, however, in what naive belief doubt finds origin. It is only necessary that there shall have been a belief in something. Naturalism unexamined is as ready a medium for skeptical growth as supernaturalism, and just as inevitably a producer of misgivings. Skepticism is generated only by the formal fact that one has been committed to some belief or other, no matter what. It is a position perpetually regenerated as new knowledge becomes customary or hereditary. In skepticism there occurs the alienation of thought from its object, and so, in all times, the rediscovery of the solitude of thought itself. This transition does not, and cannot, occur where one is thoughtless, without a stake in some view of man's qualities or nature's order. Only the man with a theory, with some, perhaps unclear, universal belief, can suffer this disturbing disillusionment. Experience, when articulate and possessed of some formal order, however elementary or sophisticated, must pass down the road of self-discovery. One has trusted sense, or judgment, or revelation, tradition or reason. But somewhere one has given one's faith.

To show that all philosophical ideas emerge from the pressures of commitment could require prolonged exhibition in many types of philosophical study. For I do think it is at last a matter of exhibition, rather than of abstract argument. Still, the career of a commitment may be carried a step farther in considering the historic fate of skepticism itself. Being a product, it is itself transitional, an advertisement of limit and instability. Something more is called for. Perhaps one inspects this lonely self and finds that it veils a further unexamined assumption, perhaps that of a thinking substance. This, however, also vanishes into the phenomenal data, and one comes to the question of the radical empiricist: "Does consciousness exist?" Still, it is hard to ignore the base degrees by which one has risen to nonentity and annihilation. So long as any position is taken, even a denial, even the stream of consciousness, one still maintains some outlook, however desperate and impoverished.

This is the part of the record that thereupon produced the essay of Immanuel Kant. It is always difficult in dealing with the history of philosophy to demonstrate that a figure in a standard textbook ought to be in the textbook. There are those who would stop the story with Thomas Aquinas, and others favor John Locke, holding, with James, that philosophy goes around Kant, not through him. It is not simple to show just why Fichte, for example, belongs in the history of philosophy and why the position of nature received from him a treatment enforced by the commitments of his predecessors. But throughout one must, I believe, maintain this attitude of tension and desperation in order to keep one's discourse historical. Not every word spoken in philosophy can hope for such distinction.

It is, consequently, a great mistake to quarrel with the figures who make history. One does not stand outside the issues of philosophy and judge them. They are judged by history alone, that is, by any successor who had embraced prior commitments, made them his own, and suffered their bewilderment. If he thereupon accepts his task, maintains the validity of the problems that produced confusion, he may hope to add something to clarity. The philosopher, like the artist or statesman, must settle with some actual and self-defining difficulty and speak to its demands. One is entitled to suspect those reformers who see in the past the record of errors and confusions that might have been avoided in a fuller possession of ahistoric truth. For them there is no history but only static and intellectual truth.

In a broader sense, all history displays this equation between selfhood and actuality. This is the stage on which all action occurs. Action announces limit. Infinity cannot act, and speculation need not. In the present time we face great issues, greater and more searching than ever before in the history of our country. If we can find the actuality that is for us self-defining, and hence absolute, we shall know what to do. Otherwise we may well suffer disintegration and defeat. But what we are is what we have come from. There we find our necessary meaning, because there we find the meaning of our problems and of our finitude. From that process and its results we cannot escape.

I have felt that this idea of commitment, of an absolute though finite actuality, exerts considerable appeal for young men, especially those who have interposed their bodies and their wills between their country and its enemies. It seems to me shameless to suggest that the soldier faces destruction and deals it out, or that he could be asked to do so, for any but a final cause. And it seems to me no less inhuman to engage in these undertakings for theoretical ends. This is the locus of our confusion over the actual. We are intellectualists, we are spectators, and cannot therefore conceive of the absoluteness of limitation. This problem has become one of morale, and of our survival. We must beware of the suggestion that our wits are sharper, our theories surer, than those of our enemies. We dare not allege that we have unveiled some abstract good, or essential virtue, and now propose to use violence in order to make our theories prevail. What we must preserve is not an abstract ideal, but limitation and finitude. We must preserve history.

The only punishment is the loss of the capacity to make history, to come to an end of a self-defining task in which lies all compulsion and all universality. These are the reasons that we cannot escape history. This, rather than the bare space of Plato, is the mother and nurse of all existence.[5] And in that medium of time is also the generation of all essence. For the universal is the form of limitation and in all its modes declares the order of critical finitude.

A great deal of effort has been expended in avoiding parochialism of both will and belief. Our loyalties, it is urged, should embrace all mankind. Arnold Toynbee[6] fears the idolatry of local attachments. In one way or another this is a familiar theme, and has often appeared in moral theory as the ever-widening circle of membership. We aspire to become citizens of the world and to embrace all men in good will. Yet the good will must also interpret itself in specific ways. No good can be accomplished where specific institutions and commitments do not shelter its growth and foster its exercise. We may well shrink from such localism. It seems to destroy, not to promote, the universal. Yet a corollary of the possibility of history occurs in the necessity of asserting the absoluteness of some actual embodiment of values. If this is narrowness and idolatry, it is also loyalty, and the condition of affection. That morality occurs in limit and only there, that it is the reaching for not a timeless value but for some present, incarnate, and imperfect good, may seem a strange doctrine. But in that way a philosophy of history is extended into the region of ethics. Ethical theory has suffered from an inability to settle for limitation and commitment, while history and the men who make it have been forced to treat every aim as called for by particular situations. Action proceeds from limit, and it arrives at no finality, but only at another defective result. Yet defect, in principle, has no critic. There is no platform beyond limit from which one may snipe at it. Defect secures no systematic condemnation.

Commitment is the acceptance of the relatively static as the locus of values, and the base of action. This may, perhaps, be illustrated by means of what Alfred North Whitehead called the fallacy of simple location.[7] No location is absolute, but it is just as true that some location must be taken to be absolute in order to make any measurement of relative velocities. This is the factor of limit. Without this limit there is no spatial or temporal infinity. For these, and all other infinities, are only the form of finitude. The same considerations apply in morals or in politics. Every moral judgment rests on the base of a current concern, on what one now identifies oneself as doing. The rules of morals can do no more than maintain that enterprise. The Kantian morality appears defective on this point. There is no duty nor any rationality until the nonrational and existent moment gives leverage to the moral law. The question "What ought I to do?" can get no answer, because it makes no sense until one is already doing something that has for oneself an uncompromising value. This is the idea of the relatively static. There can be no hope of disinterestedness in the *end* of endeavor where the actual commitments of men are not already disinterested. The sportiveness of the sequel is only the extrapolation of the disinterestedness of the origin. Only a pure actuality can propose a pure ideality. Commitment and the relatively static are two concepts that emerge from the problem of history. They are articulations of finitude, and they are ontological categories.

In this situation one must, of course, discover the dark depths of the nonrational immediacy. Our acts engage with universality only in one or another of its dimensions. It is this situation that Paul Tillich calls the demonic.[8] When we identify ourselves in any way with the actual, it is in some partial aspect of the actual. For example, we may operate on the assumption that the economic order as it occurs in the marketplace embodies the pattern of our social life and private will. Thereupon the pursuit of commodity threatens to override other interests. It becomes demonic. It may violate other dimensions of our society and of our private wills. It generates ruthlessness and a remarkable opacity to the common humanity of employees. It obscures art, science, religion, or politics. It generates conflict. And yet, this dark partiality of the economic demon is the condition for testing both its own authority and the authority of other interests. For they too may, and I believe must, become demonic. This has happened to religion, to nationalism, and even to education. History rides on the vehicles of partial truth, but their demonry is the sole condition of discovering their force. This is a situation analogous to that in psychology, where the drives or instincts of men can be separated from vagrancy and whim only as they generate conflict and the resultant requirement for a controlled integrity. It is only a philosophy that endows limit with ontological status that can turn conflict to constructive use. The use of conflict is the disclosure of the necessary. To make that disclosure is the labor of history.

These considerations centering on the structure of commitment and leading to the idea of conflict may be carried further in raising afresh the question of universality in history. For history shows men divided among themselves and within themselves. The philosopher has traditionally sought the universal. History in its emphasis on the local and actual seems to disregard the universal. History divides; philosophy unites. History defines relative disorder; philosophy aims to dispel disorder in a coherent picture of all experience.

It is indeed the discontinuity of experience that may first arrest the student and lead him to wonder about its structure. One discovers, for example, that one may not find it easy or possible to comprehend the Greek world, even as it is presented in its literature, or represented by scholars We do not offer human sacrifice like Agamemnon, worship nature gods, construct ideal societies without mentioning "rights" as did Plato, or believe in final causes with Aristotle. It is not so much a question of approval or disapproval as of understanding their world, or their outlook. The Greeks are not modern people with recognizable idiosyncracies, but in many respects unrecognizable. Similar considerations apply to all the great formulations of the past. There is a sense of helplessness when the teacher, making a reference say to the Book of Genesis, or the Book of Job, or the seven deadly sins, or to sin itself, discovers that some students meet these indications with complete blankness. There seems more afoot than an absence of information. Nor can one quickly proceed to inform the ignorant one of the factual content of Plato's *Republic* or the Book of Job. One can't just look something up in the *World Almanac* or the encyclopedia. Facing the past we all have our shortcomings, and they are more grievous than ignorance. They suggest an incompleteness in our selves, in the degree to which one has objectified one's own axioms and habits. The past is historical because it is always relatively discontinuous with the present. Oswald Spengler, making it absolutely discontinuous, at least in theory, offers in the end an ahistoric account of past time. Yet, when one first meets the Greek or the medieval mind one may be deeply puzzled, wondering what common humanity unites our day with theirs. History, which vanishes if the discontinuous be made absolute, confronts us with problems of continuity. On the other side, if the past presented no puzzle, all transactions in time would appear transparent to a single perspective, and to any perspective.

The humane scholar cannot but experience a sense of shock when the emancipated critic ventures to either approve or condemn the past, its ways and beliefs. Nor is this feeling due to any agreement with those ways. They are gone, and they are not ours. The shock appears because of the implications of such judgments. For they condemn history to the ahistoric. History is more than the sympathetic apprehension of the deeds, thoughts, and feelings of others. It is the activity by which such sympathy can become actual. And that requires effort. This effort is launched by the obscurity of the present itself. Of this need of the present for the clarifying power of the past, the common law seems to me as good an illustration as any. What we mean by rights, for example, is discovered in the crises that have led to their assertion. The concepts employed in the law find their meaning in constitutional history and nowhere else. There is no merely present legal system, none that lacks the continuing pressure of the will that still sustains its functioning. Similar considerations apply to philosophy, where every controlling term means what it has come to mean in the controversies that alone give it authority. An idea must make good, it must make its way. No problem in philosophy is innocent, none is timeless, none is launched from a point of view without environment. That environment is ideal, because it is historical.

We cannot escape history, and we cannot escape the study of history. Nor is there any history at all apart from the thrust of present meanings into their yesterdays. History is a category because it is a necessary condition of the present. In history time is efficacious. This is not so in physics. The efficacy of time occurs only in the strenuous preservation of the present. One is not at liberty to refrain from the study of history. To do so is to court the punishment of which Descartes spoke. Like all proper philosophic punishments, it is radical and destructive, for it means that one has sentenced oneself to ostracism from every compulsion, and hence has lost one's freedom. For freedom is the self-control and the self-revision of thought in the modes of necessity.

In summary: History avoids finality, establishes finitude, defines the relatively static, emerges from commitment and conflict, allies us with evil, and presents the universal as self-revision in terms of the necessary. It is the locus of punishment of a systematic sort, and thus becomes an ingredient in any account of the real. It is the most concrete of all categories, and one of the latest to emerge.

The literature of the philosophy of history grows apace, and has captured a remarkable degree of popular interest. This fact should lead to no implication of any lack of technical complexity or philosophic importance. Our times face the broad problems of morale without the traditional comforts of a supernatural support, or for that matter, the support of a rational order of nature that offers us both emancipation from superstition and

unlimited means of private satisfaction. We are on our own. In consequence, our acts and purposes lack adequate authority. Since they are
identifiable only in time, they seem insubstantial and ephemeral. There
has resulted a great sense of loneliness so that the return of any public
man to the church makes news and seems arresting out of all proportion
to the record of mankind in taking it for granted that time is not of the
essence. Without a moral universe, men become lonely and pessimistic,
and sometimes merely trivial. But a moral universe is something more
than a cozy refuge from uncertainty. Such an interpretation does less than
full justice to the motives that seek it. To be moral is more than being
good, or being secure; it is rather being effective. The effectiveness of finitude is the great metaphysical heresy, and, on the whole, the idea of action
has fared badly in ultimate formulations.

The idea of a moral universe is not the same as that of a benevolent
universe. It is rather the idea of the primary influence of the forces that
discover the meaning of good and evil, and therefore include both. This
distinction is generated by time, and in time attains progressive refinement. Such a statement is plausible only if time itself may be endowed
with the status of an absolute. Where time is invalid, its fruits are tainted.
Moral theory apart from history has become, I believe, stale, flat, and
unprofitable. We play moral finger exercises with hedonism or with obligation, but make no music so long as action is itself disqualified.

Of the bearing of this idea of a moral universe on the philosophy of history I can give only these shabby indications. But the main lines of the
problem have been plotted. The phrase *moral universe* is probably not
gladly heard, and, for my part, not gladly used. It seems pretentious. On
the other hand it seems absurd to look away from the issues that reintro-
duce this concept, and to condemn them in advance because of their outcome. Apart from some essay at establishing a bond among men, moral
theory has little to say, and probably makes no sense. The idea of history
proposes that this bond lies in no finality, but in the overcoming of those
systematic and structural discontinuities that generate both conflict and
reconciliation. There is no morality where nothing finite possesses
absolute status. Clearly, such a claim threatens idolatry, but with no less
clarity it is also the condition for discovering idolatry. Only what is itself
absolute can discover an absolute antagonist. This is the dialectical
process of history, and this mode of our being is itself a discovery of time.
For this reason it was said earlier that history is radical empiricism, and,

I believe, the only form that clothes disorder with unity. Scientific empiricism, when radical, generates nihilism, and leaves even hypotheses and postulates in a perilous position, at most handy, at worst without meaning, in any case without authority.

History, morality, and truth conspire to elevate the particular and the local. For this reason there is no universal history, no synoptic vision of man in all his attitudes. All history, like all measurement in nature, must have its local absolute. Consequently, American history must have for us a peculiar authority. We levy on others for the illumination of our own meanings, carrying the lines of inquiry as far afield as may be. It is only in terms of our own forces, and of our own responsibilities, that we can make history. The point of view that makes history is also the sole point of view that can study it. Indeed, there is no reason for studying history at all except for the sake of making it. For only in making history can the past secure efficacy. This localism is not barred from universality. On the contrary, it defines it in its own self-maintenance. Nor does this seem to me to imply any lack of reverence and respect. One shows no disrespect in inquiring of a man or of a culture how it contributes to such affirmations as one may make and must make in order to preserve one's own point of view, and hence one's capacity for criticism and revision. The past is important because it contributes to our self-comprehension, but it does not do this in general, but only apropos of our present meaning. This, I submit, is not arrogance or provincialism, but rather the sole evidence of our own sense of responsibility. In history the moral bond becomes practical. There alone it becomes imperative, because defined through the dark determination to give here and now illustrations of the law.

There is one essay in Ralph Waldo Emerson, the one called "Experience," where for a moment the shadows of limit qualify his happy light.[9] For a moment experience appears in a tempered chiaroscuro. "We live amid surfaces," he says, "and the true art of life is to skate well on them. . . . Men live in their fancy, like drunkards whose hands are too soft and tremulous for successful labor. It is a tempest of fancies, and the only ballast I know is a respect to the present hour. Without any shadow of doubt, amidst this vertigo of shows and politics, I settle myself ever the firmer in the creed, that we should not postpone and refer and wish, but do broad justice where we are, by whomsoever we deal with, accepting our actual companions and circumstances, however humble or odious, as the mystic officials to whom the universe has delegated its whole pleasure for us." In this essay the polarity of the individual and universal, the steady Emersonian theme, is viewed from the position of the incomplete individual. It is a remark that may serve to point up the requirements of the attempt to make the secular sacred.

There are, of course, many questions bearing on the idea of history that have not here been mentioned. Something about the meaning of causality, controls, determinism, would be in order, and also a great deal on the function of the artifact or symbol as a factor in defining nature as well as man.

In brief summary: A problem is set for the idea of history by the traditional aspirations of philosophy and by the consequences of that ideal whether speculative or empirical, dogmatic or skeptical. History poses a problem about the centrality of action, and draws into the orbit of strict philosophy all the terminology that gives form to finitude. Above all, it enforces the absoluteness of limit, and makes liaison between the authority of our concepts and the hazardous acts that give them standing room in time. It is, I believe, the locus of the fusion of reality and humanity. Neither God nor nature can make history, for they are infinite. It is the work of our hands and it is the portrait of our minds.

In conclusion, one may consider the association of scholarship and action.[10] There is no science of what to do next. The proper place for advocacy is in politics, where practical penalties and rewards attend practical proposals. But the scholar also wishes to be effective. A philosophy of history no more than any other special branch can tell what to do about taxes or the Marshall Plan. But it can validate the medium in which such decisions are made, and it can enforce consideration of the career of those reflectively derived absolutes that in their present relatively static form make it imperative to reach decisions. Whatever views of man and nature asperse the importance of the medium in which decisions are made invalidate both past and present. Such views will leave action subjective, and hence trivial and arbitrary. It is the function of a philosophy of history to bridge the gulf between essence and existence, and it can do this only insofar as essence becomes historical and existence ideal. This seems to me the summary view of what both motivates and controls investigation and the meaning of history.

NOTES

1. This is an allusion to Plato's *Republic*, taken here as a representative of the dominant orientation in traditional philosophy. In opposition to the principal preoccupation of classical Western philosophy to survey the real *sub species aeternitatis*, Miller is advocating an engagement with actuality *sub species temporis* (*The Philosophy of History*, p. 85).
2. First Discourse, *Discourse on Method* (1637. Paris: Vrin, 1965), pp. 9–10.
3. This is a paraphrase posing as a quotation. The source is Lecture 1 of James's *Pragmatism* (1907. Indianapolis, IN: Hackett, 1981).
4. Gilbert Keith Chesterton (1874–1936), *Heretics* (London: John Lane, 1905), pp. 15–16. James opens his *Pragmatism* by quoting in full this claim by Chesterton.
5. See *Timaeus* 50d.
6. Toynbee (1889–1975), English historian. Miller's views regarding the value of local attachments invite comparison with those defended by Josiah Royce in "Provincialism" in *Race Questions, Provincialism, and Other American Problems* (Freeport, NY: Books for Libraries Press, 1967).
7. See *Process and Reality: An Essay in Cosmology*, Corrected Edition, David Ray Griffin and Donald W. Sherburne, eds. (New York: Free Press, 1978), p. 137; also *Science and the Modern World* (New York: Free Press, 1953), pp. 49, 58, and 156.
8. Paul Tillich (1886–1965), American (though German-born) theologian. The work that Miller most likely has in mind is *The Interpretation of History*, especially Part I, "The Demonic: A Contribution to the Interpretation of History," trans. N. A. Rasetzki (New York: Scribners, 1936).
9. This essay was written after the death of Emerson's very young son Waldo. Thus, it is no surprise that "Experience" is a work in which "the shadows of limit qualify his happy thought." See pp. 478–79 of the collection edited by Joel Porte, *Essays and Lectures* (New York: Library of America, 1983).
10. These themes are developed in full in "The Scholar as Man of the World" (Part 3, below).

Mistrust of Time

In Miller's judgment, our relations with time are total and constitutive. There is no immutable, ahistoric order underlying and structuring the actual course of our historical undertakings. Time is not a moving image of eternity, but rather eternity is an abstracted image of those densely compressed yet internally differentiated moments in which a living past and nascent future commingle. That is, historical time is not an onto-logical stepchild, but the legitimate heir of a vast inheritance, the appropriation of which demands modification of both inheritance and inheritor. We are in part what our histories have made us and in part what we make of these histories and inheritances; we are truly constituted by our historical involvements and behests.

Even so, our acknowledgement of this has been halting and belated. Indeed, as Miller writes here, the "persistent and eloquent mistrust of time strongly suggests that we are not dealing here with some accidental item of experience." It suggests a deep-rooted, long-standing exigency. This mistrust of time has meant the resistance to "the identification of our own actuality with time and deeds." Our innermost self must, we feel, somehow transcend the vicissitudes of time and defeats of history; we must be allied with a being or an order not subject to decay, not vulnerable to defeat. Hence, our "ideals have been timeless and ahistoric. They offered no constitutional authority to time but sought rather to coerce it into subordination to the immutable." Nor have they granted a categorial status to history. One consequence of this persuasion is that "it came as something of a shock that the rationality that we had cherished had had a career." Just as Miller in "History and Humanism" draws out the implications of his views regarding history for our understanding of philosophy, here he does the same for our understanding of rationality. What José Ortega y Gasset announced in *Historical Reason*—"The hour of the historical sciences is at hand. Pure reason . . . must be replaced by narrative reason. . . . This narrative reason is 'historical reason' "—is in this and other places also proclaimed by Miller. As noted in the editorial introduction in this section to "History and Case History," the form of rationality with which Miller is prin-cipally preoccupied is that geared toward the exhibition of uniqueness, actuality, and (in his distinctive sense) fatality. "In history we cannot disavow," Miller contends, "what we have done or said." Such disavowals are evasions of history in his precise sense of this ambiguous word. Consider one of his most exact and eloquent definitions of this term taken from "The Ahistoric Ideal": "History as a dimension of experience is the discovery of those concerns that exist only in their prolongation, enlisting original intensities in the sustaining of their destined [or fateful] revisions." What we have said and done is never contained within the instance of its utterance or enactment. It is inescapably a prolongation of what has already been uttered or undertaken; moreover, it is also inescapably an act of hurling ourselves toward a future. Any human act is part of a historical continuum defined as much (if not more) by its disruptions and dislocations as by its continuations and prolongations. As such, as Miller continues in "The Ahistoric Ideal," it is vulnerable to being judged inadequate or inept by the criteria inherent in the continuum in which it assumes actuality: "Deed and word call down on themselves the judgment their own order invokes."

For example, the fateful inadequacy of the Constitution of the United States was revealed in the crises precipitating and constituting the Civil War. The judgment called down on the institutions authorized by this Constitution issued from the very order being invoked by the framers and defenders of this document, an order instituted for the protection of freedom and the guarantee of equality. It is not at all insignificant that Miller was fond of quoting, in connection with driving home the force of his position regarding history, the words of Abraham Lincoln: "Fellow-citizens, we cannot escape history. We of this Congress and this administration will be remembered in spite of ourselves." Those moments in which we come face to face with the inescapable consequences of our defining commitments are fateful; they are crises in the etymological sense, moments in which a decision is demanded of us and ones in which our decisiveness or indecision will define us for as long as we are remembered ("The fiery trial through which we pass will light us down, in honor or dishonor, to the latest generation"). The unblinking recognition that we cannot disavow what we have said or uttered but must confront the fateful consequences of our utterances and exertions entails forging a self-conscious alliance with historical time. The motives thwarting such an alliance and obstructing such a recognition are explored in "Mistrust of Time," whereas those on the other side are the focus of "Alliance with Time," both in Part 2.

This essay was written in 1967 (Miller Papers 5:6) and was first published in The Philosophy of History *(pp. 51–60). The central concerns of this text are of a piece with "The Ahistoric and the Historic" and the other writings identified at the end of the editorial introduction to that essay. The quotation from Ortega appears in* Historical Reason *(1944. New York: Norton, 1986). Lincoln's statement is from his Annual Message to Congress of 1862. The two references to "The Ahistoric Ideal" are from* The Paradox of Cause, *pp. 158 and 160.*

Suspicion of time is a special instance of a general uneasiness over all the modes of ordered finitude. Reason itself leaves our most responsible moments contingent on consequences that come to no final termination and on premises that, if they are not arbitrary or miraculous, call for

an ever more remote support. Nor is a man's virtue unalterably established, but must prove itself again in new circumstances for which an earlier composure may be inadequate. Let a man look at any of the modes of
his articulate functioning and he will find that not one has escaped the
charge of futility. The fortress of order has become vulnerable in the
degree that its architecture and construction have been most impervious
to episodic assault. Every castle is a Castle Perilous, for it is designed as a
guard against an environing situation that reasserts its presence and its
power in the very stones that can fend off the casual invader. There is no
basis for a mistrust of time until action and thought have taken shape and
style. It is in the structured temple of delight, not in formless abandon,
that veiled Melancholy has her sovereign shrine.

There has been, indeed, many a way to arrest time, and art, not least,
draws us from our anxieties: "Thou, silent form, dost tease us out of
thought / As doth eternity."[1] The lover, the thinker, the poet, the hedonist,
are in agreement with the ascetic. None trusts to time, and each looks for
a present intensity that endows the moment with intrinsic worth. These
absorptions often appear to mark a soft life, and are looked on with suspicion by earnest persons who see them as truants from the work of the
world. But there is a lust of battle, too, where great resolve can lift men to
their finest hour. "Now, God be thanked, Who has matched us with His
hour, / And caught our youth, and wakened us from sleeping."[2] Some
seize on the day, others are seized by the emergencies of thought or of
action, but all rejoice in an absorption that asks no question about tomorrow. Even sober thinkers place some emphasis on present exertion.

Sometimes the immediate exerts its force not as an argued release but
as passion and splendor. The safety of habit may be disrupted by some
demanding abandonment. "She has heard a whisper say, / A curse is on
her if she stay / To look down to Camelot." But, then, within a bowshot
from her bower eaves there passed Sir Lancelot: "She left the web, she left
the loom," and found disaster. " 'The curse has come upon me!' cried /
The Lady of Shalott."[3] Time has no delusions unless one invites them, but
not to make this venture is to forgo not only desire but every declaration
of an instant integrity, every quickening concentration of selfhood. A
poised and aloof contemplation that sees the passions and hungers of men
as a victimization must face the counterclaim of wholeness in the summary and shining moment, whether pleasant or passionate. We cannot
very well be "up and doing, / With a heart for any fate"[4] without some

occasion that summons the will to its uttermost and thereby takes chances with a cosmic totality that, like the placid mirror, is shattered by the passage of Sir Lancelot.

Sometimes we have tried to elude time and fortune for the sake of a momentary adequacy. Even our ideals, unless they are empty, have enforced the importance of their temporal vehicles. And sometimes a rush of rapture brings a commanding intensity to a present and rescues us from a pale nonentity. And yet these enlivening moments betray themselves to their environments. Time and circumstance reassert their presence and, in the measure that we have disqualified them, spoil a finality that has borrowed its meaning from a personal past or from an evasiveness that haunts and shadows its pretended sufficiency. Horace could not count on a pleasant dinner with his friends if he had not seen to it that olives and grapes had been planted and pruned. Besides, he liked his Falernian to be well aged. One may prefer cash and wish to let the credit go, but sometimes it is a convenience to draw on one's credit, particularly if one has a desire for cakes and ale. Good credit, like good wine, is not available in the present tense. In the end it is the hedonist who is solidly seduced by virtuous regularity of conduct. The difficulty with hedonism is not that it is possible but (alas!) naughty; it is rather that even the high moment requires some environment, if only the crude circumstance of facts. And facts relevant to the supply of desire must themselves be supplied by thought and forethought.

Nor did the mystic find the occasion of flights into ecstasy until mindless savagery had been supplanted by institutional refinements, and the abrupt discontinuity of uncontrolled reactions had taken on the decorum of form, as if the intimations of eternity had to be provided by a prior grace in speech and custom. The "pure nothingness" of Meister Eckhart depends on a legacy of doctrine that included the idea that the word had become flesh and dwelt among us. Nothingness does not generate the mystical flight. "When me they fly, I am the wings"[5] applies to the manifold, quite as much as to Brahma, although the writer of the *Upanishad* seems not to have thought so, and Ralph Waldo Emerson himself never quite came to terms with death and taxes.

It seems, indeed, not possible to view time as a region that one may enter should one wish to do so, or avoid if that appears the advantageous course. If time stood as an object of intelligent choice, all these emotional essays of accommodation would be much overdone. My friend who lives in Vermont finds the winters there pretty rugged, but he knows quite well that he could move to Massachusetts, where twenty-five below zero Fahrenheit is more rare, or to Florida, where it is unknown. There are some particulars that one cannot usually evade, such as one's height or complexion, but these do not arouse the interest and eloquence of poets, philosophers, and theologians. When such particulars constrain attention, they stifle rather than enlarge the imagination and restrict feeling to an obsessive narrowness.

Our relations with time are total and constitutive. The emotions and theories that have been provoked when time has seemed unsatisfactory permeate the whole man and affect his entire outlook. Remedies for the ills of time are not analogous to those appropriate to particular uneasiness. Limited ills respond to specific remedies, but limitation itself, as an overall condition, can hardly be amended by some patent medicine or by a change in diet. We can with some plausibility abandon our purposes, declaring all of them unprofitable, but what we cannot do is appraise the whole region of purpose from a point of view that itself expresses any finite purpose. Where one has a constitutional problem, no "theory of types," no more inclusive tentativeness, is of the slightest use. And so we have tried to arrest a fickle fortune in oblivious pleasure or by reaching for a steady "reality" where, in the absence of a perilous present, there are to be no yesterdays and no tomorrows.

Such desperate remedies indicate a vague and troubled uncertainty over the identity of the actual person, not a reasonable choice among more or less advantageous alternatives. Choice, deliberate and informed, has its place; but it is not, as many have said, the avenue leading to emancipation. It is a dubious therapy that can only perpetuate the conditions of distress. The frustrations of the practical man have practical remedies, but those of the thoughtful egoist who has questioned the competence of time to furnish him with satisfaction entail remedies that are constitutional and philosophic. One can always withdraw from a situation with which one is not identified. Indeed, the accidental is not a neutral or impersonal fact, but is disclosed in this very reserve of the individual who is not ready to settle for the arbitrary and ephemeral as the center and actuality of his own existence. Anyone, then, who does not find time constitutional and self-definitive must look elsewhere. He must look before and after and pine for what is not. The romantic soul is aware of a schism that is more than a disappointment over his investments in the market.

Mistrust of time expresses no calm and tentative pondering of the superior advantages of refraining from giving hostages to fortune while sensibly pursuing one's purpose in other, more profitable ways.

It is not easy, then, to divest oneself of time and to renounce all interest in it, even if one wanted to. Nor is this difficulty plausibly ascribed to the allurements and seductions of natural objects and to the weakness of the flesh, as if a man's lower nature subverted his higher faculties into eating his dinner, dragging him down to an interest in learning, to a nice competence in his craft, to honest solvency in his enterprise, or to love of a woman. Neither are these activities under the direction of timeless perfection, as if a person in no way identified with eating and drinking, in no close intimacy with books and politics, viewing them all from a superior distance, decided for no earthly reason that he would like some tea and toast. Such a plunge into the concrete could only be regarded as a miracle. This estranging dualism suggests an ability to weigh time against the timeless as if the discriminating shopper, who reads a consumers' magazine, were identified with neither. And so one is led to wonder where one stands when recommending so absolute a preference or when apportioning the proper measure of concern in each. What is the apparatus of this judgment? And, for that matter, why make the choice at all?

It is an overlooked property of choice that one can always decline the gambit. If you ask me whether I wish to go to Boston or to New York this weekend, I may decide to stay home, satisfied with what I have. To urge a choice between good and evil is to imply a possible indifference to the distinction, and the more portentous the choice is made to appear, the more one may be inclined to cultivate one's cabbages in tranquility. What is more, the consequence of a choice is untrustworthy. Tomorrow's newspaper, the latest book, the word of a friend, may lead one to think that one has been hasty in the balancing of advantages. It is worth noting, too, that choices lose importance and clarity when not operating as the implementation of resolve. Indifference does not choose. Before Caesar, many had crossed the Rubicon, but they had not cast the die. Choices are tentative, not absolutely but with respect to the resolve that sets the stage for their urgency and for their intelligent propriety. Choice, after all, is not on the loose but is restricted by the self-identifying functioning of an actual person. There it finds its occasion, its necessity, its specific tentativeness, and its intelligent modification in the sequel of particular experiences. Only so can it then be said that the choice was either wise or incautious.

The persistent and eloquent mistrust of time strongly suggests that we are not here dealing with some accidental item of experience. Time poses a problem of one's identity and nobody wishes to be identified with unessentials. So long as we viewed temporal change as a region in which mind and individuality were not to be discovered, we could properly bewail its mutability, seeking for ourselves a steadier reality beyond unstable fortune or laying hold of some untroubled hour of inconsequential pleasure. But historians, perhaps with more enthusiasm than deliberation, have concerned themselves with the past as if with materials in which the character of man had been revealed—as if, like other scholars, they controlled some way of telling a coherent story about a distinctive factor of experience.

It was not until the record of acts had been set down in documents and these had been accepted as genuine disclosures that the identification of our own actuality with time and deeds acquired not only plausibility but a powerful authority. We grew into our past without prior deliberation, without philosophic sanction, and then found that we had no way of accrediting a dimension of learning that contained all that we had ever done, all that we had ever thought, and all that had given occasion for our specific actuality. Then for the first time we could turn on this pretender to knowledge and ask for credentials. There was not much to offer. Our ideals have been timeless and ahistoric. They offered no constitutional authority to time but sought rather to coerce it into subordination to the immutable.

The old and traditional mistrust of time has not, in short, resulted from some defect of history, for there has been no constitutional structure to the past. History was not so much a defective mode of experience as no formal mode whatsoever. The past, and therefore the present that had generated it, stood together as manifestations of psychology. What we said was opinion; what we did was impulse. We could learn about particulars and acquire useful skills, satisfying an irrational propensity. Our skill in warfare has been considerable, but the preservation or extension of individual power has been ascribed to an instinct of pugnacity or aggression, backed by other drives and urges such as sex or food hunger. On a social scale war has been declared a manifestation of tribalism, beset with prejudice of race or creed, and obviously nothing that a person not victimized by nature would undertake. The political liberal has wondered on what basis he could declare himself and take a stand, since action abandoned the felicity of a critical aloofness, brought down on one a partisanship that suspended an evenhanded deliberation, and put one in the uncomfortable position of being observed by the superior person as no better than any other psychological oddity. Absolutism in all its forms reflects an unwillingness to be identified with finitude in its opinions and desires. And so we have vacillated between the high absorptions of the moment and the repudiation of all such deceptive sufficiencies. If history is psychology, then the modes of the accidental take charge of it and explain it.

The alternative has been the ahistoric, beliefs not proposed or proved by experience, acts not motivated by circumstance, morality that sees defeat in any alliance with our finitude. One need but read the daily paper to find evidence of the scope of this intimidating absolutism, as when, for example, political rights are talked about as if they had a sanction in the arcane depths of the individual, and owed nothing to the actual community of resolute men or to that long and arduous career of our essays in functional interdependence. These attitudes are themselves the revelations of time. No one mistrusts what he has not embraced and found wanting in terms of its own pretensions. Psychology cannot recommend "adjustment to the environment" and then elevate our adaptations into finalities. Engulfing desires come to no enduring satisfaction in the accidental, and accidental desires pass with no more reason than authorized their arrival. It is not history that we have repudiated, but prehistoric and dissociated moments.

History made its appearance in a world that the most responsible thought of man had already shaped into various modes of unity and order. Change, multiplicity, and the fierce concentrations of finitude had all seemed deficient in that universality and stability which bespoke the disinterested reason of man and the integrity of his world. It came as something of a shock that the rationality that we had cherished had had a career. It was even worse to entertain the idea that without the career there could be no rationality that we could identify as our own. These considerations were slow in making themselves felt. There persisted, and still persists, the attempt to bring history under some alien unity. There was the record of what men had done and said, but what sense did it make and how were we to call that "knowledge" which lacked a rule of unity? How was history to be brought under the classic pattern of the ahistoric cognitive ideal?

Peculiar faculties not themselves caught in time had to be invoked as the implements of criticism. An aloof "reason" was to preside over thought, and a supervising "conscience" over every wish and every act, over all our undertakings and institutions, over all mortal emergencies. The warders of our finitude, if there were to be any, were necessarily not themselves part of our own cumulative experience. The universal in the object appeared as the consequence of the universal in the subject. When, as with the psychological empiricists, no universality could be found in our own experience, none could be attributed to the objects of experience. But if we ourselves can employ an innate universal, then the rational ideal discloses its nontemporal character in the very equation between ourselves and our nontemporal faculties. The rule of order led to powers within us that for their own satisfaction demanded analogous powers beyond us. And so we looked behind, beneath, or above all the shifting changes of time for a constancy that complemented our own demands. The gaze of man was to be directed—could not avoid being directed—toward foundations not actually in sight or toward a splendid superstructure never to be reached by the measured gradation of a continuous approach. It has seemed, indeed, that the force of the cognitive ideal must carry beyond all possible mutability. It was a major moment in the life of reason when the security of the grand object of thought failed to establish itself in the actual, so that a superlative reality, an *ens realissimum,* had to be accepted as the guarantee of the eventual order of any present event. To be quite pure, reason had to lead on to a situation that stood apart from whatever happened. The timeless universal could not consort with time. It could not be part of history.

Given the problem of order as one of unity, and given diversity and change as the helplessness of understanding, what would one do if not project into its ultimate consequences such organization as we already possessed? Certainly no one concerned with history could fail to be sympathetic to these formidable essays. But no one interested in history can renew absolutism by dispensing judgments of true and false. He would disqualify history in that gesture of intellectual superiority. In history we cannot disavow what we have done or said. It is not merely a question of ignoring or denying what took place; it is rather that the past act is a progenitor of the present, a source to which we must look if a present is to be understood. The cognitive ideal is not, then, merely opposed to history, but is a condition for raising a question about its meaning and authority. If we are puzzled about history it is because we have entertained a view of knowledge that gives no obvious certification to an alleged order among dated events.

NOTES

1. These lines are from "Ode to a Grecian Urn," by John Keats (1795–1821).
2. The lines are from "Peace," one of Rupert Brooke's (1887–1915) sonnets in *1914 and Other Poems*.
3. "The Lady of Shalott," by Alfred Tennyson.
4. These are lines from "A Psalm of Life," by Henry Wadsworth Longfellow. The concluding sentence of Ralph Waldo Emerson's "Experience," on which Miller comments in the previous chapter, expresses a similar attitude, in particular with respect to the fate of the irrevocable loss of a loved one: "Never mind the ridicule, never mind the defeat; up again, old heart! . . . there is victory yet for all justice; and the true romance which the world exists to realize will be the transformation of genius into practical power" (*Ralph Waldo Emerson's Selected Essays*, Larzer Ziff, ed. [New York: Penguin, 1982], pp. 310–11).
5. "They reckon ill who leave me out; / When me they fly, I am the wings; / I am doubter and the doubt, / And I the hymn the Brahmin sings." These lines are from "Brahma," by Emerson.

The Ahistoric and the Historic

This essay is one of Miller's most polished and compelling statements of his distinctive outlook. "Our relations with time are," as he states in "The Mistrust of Time," "total and constitutive." The realization of this, however, took time—indeed, centuries. For our actual history is one in which the actuality of history in its full significance and authority has been systematically evaded. "The disparagement of time is no fitful impulse," Miller writes in "Alliance with Time." "It draws its strength from the orthodox and traditional background of our most systematic thought." This ahistoric ideal José Ortega y Gasset called Eleatic, from the city of Elea "where there appeared a number of men who argued, with originality and brilliance, that change was illusion and not reality." This ideal has shaped our understanding of rationality and much else, so much so that the essence of reason seems wedded to a commitment to the eternal, the necessary, and the immutable. The transitory, the contingent, and the alterable seem unworthy objects of such a noble capacity. At any rate, reason, as Miller writes here, "has led us into some Eleatic Absolute, mundane or celestial, to some reality where time and finitude are absorbed, where they lack authority and become subordinate and derivative, the manifestations of another power, and so without original jurisdiction of their own."

Miller's efforts aimed at investing the finite actualities of our historical inheritance with immanent authority and absolute value. History "is a constitutional revision of all systematic identity." Hence, his efforts are part of a radical revision of our self-understanding. We must try to define ourselves, far more self-consciously and self-critically than we have yet done, in terms of the actual histories in and through which our determinate identities have come into being.

In doing so we will sharpen our sense of the extent to which we, as Miller observes in *The Philosophy of History*, "are the heirs not only of past wealth, but also of past debits." We will come to see what we characteristically overlook: "To a larger extent than we are aware we live through the past tense. The modes of this continuum are obvious enough, but they lack accredited status. We need a new epistemology, one that does not shrink from giving ontological status to artifacts. The past rides on them, and they are symbols and voices." In "The Ahistoric and the Historic," Miller principally explores the *historical* continuum exemplified in any human utterance (scientific, humanistic, or artistic), whereas in "The Midworld" he more fully makes a case for granting an *onto-logical* status to the symbols and artifacts making up the midworld. All expression is a discipline and a destiny. Accordingly, "it is time that we abandon the nonsense of sup-posing ourselves antecedently in possession of a world of which" language "is only a handy memorandum"—as if we knew about freedom apart from the institutions that have historically emerged as its indispensable vehicles, or about humanity apart from its history. Language in an inclusive sense is granted a status and authority seldom accorded it in the history of philosophy, even (perhaps especially) by linguistic philoso-phers of the analytic persuasion. In its actuality, language is, at once, legislative and dis-closive. Miller's insistence on the legislative aspect of our constitutional utterances points to his kinship with Immanuel Kant, but his rejection of any dualism between appearance and reality indicates an important respect in which he is allied to G. W. F. Hegel, on the one hand, and various phenomenologists (especially Martin Heidegger and Maurice Merleau-Ponty, who likewise proclaimed the centrality and irreducibility of history), on the other. Language in the sense intended here does not provide the means for identifying antecedently determinate affairs, but rather the dynamic forms by which these affairs are instituted, preserved, and altered in the course of their histories. In other words, our language and our world are of a piece; they are inseparable (a point addressed in the following chapter).

The historically authoritative ideal of viewing reality *sub specie aeternitatis* is being challenged in this chapter, in the name of the historically emergent imperative to con-ceive actuality *sub specie temporis*. The perspective of the disengaged spectator, pre-suming the ability to survey all time and existence, is being displaced by that of implicated agents, forced to come to terms with their finitude but not thereby either imprisoned in the present or deprived of the resources to evaluate their inherited prac-tices and historical institutions. No less than figures such as Plato or Hegel in mind, Miller writes here, "Eleaticism is an imposing and a moving monument; but as a final-ity it is a denial of the energies which so gallantly sought some significance in the moment," to accord in some respects cosmic importance to the finite struggles of human agents. Miller's own essay is an affirmation of these energies in their finite actu-ality and, hence, in their constitutional incompleteness. It is one of the places in which he resists allowing the self-revisory actualities of history to be absorbed into the self-same immutabilities of some transcendent order. It is also one of the places where he clearly manifests a pious yet critical attitude toward his philosophical ancestors.

This essay originally appeared as the Afterword to José Ortega y Gasset's History as a Sys-tem and Other Essays toward a Philosophy of History *(trans. Helene Weyl [New York: Norton, 1961], pp. 237–69). A sheaf of Miller's notes from the early 1960s regarding Ortega, at least some presumably composed in preparation for this essay, is located in the archives (Miller Papers 17:15). The quotation from* The Philosophy of History *appears on page 188. Some of the texts with which this essay is most profitably read are: "The Ahis-toric Ideal" (*The Paradox of Cause, *pp. 130–60), "The Static Ideal" (*Philosophy of His-tory, *pp. 44–50), and "The Constitutionally Incomplete" (*The Midworld of Symbols, *pp. 118–26).*

I THE AHISTORIC

W e need not take too seriously the current objections to metaphysics. Anyone who looks farther than his nose may find himself wondering what lies over the horizon. No one takes satisfaction in the narrowness of his outlook nor could he appear to do so without a disguised pretentiousness like that of Antisthenes the Cynic, to whom Socrates commented that his pride showed through the holes of his ostentatious rags. We like to inhabit a world, and indeed are sure to do so if we enjoy so much as a local habitation and a name. The first personal singular pronoun is no denotation word corresponding to some object of consciousness; it is rather a reflective word, a mark of self-consciousness and therefore of an equally ideal environment in terms of which the self articulates its identity. The traditional distinction between appearance and reality is no more than the attempt to establish the personal pronoun, to make it articulate, and, at the same time, to avoid the victimization that threatens any extension of the immediate into its environment. In all pretensions to finitude there lurk the conditions that allow it to be identified. We are told from early years that infinity is a mystery and that we do not understand it nor can hope to do so. But no infinity is any less a mystery than the finitude of which it is the condition and the meaning. Apart from that no infinity could be suggested.

The motive of the many endeavors in making and characterizing this distinction between appearance and reality has been not intellectual but voluntaristic. Immediacies seemed unorganized and therefore a threat to the powers of the self and to the clarity of objects. It is not only an ideal object that metaphysics has been charged with proposing, but also an equally ideal subject. There was no secure antecedent self and then a casual interest in an environing world; the question has been, rather, how to establish the self by providing the sort of world in which it could function. In "The Sentiment of Rationality," William James proposed that no acceptable philosophy could disqualify our cognitive and moral powers. He would have as our world only that situation which warrants and fulfills our own energies. In this abstract form his proposal was not novel, but for the sake of meeting this basic demand he did not shrink from proposing a pluralistic universe, aware as he was of the oddity of such an adjective.

Metaphysics, then, is no attempt to evade immediacies. It aims rather to get them established. This aim has never been undertaken in cold blood, but always with an intensity and ardor that to many has seemed not the least count in the indictment. Yet one may expect something more than prosaic sobriety when a man tells what he is or what he is up to. A man is not disturbed in his world if he is not disturbed in himself.

The mistrust that philosophy has frequently encountered appears on the surface to be the consequence of extravagant conclusions; but its deeper source lies in the dislike, or even the dread, of maintaining the actuality of limitation. For that is self-consciousness and reflects its urgencies and responsibilities. A search for reality has also been a search for the self. And where the self is not actualized in that search, it has not yet put in its appearance. When, however, through adopting the thought of others a reality appears ready-made, the self becomes conventional, irresponsible, and dogmatic. That the world be ready-made has even seemed at times a philosophic propriety. Its typical form is realism. The reaction to realism is skepticism. The skeptic sees no continuity between himself and the ready-made world. Then appearance asserts itself as no less absolute than reality but lost in its isolation and impotence. Idealism occurs as a reaction to both realism and skepticism; and its characteristic quality is found in a reversion to an ancient definition of the world as the perfection of an ordered finitude. In all these instances, appearances draw their status, their authority or lack of it, from a reality that exceeds finitude. When that environment has been viewed as absolute it has become ahistoric, including time or casting it off as illusion, but in either case denying it a constitutional status.

Historicism is the affirmation of the constitutional interdependence of center and environment; this relation includes all the efforts that have been made to define it. It is the view that historical time, that is, dated-time, is constitutional and not derivative from any antecedent account of a timeless situation. Obviously this can be the only basis for a philosophy that proposes to include history as a category. Let history be derivative, let it be irrelevant to the maintenance of the distinction between appearance and reality, and one deprives it of ontological force. If thought has taken flight into very remote regions it has done so in order to illuminate the closer immediacies that, unenvironed, present neither a world nor any coherent finitude. Then we have conjured up visions more vast than dreams and much more persistent. For now as in the past we call that our world which gives status and authority to the immediate. The record of these endeavors is history. There the modes of self-definition become explicit and serve as the vehicles for an understanding of what we have become.

Among the ideas that extend and organize immediacy, none has been more current than that of "nature." Nature is an idea, not a fact. It is not somewhere or somewhen, it has no latent heat, specific gravity, or coefficient of expansion. It is an answer to the need of understanding immediacies. It is no hypothesis explaining particulars in one way rather than in another. It is the objectivity that establishes the subject, the reality that explains appearance, the constancy that orders variety. These were the considerations that accompanied its discovery and that marked the endeavor to render immediacies intelligible.

And so, when José Ortega y Gasset says in a key sentence that "man has no nature, what he has is a history,"[1] it is plain that he is making a statement about the organization of immediacies. Whether there is a historical way of extending experience is the problem of a philosophy of history. Insofar as anyone would endorse that way, he would do so for the reason that not all immediacies find extension in nature. Why would they not? It is because nature seems not defined in terms of a past, whereas man is not defined without it. This past is not the uniformity of anonymous change where all our yesterdays have been as today. History presents a past that the present does not illustrate—indeed, the past may be darkly mysterious—so that only after many years and much soul-searching can one come to understand the forces that generated Amiens and the Parthenon, the *Divine Comedy* and *The Clouds*.

Man, thinks Ortega, is what he has become and, what is more, what he has made himself to be by his own reflective thoughtfulness. Nature is a constitutional sameness; history is a constitutional revision of all systematic identity. We stand in history only as our tomorrows will not be as today, when, indeed, our yesterdays will seem puzzling and unintelligible. Sometimes we get mildly scolded by interested parties because we have lost touch with the twelfth and thirteenth centuries or with colonial America when that "fierce spirit of liberty" of which Edmund Burke spoke was taking shape. But a historical past arises from neglect, and has to be discovered anew. That is a mark of its historical status. So long as the classical world had not been rediscovered, after having been lost and superseded, neither its wonders nor its limitations could be deliberately known and appreciated.[2] The flavor of the past is lost without the sauce of the present. There is no past except as it has been obscured and its influence reestab-

lished. One type of ahistoric mind laments the present that needs to redis-
cover its heritage. It would prefer a present that had never felt its distinctive novelty or suffered any estrangement from its progenitors, wishing
men other than they have come to be and invoking criteria of excellence
that stand aloof from time and its transforming energies. The Autocrat of the
Breakfast Table, who lived in Boston but made visits to Parnassus, observes
archly, "There was Aristoteles, a very distinguished writer of whom you
have heard—a philosopher in short, whom it took centuries to learn, centuries to unlearn, and is now going to take a generation to learn all over
again."[3] The forces once operating and now forgotten or underestimated
establish their authority only when the present requires them for the
understanding of its own constitutional confusions and for the composure
of its resolves.

The American Civil War marked a "new birth of freedom"; and in the
tight argument of the Cooper Union speech, Abraham Lincoln, who knew
that we could not escape history, set out the genealogy of the attitude
toward slavery. The denial of political equality had turned out to be worse
than had been supposed and its assertion much better. But these were the
disclosures of time. One might as well look for gravity where no object
moves in space as for historical forces that are to be discerned before their
presence, and so their power, is reaffirmed in their consequences. History
is no job for the reporter who thinks he owns the categories of description.
The historian is your true contemporary. He stands in new conditions, and
must do so, if the old are to exhibit vitality and relevance. He represents
genealogical novelty. In philosophy nothing can be more deadly than what
so often passes for its history. One cannot look for history apart from the
urgency of its present interpreter, who knows that the past has been its
own critic and therefore entails for its understanding a novel, but derived
and responsible, sequel—a perilous endeavor indeed. Not the least distinction of Immanuel Kant occurs in his calling David Hume "that great
man," although he disagreed with him and amended him. The past
derives its life from the original vitality of its heirs.

As an idea, history will seem no more clear to us than the idea of
nature. Its force will not be felt except as a reaction to the powerful
authority of the impersonal regularity and immutable constancy of the
objective world. It was nature that established the subject as a category of
experience. We have, therefore, a great stake in it, nothing less than the
identification of the personal consciousness. It is an error, then, to see in

nature nothing but the enemy of the self. Nature is its complement. Scratch the scientist and discover the devotee. Nature appeared as the great emancipator not because it saved us from illusions, but because it made possible their identification. In order to do this, the idea of nature had to establish, not abolish, the subject as the locus of illusion. In this aspect of nature occurs the reason for its remarkable tenacity as an idea. It brings us to ourselves.

The idea of nature is not confined to any particular account of what it may be that stands apart from subjectivity. Early philosophers saw the impersonal in many ways. There were the four or five "elements," atoms, numbers, the Platonic "ideas," the four causes of Aristotle, and there were also the good and the beautiful. The ahistoric has taken many forms. It seems fair to say that Ortega is not denying that man has a "nature" in order to reject materialism. What he is rejecting is the orthodox and persistent view that to understand is to invoke the immutable. This appears to be the core and center of his statement that man has no nature. What he does not want is an account of experience that omits time and self-revision as fundamental controls.

If time is not a constitutional factor of experience, it is threatened with disappearance in that truth, or in that reality, which is without yesterdays. This view of the nature of things Ortega calls "Eleatic," from the city in southern Italy where there appeared a number of men who argued, with originality and brilliance, that change, and thus time, was an illusion and not reality. To Elea there came about 540 B.C. the philosopher Xenophanes, whose native city was Colophon in Asia Minor. He was a monotheist and he rejected the current anthropomorphic view of the gods, much as we might deny that truth and reality are measured by finitude. "But mortals suppose that the gods are born (as they themselves are) and that they wear men's clothing and have human voice and body."[4] Anticipating Plato, he says further, "Homer and Hesiod attributed to the gods all things which are disreputable and worthy of blame when done by men."[5] A second and more celebrated figure was Parmenides. He says of the One Being, "It is unmoved, in the hold of great chains, without beginning or end, since generation and destruction have completely disappeared and true belief has rejected them. It lies in the same, abiding in the same state, and by itself . . . but it is lacking in nothing."[6] Plato, an admirer of Parmenides, also spoke favorably of the sort of knowledge that is "fastened as by a chain," and he searched for what remained the same—the colorless, odorless, unchanging essences; the patterns fixed in heaven. The third Eleatic, Zeno, is perhaps the best known. It was he who contended that Achilles the swift-footed, the goddess-born, could not really overtake the slow-coach tortoise once that plodding reptile had, with incautious hubris, been allowed a start in a foot race. It stood to reason, argued Zeno, that one could not additively exhaust the infinite. And since the real is the intelligible, motion that entails infinity even in its briefest extent could be no more than the illusion of appearances. Henri Bergson and Bertrand Russell have not thought it anachronistic to have a go at this annoying problem, although for different reasons and with different results. Russell retains the Eleatic proclivity to put reason in charge, whereas Bergson sees in motion an intuitive immediacy associated with vitalism and with action.

Reason unified. So it was believed. A perfect rationality would then propose a unity in which all change was absorbed into an imperturbable constancy. This unity has been called substance, Being, process, law, and much else. No literate man in the Western world, nor even an illiterate, lacks acquaintance with this way of making sense out of change. We have inclined, on the whole, to the view that it was the proper way. Reason has led us into some Eleatic Absolute, mundane or celestial, to some reality where time and finitude are absorbed, where they lack authority and become subordinate and derivative, the manifestations of another power, and so without original jurisdiction of their own.

Philosophy began as the cult of the rational. There is a story about Thales of Miletus that says that when he had at last brought a problem in geometry to a solution he went to the altar of his house and made grateful sacrifice to the god. Why should he not indeed? This was no longer Miletus, it was a world, and he the individual whose pure thought shared in the general order of spatial form that prevailed also in Ephesus and Sardis. The universal was the medium that sustained both the objective order of appearance and the thoughtful self-control of the individual. Even into modern times the philosopher has suggested the person who has thought for himself in systematic ways. Some colleges still have chairs of "natural philosophy"; and at the beginning of the nineteenth century laboratories were equipped with "philosophical instruments." Nature is not another object on which we expend a bit of attention to the imprudent neglect of household chores or to the damage of higher purposes. Nature is the articulate objectification of finitude in its impersonal mode. The infinite is the form of finitude; and, conversely, the finite is the actuality of the infinite. Form is not fact, but function.

Order, and the absoluteness it entails, has always seemed incomprehensible to the passive; while to the intense, nothing has seemed more evident than the close association of formal functioning with the reality of the self, and, on the other side, with the reality of nature or the supernatural. There is no sort of access to any Eleatic being apart from a process that is itself the antithesis of an immovable result. Confusion and darkness did not come into experience as data passively perceived or intellectually devised. They have rather been spoken of as features of a restless selfhood, inseparable from an endeavor to organize the immediate. The *Confessions* of Augustine, like Platonic dialogues that are also confessions, exhibits a search for both selfhood and order, no more for one than for the other. Eleaticism in all its forms is an egoism that has discovered the subjective without recognizing that the ideal is nothing alien, but is rather the formal condition of its own identification. When, once in Miletus, Thales sacrificed to the god, it was no common man who was moved to do so, no formalist indeed, no doctrinaire, but rather a person to whom form had become his personal actuality.

The alliance of the individual and the universal may be observed in grave personal difficulties and conflicts. A man with a universal is likely to allow it to become demonic and fanatical.[7] He will be all for unity and dead set against variety, for cause and against purpose, for the individual and against the state, for virtue and against cakes and ale. If the universal shows us a world there may be deformity and fanaticism in it. And yet what would you? Where the self is not defined in commitments, it has no actuality. It cannot be even wicked. In Rudyard Kipling's poem "Tomlinson," Tomlinson is turned back from the portals of both heaven and hell. Dante finds in the inferno one who had made the great rejection, "*il gran rifiuto.*" And the apocalyptic writer declares, "I know thy works, that thou art neither cold nor hot: I would thou wert cold or hot."[8]

Ortega sees in natural science a chief modern vehicle of the ahistoric temper. In it, too, changes are summarized in a uniformity that spreads over yesterday and tomorrow. There one deals with the impersonal and anonymous, with the repeatable. It is often held that "prediction" alone bears the mark and stamp of knowledge. There an expectation according to rule is verified by the event. This belief is part of a powerful climate of opinion. The event is in time, but the rule is not in time, conveys no date, and holds no less in Poonah than in Pisa. Prediction is the evidence that a constancy has been formulated and that as things have been they remain. There may be no final formula, but that is not the point. The point is, rather, that when we shall have come to know better it will be in terms of a more exact and inclusive rule. Only in that way are we saved from the darkness of a discrete multiplicity.

The same order that dispels confusion is also believed to save us from impotence. Power is the sign of a congruence between the act, which is local, and a state of affairs on which it can draw for desired results. A favorable outcome testifies that one's act has been addressed to responsive forces. Owen Glendower could call spirits from the vasty deep.[9] The priests of Jehovah knew how to summon a consuming fire. Now one steps on the gas and rolls a mile a minute. Yet the exercise of this sort of power leaves the operator in a condition of insecurity. Whether incantations or gas engines will "work" is not, alas, a foregone conclusion in all specific circumstances. One awaits authentication. A hypothesis must be "verified" or confirmed. Prediction stands, then, as the dependence of a subjective state on a region that is not included in the subjective consciousness. One may wonder to what extent the current search for security may be a consequence of the systematic separation of the subjective from an objectivity to which it must incessantly appeal for confirmation. Knowledge-seeking can become a sort of status-seeking. The very knowledge that, as Francis Bacon observed, brings power lacks autonomy and solicits an alien approval. Such knowledge and such power are precarious. In a paradoxical statement Bacon observes that "nature to be commanded must be obeyed." Command suggests authority, obedience, submission. When, as in the scientific treatment of man, the alleged commander becomes himself the object of knowledge, his authority is dissolved in the implied extension of objective regularity to his own behavior. Not even the subjective then retains any systematic role in the description of knowledge. Thereupon knowledge vanishes, as the tension that sustains it slackens into passivity.

The ahistoric ideal has not however prevented the return of persons to the theater of inquiry. Eminent scientists aspire to be "original" and "creative," as if the discovery of formulas expressed no formula, as if there were untrammeled forces out of which a vast and encompassing regularity could emerge. The poet, "his eye in a fine frenzy rolling,"[10] has claimed no more. A trust in the personal operator also appears in the proposal that we "reduce the degree of empiricism."[11] This is a view of the scientist's work that puts more emphasis on "policy" than on the disorderly rout of empirical sense data. (The idea of sense data is not empirical, but let it pass.) If, however we are to cross-examine nature, not to say ourselves, we must feel empowered to ask questions. A question is a formality—how many, how large, how often, with what relation to other experiences? And, of course, any question entails the assumption that the way of finding an answer is not altogether unknown. Only a good deal of study puts one in the way of asking the sort of question that opens up an area of sustained investigation and discloses the distinctive factors that control a specific discourse. It is confidence in this basis of inquiry that reduces the degree of empiricism, focusing attention and excluding those sensations and perceptions that, as psychology, have as much right as any other, and thus legislates with increasing precision the relevance of observation itself. As science has grown more "pure," more in control of quite conceptual entities and relations, less defined or not at all defined in terms of the objects of purpose and of common sense, it has transferred the order of objective nature to the order of the questions that allow a systematic inquiry. It seems plain that there are no questions and no cross-examinations without formalities.

This more or less deliberate transfer of the locus of order from what is observed to the authoritative question of the inquirer and observer is a characteristic mark of the difference between the outlook that had developed from René Descartes and that which had prevailed up to the seventeenth century. It would be a mistake not to see in this a shift in the direction of the historical. In the categories of any area of knowledge we now tend to see our own work; and this the more unquestioningly because our most general and basic concepts of order have been revised, and because these revisions have dates. Nevertheless, one has not moved from Eleaticism into history because of a transfer of anonymous uniformity from the absolute object to the equally dateless formality of a question. But the fact that it is now the question that conveys the stable and the constant does, however, put one in a position to ask about the genesis of these trusted guides. The order of that genesis is history. The chief figure after Descartes who put the form of questions in a nonempirical position was of course Kant. It was he who allowed us, and even constrained us, to construe the "nature" of physics as an organization of experience according to rule. In the history of philosophy Kant's formalism is the monumental arrest of the anarchy of Hume.

Because of the categories, radical empiricism was "reduced." After Kant, the story moved with slow and halting pace toward the genesis of the categories themselves, and of this deep change G. W. F. Hegel is the principal author. Kant had left the phenomenal world of nature quite ahistoric. It was as anonymous as you please and dealt only with consciousness in principle, with *Bewusstsein überhaupt.*

The Eleatic unity, impersonal, dateless, anonymous, has thus served to permit, not to block, the advent of history. It is great fun to see the past as a wretched mistake, and to plume oneself on one's emancipation from its darkness. But then all one's novelties are miraculous. The bankruptcy of the past offers poor security for the solvency of the present. Nor does it seem likely that a dull and nerveless ancestry will beget genius in its descendants. There is no radical revision without an equally powerful fixity. History is the revision of outlooks, not of opinions. It is not the correction of factual errors within a static control. It is a modification of the mode of making errors. The truth does not make us free; what frees us is the control of the form of truth. And that is not logic or mathematics, but history. But history could not appear until truth itself, in its fixed anonymity, in its vastness and grandeur, became itself the prison of the spirit. The Eleatic, the ahistoric, is a historical necessity. The status of the categories must be nonaccidental if they are not to relinquish legislative authority; but it must also be derivative if they are not to remain arbitrary. History is the absolute empiricism that generates the categories of truth. But that is a longer story than can be here suitably attempted.

II THE HISTORIC

The ahistoric has enjoyed much prestige, particularly for the reason that it gave status to the thoughtful individual. It seemed the region of our freedom because it carried beyond appearance and accident to the supremacy of order and so of our intelligence. There we shared the way of the world and rescued ourselves from unstable opinions and shifting desires. These adventures had their emotional side and aroused deep feeling. The need was urgent, the result often imposing. Like all aspects of self-consciousness, nature grew from tensions, from unquiet, from intensities of concentration. All the great ahistoric formulations still make this demand when we try to understand them. Nor is there any other way. Whether we seek acquaintance with the Stoics or with the powerful fervor of Augustine, we have to tune ourselves up to the hazards they faced, and to the results that appeared to them composing and validating. Emotion is not altogether psychological, aroused by accident, and so passing away with casual adaptations or with equally casual changes in the environment. There are emotions of actuality, the existential tensions of persons.

Emotion is the mark of intimacy, of promise or menace. We are not moved where nothing of ourselves is at stake, nor enduringly moved apart from some mode of attaining and preserving our functioning actuality. But there is another intimacy, that of time and deeds. The self-consciousness of early man had a temporal as well as a timeless aspect. In *The Ancient City*, Numa Denis Fustel de Coulanges presents an admirable account of early classical identity. Its keynote is piety, as Aeneas was "pious"—looking after his father and carrying his lares and penates to Latium. The person stood in his family. He had known ancestors and a household altar where he kept burning an undying flame. The slave and the uprooted stranger lacked these requisites of full personal status. These lesser beings were not involved in the continuity of time. They owned no burying ground for their dead, performed no rites, lacked the obligations of descendants and the anticipations of regard and service from their posterity.[12] Identity derived from the actual life of a particular family or tribe, and later from citizenship in a polis. Like the household, the polis, too, had its shrine and its rites. In declining an opportunity to escape from prison and prospective death, Socrates, as late as 399 B.C., voiced an ancient sentiment. For he was the son of Sophroniscus, an Athenean, and Athens herself was his civic mother. He could not see himself wandering about in Thrace without home and so without recognition. Ostracism was no small penalty then, nor is it today, although its basis has changed. The person in full force, exercising his functions, securing respect and recognition, could be found only in a temporal continuum. It is misleading to suppose that there was an objective time in which some men were persons, others not. The activities that made the time peculiar were those of the men who could act; they made the time. To be recognized as acting is to be accepted as sharing in the existence of a place and time. Objects are taken into account, or not, as one may feel disposed, but persons are there only because they cannot be ignored. Such individuals were, of course, caught up in strong feelings. Much was at stake, themselves indeed. Some may consider these early modes of identity "superstitious," but one may venture to say that superstition is only what comes to be regarded as an inadequate mode of personal identification. When, as in some modern philosophies, identification becomes in principle superstitious, nature, along with the self, vanishes in a general crash of existential order.

Identity takes time. No person, no nation, no outlook, exists in the present tense alone. In his notable but neglected *The Problem of Christianity*, Josiah Royce speaks of "Time and Guilt" and of "Community and the Time Process." A community exists in its career, in the recognition of its self-maintaining piety. A society needs to be reaffirmed—sometimes through the vicarious atonement made by those not guilty of a specific crime, avowing through their own sacrifice the absoluteness of the values that a crime has threatened. But the individual, too, needs time for the discovery of his deeper controls. Nobody can know what he has to do until his impulses disturb, or even nullify, the institutional conditions of their satisfaction.[13] We are not in charge of ourselves except as we take into account what we have done. The moving finger writes our fate only if what has been written is appropriated and becomes a source of identification. There is no other fate than this. Nature is no fate except in the history of its formulations. But this fate is the same as our finite and temporal actuality. There we maintain ourselves in those infinities that are also the sole evidence of our self-possessed finitude.

Where there is no documented history, we fall back on myth. We devise a past that gives character and direction to the present. In *Works and Days*, Hesiod wrote of the "Five Ages," the times that were gold, silver, bronze, the age of demigods, and now the time of iron—which he deplores. An underived present robs one of an attitude toward the concrete immediacy. In the *Statesman*, Plato traces present discontents to the decline that set in after the age of Cronos. This is the other side of his attempt, in the *Timaeus*, to give the state a cosmic authority. We look before and after and pine for the continuum of our present actuality. When we discover that the past is other than we took it to be, our present confidence is disturbed. Is it really possible, the student may ask himself, that Plato showed some doubt over the ability of the "idea" theory to satisfy the motives that launched it? Is there scant evidence for the story that George Washington cut down his father's cherry tree with his little hatchet and could not tell a lie about it, while there is good evidence that he did excoriate a delinquent officer in language hardly appropriate to the Father of his Country? If anyone doubts his alliance with time, let him consider the reluctance, or even the dismay, with which he receives modifications of history. It can be very upsetting, and many have found it so. And, of course, history books offer a splendid opportunity for the censor. The mythmakers are not all of them ancient. A principal reason for scientific history derives from its power to protect our identities. Personal existence is not anonymous nor are deeds facts of nature. They are individual and call for that unique continuum which extends a present—not the dateless present—into its distinctive past. He who can confuse a past brings ambiguity into the present and erodes its will. To control a past, as in a dogmatic declaration of what took place, is also to control a present. Ardors and intensities accompany the discovery of the individual no less than those that glow in the great formulations of the ahistoric.

Nature is our first explicit morality because there we are all together and no one must fabricate or proclaim. On the whole, we have by now worked into the clear on this point. History is the second morality, and its force is but vaguely felt. Individuality and history are fateful modes of the actual, and we get some idea of their current feebleness when we consider the great success of the psychological view of man as wanting to be "adjusted" to his environment. This is the erosion of intensity, the substitution of conformity for personality and of success for passion. We try to circumvent fate and call it truth. We debase great men when we see them as servants of our desires rather than as the architects and the summoners of our selfhood.

To a larger extent than we are aware, we live through the past tense. The modes of this continuum are obvious enough, but they lack accredited status. We need a new epistemology, one that does not shrink from giving ontological status to artifacts. The past rides on them, and they are symbols and voices. We know quite well that we use words and that without expression in its various forms, without ritual and ceremony, nothing of the past would be available. A large dictionary tells what a word "means" by supplying an account of the past usages that mark its career. A word means what it has come to mean. A misused word is no factual error, but an assault on one's functioning, as when the "uninterested" man is said to be "disinterested." The outlook disclosed in such abuse can halt a conversation and raise doubts about the suitability of a political candidate. And it certainly should. Your egghead is a man who can speak without abusing the language. To a lawyer the law is what it has become. The specification of actual cases when a rule has been applied and qualified, far from detracting from the force of law, adds to its weight and authority. A rule without antecedents, without liability to revision, lacks, in the end, any relevance to meaning. No articulate control can flout the medium in which it is expressed. One cannot have one's words and eat them too. Yet this is what all ahistoric views of man propose to do. There is no saying of words, as against the making of noises, apart from what has been said. He who wishes to speak must learn a language. Nor is this a practical matter between two or more persons who, apart from words, share a common world and need only put convenient labels on objects or on acts independently known. All expression is a discipline, and it is time that we abandon the nonsense of supposing ourselves antecedently in possession of a world of which the linguistic is only a handy memorandum—as if we knew about Hamlet apart from the play, or about freedom apart from the institutions that have emerged as its vehicles, about physics apart from actual yardsticks, and about man apart from his history.

Of course there are some persons who would prefer Hamlet without the King of Denmark, the murderer king, not an inspiring example to the nation's youth. Among philosophers many deplore the errors of the past. It could not be said of Hume that he endeavored to save the world for God, but he did try to keep it from going to the devil. He became, in a manner of speaking, a book-burner, saying of any work that seemed to him unreliable, "Commit it then to the flames. For it can contain nothing but sophistry and illusion."[14] One can sense the exultation with which logical positivists tell us that there is nothing to lose but our chains when we rid ourselves of words that have no "literal significance."[15] In fact, the words that they reject do have a "literal" significance and only that; and that is why they are the vehicles of ideas, and not marks on paper or tickets of admission to sense data. They are the literate words. From the point of view of the history of philosophy one cannot escape Hume, nor would one dream of committing him to the flame of purification. To see the point of that inevitability is to stand in history. There one is hospitable, never censorious from a point of view that alleges independence of time. Ralph Waldo Emerson observed, "There is one mind common to all individual men."[16] The price of the one mind is the individuality of one's own.

A rule purporting to be independent of history, aloof from occasions, operates only as a blind natural force. It can be objected to only by force. The trouble with crime, as with dogma, is that it generates no precedents. It is the lawyers who have the precedents. But the violators of the law are no more arbitrary than are the judges when the latter use words exempt from the controls of time.

Such considerations may seem homely and familiar, and one might wish for heavier themes, such as "causation" in history, the effectiveness of the hero, or the influence of the transcendent. Yet, if history is to be universal, one needs to feel its presence before talking much about it. So we need to see it around us and in the substance of our experience. Every distinctive finality is the articulation of an immediacy, not as content, but as form and so as an energy. That the form of finitude is always an infinity, and articulate, is the central theme of a philosophy of history. This is the anti-Eleatic factor of experience. Obviously, any "theory" of history is a mistake, as is also any "theory" of knowledge. Such procedures foreclose the possibility of making time a category. It is to history, not to theory, that we must go if the actual is to shine by its own light and not be obscured in the light which is also the total darkness. Philosophers have been concerned with saving the appearances; if history be a philosophical idea, it can only propose to save the moment. This is very hard to do. Ideals are fairly easy to come by and they may even seem reasonable. But a child can scatter them in the fascinated glow of some trivial absorption, thereby bringing humiliating qualms to the observer. The fugitive mind evades the conditions of the lucid moment. It shrinks from the implications of intensity. No doubt it is very difficult to let the moment declare its authority. As a general thing we prefer to regard the moment as subordinate, seeing it from some position that is never itself actual. And certainly, except as the moment operates as the point of departure of formal order, one cannot avoid trying to control it from an Eleatic position. But that is a self-deception, and it ends in conflicts and frustrations. It is hard to be in history. It is harder to make history. As a rule we prefer to be right.

It is usually said that Herodotus is the father of history. Arnold Toynbee translates Herodotus's reasons for writing *The Histories*: "Herodotus of Halicarnassus presents the results of his researches in the following work, with the twofold object of saving the past of mankind from oblivion and ensuring that the extraordinary achievements of the Hellenic and the Oriental worlds shall enjoy their just renown—particularly the transactions which brought them into conflict with one another." Of the glorious action at Thermopylae, Herodotus says in *The Histories*, "The Lacedaemonians fought in a way worthy of being recorded"; and again of Marathon, that the Atheneans "fought in a manner worthy of being recorded." Here was an interest in the past now valued for its own sake. The human spirit, its craft and courage, its weakness and power, were declared memorable and so rescued from an oblivion that would not only obscure a just fame but impoverish the heritage, dim the identity, and dull the energy of every self-conscious person— whether Greek or Barbarian.

Nor does Herodotus narrate the story of the conflict in a moralistic temper, the upright on one side, the miraculously wicked on the other, virtue and truth leading the assault on miscreants and idolators. Herodotus saw the Persian wars as a development of long-standing differences that had originated centuries ago as incidents of egoism and of trade. He was dealing with the acts of men; and he looked on them as fascinating revelations, as the naturalists had noted the planets and the stars, the seasons and the weather. The past became relevant to the comprehension of the present. This too is a piety.

Who, then, is in history? Anyone whose life has shape and who exerts himself to preserve his integrity has joined articulate forces. This need not be on a grand scale. It can mean no more than doing one's job and keeping the home fires burning. A great deal of our work is no better than maintenance. Most schooling is of that sort, and most teaching. We have a rendezvous with our time and place, and that is as much of destiny as is generally possible. Once in a blue moon one may hear an original word. Such a word is a disciplined qualification of a past. When it happens we mark a date, a moment stands out, a revelation has been made, a present glows, not with a hard gemlike flame, but with the warmth of an assured actuality. It is these actualities that, for their apprehension, impose a task. They can be grasped only as one takes the trouble to appropriate the mode of order in which they have been expressed. "Every oracle must be interpreted by the same spirit which gave it forth."[17]

The past is forever at the peril of time. It has to be maintained. But no man can be forced or cajoled or argued into history. The future, when there is one, is the fatality of the historical present, and this is no matter of fact, but a matter of will. Plainly, this is no place to look for bland placidity. All that history has to offer is our actuality. It cannot be administered. It takes nerve, or, as Ortega suggests, it is a sporting proposition.

At the outset it was suggested that objections to metaphysics are to be entertained with reserve. The universal in all its forms loses its nonhumanity when contemplated through the motives that operated to produce it, rather than through its relation to any possible specific experience or purpose. The universal lies in the line of action and of function. But Eleaticism, in its anxiety to compose appearances, overlooked the controls of its own endeavors, namely the establishment and the maintenance of the immediate. In consequence, the immediate was lost *sub specie aeternitatis*. It was sought apart from time, apart from a past, where no finitude could generate a future as the fatality of its self-conscious present. The very intensity that produced it, those arresting and distinguished concentrations on the factors of the actual moment, were lost sight of in the devouring result. But, of course, it took time to see that. The Eleatics did not know that they were Eleatics.

Historicism does not propose an alternative answer, a better one, a truer one. It notes the difficulty of setting out on a journey when the point of departure lacks articulate definition and when horizons are detached from any point of view. One cannot go somewhere from nowhere, especially if no person is there to take a step. The immediate comes into historical position when it stands in its career. Time comes of age through its own passage. Eleaticism is an imposing and a moving monument, but as a finality it is the denial of the energies that so gallantly sought some significance in the moment.

NOTES

1. José Ortega y Gasset, *History as a System and Other Essays* (New York: Norton, 1961), p. 217.

2. See E. Panofsky, *Meaning in the Visual Arts*, especially chapters 1 and 5. [Miller's note].

3. Oliver Wendell Holmes, *The Autocrat of the Breakfast Table* (Boston: Phillips, Sampson and Company, 1861).

4. Xenophanes Fragment 14. See G. S. Kirk, J. E. Raven, and M. Schofield, *The Presocratic Philosophers*, 2nd ed. (New York: Cambridge University Press, 1983), p. 169.

5. Xenophanes Fragment 15. See G. S. Kirk, J. E. Raven, and M. Schofield, *The Presocratic Philosophers*, 2nd ed. (New York: Cambridge University Press, 1983), p. 168.

6. Parmenides Fragment 8. See G. S. Kirk, J. E. Raven, and M. Schofield, *The Presocratic Philosophers*, 2nd ed. (New York: Cambridge University Press, 1983), p. 281.

7. See Paul Tillich, *The Interpretation of History*, Part II (New York: Charles Scribner's Sons, 1936) [Miller's note].

8. Revelation 3:15.

9. Shakespeare, *1 King Henry IV*, Act 3, scene i.

10. Shakespeare, *A Midsummer Night's Dream*, Act 5, scene i.

11. J. B. Conant, *Modern Science and Modern Man* (Garden City: Doubleday, 1953) [Miller's note].

12. See the early chapters of Walter Pater's *Marius the Epicurean* for a similar story [Miller's note].

13. See W. E. Hocking's excellent *Human Nature and its Remaking* (New Haven: Yale University Press, 1918) [Miller's note].

14. See the concluding paragraph of Hume's *Enquiry Concerning Human Understanding* (1777. Oxford, UK: Oxford University Press, 1975).

15. See for example, A. J. Ayer, *Language, Truth and Logic* (New York: Dover Publications, 1946) [Miller's note].

16. This is the opening sentence of "History" (in *Nature and Selected Essays*, Larzer Ziff, ed. [New York: Penguin Group, 2003], p. 149).

17. This is a line from Emerson's essays, one on which he wrung several changes (see, for example, "Nature" in *Ralph Waldo Emerson: Selected Essays*, Larzer Ziff, ed. [New York: Penguin, 1983], p. 54).

The Midworld

In this essay, not only the most important themes in Part 2 but also many of those in Part 1 (e.g., skepticism) are brought together: What we desire and indeed demand must be "not only our own, but also a *world*." This indeed picks up a theme announced at the outset of "The Ahistoric and the Historic": "Anyone who looks farther than his nose may find himself wondering what lies over the horizon. . . . We like to inhabit a world, and indeed are sure to do so if we enjoy so much as a local habitation and a name." A local habitation implies nothing less than a cosmic locus, while a self-identifying word or expression implies nothing less than an encompassing scheme in which a complex array of alliances and antagonisms are at least implicit. The here-and-now bears within itself traces of the there-and-then, just as the I and me (the self as an active, appropriative being and as a solidified, sedimented inheritance more or less in possession of itself) bear testimony to the you and they. What I demand is nothing short of a world, though the historically authoritative conceptions of the world have overwhelmingly tended to be personally annihilative conceptions; for they have not accorded individual agents as such cosmic status.

In our desperate efforts to affirm our irreducible individuality and cosmic uniqueness, we have been driven from the outer world into the hidden recesses of our psychic interiority, most often, our private imagination. Here at least human selves can have the status and significance they accord themselves. But a purely imaginary world is no more tolerable than an utterly alien one: The human spirit demands nothing less than a world of its own, one in which the foreground of human engagement is felt to be but a fragment of an encompassing totality but also one essentially linked to my exertions, competencies, and even aspirations. (As Miller writes in "Purpose," "Any environment not defined through me, and by my consent, is a prison.") The actual world is the world insofar as it is generated, maintained, and revised by the actions of individuals or egoists, agents who have come into possession of time because they have appropriated the histories in and through which they are defined (our relations to time are, as already noted in another introduction, comprehensive and constitutive). In light of our historical evasions of the actual, we might be inclined to say that *despite* its derivation from our modes of acting it is nonetheless a world; but in a fuller reconciliation with the finite actualities on which both claims to being a self and having a world rest, we should say that it is a world *because* of this derivation.

In any event, the actual world is the historical world. But the historical world is truly a world, though many will feel that the finitude and alterability constitutive of this world rob it of its objectivity. Others will feel that because the historical world makes human agents so deeply beholden to inherited institutions, it robs us of our originality and freedom. Miller was convinced that a proper understanding of the finite actualities of such functioning objects as the human body, natural languages, religious rituals, experimental procedures, and political processes would provide us with adequate resources for a compelling account of objectivity, originality, freedom, and much else. His ontological historicism was intended as anything but a reductionistic perspective. The reduction of the historic to the ahistoric, of history merely to case histories, entails a loss of the actual. In contrast, an affirmation of the actual makes possible and intelligible just how the telling differences (truth versus error, objective versus subjective, reality versus appearance) can effectively be told. Grant present active participles their full authority and necessary media, give the midworld an ontological status and authoritative function, and then one can show how a mistake *was made*, or how the appearance of an object from only one perspective involves a systematic distortion.

Facts are neither absolute nor arbitrary. "There is," Miller contends in the present essay, "no fact without artifact." Language, or expression in the most inclusive sense, is the locus of the union between subjectivity and objectivity. By virtue of expression, subjects are constituted and objects disclosed. Given the importance of language, Miller devotes the concluding section of this essay to language and communication. "Communication implies," he notes, "a limited world and a vulnerable one"—a world susceptible to not only minor disturbances but also constitutional crises. Such a world has prompted the quest for unshakable certainty, itself a quest for absolute assurance. "To see the invulnerable in nature, in the supernatural, or in some other coercive symbolism is to destroy all signs, and all functioning objects." Despite what many are tempted to suppose, the midworld "robs no one of nature." Nature in its otherness is not compromised, much less effaced, by acknowledging the ontologically irreducible status of the midworld. Rather the midworld is the sole "means of saving nature from arbitrary dominance" or skeptical dissolution. It alone accords nature the ontological status and cosmic importance nature has come to possess in the actual course of our historical investigations into the physical, chemical, biological, and other dimensions of natural processes. In contrast, the nature of the reductive naturalists and materialists does rob us of history and, along with it, the authoritative bases of our historical practices (including our natural sciences).

This essay helps to prepare us for the selections in Part 3, for the midworld provides the sole "basis of a responsible humanism." The midworld "generates infinities, but only as the form of an actual finitude and an ideal finitude." The finite actuality of our various means of articulation contains within itself the indeliminable ideality characteristic of human utterance: To inherit a language is to be initiated into a world with an integrity and tenure of its own, a world in many respects outstripping our present comprehension. Not only does one word lead to another, but language opens onto a world. It is no prison house, but a revelatory medium of unrestricted scope.

Miller did not simply try to show, via narrative, how the midworld provides a basis for humanism; he also endeavored to provide a somewhat detailed account of responsible humanism. The essays in Part 3 can be read as providing a sketch of this account. Miller's approach to the midworld drives toward an ever more concrete, thus ever more detailed account of the historical institutions, practices, and discourses by which a self-critical humanism establishes itself as a self-imposed task. Such humanism is a historically rooted, constitutionally incomplete, and truly fateful undertaking. What is at stake in this task is the affirmation of self-and-world, our selves and our world in their finite actuality and utter uniqueness.

Published first in a slightly different form in The Paradox of Cause *(pp. 106–23), this essay was originally written as a presentation to the Harvard Philosophy Club in 1952 (Miller Papers 2:1). The quotation from "Purpose" appears on page 128 of* In Defense of the Psychological. *Some of the main themes and topics explored here are also illuminated in "Some Notes on Language" (*The Definition of the Thing, *pp. 171–89), especially in the selections titled "Language" (pp. 171–75) and "Symbols" (pp. 186–89). Of course, a number of the chapters in* The Midworld of Symbols *bear directly on these themes and topics, but "Philosophy Is Just Talk" (see Part 1, above), "'Explaining' Language" (pp. 66–75), and "A Few Outlines" (pp. 154–70) are especially noteworthy in this regard.*

I

What I propose is that we consider the price to be paid for enfranchising discourse. Discourse needs authority. It is this concern that lies at the core of the philosophy of history. History deals in what has been done in one way or another. Its materials are the residue of deeds. They are artifacts of every description. The region of artifacts may be called the "midworld" since it is exclusively neither the self nor the not-self, neither consciousness nor its object. This inquiry concerns the status of language, of signs and symbols in their widest sense. It lies between epistemology and metaphysics and is the bridge between them.[1]

History does not study "nature" conceived as object, or as the region of objects. Nor does it deal with the supernatural in its recondite perfection, although the alleged signs of the supernatural do concern the historian. Nor does it study the stream of consciousness, that is, psychology. For all these reasons it separates itself from the usual patterns of truth, which are stories about quite impersonal reality. No statement in history concerns the timeless and invariant. As for those sciences that deal with ahistoric modes of order, history regards them as the record of experience, not as true, but as the expression of what we have regarded to be true.

It is concerned, therefore, with finitude and its career. But in this respect, history seems to alienate itself from the traditional concerns of philosophy, which have tended to stress the timeless and the ahistoric, treating time as a derivative and secondary. The true heavenly city, we have supposed, is not built by hands, and the true forces of nature sweep man and his deeds into the invariance of their own law. We have been trying to see all things under the aspect of eternity. It cannot be denied that such conditions of rising superior to time have their attractions. Yet many have felt that they must settle for something closer, finding a sharper and more self-possessed life within limitation.

Limitation has not been accorded an equal place at the high table of philosophy. It sits well below the salt unless, indeed, it has been only a servant in the festivities of its betters. This is what the historian knows and so, metaphysically homeless, he has maintained a stubborn or even sardonic independence, occupied with the identification of individual moments. It would appear, and I would propose, that unless history be a "category," there can be no philosophy of history. But if it be such, then the region of its concern, artifacts, or the midworld, must be accorded a place among the constitutional elements of being.

This need of providing for artifacts is the specter that haunts philosophers and their discourse. And it seems plain that one could not exorcise that perturbed spirit by further incantations.

II

In this way, arrested by the insecure status of our own words, we encounter a variant of skeptical mistrust. In philosophy we must use language. We speak our minds. We speak them, too, in practices and institutions, themselves artifacts—church, state, art, science, and language itself. They confront us as the loci of both order and confusion. In discourse we no longer deal with abstract appearance and abstract reality, but with a midworld that is also our own deed. And so, being our own, it is threatened with a lack of ontological status.

Skepticism traditionally occurs as self-mistrust. We are skeptics, however, not because we make mistakes, but because we can no longer trust the means of deciding. Nobody is less skeptical than the canny person who

knows wooden nickels when he sees them. Skepticism is no grubby cau-
tion. It is a point of arrest where we are thrown back on our own
resources. And those we have no reason to trust. On the other side, neither can we trust anything else. It is in this situation that the properly
emotional and distracted mood of skepticism appears. We cannot bridge
what J. B. Pratt called "the epistemological gulf" since we are incapable of
moving either way between appearance and reality.[2] It is this situation
that some have thought to identify as the province of epistemology.

In this way skeptical insecurity marks the experience of elementary
self-assertion, the disclosure that we are parties to our affirmations and
denials, although, of course, we hardly see how that leaves us with a satisfactory result. But this is also the threshold of responsibility, a stage of
all thought as it passes from confident innocence to the dark menace of
egoism. Skepticism shows, too, that thoughtfulness as a power in the
world is first identified in the threat to its own trustworthiness. Confidence in thought and its works cannot be original. It must be twice-born.

But while no original position, neither can skepticism be final. So we
have to look for ways out of it. These ways have not, characteristically,
given finitude an ontological status. In realism and mysticism discourse
lacks constitutional authority. Both confront thought in the end with some
overpowering and absorbing reality. In realism the disparity between
appearance and reality is allegedly maintained, but not bridged. In mysticism, the disparity is abolished.

A solution should not only unite the factors. It should also *keep them
apart* as the price of the problem. Until separated they cannot be reconciled. It has sometimes seemed that the division represented a miscar-
riage of thought, that it ought not to have occurred, and that it exhibits
nothing more than the folly of metaphysics.

Of the confusion there can be no doubt. But its necessity is no less obvious if thought is to be discovered as an efficacy, and its works accredited.
The primary efficacy of thought is to discover itself, something that could
not occur in bland security or in complete rational fluency.

But, then, this situation is as long as it is broad. For neither could the
object be discovered in principle until it became systematically elusive. That
the self is elusive many have been pleased to note, and, indeed, its fortunes
as an entity, or as a content of consciousness, have been pretty dismal. But
the object is no less obscure. Nothing is object by virtue of any specific

attribute. Object like subject is an omnibus word. If it is to be useful it must be identified through a formal order, as constitution, not as datum or even hypothesis.

It is the *necessity* of the distinction between object and subject that was neglected by traditional skepticism and, as it turned out, by the psychological empiricism that was its offspring. The ground of the distinction could not be some matter of fact, some clear or naively apprehended object. The troubled experience of skepticism is not to be understood in calm passivity. It falls within no placid environment of any sort, natural, psychological, or logical.

In this way it is the deepest frustration and the first compulsion. It is the birth of responsibility because it forces us away from abstractions into a more concrete account of its occasion. It does this because it can give no account of itself *in terms of the absolute disparities that generate its impasse.* It is a conflict without ground in the articulate. It can become articulate only as it is reinterpreted through limited and actual modes of imperfect order.

A classic illustration of this blockade of abstractions occurs in the *Theaetetus*. I will quote a few lines to show that the above dialectics are not without provocation.

The problem of the *Theaetetus* is that of establishing knowledge, but it is presented as an inquiry into the possibility of error. Plato, it seems to me, is clear on the locus of the difficulty, namely the exclusiveness of the distinction between knowledge and ignorance. He asks:

"Where, then, is false opinion? For if all things are either known or unknown there can be no opinion which is not comprehended under this alternative, and false opinion is excluded."[3] At the end of the dialogue he observes: "But how utterly foolish when we are asking what is knowledge, that the reply should be, 'right opinion with knowledge of difference' or of anything!" This, he says, is to "go round and round" and to be "as the blind directing the blind."[4]

III

We need an articulate basis for skepticism and it will furnish, I hope, a first hold on the midworld. What seems called for is something more concrete to work with than appearance and reality, or knowledge and ignorance. The defect of such terms is that they furnish us with no ordered materials, mere appearance that is states of mind, and mere reality that nobody knows anything about, or, if he does, he can't say what it is without adulteration. It is not the case that Plato's difficulty resulted from the conflict of relatively ordered areas of experience; it resulted from a total *lack of order* and of actuality, a lack of both of them. Conflict needs an articulate vehicle.

That is the price of conflict. Each factor must exercise some hold on us on an already established area of reason and control. At the same time, neither can be adequate to the whole scope of our practice and belief. Reason never occurs in any actual integrity, but is pluralistic and partial. That is why we are involved with it, and why we know about it. We don't have, and we can't have, an infinite organism. We find ourselves, for example, somewhat involved in the practices and beliefs that turn on value control, that is, where events find their explanation in ends. So we have a rationale in ethics, politics, aesthetics, in the maintenance of individuality and free government. On the other side, it would be difficult to disavow our profound commitment to impersonal types of change where, as in physics, value control is excluded. In consequence, we stand divided in our needs and loyalties, in our practices and beliefs.

In this situation, each component of conflict carries some claim to order within itself. There is the control of value, and of causality. There is the integrity of the individual on his own, and there is the vast impersonality of nature's laws. Here is plenty of difficulty, but however reduced to abstract terms it draws its vitality from actual and concrete organizations of experience.

It follows from this that the occasion of an articulate skepticism is retrospective, as indeed are all reflective moments. Something reasonable and self-defining, as well as nature-defining, is already established. Our unease reflects also our previous grasp. This is the embarrassment of skepticism, its self-consciousness and awkwardness, its misery and also its progress from the naive. But this self-consciousness is not analogous to the presence of an error. Where we find ourselves in error we presume we have command of the order that has been violated. But here in skeptical self-consciousness, the threat of confusion becomes systematic, because it is the confusion of what we most trust, modes of reason themselves.

It may be useful to remind ourselves briefly that this concrete skepticism depends on no specific conflict. For one person it marks the impasse of empiricism and rationalism; for another the impasse of home influence and college-learned doctrines. But in all cases it appears as the conflict of commitments each of which is articulate, although a vehicle of but a partial reason. Thus, the *occasion* of skepticism, *not just its solution*, as René Descartes proposed, is existential. It is not theoretical merely. It is not merely tentative, passive, and receptive. It is not positivistic but the consequence of universality in the actual. It is not the consequence of a vaulting ambition that o'erleaps itself, but of something far more modest and far more turbulent.

I hope it is plain that I set some store by the necessity of skepticism. Of course, I do not mean by this necessity that skepticism falls within an environment that produces it. It is rather *the loss of confidence in whatever one regards as environment.* Nor, of course, would I suppose that there is any intellectual technique for producing it. One can't be argued into it. All that is question-begging. Skepticism is rather the point at which necessity occurs as an idea, for there one is threatened with the nullification of such actual control as everyone in a degree possesses. But it has great heuristic value in bringing to notice the condition of its occurrence.

Finally, one would not want to say that skepticism occurs as a conflict among or between abstract absolutes. Yet, in itself it is the actuality, and so the absoluteness, of conflict. That is a distinction worth making. There are philosophies averse to all assurance, and others that would not care to find their origin in conflict, with all that is thereupon implied. Not all will see necessity in the conditions for maintaining the order of finitude.

In broad summary, skepticism is difficult to define because it is throughout reflective. It occurs as conflict. This conflict is not between abstract appearance and abstract reality, but between already ordered modes of experience. In these we have a stake, and to them we are committed precisely because they are the vehicles of as much grasp and comprehension as we already possess. Skepticism is retrospective, and it is existential. It occurs through no specific opposition, but through any systematic opposition. Consequently it is the occasion for discovering what one does actually consider orderly and systematic. At the same time, by demanding a decision as to the true order, or as to the relations among modes of order, it forces on us responsibility for our world. After skepticism, our commitments are deliberate and cannot be disavowed as not our own.

IV

Assurance must assert its force in the very materials that permit articulate doubt. Otherwise it will again take wing into some noumenal or transcendent region and so relegate finitude and its actual expression to further metaphysical ostracism. Of that there has, it seems to me, been quite enough. In a time of decision, philosophy can hardly allow itself to become an adventure into enervation. Nor, in a time when arbitrariness has taken new and dangerous forms, can philosophy avoid seeking a humanistic solution to problems of authority. Like other responsible studies it must, I believe, express limitation, but in its particular case limitation must stand its ground as the actual locus of responsibility. It seems to me that nothing else could be proposed by men who wish to be both resolved and critical.

There can be no question that nature and society do, in structure and content, enlist our thought and will. How, then, do they come to possess such authority? This is the crux of the problem, and it leads directly to the artifact and to the articulate regions that depend on the artifact for their order, and are allied to it in content. The thesis takes some such form as this: *There is no fact without an artifact.* Language, or expression in its widest sense, is the *locus of the union* of the abstractly subjective and the abstractly objective. It is here suggested that apropos of this union limitation acquires ontological status. There the subject is embodied, and the object becomes the vehicle of meaning, and in some cases of quite formal and ideal meanings. There are different sorts of artifacts, notably signs and symbols, but for the moment I will leave those distinctions in abeyance and deal with the situation more generally.

Perhaps an illustration would serve to carry the reflection that voices the theme. Space, a property of articulate nature, occurs in measurement. It is the order of simultaneous diversity. Things are at a distance and a determinate distance. But while such ideas as "distance" and "measurement" seem common enough, they have given a good deal of trouble. One reason is that they have no psychological equivalents. There is no sense organ for the apprehension of space. It is no specific quality, no datum of a discrete and peculiar sort. It is not here or there, now or then. It is no accident, falling within some already defined situation identifiable and organized without benefit of space. Nor is it something remembered, or something imaginatively constructed from materials devoid of it. Then there is the view that space is a universal and a priori form, pervading all experience, distinctive of none.

For some reason, and I am convinced that there is a reason, "space" has rated more tolerance than other universals or a priori forms, such as substance, causality, or mind. One might wonder how one is to play favorites among them. At any rate, while the critique of cause has proceeded with a good deal of vigor, space has enjoyed a relative respectability. This immunity has been especially notable in view of the highly rated rule that no concept that fails to make a local and specific difference can win full faith and credit as a factor of the actual world. Of course, no constitutional universal could meet that demand if what one requires is a distinctive appearance.

Space, however, does have a finite actuality as well as a universal ideality. In the case of space this limited actuality is the yardstick. At first sight this may seem absurdly simple and inadequate. The yardstick is an actual object, a *functioning object*. One can, and indeed one must, take it in hand. It is palpable. It is a piece of pine or maple, and so part of the whole collection of objects. It may, of course, be made of any other material, a textile strip or a steel tape. It is not by virtue of one material or another that the identification "yardstick" is made. Nor does it possess any peculiar sense qualities. Good workmen, and men of science, shrink from using it as a tool, as a device for propping a window or poking the fire. That is not to use it, but to abuse it. Yet such abuse is surely not any consequence of its material composition. It does very well to prop a window. Nor, though not to be used as a tool by any decent man, is it a fetish, something not to be handled, or handled only with sentimentality, or with awe, or for the invocation of occult powers. If it is no tool, it serves no purpose and is quite destroyed when treated as an aid in getting adjusted to the alleged environment.

Nor is a yardstick a yard long. A piece of cloth may be a yard wide, or a target 500 yards away, because one has determined their spatial extent through application of the yardstick as a unit of measure. Nor, of course, must that unit be a yard. Horses are said to be so many "hands" high. "Full fathom five thy father lies." "Give him an inch and he'll take an ell."

There are other peculiarities of yardsticks and I submit that as one considers this apparently absurd simplicity it may be said to take on dimensions, and indeed to become a first-class puzzle. One may note that the yardstick cannot be produced by what is called "ostensive definition." It is no illustration of a prior subjectivity in a prior objectivity where there already exists a here and there and every sort of spatial order. It conforms to no idea in the mind where, by hypothesis, the mind is furnished with plenty of other ideas unaffected by spatial order. It is not a possible idea like the Loch Ness monster whose appearance coincides with the tourist season, nor is it like the celebrated sea-serpent with red wings. It is no possibility belonging to the null class, nor yet in a class with members. And neither does it exist in the pure infinity of universal space.

Nor is it a convention. That is a question-begging term in this context. A particular unit may be a convention, but not the unit in principle. Conventions do not define the situation into which they are introduced; red and green lights do not define roads and vehicles or account for them.

With this budget of characterization before us, some reflection on the numerous peculiarities of the yardstick seems in order. Of central importance is the union in this familiar instrument or symbol of both subjective and objective factors. Here is all the psychology that anyone could ask for in the apprehension of an object. Here, similarly, is all the neutrality to psychology that appears among the common objects of nature. But the yardstick conveys a further property, that of its *ideality*, and that is the feature I wish to underscore and, if possible, make clear. This ideality turns on the function or role of the yardstick. Through it, nature, in respect of its simultaneous diversity, gets established. Nature as space occurs as the actual operation of measurement. In its infinity, it indicates the endless extension of an actual and finite object in its use and function. One cannot ask of a unit of measure whether it has application. It is such a unit precisely in that application and for no other reason. Spatial infinity is the order of finitude. But finitude has no order at all unless some *object*, something here and now, is invested with an ideal meaning. Nor has infinity any order until the artifact or symbol becomes its vehicle and present reality.

The region of which the yardstick is a part is itself dependent on measurement for its order. For that reason the region of objects exerts a stubborn tenacity, and resists attempts to reduce it to psychology, or even to phenomenal status. This stubbornness of the objects of nature and of the perceptions associated with nature derives its force from the union of subject and object embodied in the artifact and its implications. Otherwise we might easily let nature go.

On the other side, the transcendent *fails* to exert this spontaneous hold on us. In its traditional forms it is not defined through us, nor is it sustained through the order of symbols, as are all modes of articulate and ideal infinity. Consequently, the perpetuation of any infinite being as an object of regard, involving as it does the disqualification of limit, becomes a *tour de force*. Education then operates as training and indoctrination, and belief is enforced by reward, punishment, and abnegation. Here, indeed, we will find ritual and symbolism, but the symbols will not be those objects through which nature secures articulation and the mind its exercise. This is a theme capable of some extension as one respectfully considers those vast endeavors to express and summon the energies of men in terms of the symbolism of the transcendent. The yardstick, the monument, the word, in contrast, are the *functioning symbolism of finitude* and propose the infinity of both nature and the resources of soul.

But, while functioning objects illuminate no hypostatized infinity, neither do they assist in giving order to that version of finitude which leaves it nominalistic. These two—an infinity that is a *fait accompli* and a finitude without universality—are *alike* in their repudiation of actuality that is also ideal. Neither is articulate because neither accords organizing power to, or has any ontological place for, yardsticks. Each, in its own way, can do nothing with discourse but leaves it arbitrary, and therefore nonrational. It is the functioning object that unites the particular and the universal. They are united in function, or in use, in the embodiment of form. The embodiment of form is function.

The reality of a world is a consequence of the reality of its functioning parts. Where nothing finite is real, and I mean metaphysically beyond question, neither is anything infinite comprehensible. That is beyond question which permits questions to be asked, and any question is the mark of limitation, yet of reason and articulation too. In stressing the priority of the whole, philosophy has been driven to devices to account for the parts. Their generation was a mystery, their order at best phenomenal. On the other side, parts without order are in no better case. A *determinate infinity* rests on the actuality of its ideal symbol.

Not to apprehend objects as the reality of formal order is to view them subjectively. For the intellect they become mere appearance, and for the will mere desire or aversion. This is what José Ortega y Gasset fears in *The Revolt of the Masses*, the reduction of the complex world of the past to appearance and appetite. He fears the assault on reason and on persons, those who have spoken in the significant forms that make up the actual and intelligible world. It has seemed useful to cast a passing glance at this negative side of the picture in order to make plainer our involvement with the midworld and the stake we have in it. For it must be admitted that so fragile and even commonplace an object as the yardstick hardly promises, when first regarded, to illustrate a point of some importance, as I see it, in the establishment of a metaphysical foundation for history and all other modes of man's deeds.

Order, once said to be heaven's first law, and then alleged to reside in an objective nature or in a phenomenal vision, we must now, I propose, relocate in the midworld. As a matter of fact this, and nothing else, is the material of all studies. Physics, for example, studies no order except that of its instruments. The order of physical nature is the theory of their use. History is wholly confined to things done, although theories about history sometimes attempt to force it into dependency on psychology, physics, or theology. It may be noted, too, that the persuasion of realities disjoined from man and his deeds has grown apace with the enlargement of his own articulate powers. Heaven seems never so sure as when the pealing organ blows, or when the arguments of a Thomas Aquinas or a Jonathan Edwards exert their compulsions.[5] Nature, similarly, seems now well established, so that it seems folly to propose a midworld as its condition. But this is a systematic illusion and it is surprising to see how rapidly it collapses once we suppose that, as a matter of course, our most solid realities would, of necessity, be precisely those whose infinity echoed the order inherent in the finite symbol. The midworld, I believe, robs nobody of nature. On the contrary, it is the means of saving nature from an arbitrary dominance, and of then preventing its inevitable dissolution in the acids of skepticism.

Here too, I venture to suggest, empiricism can take authority, no longer groping for an order that its own requirements have forced it to disqualify, but without which its critical pretensions are absurd. To save us from the unverifiable it has bombarded all our citadels, with the result usual in bombardments, reduction to rubble. The assumption of criticism is that we shall have a world of our own, and should that *not* be the outcome it won't matter much what that alien world will be. But what we must have is then to be not only our own, but also a *world*; and so empiricism has exhausted itself in trying to have it both ways on premises that make it impossible to have it either way.

The broad demands of a philosophy of history require the authentication of discourse and a construction placed on *functioning objects*. But discourse is language and it is a deed. Accordingly it is limitation. The knowledge of limit as a systematic factor—and it can appear in no other way—occurs in skepticism. Traditional skepticism posed the problem of uniting appearance and reality, but the complementary problem of holding them apart is no longer pressing. In fact, actual skepticism always involves relatively rational and concrete conflict. When that is unrecognized, solutions take the form of reductionism or phenomenalism. The ground of the distinction between the skeptical absolutes is the artifact, or the symbol, because it is the local and actual embodiment of ideality and of criticism. It generates infinities, but only as the form of an actual finitude and an ideal finitude. It is the reason for the stake we have in nature and institutions. In its extension it is the midworld, the basis of a responsible humanism.

V

By way of further illustration of the midworld, something should be said about words and language. Here, again, the problem is to discover the part played by words in making possible the order of subjects and objects.

It was once supposed that words possessed magical properties, and very likely something of the sort is true. They were supposed to exert forces, or to be capable of summoning them. "I can call spirits from the vasty deep," said Owen Glendower.[6] One gives one's word, no small thing to do. Robert Frost, in "The Code," shows how New Englanders of rural habit watch their words.[7] Jacob sought his father's blessing, and was willing to play a trick to get it.

In any case one can hardly be casual about words. They are mysterious enough. As they occur they seem quite ordinary sounds, like wind and wave, or, when written, sights, like sticks and stones. Their perception enlists no strange or unusual faculties. Shall we then say that words fall into the same order of appearance as other objects?

There are difficulties. The objects of nature rest in their own invariance. They are what they appear to be and nothing more. Nature, so regarded, tells no tales, proposes no points of view. It is infinite in its integral impersonality. So, it has no language and makes no sign. This aloofness has often enough been noted. In nature as object there are no confusions, mistakes, truths, virtues, or conflicts. It exhibits no historical changes. Language and artifact are what nature, as object, cannot produce. Naturalism finds no *subject* among the objects. But it seems more serious not to find an artifact. For, while the sufficiency and order of nature might be menaced by the *presence* of spirit, they are even more menaced by the *absence* of a symbol.

Language seems an intruder among proper objects that, in their well-mannered regularity, exhibit no feeling and make no errors. Their ways are not modified by signs, and so are not established by them. How language managed to enter that region has seemed to call for a theory. Such a theory should not, however, invoke for language any environment that is itself identified through artifacts. That would be begging the question. What is more, it would fail to account for exactly that aspect of an artifact which makes it a sign, rather than another object or quality of an object. This situation seems to me a recurrent one in philosophy. All the embodiments of finitude, a work of art, the constitution of a state, the processes of history, seem incidental to the quite impersonal region in which they are episodes. All seem to need a theory to explain them, and all need the same sort of theory, one namely on terms quite other than their own. The inarticulate, however, can hardly be proposed as the control of the articulate.

In passing, it might be amusing to consider why we might not set out to abolish language. For, if language were really an *incident* of experience, we might hope to control its occurrence, as we take antitoxin for typhoid before going on a journey. It seems hard, just because one is dealing with language, to deny that what has a causal genesis in an environment cannot be controlled in its causes. Knowledge is power. Nature to be commanded need only be obeyed. But I do not think we will be able to put a stop to it. At bottom, the reason is that to do so would be to abolish nature as an identifiable region and also in detail.

Discrimination among objects depends on identifying them through names, a point made with uncommon clarity, I think, in Susanne K. Langer's *Philosophy in a New Key*.[8] Perception is never direct. It is something more than a combination of sense data plus the psychological functions of memory and imagination. An object with a name is consolidated. It possesses a unity lacking in passive perception. It acquires that unity through the factor of action. Names are our deeds. Objects acquire names as part of our control over them. No appearance has any significance when it lacks association with the act that establishes its place in the economy of mind. One sees little in a walk through the woods if the names of trees, plants, birds, or conformations of terrain are unknown. The long analysis of perception into passive ingredients, purged of dreaded distortions of the subject, led to the denial of necessary connections and to the insignificance of appearances. Action places the object in a continuum of other objects and endows them with its own order.

Action is never direct. An object isolated from a situation in which no prior marks of action can be found calls for no specific response. One does not know what to do about it. Suppose one is lost in the woods and one is thirsty. A slope suggests a brook at the bottom. The slope becomes a sign of water. But this is not because there are sensible qualities about a slope, rather than about a peak, to offer the suggestion. It lies there like any other object. As object alone it gives no sign. But if one has ever walked down a slope to water, if the slope is mixed with action, it takes on an added quality of significance. The general rule is this: A sign occurs only through prior action.

A sign is both the occasion of an act and the evidence of a prior act. Our acts, in turn, are known to us in proportion to our identification of objects. The slope is a sign. It is also an object. And it is also an appearance. *The sign is an appearance that controls the production of other appearances.* Nature is controlled appearance. This is the foundation of our trust in experiment. Even observation is not an unguided receptivity. It is a controlled receptivity through signs and through functioning objects like microscopes, or a compass.

The control of appearance is the same as the objective. That is the only ground for the revelation of objects in principle. *Objects are those appearances that I can produce by action guided by other objects, which, already touched by action, serve as signs.* In passivity there are no objects or any subjects either. That is the well known and quite proper result of that empiricism which is based on analysis alone.

Language does not supervene on nature or on the self. It is the evidence of control, and only in terms of control can either of the two abstract components be identified. Without it both are lost, along with every vestige of order. It is not unusual to treat language as formal within itself; what seems less usual is to assert that language is in principle a formality, a type of order dialectically related to the order of nature and self and necessary for both.

Language is not a uniform and unambiguous symbolism such as one finds in mathematics and symbolic logic. Signs as language are always the marks of broken worlds. There is not one language, but many, and each person and society has to some extent his own. This is one of the true bases of pluralism, of the actuality of finitude. Communication is the mark not of complete agreement, but of partial agreement. To seek for monism in language is to betray oneself as occupying the ahistoric bias of traditional philosophy.

Communication implies a limited world and a vulnerable one. To seek the invulnerable in nature, in the supernatural, or in some coercive symbolism is to destroy all signs, and all functioning objects. There is no communication through objects viewed as wholly impersonal, or yet through subjects viewed as wholly personal. The role of communication is disclosed in its collapse. The disclosure of its function and properties occurs in those conflicts that threaten it in principle. Those conflicts, on the side of the psychological, lead to madness, with all its inaccessibility. On the side of relatively controlled reality they appear as the disparities of outlooks. It is at that point, and not short of it, that we feel the menace of privacy. Then, for the first time, the relation of speech to nature and to other men looms with existential force. That is why I regard philosophy as the deliberate concern with the loci of systematic conflict. It is the function of language to permit such conflict to occur, and thereby enforce the acknowledgment of its role in history.

For history is the revision of outlooks at the point of conflict between them. It is the process of putting us in rapport with each other, and with those monuments of expression that are the substance of civilization.

So, at the end, we move, it seems to me, once more into finitude that, because of language in its widest sense, operates as the maintainer of the distinction between self and nature and between selves. This is the locus of all criticism, of all disorder and so of all control. It is a concrete situation, but at the same time defined throughout in form and ideality.

I may say in conclusion that I have found this general position fruitful. How are philosophers to look with tolerance and even with envy on each other's specialties? How is one to bring discourse about history, the state, aesthetics, or logic under a common roof? What I missed in the realisms current in my student days and for some time thereafter was an ability to open pathways to those varied areas. Each appeared as a novelty and some as illicit. But it seems to me that in terms of a view based on the ontological status of finitude, all the forms of discourse that exhibit limited but actual essays in orderly language can find a home. On the other side, the majestic idealisms, learned and humane, sympathetic and hospitable, seemed to ignore precisely these dark emergencies that are the occasion of desperate attempts to maintain civic order and personal integrity. For these very good general reasons, as well as for the more specific reasons of this essay, it seems to me that one could do worse than consider the ontological status of the midworld. In its disciplined energies, ideal and finite, all expression can be interpreted. Otherwise we shall go on doing violence to our deeds as we force them into alien contexts, or else leave them in the limbo of phenomena.

NOTES

1. If this essay were to be rewritten today [1978], the term *functioning object* would generally be used where the term *artifact* now appears. The next essay offers a brief discussion of the distinction between the terms. [Miller's note. The "next essay" Miller here refers to is chapter 9 (pp. 124–29) of *The Paradox of Cause and Other Essays*, "Functioning Objects, Facts, and Artifacts," reprinted above as the third essay of Part 2.]

2. James Bissett Pratt, Miller's senior colleague at Williams College and vigorous defender of epistemological realism.

3. *Theaetatus*, 187d–88c.

4. *Theaetatus*, 210a–b.

5. Thomas Aquinas and Jonathan Edwards were two theologians who devoted painstaking attention to arguments concerning God.

6. Shakespeare, *1 King Henry IV*, Act 3, scene i.

7. *Frost: Collected Poems, Prose, & Plays*, Richard Poirier and Mark Richardson, eds. (New York: The Library of America, 1995), pp. 71–74.

8. Susanne K. Langer (1895–1985), *Philosophy in a New Key: A Study in the Symbolism of Reason, Rite, and Art*, 3rd ed. (Cambridge, MA: Harvard University Press, 1957). For the point for which Miller is appealing to Langer, see especially chapters 2 ("Symbolic Transformation") and 10 ("The Fabric of Meaning").

The Owl

In a famous passage, G. W. F. Hegel claimed about philosophy that, "as the thought of the world, it appears only when actuality is already there cut and dried after its process of formation has been completed." Philosophical reflection is thus essentially a retrospective comprehension of a dead or dying world. "When philosophy paints its grey in grey, then has a shape of life grown old. By philosophy's grey in grey it cannot be rejuvenated but only understood. The owl of Minerva spreads its wings only with the falling of dusk." The owl is the image of a spectator looking on a scene in which it is not itself a participant.

What if actuality is, however, not conceived as a *fait accompli* but as a living process in which philosophical reflection is ineluctably caught up? What if the perspective of the implicated agent were granted the authority previously reserved for the aloof spectator? These are among the central questions of Miller's last decades; they are addressed in this essay in an informative and insightful way.

In addition, this article expresses one side of Miller's ambivalence toward Hegel and, more generally, toward the dominant traditions in Western philosophy. On the one hand, Miller felt such deep respect for the monumental character of the great works in Western philosophy that he did not hesitate to give this respect its proper name: piety. Only barbarians chip away at monuments, Miller observes in "The Sense of History," in time often annihilating them completely. This can happen to textual as well as architectural monuments, Plato's *Republic* no less than the eloquent ruins of an ancient city. "It is as barbarous to chip away at Plato as to knock a bit of marble off the Parthenon," Miller writes in *The Philosophy of History*. "One may, and one must, allege that the concerns that animated Plato were not there brought to completion. But that is a judgment of history [and indeed a judgment made from within history itself], and not of an undefiled ahistoric omniscience." Neither our entangled histories nor the monuments in which their momentum is gathered and, indeed, given arresting form, memorable articulation, are instances of a *fait accompli*. History and its various articulations are unfinished continua encompassing trajectories to be advanced and tasks to be joined. In *The Philosophy of History*, Miller writes that history is, in this context, a career in which "the present has joined and embraced its past." Miller took Hegel's writings to be themselves monumental: Only an intellectual barbarian would treat them dismissively. At the same time, these texts project a present still in the making, concerns not yet brought to completion. Miller was thus deeply appreciative of the truly monumental status of Hegel's philosophical achievement.

On the other hand, the dominant temper of Western culture has been Eleatic: There has been a deep mistrust of time and an even deeper aversion to history. To affirm the actuality of history is of course to embrace historicity as much as actuality. "The current need of philosophy is to do away with owlishness," Miller writes in this essay. But not until the voice of philosophy declares the articulate present can it hope to overcome its owlishness; only then would philosophical discourse be an integral part of the articulate present. Miller's philosophy is at bottom not simply a plea for declaring such a present; it is a declaration of actuality and an acknowledgment of the price to be paid for such a declaration. "The plague of the contemporary world is that it has accepted a midworld while not endowing it with ontological status. . . . The basic impiety is the objectification of the actual."

What does it mean to endow the historical world with ontological status? How is the objectification of the actual to be avoided? Given the hold of such categories as the objective and the subjective, how can a campaign against such objectification avoid aiding the cause of subjectivism? The answer to each of these questions involves appreciating that present active participles (perceiving, speaking, writing, measuring, bartering, negotiating, etc.) are the loci of actuality and control. Such participles are examples of *embodied* activities; moreover, they are instances of living, rather than true, utterances. They are the loci of self-transcending, because self-critical, actuality. Miller in "The Owl" clarifies the meaning and conveys the force of these claims.

Written in the 1960s (Miller Papers 5:11), this essay first appeared in a slightly different form in The Transactions of the Charles S. Peirce Society *24(3), 1988, pp. 399–407. The quotations from Hegel are to be found in* The Philosophy of Right, *trans. T. M. Knox (1821. New York: Oxford University Press, 1967), pp. 12–13. The quotations from* The Philosophy of History *appear on pages 83 and 179. It is instructive to read "The Owl" in light of "Spectacle and Spectator" (*The Midworld of Symbols, *pp. 31–47) and "The Ahistoric Ideal" (*The Paradox of Cause, *pp. 130–60).*

The owl of Minerva, observing the past, supplied G. W. F. Hegel with an apt metaphor. The owl is a spectator, not an agent. He utters no commands, no pleas, no "Drink to me only with thine eyes," no "As I sat on a sunny bank," no "Rouse for King Charles," and no *de profundis*. For Hegel the present has no systematic status even as a matter of style. He has no contemporary world in terms of the controls of action.

A present, however, is not observed; it is enacted. The poet, the statesman, the lover, establish a present and that is the reason for their authority and attraction. The wisdom that does not express itself in the present omits the here-and-now as part of itself.

Among philosophers, both professional and amateur, praise of Plato is fairly unanimous. It is sometimes overlooked that the source of his charm is in the remarkable concern with the present. His problems turn on this maintenance of an actual command. The emergency is here and now in the speaker, or in the act of a man who is on his way to town in order to accuse his father of murder, or in the reliability of a teacher of virtue as a guide for a young man whose enthusiasm gets him out of bed very early in the morning in order to attend the lectures of Protagoras. This orientation is more than a rhetorical device. It is part of the substance of what is being said. Translate Plato out of his emergencies into abstract argument and one has only another example of futile contentiousness, frequently not very well sustained. But something besides argument is at stake and this is the immediacy of the person and his acts.

That the present lacks such metaphysical authority is an old and persistent view. It is this lack that troubles any philosophy of history. The spectator in viewing the past has not been able to assure his own authority. It is common to find a historian of a century ago "explained" as a man of his time, where that time is itself part of a process that embraces all epochs. Edward Gibbon, for example, is said to write like a rationalist, that point of view then having been prevalent.[1] In this way the authority of any point of view is lost in some wider process. We have looked to an environment to explain an immediacy, but in immediacy itself we have found no finality. To do that would lead to mysticism or to some arbitrary intuition claiming to be clear of circumstance. Or, it may lead to dogma and to fixity. The appeal of dogma is a corollary of the nonontological status of the actual immediacy, whether cognitive or volitional. The emancipated intellectual takes no immediacy seriously. He explains it and so destroys it. We have heard the cries of the existentialists who long for a valid immediacy and end in defeat and in search of an exit.

Like the owl, philosophers have been night birds. They look at a present as if it lacked constitutional authority. Every vast affirmation is the corollary of an equally vast rejection. Does one dare trust the senses? Is not perception "conditioned"? Are not loving and hating the manifestations of mere instinct, of human "nature," or of chemistry? Is not speech a "convention" or a "tool"? Is one not adjusted or maladjusted to the environment, and may not any alleged environment be only a fiction, an exhibition of "animal faith"?

And so Hegel writes a Phenomenology. It is a story of appearances. Back of it, in owl language, is what he calls "*Geist*." It was no misunderstanding that led the auditor to see Death in Hegel, a man who had neither a cosmic finality nor an actual one. Death is the spirit that surveys the actual. It is the spirit that takes a flight after dark. It is the spectator. It is the voiceless silence because no voice is authoritative and ontological.

The philosopher who hears all voices hears no actual voice. He does not hear his own. An actual voice is one that is never fully understood but, for all that, establishes the moment, projecting its prospect and its heritage.

The finitude that is constitutional is no abstraction. It is individual, not particular. It is actual, the here-and-now. It is the center of any orderly discourse, and this center is essential. The owl was no participant. What he saw was not in the seeing but was *ex post facto*. This was called "objectivity." But where there is no subjectivity as a constitutional factor, neither is there any objectivity. The owl is the symbol of inactive nonparticipation. Observation generates no actuality.

The nonobserved appears somewhere in any philosophy. It has had many names, usually owlish, such as God, ideas, atoms, natural law. All have the effect, indeed the intention, of enclosing the moment in a reality that devours and destroys it even as that reality is said to preserve it. One may give some respect to a frankly dogmatic religion that puts mystery into the salvation of the individual or in his damnation. To an owlish observer, the individual, the here-and-now, is obliterated. A world in charge of *Geist* is not in my charge. That is the basic objection of William James to Hegel.

There is in Hegel the fallacy of composition. The whole of phenomena is no phenomenon. Kant was surer; the whole of natural objects was no object. No tracks lead outward from the lion's cave, but neither do any lead to it. The phenomena of any absolute are a mystery, as is notorious. Whatever explains everything explains nothing in particular, and only the particular explains the particular, and only the particular calls for explanation. Of all things, *Geist* has no phenomenology.

The distinction of the phenomenal and the real is a corollary of the actual. Immanuel Kant at least tried to preserve the contrast between phenomena and noumena. He had, alas, no basis for the distinction. Hegel rejected Kant's distinction in favor of an internal control that, however, had no fulcrum and so fell subject to a pervasive spirit. The actual as a fulcrum of all self-possessed enlargement received no acknowledged authority. Even the hero does what his time requires; but what does a time require? No owl can say.

The actuality of a category is in the present active participle. Thus, space is measuring with a yardstick; time is telling time by the clock; cause is controlling or preventing effects proposed by purposes. Every category requires a vehicle. The vehicle is a "functioning object." There are, then, questions about categories like being and nonbeing: What is their vehicle? What is the vehicle of negation? Could it be the word *not* itself? What else? But much more needs to be tried before one can speak in a civilized way about those vehicles that are neither subjective nor objective, neither phenomena nor noumena, neither appearance nor reality, but the actuality that permits, generates, and enforces these distinctions. The owl has no language; it can only hoot.

It is a serious matter to be "understood." One may properly fear, and so dislike, anyone who claims to have understood one's ways. Owls claim to understand. What is wanted is to have a continuation of energy and enterprise that *nobody* can objectify. To say of a person that he behaves like a city-dweller or like a countryman is to take something away from his independence. In all ages asceticism is an essay in independence. If to be limited is to be enslaved, then it is not unnatural that one shall try to evade limit. We resist being the phenomena of any alien power. Insofar as we are peculiar we find cosmic reasons for a condition that others view as an oddity. And so a city is licensed by Athena or Diana, a race by Jehovah or by the sun-god. The man of money likes to think that all other interests are dependent on his activity. To the farmer the city-dweller has seemed a parasite who rudely disregards his dependence and puts on an offensive air of superiority and sophistication. The physicist does not relish the suggestion that his science is really a subdivision of psychology nor the philosopher acquiesce to being the *ancilla theologiae*. We slip away from being anybody's phenomenon. If too hard pressed, we will take to dreams or to defiance. We will not be phenomena. We will not surrender local control. The world is answerable to the here-and-now.

Intimations of this self-reliance appear in Ralph Waldo Emerson, who far surpasses Hegel in his grasp of the ontological status of the actual. In the end Hegel did not make good on his claim that he had found an energy internal to the spectacle. His control was not a local control. The local is *the same* as control. *Geist* is not a local control. But I am a local control when I "tell" a tale, or tell time, or make a mistake. Egoism, the sense of local control, is no force in Hegel. The baffling problems of egoism are a consequence of an imposed order, whatever the manner of that imposition, by whatever force. But egoism is no problem when the local is the same as the enactment of order in function, in the functioning object, whether yardstick, grammar, logic, or dialectic. In each case the actuality requires the medium. There is the cure for any vagrant egoism, and it is the only cure.

The current need of philosophy is to do away with owlishness. The philosopher must be a universalist but also a localist and the localist is not to be patronized. The repute of philosophy has suffered because it has had no way of combining the universal with the local. Their common element is the medium, the functioning object, and that is always an utterance that is a self-extending immediacy. This immediacy is no datum, no concept, but an action. The very vehicles of order, its actuality, have been objectified as a means, treated as tools, conventions, or phenomena. Spinoza is a prime example of a man whose voice was drowned in a substance that had no voice. I will turn away from the murdering logic that will let me hear no authentic voice. Such views are to be met not with argument but with whatever acts establish the conditions and the practice of acknowledged authority even in the plainest man and in the simplest functioning object. No owl hears a living word nor utters one. Hegel was quite conventional in proposing the owl and that has affected the ontological force of the result. He was conventional in his night-view, which is only the shadow of the absolute light.

The spectator is bound to become pretentious in order to compensate for his frustrations. The actuality of function is the immediacy that has not been accredited. This is the immediacy that is not mediated. Measuring has no spatial environment and the word has no denotation in a region not already touched by words. In the Schematism Kant nearly upset the *Critique*.

The owl is a spectator, not a participant. He has no present. He looks for, and claims to find, a control within the spectacle. But this reverts to what is not local but all-embracing. On the positive side, there are reasons for owlishness: the failures to give the local an ontological status and to recognize in the functioning object the vehicle of all control and of all failure.

Owls are birds of prey and their prey is the actual. What they devour they first kill if, indeed, it ever was alive. And yet, a reporter is a man not necessarily without honor. There persists the feeling that a neutral report is possible and that it is essential. True stories about nature and the past require this. Even the skeptic and the cynic pose as men who have found out the true state of affairs. The very man who mistrusts his own story and despises the story of another offers some credentials. René Descartes felt that he had been often deceived but, like most philosophers, he was not merely asking that we take his word for it but went further and tried to make his mistrust plausible in view of the nature of things. Somehow report fits the scene, even the sour report of the skeptic and the cynic. Report is possible only when nonpartisan. That is the ancient lore. The problem has, accordingly, been made quite simple for the philosopher: Can he give report an ontological status? If he cannot, let him invoke *Geist* or another absolute. But if he can, let him settle for the ontological authority of utterance, for the living word and not for the true word. Then the vehicle, the medium, the functioning object, become essential as the sole locus of a self-extending and of a self-critical actuality. Ask a reporter how he came by his story and he will say that it was in terms of some functioning object, and he will say that it was by seeing, counting, measuring, hearing words, reading a book. All report proceeds through this midworld, which is neither subjective nor objective. How would one detect an error if not in a malfunctioning? To function badly is to lose not the ideal but the actual, the moment, the here-and-now. A passive empiricism is as miraculous and as arbitrary as any dogma. The midworld is the great neutrality. Would one allege prejudice if a man can count or measure or speak grammatically? All criticism derives its force from the loss of such controls. These are the liberal arts where self and object become articulate under no compulsion but their own. Because they fix the moment they are the sole vehicles of history.

Civilization is respect for the midworld. That is its energy and its self-respect. Barbarians make an object of the functioning object and therefore they enslave men, burn books, and convert marble statues into useful lime. Poets are true civilizers because they deal in nothing but words. Philosophers, alas, have used words that have no use, but are only functional actualities, in order to lead us *away* from the actual. Are the preachers of life any better than the preachers of death? Not until the voice of philosophy declares the articulate present can it hope to lay aside its owlishness. Philosophy would then become the articulate present.

The great Kant told a story of the structure of experience that joined form and content in the intelligible. The "epistemological object" of the realists faded into vagueness. Traditional epistemology had permitted an inference from the facts found in experience to the transcendent. That argument lasted for centuries and is still used. But Kant put up a barrier to a rational ontology. It was tremendously effective and brought down on him the anathema of all realists, secular and theological. Samuel Johnson could make George Berkeley look a bit silly, but Kant was not silly; he was dangerous.[2] He turned out to be no more the prop of idealists than of realists. The idealists wanted some connection between experience and reality. To be masters in the house of experience it was necessary to accept the idealization of quality and of judgment. Still, the world could not be exhausted in phenomena. It was enough to say "phenomena" to prove that phenomena were not enough. Cognition in principle omitted one's own cognition. There was no transcendental psychology any more than a transcendental ontology. There was no center, as well as no periphery. Consequently the idealists proposed the absolute as the validation of finite experience. This was the rescue from a floating phenomenalism. On this point Josiah Royce made the great argument. The world was the answer to my problems, and those problems had to have an answer if they were not to revert to the trivial. Without the answers, the house of experience was built on sand. The absolute had those answers, and it had them *now*. In effect, this amounted to the reintroduction of an authoritative present as the price of an orderly world, and of any world that one could call one's own. A man wants his supper, his woman, his children, as well as synthetic judgments a priori. It is his living room that is 15 feet wide, and the universe that dissolves this present fact into idealized space is not his own. On the premises, Royce's problem was a proper one and his solution had force and scope.[3]

Arthur Schopenhauer faced this same problem. Phenomena were not enough. But he looked for imitations of a present reality in the will, rather than in the extrapolation of cognition. A mighty force, rather than a mighty mind, rescued the here-and-now from a phenomenal exile. In both cases a present sought alliance with finality. In both cases the personal present went begging for a validation to a cosmic present that was not its own. This has been the classic posture of philosophy. It is the wild and thoughtless man who seizes the moment. From this heedlessness he is to be rescued. He is to be brought to heel. There is no health in him. And then one hears the resounding cry of St. Paul as he struggles with the meshes of the law.

But meanwhile a present that is not lawless has been declaring itself. This has caused alarm and consternation. Once a word is spoken, the fat is in the fire. Error, illusion, wrong, and inadequacy came to be functions of local control. The stone rejected became the keystone of the immense arch. So long as the local was experienced not as control but as the absence of control, the dogmatist found a leverage and the philosopher could counsel synoptic visions. To the theorist this self-declaration of the present as actuality is foreign. It is easier to find a man acknowledging that he is eating bread than that he is eating. We like to stand off and to say that bread is a very good food, or that one should not eat too much of it because it makes one fat. Such statements seem eminently sensible, even scientific. But eating itself may become, and has become, a metaphysical problem: what to eat, what never to eat, how much to eat, and whether the wise man ought not to deplore so actualizing a propensity. All such immediacies have been examined and usually rejected, patronized, or tolerated. We have, in fact, been eating, using the senses, loving, fighting, singing, under license. But meanwhile these spontaneities have developed a self-defining discipline and we have natural science, the free state, the arts, and history. We have, in fact, a midworld where function generates environment, but one that is articulate and as much local as universal. The actual is enacted before it is identified. But one is now a doing when one comes to recognize the ideal as the form of the actual, and the universal as the mode of a present functioning.

The plague of the contemporary world is that it has accepted a midworld while not endowing it with ontological status. The air is still full of dismal stories *about* man in which no man appears. The basic impiety is the objectification of the actual.

NOTES

1. Gibbon (1737–1794), English historian and author of *The Rise and Fall of the Roman Empire*.

2. Johnson is famous for refuting Berkeley's idealism by kicking a stone. See James Boswell's *The Life of Samuel Johnson* (1785. London: Everyman's Library, 1992), where Boswell recounts Johnson's refutation.

3. The work by Josiah Royce to which Miller is most likely referring is *The World and the Individual* (1901. Gloucester, MA: Peter Smith, 1976), two volumes. See, e.g., volume I, pp. 40–42.

PART 3

The Maintenance of Community

We know another mind primarily in the acknowledgment of the symbol. No one can announce himself to another in any other way. Language of all sorts is not the *means* of communication, but the *actuality* of communion. Our discovery of ourselves as minds is identical with our discovery of these functioning objects that regulate and explore. Then for the first time we are united with others. Then for the first time we can influence them, or be influenced as minds, not as appearances to which our own responses are violent because lacking a common base.

—*The Definition of the Thing with Some Notes on Language*, p. 189

INTRODUCTION

The theme of community organizes this third part. The idea of community is, in an important sense, a vehicle for elucidating the concepts of philosophy and definition from Part 1 as well as the concepts of history and symbol from Part 2. Yet it would be a mistake to see ethics and politics as mere applications of key concepts of Miller's historical idealism. While the parts of this book are ranged 1–3, and community follows on philosophy and history, it must be kept in mind that philosophy is always an intersubjective activity and history cannot be understood apart from the careers of shared practices, common institutions, and social and political communities. Community is the basis of philosophy, establishes the symbols of the midworld, and founds criticism even as the actuality of community is defined by these elements. As one finds throughout Miller's philosophy, these critical relationships are dialectical.

The *maintenance* of community, then, is no dull affair. As goes community so go philosophy, criticism, and history—all of which are basic to our sense of personhood and agency. The form of community addressed here is that of the liberal democratic state. In Miller's estimation, it is the liberal democratic community that best reflects and effectively contributes to the philosophical practice and historical consciousness basic to his variant of idealism.

In the pages that follow, one finds perceptive essays on significant aspects of the liberal democratic community—for example, morality, freedom, tolerance, utopia, scholarship, citizenship, and art. Taken together, these essays form an incomplete composite, an imperfect account of Miller's social and political philosophy. Miller wrote no definitive or summary statement of his thought in this field. Yet we know that he was guided by a conception of a *metaphysics of democracy*—the phrasing borrowed from Walt Whitman, but the idea wholly Miller's own. These essays provide the critical concepts and basic form of this metaphysics.

Management

In these pages Miller addresses his philosophical commitments to action, history, and the midworld in the context of politics. The examination is implicitly connected to the question posed in "Freedom as a Characteristic of Man in a Democratic Society": "On what conditions, then, can one tell the story of man as the locus of responsible power?" How one answers, or fails to answer, this question traces the division between politics (which implies freedom and responsibility) and management (which denies both freedom and responsibility).

The crux of politics and political authority, in Miller's estimation, is stated with clarity in Aristotle's account of the "double capacity" that defines a citizen in a democratic state. A preliminary definition of the citizen relies on a description of a person's role within the apparatus of the state: "The citizen in the strict sense is best defined by the one criterion, 'a man who shares in the administration of justice and in the holding of office.' " A more essential definition, also found in the *Politics*, addresses the quality of the democratic person's character that Aristotle describes as knowledge of "how to rule and how to obey." This knowledge, essential to political rule (i.e., rule over equals), is acquired by learning to obey the commands of other citizens.

In "Idealism and Freedom" and "Freedom as a Characteristic of Man in a Democratic Society," Miller draws on these ancient insights as he develops his idea of a democratic community. What we find in the present essay is a sustained attack on a whole class of theories that defines rule as management and reduces the idea of democratic government to complete nonsense (e.g., B. F. Skinner's behaviorism). *Act, assertion, word*—these are the conditions of authority and these must be maintained if personhood and community are to be meaningful and effectual. As "The Portrait of Man" in Part 1 makes clear, material reductions cannot provide adequate accounts of persons or political associations. The maintenance of community thus begins in the effort to preserve the integrity of the very idea of community by limiting the pretensions of empirical theories.

First drafted as a letter dated September 22, 1971 (Miller Papers 20:7), this essay originally appeared in a slightly different form in In Defense of the Psychological *(pp.*

139–43). The quotations are from Aristotle's Politics *(trans. Ernest Barker, New York: Oxford University Press, 1995), Book 3, chapters 1–4 (pp. 1274b33–1277b33). Two other essays from* In Defense of the Psychological, *"Behavior" and "The Behavioral View of Action" (pp. 50–63 and pp. 90–98, respectively), elaborate the critique of behaviorism.*

The free Greek did not equate freedom with vagrancy or anarchy. Action needed control. The four classic virtues present action under control. So there is nothing new in a proposal that action be controlled. Moses proposed it.

There has persisted the view that action *precedes* its control. A brook flows; it is not under control; one builds a dam or a new channel—flood control. To see the control of action in that way is not unusual. People need advice, directing, counseling, "guidance." In various ways we say, "Beatrice Fairfax tells me what to do."[1]

To this view there has long appeared a contrasting claim. It is that action does not take place where there is no concomitant control, but that this is self-control.

It is agreed by all that action needs control. But it has been held that this control is not subsequent to the act, but is *inherent,* that no act occurs in the absence of self-control. The free act is then the inherently controlled act. The expression "free act" becomes a tautology. To act is to be free; and to be free is to be self-controlled, not to be without control.

There is today a readiness to believe that neither of the traditional views of act is acceptable. To be summary: Nature appears only as act is excluded. Act is "myth," not an "error" of fact, as if there might be *act* but that it is not found.[2] Act is not possibly found. This, I believe, is today a powerful persuasion.

The ideal of *knowledge* has long been that we keep out. Any personal participation contaminates knowledge. We are to be passive, receptive, and innocent. The prestige of revelation and also of data derives from this persuasion that such knowledge is none of one's own doing. Skeptics see no escape from a private or personal factor. Mystics of certain sorts propose a reality with which we have nothing to do as individual persons.

The knowledge in which we presume to take a hand is illusion. It is not truth. The claim "I see the speaker in what is said" is enough to disqualify the saying. It is a very common ploy. Truth-tellers protest that they are not speaking as themselves. The news reporters protest their innocence.

They are not "subjective." Butter would not melt in their mouths. No one may personally appear in what he alleges as his knowledge.

Why not, then, apply the same rule to action? This has been done. The poet invokes the inspiration of the Muses. Prophets and priests act for a god and disavow the act as merely their own. Crusaders march because "God wills it." Such acts, *not* one's own doing as an individual person, are the *best* acts, just as the knowledge with which one has nothing to do is the best knowledge. Let a man once suppose that he acts for himself, and he invites the devil to tempt him with pretty tunes. Where I do not pretend to act for myself, the devil has no leverage. It is the classic claim. Our first parents took the liberty of acting on their own motion instead of resigning to the will of Jehovah. In the true reality there was no place for the personal act. The wise man divests himself of the pretension to act as an autonomous individual. It is a point on which both science and theology agree.

Why, then, should B. F. Skinner be regarded as an innovator? Instead of trying to account for Skinner it would appear more in order to account for *those who find him disturbing*. Do they lay claim to autonomy? Who denies that "slums make people" and affirms that "people make slums"? Who repudiates psychiatry with its unconscious controls of action? What scholarly biographer does not "explain" a character in terms of "influences" that account for his temper, beliefs, sayings, and acts? It is standard practice. Only a divinity is autonomous. To hold so is also the standard way. For the Christian there is only one autonomous Person.

So, what exactly is the basis of any objection to Skinner? His position seems normal rather than odd. The objectors remind me of the objectors to Bishop George Berkeley. They do not like Berkeley, but they cannot say why not, especially if they are empiricists believing only the avouch of their own eyes, "the sensible and true avouch," as Horatio says.[3] I doubt that Samuel Johnson, refuting Berkeley by kicking a stone, would pretend to a divine autonomy in that act.[4] Short of that, however, Berkeley could smile at the doctor's opacity. So there are mutterings about Skinner, and very likely someone will kick a stone in refutation. Skinner will smile.

A belief in autonomy seems an unlikely basis of objection to a proposal to manage conduct or action. The study of things done—of *res gestae*—is history. I have not found history viewed as a dimension of the "real" world. Theology, physics, and psychology have laid claim to disclosing the nature of things, whereas history occupies a limbo neither supernatural, natural, nor psychological. I find that the creation story in Genesis rates rather better than the claim that no world can be described or imagined in the absence of a generative past. Dated-time, which only acts can generate, is not of the essence. Of course, even clock-time, as in physics, is alien to theological absolutes or to any totality however arrived at. As for psychology, it has no story of a past and lacks even a clock.[5]

So there is much difficulty in locating an act. A view of "behavior" on assumptions not including autonomy is traditional rather than novel.

Why, then, does a sort of common sense object to behaviorism? Because there are some acts that, although personal, are not occasioned by carrots or sticks or by specific unconscious urges. Such acts are those that are the actual vehicles of order and are so affirmed. The simplest example is in number. To count one does something, one speaks or cuts notches in a stick, one keeps a tally, that is, a tale, that is, a telling. Five fingers and five more make ten, and so do five and five apples. The sum is neutral to specific occasions. Similarly with spatial and temporal measurements. The difference between *red* and *green* has to be "told" in some way. So with *here* and *there*, with *this* and *that*, *yes* and *no*, and, of course, many others. Now I propose that common sense identifies itself with such deeds. The average man is not closed to recognizing that much of what he does is "conditioned" by advantage or disadvantage. Parents have always kept a cookie jar. But the counting of cookies is not peculiar to cookies. It is a general command. It is what one does, but it is not a particular doing. One is a counter, measurer, and so forth, in an intimate way. One continues to be. History is made by a few people who persist in the command of numbers, yardsticks, and clocks. The act becomes constitutional. It projects a *world*. Any world, any order, is the *form* of the pure act.[6] Common sense clings to those acts that define and *project* an environment.

I agree with attempts such as Skinner's to show that no act, no autonomy, can be observed as a specific phenomenon or event. On the other side, a totality of any sort, if a *fait accompli*, has always made difficulty for personal autonomy. I am proposing that the act is *itself* the immediacy that generates those distinctions. But this act is a pure functioning, as in the cases cited above. It appears in what I call the *midworld*, neither in a hidden soul nor in perceived objects, but in functioning objects.

I suggest—rather than extensively argue—that there is no egoism in such formal actualities. One surrenders to numbers and space, to much else. No one can charge that some peculiarity of *mine* appears in such action. It is anonymous. Yet it is also very much myself. At the same time it projects a world, that is, an infinity of order where even accidents are constitutional.

I think myself that the claims of Skinner clarify the issue. Either act is constitutional or else we can have no objection to what Skinner or another may propose by way of control. There can be no "evidence" for autonomy, as if one might, or might not, find such evidence. Autonomy is no *contingency*. It is no *phenomenon*. It is under no *cognitive* limits. One cannot say, "*I know* that I am free." It is no *content of consciousness* that *happens* to appear. It is not a property of any object. If one admits to objectivity, the word *free* has *no denotation*. It is excluded from the assumptions of the intellect.

Existence is functioning; functioning is original; its manifestations are utterances—numbers, spaces, words, monuments, all of which are a doing, but not a doing apropos of any specific object or state of affairs. It is a doing that projects an order, a world, a continuum of experience, an *articulated immediacy*, an infinity that is no fact or object but an actuality.

All that leads to the midworld, where appearance and reality meet in the actual. You do have to handle a yardstick, which, however, is no object, but a functioning object.

Men flee presence. They are escapists. Presence means responsible action, a burden, but also an excitement. Psychology defines no presence and so no extension of it into a world. Without such presence there is no meeting ground for argument. The futility of argument has indeed become a tenet of faith. We protest, dissent, make unconditional demands, riot, burn, murder, and proclaim "free inquiry." Nothing is sacred, nothing holy. On cognitive premises we become anarchists, and Skinner is *the answer to anarchy*, and his answer, being also intellectual, is a management. All that seems to me quite as it should be, on the premises.

NOTES

1. The reference to Beatrice Fairfax pertains to the advice column, authored by Marie Manning, which appeared in the William Randolph Hearst's New York *Evening Journal* from 1898 up until Manning's death in 1944.

2. There is a paradox involved in the myth of action. It is science and the scientific attitude that has cast suspicion on the claim that persons act. What science finds is never action (involving will and intent) but only behavior (devoid of will and intent). However, it is the *actions* of scientists that have rendered action a mere myth. Thus persons are threatened by the controls—that is, nature, scientific pro-

cedure, and instrumentation—required for the discovery and elaboration of personal power. This is a function of the pursuit of the ideal of knowledge. See Miller's essay "Spectacle and Spectator" in *The Midworld* (pp. 36–47) and "The Ahistoric and the Historic" (Part 2, above). Compare Miller's account to the analysis offered by Max Horkheimer and Theodor W. Adorno in *The Dialectic of Enlightenment* (1941. Trans. John Cumming, New York: Continuum, 1987).

3.   Shakespeare, *Hamlet*, Act 1, scene i.

4.   English essayist and lexicographer Samuel Johnson is most well known for his *Dictionary of the English Language* (1755. Robert Gordon Lathan, ed., London: Longmans, Green, 1882). Johnson's refutation of Berkeley is recounted in James Boswell's *The Life of Samuel Johnson* (1785. London: Everyman's Library, 1992).

5.   In "The Role of the Actual" (in *The Philosophy of History*, pp. 165–67) Miller notes the difference between clock-time and dated-time. Clock time is the time of physics—that is, the most basic and neutral means of measuring relations in time. Dated time is the time of history—that is, a richer conception of time involving memory, reflection, and personal change. As Miller writes in an unpublished essay: "History is the dimension of time, of an actual past, of time generating new and more complete integration. . . . History is revolution because it is conversion. It is the career of conversion" (Miller Papers 21:9).

6.   On the matter of the pure act, Miller writes: "The action which has no environment must, therefore, be *identical* with 'environment' in principle. It must be the actuality of the environment. It must create environment. . . . Pure action, absolute action, creative action occurs in the discovery and articulation *of the general conditions of specific acts*. These general conditions are the categories" (Miller Papers 21:1). The key distinction here is between pure actions and psychological or determined actions.

The Occasion of Study in Morals

The Kantian element is strong in this essay. One finds a concentrated argument, contra all forms of eudaemonism and amoral materialism, for the centrality of autonomy in our moral life. Miller seeks to enfranchise action, discourse, and finitude by establishing them not as evidence of our failure to attain a perfected state or build a utopian universe but rather as instances of our heroic attempts at self-maintenance. "We wish above all else to be effective," he writes in the opening paragraph, and we must have a conception of world and person that allows for agency.

The term *effective* can lead to a misunderstanding of Miller's aim. Effectiveness suggests that something is good for something else. This conception leads back to the utilitarian variant of eudaemonism where moral action is not good in itself but is always good *for* something else—namely, the maximization of happiness. (John Stuart Mill's attack on the deontological notion of the good will is an effort to show precisely this: Whatever is deemed good, and thus moral, is always instrumental in the production of happiness.) Miller's interest in effectiveness, however, is decidedly *anti-utilitarian*. It is his assessment that, far from being animated by the prospects of utility, ethical study "can hardly win attention for reasons that are not themselves sporting."

This reference to the *sporting* character of ethical study and the moral life is essential. It invites reading Miller in light of José Ortega y Gasset's philosophy. In turn, this reference to *sport* points toward an important distinction in Miller's thought—that is, between the *instrumental* and the *critical*. Unlike instrumentalism, criticism addresses that which is self-sufficing, irreducible, and, at a certain point, beyond justification. It concerns fundamental orders or assertions (i.e., the rules of the game) and not possible manipulations and strategies (i.e., plays in the game). In these terms it is proper to say that *action has no point*. It is the play itself, the actuality of our human being.

Action cannot be justified; it can only be made manifest. Because it is concerned with the maintenance of effective action, morality is not an instrumentality but a critical exercise. Morality, as Miller understands it, does not propose to accomplish anything but draws our attention to action, the conditions of endeavor, and the very basis of personhood. At its root, morality maintains the play itself, the conditions under which one may have particular aims and plans. Criticism is then integral to the exercise of autonomy.

Drafted in the 1940s, this essay was originally titled "Moral Man" (Miller Papers 6:13). On the topic of justification and its limits, see "On Choosing Right and Wrong" in Part 3 of this collection. Essay drafts on the topic of ethics from the 1930s (Miller Papers 9:9) are also of interest. The reference to Ortega y Gasset pertains to his essay "The Sportive Origin of the State" (1941. In History as a System and other Essays Toward a Philosophy of History, *Helene Weyl, trans., New York: Norton, 1961).*

The interest in morals derives from the prospect of freedom. We wish above all else to be effective, to count for something. We would avoid inconsequence by becoming agents and doers. From this simple origin arise all the complex problems of moral theory.

Plainly, without action there can be no morality. Yet a principal concern of our time is occasioned by the doubt that we can act at all. We are likely to assume that every event is controlled by the universe, and that no event is in the control of any particular person. Determinism is the theory that an event must be understood through a totality that includes, generates, and explains it. This totality occurs as a present completeness whether natural or supernatural. Indeed, it is not only the causal, or mechanical, order of nature that casts suspicion on the possibility of action; it is quite as much the control of events by providential design. In either case, action as free local agency is made impossible.

I

Action is an announcement not of totality but of limit. And action can be said to occur only where limit pretends to finality and absoluteness. Infinity, that all-embracing locus of energy and order, is repudiated by action. This is the egoistic core of the moral sense. Morality seeks to enfranchise limitation, and to endow it with originality of being and energy. This is the meaning of freedom. Responsibility occurs in this context of self-controlled limitation.

Here lies the heresy of morals, their inherent impiety.[1] Whether the pretension to morals more grievously affronts mechanism or theology would be hard to say. Morality involves a cessation from any utopian version of the universe, from any universe regarded as a *fait accompli*. The moralist cannot, in an unconditioned way, surrender the authorship of his act to nature, to society, or to any other obliterative agency, mundane or celestial.

In consequence, morality contains an ingredient of privacy and loneliness. Much attention has been paid to "social" ethics, but comparatively small notice has been received by the individual whose pretension to finality and freedom is regarded as a threat to community. Indeed, it seems not too much to say that morality has come to be construed as a social menace, just as it is also a denial of utopian mechanism or design. The moralist then has a hard time of it. Those who mistrust the autonomy of limitation are numerous and, of course, thoroughly equipped with the finest theories. Utopia is always the region of theory. It is a region of orthodoxy and conformity in which everything is promised but privacy. The individual is to be brought under a plan, be it political, physical, or theological. And where some meager faith in action hesitantly lingers, it is accompanied by the claim that such control as we have should take the form of assent to law not of our making. Egoism, privacy, freedom, limitation, and loneliness—all have come to be regarded as absurd or abhorrent. Yet the problem of morals is set by the close association, even the equation, of personal reality and action. And action is the autonomy of limit.

II

There seems some reason to examine the possibility of such autonomy in a time and in a state that assert the freedom of man as the basis of association and of justice. We have made it official in the Declaration of Independence: "All governments derive their just powers from the consent of the governed." Yet freedom has always been a dangerous topic. Perhaps it may be discussed today with greater safety than formerly. On the whole, our habits are lawful. Apart from exhortation to abstract virtue, our day-to-day activities enforce a large measure of thoughtfulness and personal organization. At the very least we must tend the machines that serve our purposes, and persons of no marked transcendental tendencies admit, sometimes ruefully, that alcohol and gasoline do not mix. Sobriety, care, and even ambitious thoughtfulness are enforced and solicited. There is an enormous number of honest men, not perfectionists of course, who are still broadly convinced that weights and measures should be accurate and bills should be paid. Moreover, because of the wide study of natural science in schools of every level, there exists a habitual tendency to tell the truth, to dislike inaccuracies of factual statement, and even to have a steady perception of logical incoherencies. There is abroad a new asceticism. The multiplication table may well turn out to be a far more powerful moralizer than the Ten Commandments. It seems possible, then, to scan the position of morals in our time with a measure of objectivity and freedom from any sense of crisis or evangelism.

The average man who would go so far as to consider moral theory at all is a decent fellow who is probably doing a day's work and stands in affectionate relation with his parents or with his wife and children. He is neither depraved nor stupid. He need hardly be scolded for his sins, nor yet excited to mistrust the decency of others. And yet, if ethical study is prompted by a hope of giving articulation to freedom, it can hardly win attention for reasons that are not themselves sporting. It is very strange to consider the atmosphere of seriousness, and even of menace, that marks the usual essay in moral analysis. There can, at last, be no reason for action. That would be like giving a reason for existing. Morality is useless. Give it a function and you subordinate it to another value, and none of our own. One can very rapidly read off the position of a moral theory in terms of this consideration. Whenever we are urged to follow nature, society, or eternal law, we may be sure that the outcomes will eclipse our own energies and reduce them to a derivative position. Moral study can occur only in the same atmosphere that its outcome must articulately instate—namely, the enjoyment of autonomy.

Some menace, it is true, drives to moral reflection; it is the dark dread of not being in charge of oneself. The inducement must be as absolute as the answer. Where there is no absolute inducement surely there can be no absolute answer. So many moral theories, especially some very influential ones, inevitably end by repudiating the free act because they begin with a problem that itself has no necessity.[2] No accidental problem can get a necessary answer. No accidental problem can be forced on any man. And where an individual has become obsessed with an accidental problem, we call him a madman. He should get rid of it, taking it in stride should it concern him but leaving it alone when other matters press on his attention. And there is reason to suppose that moral problems are pressing and even necessarily so.

Moral problems have a long history, and have taken the deliberate attention of every generation. They seem more than casual or episodic. They seem, somehow, problems peculiarly proper of human nature and definitive of it. Indeed, one may say that man aspires to do wrong. This is paradoxical. Yet it is critical to us to know not only the good but the difference between good and evil. To know this difference is more important than to be good. We wish to be wrong in order that we may lay claim to have acted. For when we act we advertise our finitude, and we also lay claim to autonomy. Our personal reality includes both these properties. Thus when we criticize ourselves, we take ourselves to have been agents. Only in such criticism can one assert one's agency, the pretension to have been in charge of oneself. Criticism examines an act that one cannot disavow as one's own to see how adequately it conveys one's intention.

Criticism is the activity of self-possession. It has no other meaning, and no other urgency. When we consider the allurement of ethical study, we encounter this completely free and sporting demand. Ethical study is an essay in the form of one's reality. While morality announces limit and autonomy, it must also confess the region of law and reality, the foil by which limit is revealed. The bridge in this relation is action. Without action no moral problem is posed and, what is more, no problem about nature either—whether in detail or in principle. Morality leads to the universe only because action announces the region that furnishes its particular materials and its general conditions. Moral theories have, accordingly, moved from man to the moral universe.[5] This is a universe that, broadly speaking, allows action to occur and consequently enforces value as one of the attributes of reality. The sort of world that allows action is defined through value.

III

Underneath the social reforms that have enlarged the enjoyment of commodities lies a search for power.[4] It is said that power corrupts, and of that there can be no question. It is a truism. What else could corrupt? Men require power whether or not they abuse it, as they undoubtedly will. But with power goes responsibility. Nor is that merely an added fact or a hortatory reminder. Power is sought for the sake of agency and against a power that already exists. To fall under arbitrary power is intolerable. But to assail power because it is arbitrary is to simply promise a more responsible use of it. In this quarter we have made much progress. Our practice is in advance of our theory. We have come to act on the assumption that virtue is a corollary of power, emphasizing the converse of the older insight that power is a corollary of virtue. Power, of course, generates evil, and the suspicion of power is as old as the Book of Genesis. But we have a stake in evil because it is only the corruption of power. And we always have a stake in power because it alone permits action, and so generates the distinction between good and evil. Power, like action, announces limit. It is sought not to abolish limit, but to establish it. Power gives reality because it gives effectiveness to finitude.

The only escape from limit is the rejection of action. This is amoralism. This is the quest of negative mysticism, which sees in limit the unreality of the person. There limit is illusion. Certainly, if man does not possess originality in his acts and action is not the revelation of the unconditional, then it becomes no more than reasonable to find one's way out of the illusions of finitude. Indeed, amoralism has been very persuasive. Thomas Davidson, in his *History of Education*, characterizes these doctrines as "systems of organized weariness."[5]

It is considerations such as these that turn one's thoughts to ethical study. Action, criticism, autonomy, and power—all are central to personhood and the moral life. There are, however, no casual inducements to such study. To offer any would be the same as rendering the result uncompulsive in advance. Of course, we must train children in the best ways of life with which we are acquainted. We must even tell them the truth. To the prudent adult we recommend intelligent action, a broad consideration of consequences that he might not fail to reach what he happens to want. But to the individual who finds some call to respect, or to love, others, for all their limits, and because of them, finding his own selfhood in these revelations of original being, an inquiry into the moral aspect of human nature may have a point.

NOTES

1.   Because of Miller's interest in piety (see "Action Is Inherently Historical," *The Philosophy of History*, pp. 147–50), the equation between morality and impiety is unusual. The impiety of morality is that it stands against the scientistic pieties that

cast doubt on action, responsibility, and, indeed, personhood. The use of the term *impiety* is thus ironic and places morality in the class of other necessary heresies— for example, of personhood (Miller Papers 9:9), history ("History and Humanism" in Part 2, above), and liberalism (Miller Papers 21:2).

2. Miller is sympathetic with José Ortega y Gasset's assertion that "the life of man appears essentially problematic" (*History as System and Other Essays Toward a Philosophy of History* [trans. Helene Weyl, New York: Norton, 1961], p. 115). Yet Miller's interest is with *necessary* problems—that is, those that concern fundamental orders such as law, logic, and physics. Accidental problems, by contrast, concern the troublesome details of our experience such as missing cooks, assignment deadlines, and how to put dinner on the table. See "Idealism and Freedom" (Part 3, below) for more on the role of problems in philosophy.

3. The theme of the moral universe is most prominent in Plato's *Crito*. Miller is careful to distinguish the *moral* universe from a *benevolent* universe. The moral universe establishes the meaning of *good* and *justice* but does not assure any actual outcome. The concern is with structure, not content. Similarly, the necessity that one be a *moral* person is different from the imperative to be a *good* person. Miller is not making the stronger, and more dubious, claim that insofar as one is a person then one must act according to the moral law. That is a more strictly Kantian point. The actualist position more modestly asserts that personhood is synonymous with *having the moral question before oneself.*

4. The idea of *power* must always be placed within the normative context of "the community of power" (see *The Definition of the Thing*, p. 189), a community in which one acts as ruler as well as ruled and in which each increase in an individual's power does not diminish the power of others. This power is fundamentally political and not strategic or instrumental. See "Idealism and Freedom" (Part 3, below), where Miller writes that the key issue of the future will be "the problem of winning power for each man."

5. *History of Education* (New York: Scribners, 1901).

Idealism and Freedom

The ethical and political implications of epistemology are a central concern of Miller's writing. There is no detour around epistemology if one wants to arrive at a reflective consideration of ethics and politics. This is so not because Miller conceives of epistemology as prior to ethics but rather because epistemology and ethics are *dialectically* related. Any inquiry into action is possible only on the basis of certain epistemological principles. Similarly, the investigation of the status of knowledge can be conceived only in the context of intersubjective and, therefore, ethical relations. The common root of epistemology and ethics is the act. The vitality of both areas of inquiry is discerned only in terms of the historical career of action.

In a condensed form, Miller explores the unity of epistemology and ethics exemplified in the systematic project of Kantian critical philosophy—that is, limiting knowledge to make room for freedom. Miller goes on to offer a revision of the Kantian project by situating idealism within history. (This move defines Miller's thought as a form of *historical idealism*.) The form of autonomy derived from Immanuel Kant's transcendental idealism is translated into a mode of historical criticism. Such criticism is oriented toward taking responsibility for one's historical circumstances in the form not just of inherited beliefs and folkways but also those public institutions and formal practices that define, for example, our common political and scientific endeavors. These historical circumstances are not mere happenstance but are what Miller refers to as the "factors of structure" and "elements of organization and criticism" at the root of our "necessary conflicts."

What was for Kant the sphere of heteronomy (i.e., nature, history, and public life) is refashioned by Miller into that which is necessary and thus the realm of autonomous action.

At this crucial turn from transcendental to historical idealism, one finds Miller's statement appropriating Walt Whitman's challenge to forge "a new Literature, perhaps a Metaphysics, . . . the only sure and worthy supports and expressions of the American Democracy." Miller hardly lingers over this phrase drawn from *Democratic Vistas* and devotes but two pages to the exposition of the idea. Yet the concept of a *metaphysics of democracy* describes a leading tendency of Miller's thought. Just as Kant stipulates that freedom needs the assistance of philosophy in the form of transcendental idealism, for Miller democratic political institutions require a metaphysics that clarifies their fundamental presuppositions and aims. In sum, our public life is in need of philosophy—that is, a reflective apprehension of the actual and historical conditions of our endeavors.

A more basic dialectical relationship between philosophy and democracy is uncovered in Miller's prevailing suggestion that the activity of philosophy is both a model for and the expression of democracy. In a democratic community, as in philosophical discussion, each person exercises power, recognizes the power of others, and reflects on the presuppositions and responsibilities of power exercised by each participant. Democratic processes are like philosophical discussions in that they are fundamentally activities of criticism. By formally organizing the activity of criticism, liberal democracy becomes, as Miller writes in "Utopia and State," "a school of the will" and thus an adjunct to philosophy.

Originally published in a slightly different form in The Paradox of Cause and Other Essays *(pp. 64–74), the present essay was composed in March 1943 (Miller Papers 1:11).* Democratic Vistas *(1867), noted above, appears in many editions of Whitman's work, including the collection* Prose and Poetry, *edited by Justin Kaplan (New York: Library of America, 1982). (See page 984 of Kaplan's edition for the phrase of Whitman's quoted above.) On the topic of the dialectical relation of epistemology and ethics see an untitled essay draft of Miller's dating from 1932 (Miller Papers 9:9) and the essay "Knowing Other Minds" in* In Defense of the Psychological *(pp. 163–72). Miller concisely states the political implications of idealism in the chapter "In Sum," which closes* The Midworld of Symbols and Functioning Objects *(pp. 185–92).*

I

Idealism occurred historically as the outcome of the attempt to mediate between skepticism and dogmatism. This attempt finds its modern beginning in Immanuel Kant. David Hume had aroused him from his dogmatic slumber. How did this come about? Why should Hume have had the power to awaken the tranquil dogmatist?

It occurred because Hume had denied necessity. This was equivalent to the denial that any aspect of consciousness could be more than accidental. All experience derived from "impressions." Every impression could be some other way. Between impressions there were no connections capable of enforcing consequences. Any impression could follow any other. Among impressions there was no unity, actual or ideal. Nor was there any unitary self, or soul, as the central recipient of impressions. Bishop George Berkeley had already stated that there was no "idea" of the soul;[1]

Hume now added that there was no "impression" of the soul and, by implication, no "notion" of it.[2] He allowed unity neither in objects nor in the self. Atomic impressions were the sole data of experience, and experience was confined to data.

Such a claim attacked dogmatism at its root. Dogmatism had asserted existences and unities that experience did not contain and that it could never certify. Thus, matter, soul, God, causality, logical order, obligation, were not contents of consciousness. They were either objects beyond all actual and possible experience, or else alleged universal laws of experience. Where all experience was confined to "impressions," there could occur to it neither such transcendent objects nor any such universal laws.

By Hume's time induction or empiricism had acquired great prestige. The scientific method was winning great victories. The naturalism of the eighteenth century was, however, still dogmatic. The causal argument was still used to establish both the rational order of nature and the existence of God as the author of nature. Hume's position was not that of the empirical naturalist. The naturalist was dogmatic both in his assumption of a logical order among the objects of nature and in his conclusions based thereon. This vast structure Hume struck down. He did this by undermining its rationalistic foundations, namely the universal laws that both organized experience and then permitted the transition from nature to God.

Kant took seriously this reduction of all experience to the stream of consciousness. Himself something of a scientist, he had the scientific conscience. He believed that all statements about the content, or objects, of experience must be inductive. He saw that induction alone could generate no universal. Empirical procedure could not, he held, make verifiable or even meaningful statements about transcendent objects. Those two factors in traditional philosophy could get no support from an empirical method.

So far Kant went along with Hume. By doing so he abandoned dogmatism.

But Hume had destroyed more than dogmatism. He had also destroyed empiricism. At that point Kant balked.

To be empirical, said Kant, is to judge. Empiricism, as he saw it, was not the total absence of criticism. It was rather the restriction of criticism to the accidental, to impressions, to the content of consciousness. So much the psychological movement had made clear. But concerning that passively received psychological content, Kant differed from Hume, alleging that it always exhibited elements of organization, or of form. By denying form,

Hume had made empiricism impossible. However correct Hume may have been in restricting knowledge to impressions, he was wrong, according to Kant, in supposing that those impressions were vagrant, unrelated, and without unity.

In proposing the categories as the form of impressions, Kant was not repudiating empiricism. He was seeking, rather, to establish it. In effect, Hume had denied the possibility of judgment, since judgment entails compulsion. Without compulsion empiricism is reduced to indeterminism. Hume had made definition impossible because he had made all things possible, and definition means the rejection of some possibilities.

II

By this stroke of accepting empiricism while insisting on formal order, Kant presented a new idea of first importance for the history of philosophy. It was that quite within the domain of thought itself there lay responsibility. Thought could police itself. Nature lost its status of opposition to thought, and became the ideal or theoretical meaning of any given perception, the extrapolation of the inherent form of any datum. The order of nature became the same as the order of judgment, or of criticism.

Both skepticism and dogmatism deny the self-limiting capacity of thought.[5] The skeptic rejects the possibility of an alien control and finds none within himself. The dogmatist likewise finds no inner regulation, yet asserts a control exercised by laws or objects independent of thought. Both deny the autonomous authority of criticism. In the view of Kant, it was possible to stay within the confines of experience and still be critical. One could be mistaken. One could be limited and incomplete because of the formal order and the infinite relativity of thought itself. One needed to be faithful to the lawful form of one's own experience. In contrast to skepticism and dogmatism, thought was given power over itself. To have such power was its nature, a power inherent in every datum or impression.

A frequent misunderstanding of the Kantian position occurs in the charge that it is subjectivism. On this point Kant is clear. It is true that the criticism of appearances occurred solely through the operation of ideal form, and not through an appeal to laws, or to objects separate from the content to be criticized. This was not however the reduction of all thought to psychology. It was rather a claim that not all components of thought, or of experience, could be found in psychology. He urged a nonpsychological aspect of experience, namely form, something not sensory, not accidental, and not biographical. While unintelligible apart from content, it remained wholly ideal, the structure of content, its law, and its organized pattern. In this way accidental content became at once limited in fact and, at the same time, infinite in its ordered relations. Limitation was combined with infinity through the law. Empirical statements became also responsible statements. Subjectivism is not the view that all experience possesses a lawful and ideal form; it is rather the view that all experience, being only psychological, lacks such lawful form. From the standpoint of psychology there are no universals. Kant asserted universals by denying the claim of psychology as the exhaustive account of experience. His claim was this: No experience without law, a law inherent to experience itself. The factor in Kant's position that has often been an obstacle to philosophers is just this presentation of a nonpsychological element in empiricism. This is his resolution of the conflict between an atomic empiricism devoid of formal limitation and a dogmatic assurance devoid of the limitation of accidental content.

The charge that Kant was a subjectivist is too weak to warrant much consideration. A much stronger charge is that he was not subjective enough. He spoke of his phenomenal world as "consciousness in principle."[4] Yet consciousness occurs only in the individual. Kant left obscure the place of quite personal experience in his highly impersonal account of nature. One may doubt whether idealism has been clear on this point, especially in its more popular versions. Idealism has been tolerably successful in claiming ideality for law; it has not been equally successful in relating that law to biography and to history. Its characteristic difficulty occurs in its omission of individuality and finitude, rather than in an exaggeration of the personal stream of consciousness. It was for this reason among others, that William James objected to Josiah Royce's Absolute, and Royce himself saw the need of avoiding the obliteration of the individual in the world.[5] It would seem that the usual charge against idealism is not subjectivism, but rationalism, its tendency to eventuate in some dogmatic completion. Idealism, it is often held, slights the factor of the accidental, of the finite, of the nonrational. Arthur Schopenhauer found that fault with G. W. F. Hegel, while James urged a pluralistic universe and a finite God. Of course, there are many philosophies other than idealism that attempt to "explain" the finite and the accidental by treating them as properties of appearance, but not ultimately of the real. All such "explanations" of the accidental are necessarily dogmatic. The agnostic element in Kant registers his recognition of this result.

III

Idealism after Kant consists in the discovery and exploitation of the non-psychological factors of experience. They are the factors of structure, and consequently of criticism, for criticism is nothing other than the self-maintenance of structure. It seems tolerable to assume that the denial of structure is all the same as the denial of criticism. It seems equally persuasive that the authority of criticism depends on the necessity of those structures in accordance with which criticism operates. Let it be urged that the modes of criticism lack equivalence with the real, and it follows that authority itself is only appearance, animal faith perhaps, or a convenient code for getting a little order out of the mess of running experience.

The sticking point in the understanding of post-Kantian idealism is precisely this claim that structure is absolute. It seems clear that no absolute can secure logical demonstration. There can surely be no point of view that could ever *certify* the pretension of necessity. And we are accustomed to suppose that what has no environment is the very essence of the arbitrary.

The idea of statements having no environment is not, however, totally unfamiliar. The scientific honesty of our time has scrupulously explored those elements of knowledge that are asserted without evidence. Especially has this been the case in logic, mathematics, and physics. There one encounters the "postulate" in all its underived primitiveness. Granting disputes over the precise postulates of any one of these areas of orderly study, still it seems agreed by all hands that what allows order and responsibility is some such list of unverifiable assertions. All postulates refer to order and its elements. None refer to particulars.

An unverifiable assertion, since it is about nothing in particular, is a very peculiar idea. Assertions about particulars are contingent. They owe their meaning, and their contingency, to the sort of organization that identifies specific situations. They are not about structure, for structure is neutral to all possible particulars. This state of affairs has given the positivists their inning.[6] Assertions about nothing in particular, they say, make no sense. Since no assertion can secure verification apart from particular differences, it is obvious that wholly formal statements are, for positivism, without meaning.

Nevertheless, from the beginning of philosophy there has been a search for these *organization words*. Words having denotation have seemed not to concern philosophers. But what authority have organization words? Indeed, what is the peculiar urgency that invents so perverse an idea? At any rate, their authority and their meaning must be related to that urgency. Their authority will depend on the absoluteness of that urgency.

IV

No one will be in accord with an answer to a question unless he accepts the validity of a problem. And, certainly, no answer can be viewed as necessary where the problem is believed to be accidental or gratuitous. At the same time, neither can an answer be accepted as necessary when the problem has an environment apropos of which it occurs. The foundations of thought, and the character of reality, would then, of course, revert to the scheme of that environment. Consequently, any problem about reality must be identical with reality. The problem must be unconditioned if it is to convey an unconditioned answer.

Instead, then, of proposing the unconditioned as an answer, let it be considered the property of a problem. This would be a problem about structure, for it is only in structure that thought shows its authority. Only in a problem about structure could this authority be seen in its urgency and in its origin.

A problem marks disconcertment. It is the claim of idealism that some disconcertments are constitutional, not accidental. They occur as a threat to control, not to a detail within controlling law. Incoherence of a radical sort means a systematic inability to deal with particulars, a confusion of procedure. It threatens thought itself. By the same token, it threatens nature itself, for the order of nature accepted at any historical period reflects the modes of making sense out of experience.

This threat to thought must, of course, turn up within thought. It occurs as conflict, the conflict of unreconciled demands of modes of apprehension. Accordingly, the origin of Western philosophy records the first self-conscious conflict. It was the problem of change. Events without unity made no sense. It was not until Plato's *Parmenides* that we received a document delicately aware that the ideal of complete unity would be no less frustrating than absolute variety. The history of philosophy is the record of such necessary conflicts.[7]

They are necessary because only in them is the presence of thought revealed. It seems plain that thought as "consciousness" has never been given a clean bill of health. Consciousness remains hidden, or else one finds it reduced to unconscious nature. It is only in self-consciousness that thought draws its own portrait. If it is possible to know thought it could be only by means of itself. Yet were thought "consciousness" it would be, as it has been, elusive, not capable of distinguishing between itself and nature. That was the position, and it is the meaning, of Berkeley. For Berkeley anticipated Hume in holding all "ideas" passive and hence without structure. The mind, or soul, alone was action, he believed, and for that reason could not show itself. Since what did show itself was only idea, the soul remained in Berkeley a dogmatic residuum. Allegedly active, its activity was recondite, never mirrored in the very content of consciousness.

It was Hegel who undertook a systematic study of conflicts. They are the phenomenology of the spirit, the modes of thought's reality and self-consciousness. The solution of any conflict, or rather its resolution, lies in realizing the necessity of the conflict. Each factor is highlighted by its antagonist, disclosing its imperative role only to the degree that it meets frustration. Consequently, each factor has a stake in its antagonist.

For example, *purpose* has a stake in *cause*. No purpose can define itself, nor can it secure execution, apart from the order of nature. Similarly, cause has a stake in purpose. No cause can be discovered in passivity and none can be demonstrated without experimental control. Each needs the other, and thought needs both. In its concreteness, an event in nature appeals elliptically to the purpose or the act by which it secures organization.

Consider the position of skepticism as a further illustration. The skeptic denies affirmation. The verb *to be* equals the verb *to seem*. Yet skepticism must live in a haunted house, forever invoking the ghost of nature as the means of securing its own vivid isolation. It is haunted by its denial. At the same time, skepticism is the very position that thought must first take in order to distinguish itself from nature. It is the systematic and necessary discovery of the omnipresence of thought. No one can be a philosopher who has failed to experience the force of skepticism. Dogmatism is only the illegitimate escape from skepticism, a very common procedure. Until thought finds its own features in its antagonist, dogmatism and skepticism remain the two unavoidable basic philosophies, although their forms be protean.

These conflicts bring out the factors of structure in discourse. They indicate the ways of thought, and hence the elements of organization and of criticism. They are the evidence of responsibility because they are a threat to one's own coherence. They have no imperative except that of one's own self-assertion. One cannot induce anyone to accept such conflicts. They reveal their imperative quality only because they cannot be induced in others. It seems plain that no one can feel as his own predicament what his very self does not propose and demand. The practice of teaching philosophy by argument is widespread. But any such procedure is the plainest evidence that nothing necessary can result. The quality of philosophy is not strained. Its authority and compulsion must wait on each person's acknowledgment of his own identity with its problems. Its force is derived from the discovery that all compulsion occurs as the demand of some aspect of organization. The willingness to assume risks of disorder for the sake of allowing imperatives to make themselves clear is the mark of the philosophic spirit. There is no conventional philosophy, but only the free discovery by the individual of his own reality through a wholly free activity.

Consequently, the progress of philosophy must wait on historical events. As we build lives and states on some view of order, we let loose on ourselves the consequences of any flaw in that view. If a man's world runs smoothly he can have no philosophic problems. Only as events with which he has identified himself and his hopes threaten his own outlook with destruction can he begin to take stock. This is the rationale of the comic and the tragic.

V

In politics we are today struggling to secure free institutions. But it is obvious that, to use a phrase of Walt Whitman's, we have no "metaphysics of democracy."[8] Indeed, our currently successful doctrines repudiate metaphysics, alleging that democracy is the triumph over such fantasies.

Yet even the democratic man must have dignity. Sovereignty, whether monarchial or democratic, needs sanction. This sanction turns on the responsibility of the sovereign, and on reverence for his pronouncements. One does not escape tyranny by multiplying irresponsible and subjective arbitrariness. Every man may be a king; but in our time a king must be a constitutional authority. He must carry responsibility in his person. It is a great illusion to suppose that government will protect rights when actual individuals display nothing but desires in their wills, and nothing but opinions in their minds. Such doctrines paralyze resolve. They are degenerate, and they invite the conqueror and the despot. What shows men to be free is their capacity to recognize and revise the grounds of their choices and of their opinions.

There is just one quality in every man that he must change at least once; he must change his philosophy. Only in the discovery of some fatal threat to himself in the framework of his inheritance can he discover freedom. There alone does he confront a necessary and an absolute problem, one proposed by himself and suffered in himself. Freedom is not, as so many have said, in choice; it is rather the revision of the basis of choice. What a man chooses, what he believes, can easily be reduced to psychology and to circumstance. But the complex structure through which choice occurs can never be. Psychologists know this. That is why psychology denies meaning to the universal and the critical.

Philosophy must join men of action, the history-makers. But philosophy is too ancient and too informed to suppose that history is made by the moralists or the purveyors of circuses. It is made by those who have not shrunk from the conflicts that challenge a present outlook, who have seen those conflicts through in physics and in politics. Those conflicts are the phenomenology of the spirit, the stations of its career, the secular stations of the cross. It is this story that is both history and philosophy. Argument saves a man from himself, from the ultimate loneliness where he finds his freedom.[9] Argument is never fatal. It makes no history. But philosophy is the actuality of those conflicts that establish the grounds on which arguments occur and by which they are regulated. That lies beyond argument and proof. It is the career of the self-conscious and the generation of outlooks.

This, I suggest, is the base of a philosophy of freedom. This is the only universal common to all minds. One need respect no man because he eats and drinks. One is not compelled by his psychology. But one must be concerned with him insofar as he stands forward as one who has come to himself, and through his conflicts has paid the price.

Politically, the future will be oriented on the problem of winning power for each man. This is not power over nature, but power of one man over another, and every other. But power of that sort can never be physically enforced. It must proceed from respect. And respect can be bought only at the price of that inner conflict through which a man's life becomes the forfeit of his truth.

What Kant proposed was the capacity of thought to police itself. He did not carry out that idea. Since then it has grown. Since then the idea of history has been brought into the open. History is the order of the unique. It declares the efficacy of time in the meaning of events. Physics and logic do not do this. History is the vindication of inwardness, the record of its daring and of its transforming victories. The idealism of the future will be a philosophy of history, of action, of a self-generating, lawful finitude. Such are the conditions of a metaphysics of democracy.

NOTES

1. Introduction to *A Treatise Concerning the Principles of Human Knowledge* (1710. Oxford, UK: Oxford University Press, 1998).
2. *A Treatise of Human Nature* (1739. Oxford, UK: Oxford University Press, 2000), Part 4, Section 6, "Of Personal Identity."
3. This "self-limiting" capacity is *criticism.*
4. See "The Transcendental Deduction" in *Critique of Pure Reason* (1781, 1787. Trans. and eds. Paul Guyer and Allen W. Wood, New York: Cambridge University Press, 1998), with particular emphasis on Kant's account of the transcendental unity of apperception.
5. See Royce's *The World and the Individual*, Series 1–2 (1899. Gloucester, MA: Peter Smith, 1976).
6. The brand of empiricism most prominent in Miller's day was *logical positivism.* Logical positivism attacked metaphysics and emphasized the logical analysis of scientific knowledge. What is termed the *verifiability principle* did most of the philosophical work for logical positivists. This principle sorted legitimate knowledge into two classes: (1) mathematics and logic (analytic and deductive) and (2) empirical science (synthetic and inductive). Philosophical statements, because they do not fit into either of these categories, were dismissed as meaningless. The new, positivistic philosophy claimed not to make statements but rather to clarify the statements made within the two classes of legitimate knowledge.
7. As Miller makes clear in "The Scholar as Man of the World" (Part 3, below), philosophy is interested in these conflicts because they "are the fatalities of thought and it is the philosophical task to lend itself to these fatalities in order to understand them, and so to reconcile them. The pathos of our deeper antagonisms lies in this fact, that they are always the signs of what we must respect, namely some essay at a rational world. Philosophy is the reason that seeks to comprehend the loci of the breakdown of reason."

8. Whitman's reference to a metaphysics of democracy is found in *Democratic Vistas*
    (1867. In *Poetry and Prose*, Justin Kaplan, ed., New York: Library of America, 1982).
    Whitman writes that "a new Literature, perhaps a new Metaphysics, certainly a
    new Poetry, are to be, in my opinion, the only sure and worthy supports and expres-
    sions of the American Democracy" (p. 984).

9. The themes of existentialism (for example, loneliness, individuality, responsibility,
    and action) pervade Miller's work. In an essay titled "Motives in Existentialism"
    (Miller Papers 3:1), Miller makes it clear that he appreciates certain qualities of the
    existential temperament and recognizes how this philosophical movement fits the
    post–World War II era. Miller's sympathies are limited, however. Because of his
    stress on community and rationality, Miller could not subscribe to the sense of iso-
    lation and of the absurd so prominent in existentialism.

Freedom as a Characteristic of Man in a Democratic Society

Following "Idealism and Freedom," this paper develops the idea of a *metaphysics of democracy*. Such a metaphysics articulates, as Miller states here, "those conditions in which men can influence others insofar as those others are in charge of themselves." Echoing Aristotle's words from the *Politics*, the present discussion deepens the basis and the implications of the equality and reciprocity underlying that ancient description of citizenship.

The problem posed by Miller is a standard one: How, in an age committed to empirical science and its often reductive descriptions of human activity, can political *science* account for freedom and responsibility even as it details the order and structure of human affairs? While the problem is standard, Miller's response is not. Charting a course between empirical and rational accounts of intersubjective relations, his aim is not to dissolve the difficulty. The intent is to maintain the difficulty as a productive and revelatory tension residing in as well as between individual persons.

Availing himself of the resources of a historicist and semiotic vocabulary, Miller offers an important sketch of democracy understood as a *community of criticism*. This community is one in which persons are defined by and invested in common symbolic instruments, practices, and institutions whereby persons simultaneously exercise control and are subject to control. Because they are mediated by the midworld of symbols and founded in the historical career of their critical revision, the most deeply held personal commitments turn out to be the most widely shared. Elsewhere Miller refers to this form of relationship and association as a "community of power."

The occasion for this essay (Miller Papers 1:7) was a meeting of the American Political Science Association that occurred at the University of Chicago in 1948. Along with the other presenters at the conference, Miller was invited to read a paper on the topic of freedom. The text of this essay first appeared in a slightly different form in The Paradox of Cause and Other Essays *(pp. 97–105). The phrase "community of power" appears on page 189 of* The Definition of the Thing with Some Notes on Language.

I

It may seem plausible, or even obvious, that any view of man that qualifies him to establish a democratic society will endow him with reason and self-control. And yet, the common phrase *human nature* likewise suggests that the defining trait of man is not his autonomy, but rather a set of fixed properties found by observation and experiment. These properties, one supposes, can thereupon be exploited by the social engineers. And so I wish in the first place to examine the status of "nature" and of things that have a "nature" in order to relate the concept of man's "nature" to that of his freedom.

A principal feature of modern man is his control over the immediate environment. The manifestation and proof of that control are found in technology. For us, as men of this time, the real world is the region of controllable objects and predictable events. To that region of experience and knowledge we give the name *nature*, and most of our pedagogy assumes this region as the suitable locus of reliable inquiry. We are likely to feel that all knowledge has nature as its content and object. Furthermore, we are committed to a procedure for getting knowledge that directs our attention and our criteria on this common objective order.

Insofar as we discover what we call *facts* we appeal to that region, and what is not found there meets suspicion. Its general properties we take to be described by physics, and, although there appear to be living "organisms" among the dead "mechanisms" of nature, we are intellectually disposed to reduce the living to the dead. The reduction of biology to chemistry or physics seems a proper conquest of knowledge, and so an opportunity for power and control. In general, we suffer intellectual embarrassment in proposing as knowledge any story that employs an organizing vocabulary other than that suitable for the region of objects.

We want knowledge to be only report, in which every element of value has been laid aside. In this way, a study of human nature becomes at best a description of a peculiar sort of objective event.

Of objects, or types of objects, we say that each has a *nature*. By this we mean that it is identifiable through the uniformities of its changes and in its consequent entanglement with other changes in a single and infinite order.

If we speak, in this context, of human nature, consistency and analogy suggest that man, too, is an object of knowledge, and consequently controllable, as are all other facts of nature.

Politics, being a control of human nature, rightly seeks an understanding of what is to be controlled. And when politics comes to be called "political science," there is a strong presumption that human nature would best lend itself to management if it were to have a fixed, objective, and reportorial character like salt or marble, or the motion of the heavenly bodies. It is not uncommon to look for such a fixed nature in psychology, as in lists of instincts and in the laws of the learning process. What to attempt in society or politics becomes a corollary of what man in fact is. Just so, in laying up a wall one takes into consideration the proper mixture of sand, gravel, and cement.

For example, the well-known solution of Thomas Hobbes to the question of government turns on his unflattering view of human nature, the life of man being "solitary, poor, nasty, brutish, and short."[1] Hobbes did see man as possessed in fact, whether one liked it or not, of a measure of reason, whereby man could manage his more anarchistic tendencies to his larger advantage. I mention Hobbes only to furnish an example of a typical procedure, namely one that begins by showing what man in fact is, in order, secondly, to bring him under control.

There is no doubt that this sort of approach to the question of political order has great influence. Control, we rightly assume, depends on knowledge, and so in turn on an objective report of a "nature," in this case human nature. Yet this procedure causes misgiving, since it places human nature in the same class as all other objects, subject to ambiguous manipulations in the interests of ends that it does not, as object, define. So neither does salt determine its use as condiment or preservative, or calcium carbonate as doorstep or gravestone. Although devoted to scientific procedures, we hesitate to accept the status of an object. This is the difficulty imposed by assigning to man a "nature" and then subjecting it to control.

This difficulty involves an old ambiguity. For the concept of human nature appears at both ends of a transaction. It appears first as the factual and objective "nature" that is to be managed, and then secondly as the very source of the values that are to exercise direction and control. To preserve the problem it is necessary to make this distinction, while to keep the distinction is to abandon the essay at strictly objective definition of human nature.

There have been many attempts to avoid this dilemma by viewing the values and the controllers of society as themselves nothing more than examples of quite factual or natural instincts or propensities. This is a technique that casts doubt on the validity and authority of all control by man over himself and others. The hero's alleged authority reduces to the facts about human nature, and therefore converts power into impotence, vision into blindness, and control itself into passivity. It is a case of the blind leading the blind.

The frequency of the *argumentum ad hominem* in political controversy discloses the prevalence of this method for the understanding of human nature.[2] We find the free economy represented as a conspiracy to secure profits; the national state we see as a plot that, by means of fraud, force, and favor, and by use of suitable seductive symbols, lures men away from the scientific truths about themselves. But, on the other side, those who promise to make "every man a king" are in no better case. They themselves are victims of a ruthless lust for power—seductively disguised as benevolence. Whether one be counted as right wing or left wing, there seems always ready at hand an explanation in terms of the nature of man, for example, that rightists are a greedy lot, and the leftists pathologically adrift, frustrated men in a world they never made, who must destroy every vestige of independence in others so that their own personal nonentity can never be discovered. In these ways, good and evil alike become meaningless to the reportorial method. And so the problem of the fitness of human nature for democracy, or for any other final end, becomes absurd.

It was Francis Bacon who proposed that "knowledge is power." He, likewise, took knowledge to be confined to nature, and he died, it is said, from a cold contracted in an experiment to test the preservative effect of refrigeration on meat. Since Bacon's death in 1636 we have come a long way in knowledge and in the type of control it yields. Today, our knowledge of nature threatens to destroy us all, and our knowledge of man reduces control to an illusion and a menace. How far this mistrust of knowledge has moved can be gauged from the frequent and derogatory use of the phrase "power politics."

To mistrust power is to mistrust knowledge. Except as will-less contemplation, knowledge can result only in action, that is, at an attempt at control. It is this dilemma that underlies Arthur Koestler's book *The Yogi and the Commissar*. One can do anything one likes with knowledge of objects except one thing: One cannot by its means define the free man or the democratic society. So it comes to this, that man fears destruction from his physics and an emasculated will from psychology. Nor should we flatter ourselves that the sharp-eyed explorers of illusion can offer a remedy. For their truth is that of natural knowledge, and they can only stare at the facts where no trace of value can either define aspiration or guide fulfillment.

In summary: "Nature to be commanded must be obeyed."[3] The obedience, however, is for the sake of the command. Knowledge seeks power, and conformity, control. It is command, power, and control that are difficult to define in the context of report.

II

The average citizen exhibits complacency rather than distress over the democratic process. It is those with a theoretical bent who sometimes express misgivings and even despair over the meaning of such words as *freedom* and *self-direction*. For these words do not find definition in the context of scientific report. They suggest willfulness and egoism, and allege a type of control neither statistical nor causal. How is nature, particularly human nature, to be commanded?

The problem of power in a democracy involves the control of men over each other. Yet, one may distrust all such power. It has often been remarked that power corrupts. Consequently, it may be proposed that men be stripped of all power over each other. It is, of course, true that power corrupts. Nothing else can. Impotence can do no harm, nor, of course, any good. Politics is a science of the power of men over themselves and over others. Its meaning vanishes when human nature lacks self-assertion and the passionate egoism that is the spring of all control.

There occurs in this most individualistic age a deep mistrust of power, as, for example, in the national state, even though it be democratic. It is felt in various quarters that the state must wither away, leaving either a bland anarchy or a parliament of man, where nothing is intolerable except having a will of one's own. Such proposals reflect the suspicion we feel of the power of man over himself and over others.

Insofar as man is described as having a "nature," these suspicions seem to me entirely proper. There is no account of man as a fact, or as a part of the region of objects, that can exhibit him as possessed of both power and responsibility. Natural forces are not responsible forces. The naturalistic account of man can only view every pretense of power as an illusion and as a menace. Political science on those premises can set for itself only one task—that of stripping man of this irresponsible illusion. This is a purpose in which, by a curious irony, both naturalists and supernaturalists are in agreement.

Whatever view of man deprives him of power over himself and others solves the political problem by abolishing it. When men are viewed as objects, command becomes simply a mistaken idea, for it violates the condition on which human nature is presumably discovered, namely, as fact and uniformity. Man becomes lost in his "nature," and so far from being in a position to rule others, he cannot even rule himself.

III

On what conditions, then, can one tell a story of man as the locus of responsible power? In terms of the preceding analysis one way of answering this question is barred. It is the way that would look for political and democratic qualifications in objective peculiarities.

A clue to those activities that incorporate both power and responsibility may be found in the identification of the occurrence of tyranny.

One locus of tyranny is revealed in obstacles to the investigation of nature. Science is power not only as a means for technology, but as a primary exhibition of responsible thought. Wherever men by doctrine or by law forbid or hamper the investigation of nature, we detect the mark of oppression and degradation. For science is much more than an enlargement of animal learning. It is also the primary and the most solid region of community. It is not a community of custom, ritual, or habit, or an anthropological pattern of behavior. It is a community of minds in which men exercise power over each other through their vulnerability to criticism. And it is through this freely assumed liability to error that respect is established and men become ends in themselves. No threats, not even those of death and hell-fire, have stayed the mind of man from these adventures. Nor can any promise of bread and circuses summon the energies for the disciplined and ascetic clarification of our common world.

Nature is sometimes debased into a static fact. Any such premise is fatal for the political guidance of free men. Nature is, on the contrary, a historic achievement, always changing in its outlines, and even in its logic. The political scientist who bases his view of man on what he takes to be scientific truth is making a grave error. For all views of nature are achievements, and the mechanical view, itself only three centuries old, and now assailed by positivism, is itself a product of reason. One finds human nature not as an episode within the latest account of physics, but rather, I believe, in those energies and values to which physics owes its genesis and its historical transformations.

I would ask you to consider how a person feels his own reality. Is it otherwise than in effectiveness, that is, in the exercise of power? Impotence and freedom are mutually exclusive. A premise of the democratic man is his individual reality in the exercise of influence on others. This, I submit, is the goal of politics for free men—*to create those conditions in which men can influence others insofar as those others are in charge of themselves.* This need is at the bottom of our liberties, of our rights, and of our nonarbitrary powers.

Above all, what characterizes the free man is his capacity and determination to make history. It is not the static truth that makes men free. In that static guise the truth always enslaves. It is rather in the *revision* of truth that freedom is found. Furthermore, static truth abolishes community. The revision of truth is the maintenance of community, not, of course, the anthropological or sociological community, but the community of free men. One cannot argue or deal with static modes of truth. In history, we see the awful, but responsible, spectacle of man's reinterpretations of himself and of nature, and reassessment of our heritage. One can inherit neither truth nor freedom. Every heritage must be understood in its own creative motives and then overpassed in amendment and revision. We cannot escape nature, but neither can we escape history.[4]

These general properties of the democratic man entail many corollaries. As a first consequence may be mentioned the maintenance of systematic thought or inquiry, since only order can be revised, and only the pretension to responsible order can create both humility and accessibility.

A second corollary is this: There must be preserved nonpolitical sources of power, as the centers of privacy and as the authority for the criticism of political institutions. Government is the form of community, but not its substance. It is the sign of the absoluteness of a self-regulating privacy. Politics waxes exuberant and possessive. Modes of nonpolitical self-assertion occur in science, social groups such as the family and private clubs, and in religion and commerce. Man is indeed a social animal, but it would, I believe, be a mistake to interpret his primary sociability as political. When that mistake is made, there is nothing for it but to treat man as an object, and then he is devoured by the managers who, one hears, know best how to establish community. The state is rather the organization, and the express recognition, of the nonpolitical modes of personal actuality and influence. From this condition flow the authority and the mission of the free state. To extend this recognition is the history-making task of free governments.

A third corollary can be offered: Democratic man seeks responsible power without asserting a fixed goal.[5] This is the quality of risk. Security of any sort, made absolute, is the stifling of freedom. A risky but creative adventure is the man himself. When, by means of action, including experiment, we define our world, we see only oblivion in security. Cosmic security is an anachronism. Personal security is the denial of adventure, the obliteration of personality.

In summary, human nature has no static, objective, or merely cognitive definition. Knowledge is power, but the sort of knowledge sought in politics concerns those traits that allow one, insofar as one is in charge of oneself, to influence others insofar as they, too, are in charge of themselves. Science and history-making are among the major actualities of such power. In consequence, three corollaries were mentioned—the need for systematic thought, for nonpolitical loci of self-government, and finally for risk or adventure. I may conclude with a sentence of José Ortega y Gasset: "Man has no nature; he has only a history."[6]

NOTES

1. See *Leviathan* (1651. London: Penguin, 1985), Part I, chapter 13.
2. Argumentation *ad hominem* (against the man) is, to Miller's mind, not always a fallacy of logic. Argumentation must address each person and so, in a conflict, must also in some important sense be *against* that person. The attack presumes the authority that resides in the person. The sort of ad hominem argumentation that Miller supports addresses our fundamental (and deeply personal) commitments to forms of order such as logic, language, and law.
3. The allusion is to Bacon's statement, in the third aphorism of his *Novum Organum* (1624. Trans. Peter Urbach and John Gibson, Chicago: Open Court, 1994), that "nature is only subdued by submission."
4. See Abraham Lincoln's Annual Message to Congress of 1862, in which he prepared Congress and the nation for his final Emancipation Proclamation of 1863 (in *Speeches and Writings, 1859–1865*, Don E. Fehrenbacher, ed., New York: Library of America,

1989). Lincoln stated near the close of his 1862 address: "Fellow-citizens, we cannot escape history. We of this Congress and this administration, will be remembered in spite of ourselves. . . . The fiery trial through which we pass, will light us down, in honor or dishonor, to the latest generation" (p. 415).

5. One of the fundamental commitments of democracy is to procedure. In "Utopia and the State" (Part 3, below), Miller writes that the liberal state "describes no fait accompli, but an endeavor, and a procedure." Authoritarian states determine the ends and rig the process to achieve these ends. Liberal states, like other formal communities of inquiry, establish principles and procedures and then allow those procedures to do their work. This is, at root, what John Rawls meant when he wrote of "Justice as fairness" (*Justice as Fairness: A Restatement*, Erin Kelly, ed., Cambridge, MA: Belknap Press, 2001). For Miller, another level of procedure is the self-critical process where a community of inquiry revises the basic terms of inquiry. In the liberal state this translates into the revision of the political constitution.

6. Ortega y Gasset makes this statement in his essay "History as a System," in *History as a System and Other Essays Toward a Philosophy of History* (1941. Trans. Helene Weyl, New York: Norton, 1961).

On Choosing Right and Wrong

In "The Absolute Authority of Criticism," in Part 1, Miller describes his methodology as the "rigorous analysis of the finite point of view." A fine example of this mode of philosophizing, these pages combine the transcendental style of questioning into the conditions of experience with a dialectical form of inquiry. At once Kantian and Socratic in spirit, this form of analysis is a hybrid methodology. Here it is employed to make a fundamental point about not only moral experience but also experience as such.

As for moral experience, Miller asserts that one must resist thinking of right and wrong as if they were *choices* of action. Illustrating his antipathy to those doctrinaire types for whom being right and telling the truth are ultimate values, Miller resists making morality into a matter of moraliz*ing*. (In this regard, something important is shared between Miller's outlook and Friedrich Nietzsche's *Beyond Good and Evil*.) This is not a premise in an argument for amorality, however. One cannot be indifferent to the distinction between right and wrong. Rather Miller sets the dyad of right and wrong *beyond* choice precisely because it is a condition of moral experience. Each of us has the responsibility of discerning the right in particular situations. None of us, however, has a choice but to think and act in light of the moral terms constituting the "form of finitude," one's actuality, of which the dyad of right and wrong is a part.

The actuality to which Miller refers can be compared to those environing customs, laws, and institutions that G. W. F. Hegel gathers together under the heading of *Sittlichkeit*. Yet it must be noted that this concrete ethics contains and is in an important respect formed by an intuition of *Moralität*. "The interest in morals derives from the prospect of freedom," Miller observes in a relevant passage from "The Occasion of Study in Morals." "We wish above all to be effective, to count for something. We would avoid inconsequence by becoming agents and doers." Terms such as *right* and *wrong* are not only part of the fate of being a member of a community but, properly understood, mark out the grounds for the sort of effective action to which we all aspire. This is the import of Miller's call to maintain the *conditions* of choice.

The analysis of moral experience holds important clues for understanding experience as such. Implicit in this argument that right and wrong are beyond choice is the larger but analogous claim that the basic conditions of all our common endeavors are not precisely chosen and, thus, are in an important respect beyond reason. Just as Miller's statement on moralizing cannot be interpreted as a plea for immorality, this assertion regarding reason does not amount to an argument for irrationality. The "form of finitude," the actuality of which Miller writes, is certainly not rational insofar as *reason* is equated with the construction and carrying out of hypothetical imperatives—that is, practical reason in its Habermasian sense. Nor can it be considered to be rational if *rationality* is defined as that which is subject to causal explanation. Actuality cannot be approached by reason in these modes because it is a necessity or fate—that is, the fund and burden of meaning that one inherits as a member of a community. (It is one's *world* as Miller uses that term in "The Scholar as a Man of the World.") This fate is structured by thought and action, and it comes to our attention, as Miller notes in the unpublished essay "History and the Sense of Fate," "where our own activity, whether thought or will, encounters systematic restriction." Not amenable to the tinkering of practical reason or liable to causal description, fate is open to understanding, interpretation, and revision carried out by reason in its philosophical mode. It is precisely this form of reason that this essay brings to the fore.

Dated December 27, 1956, this essay (Miller Paper 4:22) previously appeared in a slightly different form in the journal Idealistic Studies *(vol. 21, no. 1 [1992]: pp. 74–78). Pertinent to this discussion of choice is the 1954 essay "Ends and Means: The Realm of Means" (Miller Papers 14:8). The essay "Truth Tellers and Story Tellers" of 1971 (Miller Papers 55:3) addresses the difference between morality and moralizing, while "History and the Sense of Fate" of 1955 is another relevant work (Miller Papers 4:15).*

It is a dreadful thing to see men, especially men in public life, parade the superiority of their moral choice. It is dreadful because it leaves one helpless. One knows one can't differ with them on the basis named, namely a choice of good over evil. You can talk to a man who chooses IBM for a rise in the market, but not to a man who chooses right or wrong, or says he does. Discourse collapses.

Choice requires alternatives, that is, alternative acts, one's own or another's. One chooses to do this rather than that, or to have it done by someone else. The choice of alternative acts is quite without parallel in the ideas of good and evil. The choice of ways of going to New York City—and all true alternative courses of action—is based on a specific purpose. Going to New York is not investing one's money or cultivating a garden. But there is no specific purpose that occasions the alleged alternative of good and evil. Neither of them is the prolongation of an act already in existence.

Right and wrong, or good and evil, do not then stand for alternative possibilities of action. An alternative represents at least two programs of action, either of which could be executed. If I am going to New York City I can go to either Albany, New York, or Greenfield, Massachusetts, get to the station at the appropriate time, board the appropriate train, and so on. I could do either, and either act is compatible with the order and security of the world and of my experience. The choice is made apropos of my purpose to go to New York. The purpose guides me to the alternatives. In the case of *good* and *evil* there is no analogous situation with antecedent concern and two eligible alternatives. By the same token, neither *good* nor *bad* is a specific mode of carrying out a purpose. Choosing good is to make no actual exclusion of acts or programs. But taking the train is very different from buying 100 shares of mutual stock or spading a corner of one's yard.

I

It is usually supposed that a choice of good and evil is very important. The very heavens are involved. Not so with actual and practical alternatives. There was no great consequence, for example, in the fact that I did not go to New York. Indeed, most people in the village did not go. It is usually supposed, too, that a choice of good and evil is a peculiar mark of man. But many do not choose to go to New York and yet suffer no loss of human status as a result. It is also usually supposed that the choice of good and evil is somehow forced on one. But any usual and specific choice is not forced. I do not have to decide about taking trains from Albany or Greenfield. Why not, if there be an analogy, ignore the choice of good or evil? Why can one not have other business than is involved in making *that* choice?

The difference appears to lie in the fact that purposes that propose the need of choices can be changed. When the purposes are changed, the particular choice is not even proposed. But the alleged choice of good and evil is always relevant, so that it again bears no similarity to choices based on purposes that are specific. Its seems, too, that some value factor (good and evil) is present in *all* acts. Acts involve preferences, appraisals, acceptance, and reflection. But taking the train from Albany is not a factor present in all acts. Good and evil, by contrast, somehow define the possibility of any action. No choice-worthy alternatives do that. Where there is choice there is only the possibility that action will involve either alternative. But good and evil are, in contrast, part of the actual, that is, of the meaning and existence of an act, of any act.

Further specific differences can be noted.

All normal and specific choices come to an end. One goes on to something else. But there is no way of defining the performance of good and evil alternatives so that they terminate. They never terminate. But a train from Albany arrives in New York and one gets off.

Ordinary choices are proposed by one's fortune and by what one happens to be, and by what one happens to know. In contrast, the choice of good and evil is alleged to be made by all regardless of fortune or accident. Ordinary choices reveal what one is in particular, but the alleged choice of good and evil never does and is, in fact, explicitly declared to be universal.

In ordinary choice, the alternatives, although different, are both eligible. That is, all alternatives contribute to the purpose that proposes them. One can go to New York by Greenfield even though one can prefer Albany. In the case of good and evil, the situation is not parallel. A *good* way and an *evil* way are not both eligible activities in continuation of a purpose to which either contributes. One renounces the devil and all his works and pomps, but one does not renounce going to New York by Greenfield. It might prove agreeable some day, and properly, soberly, and easily so. No choice-worthy rejection is ever absolute, nor is any choice-worthy acceptance, either.

A similar consideration is to the effect that no choice-worthy alternatives are annihilative of each other. They are different, but not destructive. You do not have to discontinue the route from Greenfield because you are taking the train from Albany. The situation that allows for Greenfield is not inimical to the Albany route. Drinking tea and drinking coffee may be two compatible acts, that is, compatible in the same world, and even supportive of each other. But good and evil are not only different means to achieve a common end; they are mutually exclusive. This is contrary to the situation of choice.

In ordinary choice, furthermore, the activity proposed in the choice may lead to a revision or even removal of the launching purpose. I may find that it costs too much to go to New York, that it is troublesome to find someone to look after the house, that I do not want to borrow, beg, or steal the money for the fare, or that I would prefer to use the money in another way. Every chosen action is, then, hypothetical and can lead to the revision or removal of its urgent purpose.[1] Yet, assuming that it made sense to set about doing good, nobody suggests that in doing good one may find the game not worth the candle. (Nobody, that is, but the amoralist.) If virtue were a choice it should be possible to find that it could force one to drop or revise the interest that recommended, or indicated, the choice between acting virtuously and acting viciously. But in fact virtue or good are not similar to ordinary choices in their capacity to recognize and then to revise or drop the very interest that proposed the choice.

II

Only if the purpose that suggests choice is itself tentative can the choice be rational. For an absolute purpose the choices of execution or fulfillment are equally absolute. That is to say, choice, as a selection of alternatives, is irrelevant to an absolute purpose. To go absolutely to New York may take one by way of Tokyo. Why not? What can one say against it? One can say nothing against it, except as one is not exclusively a goer to New York but also a doer of a lot of other activities. Yet, pursuing the analogy, what is one other than someone engaged in that activity—whatever it may be—that leads to a choice between good and evil? If one is not other things too, the purpose leading to the choice becomes absolute and so abolishes the choice. If it is not absolute, then the choice of good and evil is like any other and can be made or not, as may be. The situation leading to the choice of good and evil is not tentative, whereas all other choices are tentative and must be so as a condition of rational choice.

One must make choices, while no particular choice is itself predetermined in its presence or its outcome. That one confronts a given choice is conditional. That one must make it one or another way is conditional also. It is like logic: One must reason, but what a particular person reasons about and what answers he then finds are conditional. In logic this recognition is explicit. *If* p, then, perhaps q or $\sim q$. Thus, both the origin (p) and the conclusion (q or $\sim q$) are conditional. Still, one must reason. Yet one reasons not about truth and falsity, but about the consequences of p, and then only *if* one considers p rather than l, m, n, and o.

Thus *if* you are headed for New York, you can consider Albany and Greenfield. But in point of fact it is you, not I, who go to New York. It is possible that I will never go there. That choice is not for me now, and may never be for me. Of course I too must choose, but if you name and specify any actual choice I may never have to make it. By contrast, I cannot reason myself into the conclusion that reasoning is a valid result of anterior assumptions; I cannot choose to be in a situation where choices are to be made.

No specific choice is then necessary. That it is *not* necessary is a necessary condition of its being deliberate, calm, and objective. It is because I do not have to go to New York that I can consider alternatives. I am free to consider alternatives, calmly and dispassionately, only if the going is also what I do and does not define myself as being. Going there is a possibility, not a necessity. Otherwise going to New York becomes an obsession. In an obsession one becomes an automaton. One is compelled. The action is a compulsion. Cost what it may, I must go to New York. The choice of means no longer functions as a restraint on the going. The importance of the means is lost. On the other hand, means, too, can, without systematic obstacles, become obsessive. How best to go to New York has no meaning where the object is absolute. One is only going to New York. That is all one is doing. Yet if one says that is not all one is doing, then going to New York becomes itself conditional, and is no longer absolute. Unless there is a reason for going to New York, no question of means can be raised. But if there is a reason for going, then the means can be contemplated as adequate to the reason or as destructive of the reason. The one thing they can't be, if there is a reason for going, is irrelevant to the reason for going. That is fanaticism, and then choice vanishes.

Thus, there can be no choice where one considers an absolute purpose. The price of choice is a conditional purpose. Every deliberate choice requires a conditional purpose.

III

The moral is the maintenance of rational choice, that is, of conditional ends, and so of conditional means, where both ends and means are determinate and specific. The nonmoral is the loss of such activities, as in children and the insane. The immoral is the treatment of a possibility without reference to the finite actuality that gives one identity and limitation. The metaphysical setting of morality is the absoluteness of the conditions that permit rational choice—that is, the integrity of finitude as one's personal actuality. These metaphysical conditions are not chosen. Nobody chooses the actual circumstances in which his morality is to be exhibited. This is only to say that the actual cannot be objectified, treated from some point of view that is itself without actuality, concreteness, and limitation. The man from Mars is not a moral agent, except on Mars, and then he reverts to actuality, a Martian, not a lunar or mundane actuality. Nobody, however, chooses to be a Martian or an Earthling.

Without actuality there is no basis of choice. Nothing in particular follows from any nonfinite absolute—no conclusion without premises; no choice without actuality. The rule of cause explains nothing in particular.[2] Only the particular explains, justifies, and certifies the particular. No experiment in a lab is "true" because of the causal rule. No act is right or wrong because of a moral rule. Reason maintains the articulate thought; morality maintains the articulate act.

The difference between right and wrong (or truth and falsity) is entirely formal. Neither right nor wrong can be objectified. There is no position that can be made articulate that is neither right nor wrong in terms of which each becomes tentative. No actual man can step as onto an Archimedean platform, apart from his actuality, praise it, condemn it, or ignore it. To have no stake in any actuality is to forbid judgment on any actuality. Right and wrong are aspects of actuality and develop from it.

IV

If the wages of sin are death,[3] then there is more reason in the maintenance of life than in its abandonment. Reason and choice deal in possibilities, but neither is itself a possibility. Virtue can't be certified; it has no rational alternative. It is not, like a particular choice, what one could defend. A choice, however, can be defended. It is the defended alternative. And, as above, if not defended it is no choice, but an automatism or obsession.

No man knowingly does evil, that is, chooses evil.[4] But that is not because he chooses good, but because he chooses neither good nor evil. It is a characteristic of Plato that he was in no position to articulate this common irrelevance. He did feel its impropriety, in saying that the enthusiast was superior to the sober man, and in preferring dialectic to understanding. Perhaps this is the difference between Socrates and Plato so far as articulation goes. In spirit, even Socrates simply maintained the vigorous life.

The very essence of ethics is to show that good and evil are not choices. This is the lesson of moral history. It is people who allege that they can choose who are either weakly unsure or harshly overbearing. What you choose is tentative. It can be revised. It must be, if rational, in a position to be revised. But am I to conclude that I might better have chosen wrong? And, if wrong is a choice, how could one deny that possibility? I say it is impossible to choose wrong, and also that it is impossible to choose right. This is an altogether meaningless frame of reference.

I remember when I was a boy reading about a saint who said that anyone who had once perceived the glories could not but follow them. This puzzled me because I had been told that one chose. But I am not a moral Cartesian. I do not withdraw and choose. It is correct to say that nothing great is chosen. One does not choose to know math, logic, or art. Man is not to be managed, by others or by himself. He manages apropos of his actuality, but not by objectifying it and coming from Mars to see whether he will, on the whole, opt for virtue or for vice.

Responsibility is not chosen. Rule is not chosen. Nor is it simply arbitrary and irrelevant to finitude. It is the form of finitude. Right and wrong are formalities, wrong the destruction of formal conditions, chaos. But they are no more an option than are any other formalities.

Morality is the maintenance of the accessibility of minds. Education seems to make a mind accessible to mind. *"Il gran refiuto"* is the repudiation of that universal medium.[5] "There but for the grace of God go I" is a surly rule. "There, by the grace of God, I see myself too" is the moral and human rule.

NOTES

1. The reference to *hypothetical* brings to mind Immanuel Kant's distinction between hypothetical and categorical imperatives in *Grounding for the Metaphysics of Morals* (1785. Trans. James W. Ellington, Indianapolis, IN: Hackett, 1981). Hypothetical imperatives take the form of "If I want to be a concert violinist, then I must practice the violin every day." One may not want to be a concert violinist or may begin with the idea and then decide against it. The categorical imperative cannot be avoided. This is what Miller is looking for regarding right and wrong.
2. See "The Paradox of Cause" (*The Paradox of Cause*, pp. 11–18).
3. Romans 6:23.
4. See Plato, *Meno*, 77a–78b.
5. The reference to *Il gran refiuto* (the great no) is drawn from Dante Alighieri's *Inferno* (circa 1310. Trans. Michael Palma, New York: Norton, 2003), Canto 3, verses 58–60.

Tolerance and Its Paradoxes

The word *tolerance* connotes an abstention from judgment, a certain studied indifference. Examined further, one finds our habitual pleas for and appeals to tolerance to be underwritten by an intellectual and even aloof attitude (e.g., Thomas Jefferson, John Locke, and John Stuart Mill). The suggestion has consistently been that tolerance is synonymous with a general neutrality, a systematic refrain from judgment. In any given case, certainly, neutrality is possible; not all actions or commitments call forth judgments of assent or opposition. Yet universal tolerance is as impossible to maintain as are complete pacifism and total indifference. Such attitudes annihilate personhood. Miller thus seeks to discern "the other side of tolerance"—that is, the *commitments* grounding tolerance.

What stake does one have in tolerance? What cannot be tolerated by liberal tolerance? These questions lead Miller to revisit the matter explored by Josiah Royce in *The Philosophy of Loyalty*. In that work, Royce expanded the notion of loyalty beyond its more parochial, and sometimes pernicious, forms toward something he called "a loyalty to loyalty." This form of loyalty is encapsulated in the imperative that we always act such that our own loyalty to a given community or ideal augments the growth of similar commitments in others. What Royce aimed to express in this Kantian idiom was the need for loyalty to regulate itself in terms of a new form of the categorical imperative—that is, any given loyalty must not infringe on the loyalties of others; any specific loyalty, insofar as it is worthy of respect, must be universalizable in principle. The present treatment of tolerance is a variation on this theme. The twist in Miller's account lies in beginning not with loyalties that often divide us but rather with the idea of tolerance by which we seek to ameliorate our divisions. The different points of departure, however, cannot cover over the single concern animating the thought of both Miller and Royce. Both seek a form of universality that respects and enlivens individuality and locality.

In addressing this concern, the present essay stakes out a proposal that effectively summarizes the central points of the essays in Part 2 and reaches back to Part 1 for its basic principles. Tolerance is rooted in the liberal community, a community that is itself—despite its universal commitments—a particular historical order. The openness and freedom of the liberal democratic community must be, in its fashion, also a form of limitation, loyalty, and order. Liberalism embodies the paradox of historical idealism— that is, the union of the universal and the particular, the orderly and the original. The community of criticism that Miller, like Karl Popper, finds in the scientific community is a model for this dialectical union.

The present essay is drawn from an untitled essay draft penned in the 1940s (Miller Papers 7:14). Miller develops this general theme in an unpublished collection of notes written in 1941 (Miller Papers 12:1). An aspect of this discussion is treated in more detail in "Must Philosophers Disagree?" (Miller Papers 55:1). For classic treatments of the topic of tolerance see Locke's "A Letter Concerning Toleration" (1683. In The Second Treatise of Government and a Letter Concerning Toleration, *J. W. Gough, ed., Oxford, U.K.: Blackwell, 1976.), Jefferson's "Bill Establishing Religious Freedom" (1777. In* Writings, *Merrill D. Peterson, ed., New York: Library of America, 1984), and Mill's* On Liberty *(1859. Indianapolis, IN: Hackett, 1978). The work by Karl Popper most pertinent to the comparison made above is* The Open Society and Its Enemies *(1945. Princeton, NJ: Princeton University Press, 1971).*

A free country offers the opportunity for tolerated divergence of belief. Yet the idea of tolerance breaks out into paradoxes. For, on the one side, there would seem to be no point in raising tolerance to a principle of politics unless men seriously differed and, on the other side, there would seem no basis for demanding protection for one's beliefs unless one also professed an underlying identity of interest in all men.

It seems odd that the affirmation of community is most vehement and passionate apropos of the very disagreements that are most divisive. Apparently, it is the threat of making division absolute that throws us back on a darkly emotional assertion of a vague community. Christians differ among themselves on important theological matters, while Christians as a whole differ from Jews. Believers in the free economic market differ radically from communists, nationalists from internationalists, patriots from pacifists. They do not differ merely over the technical means for reaching an agreed goal; they differ in the goal itself, in the ideal they seek, and in their views of human excellence. Such varieties of attitude entail a corresponding variety in programs of action. To some extent they are antithetical and irreconcilable. Yet out of the depths of conflict we ask men to suppose that conflict doesn't fundamentally matter, that it is superficial, not ultimate.

Yet, another's program of action cannot be a matter of indifference when the success of that program would mean the extinction of all that one holds dear. Indeed, the traditional mark of character is the denial of the possibility of perpetual compromise. Somewhere one must take a stand. The history of all religions bears witness to this readiness for accepting a break with parents, friends, or state. Political reform has similarly involved the severance of diplomatic relations and the resolve to force a new birth of freedom on those who may seem to oppose it. We propose, then, to finish our tasks "with firmness in the right as God gives us to see the right."[1] To stand for nothing seems hardly the moral ideal; yet to stand firmly for a belief may entail a rejection—even a violent rejection of another's belief and program.

I

The precepts of morals appear to be in conflict with themselves. Morality seems hardly to be indifference. Yet, short of indifference, how is it possible to countenance the success of programs of action that negate one's ideals and destroy one's hopes?

The issue looms even sharper when one considers that the occasion for tolerance does not arise over mere ideas in the mind. Tolerance is a property of will, not of thought. It is true that one can be intolerant of ideas, but that happens only when ideas threaten to overthrow the basis of accepted action. A government is intolerant of such ideas as may entail its displacement; a church is intolerant of such ideas as threaten its hold, its powers, and its continuance. Thus, the need for tolerance arises over programs of action. The occasion for the maxim of tolerance is found in the conflict of ways of living, not in the region of mere ideas.

Of course, one may leave the issue to eternity. But that is abdication of the will, a confession of personal indifference to the issue of events and helplessness in guiding them. It is, further, a declaration that nothing matters in the end and so a denial of moral life. Confronted by those who say that practical arrangements do matter, is one in the name of tolerance to offer no opposition now? Is tolerance to be equivalent to a denial of earth's importance? To do the will of the Father who is in Heaven, for example, seems to suggest doing something; otherwise it would have been much simpler to counsel indifference to social arrangements, to have set no task, to have defined no properties of the moral life on this bank and shoal of time.

Thus is the ideal of tolerance a deeply paradoxical one. It is odd that it requires the immanence of conflict to suggest tolerance, that appeasement looms as most necessary where programs of action find no ground of compromise. Tolerance seems the remedy of disagreements that repudiate concessions. Its value is greatest where the reasons for it are weakest. It also seems to stand in conflict with the history of heroism and with the precepts of manly resolve. It invites a pacifism of the will, while at the same time proclaiming the need of a good will that, if it is to be different from no will at all, must launch into a deed. It recommends an ideal in behalf of which one apparently cannot act. It fixes its eye on a happy earthly condition, yet refuses to specify one condition as better than another or to act vigorously in securing its establishment. It promises to safeguard personality, yet extinguishes present deeds to overcome a present threat to personal values. In the end, it threatens to become a vehicle for destroying the privacy it advocates.

II

To these difficulties that befall the man of action and resolve the orthodox answer is in terms of thought or education. We can afford to wait. "The truth is great and will prevail. Whether men will that it prevail or not."[2]

If this sort of counsel means anything, it means that action is irrelevant to truth. It means that the truth makes its way in spite of all human programs. The appeal is to a particular conception of science. For three centuries dispassionate investigation won an accumulation of knowledge. Could only all problems be approached in the scientific spirit, could one lay aside passions and petty programs, the true answer might be discovered. For the truth is impersonal, while action expresses personal values. Indeed, there are occasional proposals to turn over government to scientific experts and fact finders. They would, it seems, know just what to do about the navy, the farmers, or the legal grounds of divorce.

This is a curious argument. It seems that since science appears to flourish in irrelevance to all human values, it is recommended as the key to all problems of value. The force of the inference is, of course, just the other way—that is, since science apparently has nothing to do with specific programs of action and flourishes by disregarding them, it has no opinion about them. Since the time when Plato first noticed the instrumental status of natural knowledge, this point has frequently been made. Knowledge of the facts is not a knowledge of values. Benedetto Croce observed that if evil were a fact it would have been abolished long ago along with serfdom and slavery.[3] But evil is not a scientific fact. Values are not natural objects. It may be that education plays a part in producing tolerance, but it isn't scientific education that does that.

And yet, we do feel that natural knowledge bears some relation to tolerance. For science, while not itself defining values, preserves them as the condition of its own activity. Tolerance for science has itself been an achievement. T. H. Huxley, Herbert Spencer, John Fiske—all of these men had no easy task in selling to a reluctant world the idea of biological evolution.[4] We have a stake in scientific freedom, but it is a stake defined not by science but by the personality of which science is a partial expression.

Scientific inquiry, scholarship of all sorts, is itself an actuality. Men go on only where the will supersedes the intellect, only where science is itself a mark of resolve. No doubt it is true that scientific freedom demands free institutions and in that way supports freedom. But it is not true that a knowledge of physics throws any light on particular programs of action. It implements, but does not determine, programs of action.

The scientific temper, however, has promoted a sort of pacifism. For more than three centuries the intellectual ideal has insisted on the elimination of personality from fact. We were to accept the revelation of nature instead of the revelation of God. Dogma was to be combated by fact. That is all very well where the dogma itself is one of fact. The genealogies of the Bible cannot be exhaustive if geology and anthropology are to get credence. But while science is admirably equipped to combat dogmas of fact, it has no equipment for resisting dogmas of value. Indeed, it can't define values. Consequently, in the measure that science has taken over psychology it has become mechanistic, and purposes have become reflexes or dark surgings produced by, say, the ductless glands. The net result of scientific study has endowed values with no authority and has even denied their meaning.

Science, recommended initially as the suitable locus of interest, concludes by denying the significance of interest. In its own context, it has promoted not tolerance but indifference. Yet the problem of tolerance occurs only where passionate interests are at stake. It will be solved not by abolishing the passions of men, but only by reconciling them. Education may point the way out of prejudice, but it will have to be an education in values and not in facts. It must be an education of the will and not of the intellect.[5]

III

Naturalism, and the education it recommends, aims to diminish the passions of men by treating them as obscurities of thought. Another proposed solution regards the passionate devotions of individuals and groups as of public concern. They are to be tolerated, but not criticized. To grant all men and all groups an untrammeled opportunity for the practice, inculcation, and propagation of their own beliefs has been suggested as the American ideal.

This is the view of tolerance as negative. Accordingly, the tolerant man would pay no attention to programs and beliefs that might destroys his own values. This tolerance consists in stirring up no antagonisms and in avoiding all denunciations. He will pass no judgment on another because of differences of belief or dogma. He will refrain from holding that a person cannot be a good American because he is a Christian, Catholic, Protestant, Jew, communist, or capitalist. To be tolerant is to define no way of life that could be incompatible with the acceptance and the practice of racial or religious dogma. The United States, so considered, is the asylum of dogmatists. Here they may practice their separation; here they may find a political form without hostility to any patterns of life and value. According to this understanding, the United States in itself stands for no program and no doctrine. In its broadest sense, a man's religion becomes irrelevant to his membership in the state. Tolerance reduces to a merely formal principle; it expresses indifference to the actual content of any belief or dogma. As a nation of free men we could see no threat to freedom in the substance of beliefs and programs. Indeed, the only threat is supposed to lie in the view that the substance of beliefs may become a public concern. Whoever ventures to say that the substance of any belief may be hostile to the form of freedom is regarded as intolerant. Whoever says that dogmatic belief is itself hostile to the form of freedom advertises his un-Americanism.

This is a widespread view. It is a view that renders affirmative unity menacing. It denies that liberalism has corollaries about the content of belief. Yet the history of the rise of tolerance is the story not of negation but of affirmation. It is true that a dogmatic state is the enemy of other dogmas, but it is not true that the liberal state is indifferent to dogmas. What the liberal state affirms is intolerance to all dogma, not to some particular dogma. For the affirmation of liberalism is the unity of men in self-critical association. It is humanism, but a disciplined humanism. It respects another's opinion where that opinion confesses its openness to dispute, its possible error, and its subordination to the kind of test available to all. It holds that whoever holds opinions not open to criticism and not defined by their emergence from the context of criticism has forfeited his right to tolerance. For no man can claim as a right what alienates him from the universality of thought. There can be no right to be dogmatic.

The distinctive contribution of the United States to the concept and practice of the good society is this: All beliefs that cannot be submitted to the methods of rational arbitration negate liberty. The beliefs on which men propose to act must establish only such institutions as facilitate the meeting of minds. Consequently, methods of arbitration become more important than specific beliefs. Our fundamental agreement is not over content, but over good form. To put content ahead of good form is to be "un-American."

Consider the alternative: If content precedes form, if one is to give final allegiance to such content, then one has denied that community lies in the reconciliation of difference, and one has asserted that community occurs only in the absence of difference. The man of firm belief is bound to work for the continuance and propagation of his specific convictions, but if his convictions pertain to substance and not to form he owes no allegiance to form. He will and must override it. If he does not, the belief in good form will threaten the overthrow of his specific doctrine. For the radical enemy of doctrine as substance is not another substantial doctrine, but the claim that all particular beliefs must submit to criticism.

Liberalism is the community of criticism. The laws of community are the laws of criticism. Beliefs not engendered by criticism and not held because of their fidelity to critical causes define the dogmatic. They define a repudiation of the only universal factor in human nature. For men are not at one in the substance of their beliefs; there they are divided. But they can be at one in the critical form that examines beliefs.

One need fear no man whose specific belief expresses his humble effort to come under the law he now shares with all others. That is why differences of opinion among scientists raise no problem of tolerance. Every scientist is eager to learn about new and revolutionary conclusions; he can be eager because he has a stake in the methods of reaching conclusions. His own beliefs are held apropos of those methods and have no other persuasion. He will passionately defend that method because the alternative equals destruction of scientific enterprise. He is a scientist only in the society of scientists; by himself he is only a dreamer or a dogmatist.

To what extent we have accepted this axiom, that form unites and content divides, I do not know. As stated before, sometimes one gets the impression that the United States has to be regarded as an asylum for dogmatists, and that here is found a state that tolerates dogma where elsewhere dogmatic beliefs meet the hostile impact of other equally dogmatic views of life. Where such views prevail it is fair to conclude that dogmatists do not love liberty for its own sake. Free institutions become a means, not an end. But wherever liberty is not valued for its own sake it becomes imperiled. If what is most important be the substance of dogma and not the form of criticism, then the universality of human nature for which the United States stands is denied at the outset. For men are not now and never have been together in the content of their beliefs. Nor within any man's own mind are all beliefs consonant with each other. But the condition of conciliation is this—that there be no other purposes put before it. That is the postulate of tolerance. It is not certain that we have accepted it. Tolerance is not indifference; it was not created by indifferent minds; it will not survive that way. It too has its affirmations. They are the other side of tolerance.

IV

Without tolerance there is no freedom. Something has been won for liberty in the acceptance of that important rule. In this negative form it expresses the lesson of much political experience. It means that men can have no political loyalty to the state insofar as individual aspirations and beliefs win no respect nor any chance for making themselves effective. Whatever destroys privacy also destroys the free acceptance of authority. This is the difference between freedom and oppression. Freedom is not the denial of authority; it is the assertion of such law as may be necessary for the creation and preservation of privacy. It is the peculiar prerogative of freedom that it alone asserts the law. The free man invokes the law as the evidence of his readiness to set limits on his caprice, and in so invoking the law he proclaims his responsibility, his capacity for self-criticism. The law is the evidence of his freedom. To be under the law is slavery; to have no law is brutality; to assert the law as one's own is freedom. It is not the case that one is free in the measure that one feels no limitation on desire. One is free as one can master desire by a self-asserted law. A state is free when privacy proclaims the authority that protects it, and authority treasures the privacy that supports it. In the suppression of privacy there can be no loyalty. The ground of political loyalty is privacy.

This is the lesson Americans have learned. We have not studied too thoroughly the course of events or the theoretical basis for our attitude, however. But in a rough and bulky way we accept the axiom of privacy as the peculiar merit of our own institutions and as the ground of their prestige. Although many evils beset us, we do not as a people look with favor on remedial measures the price of which is the removal of the right to privacy in thought and deed. That price is too high. We have paid for our liberty and we propose to keep it.

Political tolerance, accordingly, has two sides. The one side is repudiation of those institutions that restrict privacy. The other side is the affirmative will to secure those institutions that protect it. It is natural that the second condition of tolerance should be neglected. In the economic sphere one sees a similar difficulty. There we began with an ideal of "free enterprise"; now we see that abstracted freedom digs its own grave, and that a much larger measure of organization than would have seemed tolerable a generation ago demands acceptance. Similarly, America began as an asylum for dogmatists; now it is time to take stock of the limits of tolerance, and to inquire into the affirmations of the liberal state. Just as the necessity for economic reform raised a storm of protest, so too does any suggestion that the genius of free institutions does not define amorphous tolerance of dogmatic groups.

NOTES

1.   This expression is perhaps best known as it was used near the conclusion of Lincoln's Second Inaugural Address of 1865 (in *Speeches and Writings, 1859–1865*, Don E. Fehrenbacher, ed., New York: Library of America, 1989): "With malice toward none; with charity for all; with firmness in the right as God gives us to see the right; let us strive on to finish the work we are in . . ." (p. 687).

2.   This is a paraphrase of Thomas Jefferson's famous statement from the "Bill for Establishing Religious Freedom" (1777. In *Writings*, Merrill D. Peterson, ed., New York: Library of America, 1984). Jefferson wrote that the signatories of the Bill are "[w]ell aware . . . that truth is great and will prevail if left to herself; that she is the proper and sufficient antagonist to error, and has nothing to fear from the conflict unless by human interposition disarmed of her natural weapons, free argument and debate; errors ceasing to be dangerous when it is permitted freely to contradict them" (p. 347).

3.   See *History as the Story of Liberty* (1941. Trans. Sylvia Sprigge, New York: Meridian, 1955).

4.   Huxley was a prominent English biologist and evolutionist who wrote *Man's Place in Nature* (1869. New York: Modern Library, 2001). Spencer was an English philosopher and evolutionist who authored "The Developmental Hypothesis" (1852. In *The Works of Herbert Spencer*, Osnabrück: Zeller, 1966). Fiske was an American philosopher and advocate of evolution who wrote *Outlines of Cosmic Philosophy* (London: Macmillan, 1874).

5.   Along these lines, in "Utopia and the State" (Part 3, below) Miller refers to the state as a "school of the will." The key issue in both cases—that is, education and politics—is self-control and self-understanding. These are necessary ingredients to having a will. Education and politics, ideally, force one to reflect on and come to terms with the conditions of one's endeavors.

Utopia and the State

One of the paradoxes of Miller's thought is that it contains utopian and anti-utopian elements. In essays such as "The Ahistoric and the Historic," Miller articulates a philosophy of finitude that apparently attacks all pretensions to utopia. On the other hand,
Miller's persistent defense of metaphysics invites the charge that he is just another
utopian in but thin disguise.

Consistent with his general approach, Miller turns this tension into a source of philosophical strength and reinterprets the notion of *utopia* by integrating this no-place with the
actual here-and-now. Utopia is not a mere dream, not a phantasm divorced from action.
Ideals are ingredient to actuality insofar as they function as practical controls and provide
the basis for practical aspirations. (In this respect, the midworld is the structure of utopia
and morality is an example of actual utopian thought and action.) Utopian ideals are not
the repudiation of actual communities and persons; the price of being an individual in a
particular community is an alliance with the utopian.

The form of limited utopianism that Miller is most interested in exploring is that
associated with the liberal democratic state. The utopian element here is not, as is the
case with the polis of Plato's theory or the guiding ideal of modern autocrats, a fixed
state of affairs such as a condition of complete order or perfect justice. In Miller's estimation, the utopian element of liberalism is its unlimited commitment (in principle) to
self-assertion, discussion, and procedure. Here we find a political philosophy that
shares important features with that of John Rawls, as well as a further elaboration on
the community of criticism addressed in "Freedom as a Characteristic of Man in a
Democratic Society."

Originally published in a slightly different version in The Paradox of Cause and Other
Essays *(pp. 19–43), this essay was written in 1934 (Miller Papers 1:11). On the topic of the
liberal democratic state, see the unpublished essay of 1945 "The National State" (Miller
Papers 3:3) and M. Holmes Hartshorne's notes from Miller's 1931 class "Philosophy of the
State" (Miller Papers 22:7). Rawls's classic statement on procedural justice is found in*
A Theory of Justice *(Cambridge, MA: Belknap Press, 1971).*

The term *utopia* connotes the impractical. It refers not to plans that might be carried out but would then prove less satisfactory than some alternative, but rather to a plan that is inherently impossible to accomplish. It suggests, therefore, distinction between fancy and fact, between what might prove satisfying were the world a different sort of place, and what must be accepted in view of the actual state of affairs. To fly in the face of facts is to be utopian. And it is characteristic of thought to regard the facts as being not at all affected or determined by desire. We can only report them; we cannot alter them.

To state the meaning of utopia in this way is to condemn it by definition. The world must be conformed to; it cannot be changed. Indeed, faithfulness to the facts seems to call for a renunciation of desires, rather than for a program of action. If we can alter no facts at all there is no further problem. We become wholly determined by the rest of nature, and without any capacity for executing plans or realizing hopes. As a rule, however, the objections to utopia do not go quite that far. They permit such limited schemes as lie within practical attainment. The problem is not generally stated as a conflict between some plans and no plans at all, but rather as between realizable and impossible plans. We are to trim our sails, but we are not necessarily to lie at anchor. Some modest wishes the universe will grant, but no likelihood of complete fulfillment either now or in another world can be entertained. Plato proposed a utopia in his celebrated *Republic*; and while it constitutes for him the perfect state, even its perfection is limited, since it includes the lower classes whose minds or temper make them unfit for participation in the full insight of the chosen guardians of public affairs. Outside of theology there are few absolutely perfect societies, and even the Christian Heaven has a hierarchy of saints and of angels. So there is a factor of practical limitation even in acknowledged ideal societies. They describe the best that can be done with more or less imperfect material.

Insofar as they recognize such restricted success, such plans become less utopian and more realistic. Their motives may have been hardheaded enough, although the results proved mistaken. But in an engineering problem mistakes are always possible, so that the characteristic flavor of the utopian idea does not occur where the failure of a scheme is due rather to a mistaken understanding of possibilities than to a rejection of all limits. It is only where perfection is aimed at and where all the heart's desires have finally come to rest, leaving no residue of yearning, that the true utopian quality is present. For utopia is an assertion of the ideal, and the ideal terminates inadequacy. To do one's best and to acknowledge the poverty, the necessary insufficiency, of that best is not to be utopian, but to be simply a realistic actor. Half a loaf is better than no bread, and to be content with half seems the part of both modesty and wisdom. "I dare do all that may become a man," says Macbeth. "Who dares do more is none."[1] There is hazard enough in decidedly restricted programs, and it seems madness to entertain counsels of perfection when no perfection is attainable.

I

Unfortunately, such a view is not the whole truth, although it might be pleasant to think it so. It seems that human nature is not so easily tamed. Indeed, to suppose that one could deal with the contemporary world on that basis would be the very essence of utopian illusion. Men do not set limited goals for themselves. In fact, and in principle, there is no such sort of goal. All particular enterprises occur in the context of something other than their own limits and because of that context. I write these notes because of this lecture, but not for their own sakes. And the lecture is itself no absolute, but fits into a still larger scheme involving college and the place of the college. Any particular act can, in fact, be regarded as purposive and as fulfilling only as it becomes the local vehicle of an essentially boundless program. It is our attempt to meet confusion somewhere, to arrest it for a moment, in order to go on to the next point of challenge. One may counsel limited ambition, but no ambition is absolutely limited, and in the measure that it is strong it can derive its strength only from the desperate urgency of the enterprise into which it fits. Men can move resolutely for particular ends only as larger purposes enforce their local surrogate. Every will attempts the impossible. We are incurably utopian, since we must arm ourselves with boundless resolve insofar as we propose to reach and maintain any goal whatsoever. To cease that activity, to suppose that there is any termination of care and labor, is to entertain an illusion and to relapse into a dream. Eternal vigilance is the price of liberty, but also the price of truth. "Does the road wind uphill all the way? Yes, to the very end."

In this way and for these reasons it is not possible to maintain the distinction between the illusion of perfectionist schemes and those of merely limited scope. Neither for us as individuals nor for the social group is that possible. The very truth that we so deeply crave and so highly praise, the truth that is to recommend to us modesty of program and wise restriction of enterprise, is itself dependent on its perpetual pursuit. There can be truth only where there are no final truths. The preservation of truth requires the functioning of the same resolution that motivates every other desideratum. Truth cannot be separated from will, and to suppose the contrary is to have not truth in its fugitive instability, but dogma.[2] To recommend limited aims, the abandonment of far horizons in the interests of the truth, is to state an inherent contradiction. It is to do more. It is to suppose that one knows the truth, and that one has so thoroughly understood the place of desire in the world that one can portray the absolute. To recommend limited ends when one alleges the possession of final insight is hardly itself a modest attitude. It is, in fact, utopian, since it claims perfection of a sort. On that ground one ought not to condemn it, however, for we are bound to be utopian in one way or another. But we ought rather to consider further whether such a utopia is the true one. The condemnation of utopia can be valid only as the unlimited has been apprehended, and limitation transcended.

II

It would seem, then, that the idea of utopia is more radical and deep-seated than at first appeared. The initial contrast between the perfectionist ideal where all demands are met and the practical contentment with half a loaf is only superficial. For practice must take on some aspects of utopian perfectionism in order to launch itself effectively. It is not *practical* to engage in limited programs unsupported by some claim that they go beyond the practical. The pragmatism of William James admitted the need of human nature for some "will to believe," for some confidence not only in local enterprise but in the whole of individual life if there was to be hope of determined effort and courageous bearing in the face of difficulties.

Indeed, hazards are not only local. Life itself is a hazard, its prolongation dubious and its effectiveness undemonstrable within its own limits. Its basic hazard is absolute, and to that absolute risk there must be an absolute answer of one sort or another. Such answers have been given.

They take two forms: the denial of life, or pessimism, and its affirmation through some sort of utopian ideal.

Pessimism may best be known to the present audience in its psychological form. Sigmund Freud sees human nature as controlled by two basic forces, as irrational as they are insistent. On the one hand the egoistic appetites lead to assertion of will, and on the other side the libido craves voluptuous nepenthe. But the assertion of will only leads to an unquiet postponement of what it really seeks, namely some masterful poise that is not within the power of effort to attain, no matter how much it may be prolonged. Action, undertaken in the interest of fulfillment, meets more opposition than it can conquer, leading to all manner of attempts to compensate for deficiencies or to repress strong desires. The resultant adjustment takes the form of a retreat from conflict, and consequently seeks a return to that passivity which characterizes prenatal existence. The Freudian ideal becomes amoeboid, where infinitesimal will meets a minimum of repulse. The celebrated sexual note in Freud describes no vigorously adventurous Don Juan, but rather the decadent passivity of will-less satisfaction. Yet where there is no will at all there is no life at all, and there is no answer save in death. Life seeks the static, not the dynamic, says Freud, and even in its energies, it finds no intrinsic satisfaction. For action means opposition, and opposition is undesired. Thus Freud finds life inherently self-defeating. Desire may be extinguished, but it cannot be fulfilled. Here is an absolute answer to an absolute demand.

Arthur Schopenhauer's pessimism grows from the same type of consideration. A student of oriental philosophies, he adopted the doctrine of the futility of the finite will, and sought Nirvana in the unconscious. Max Weber writes of Schopenhauer, "Since being is synonymous with suffering, positive happiness is an eternal utopia. Only negative well-being, consistency in the cessation of suffering, is possible, and this can be realized only when will, enlightened as to the inanity of life and its pleasures by the intelligence, turns against itself, negates itself, renounces being, life, and enjoyment."[3] Schopenhauer regards the Christian doctrine as also counseling such abdication from will, renunciation of self and desire. This is probably not the case, yet there has been enough of idle dream from sensible practicality. Whatever can be said of Christianity, it is not a practical doctrine. It counsels perfection rather than acquiescence.

Pessimism found also a congenial temper in the ancient world, whose three chief ethical systems are all directed at the renunciation of effort.

Theognis—the Jean Jacques Rousseau of antiquity,[4] the advocate of a back-to-nature movement—sought only to prevent the complication of life and of desire. The Epicureans tried to beat the game by so managing satisfactions as to wring out a maximum of static enjoyment and a minimum of pain. The Stoics, caught in a vast rational providence, could only accept the universe. I am no disciple of Oswald Spengler,[5] but I am not above learning something from him, and he has with keen insight detected the essentially static and will-less character of classic civilization. Horace recommended the *aureum mediocritas*,[6] Aristotle's "the golden mean," and all adopted the maxim "nothing to excess." Man was to knock on wood and not try to compete in happiness with the gods, for that would be impious. Socrates, says G. W. F. Hegel, was not the first great student of ethics; he was rather the founder of ethics, for he faced life with a deep unclassical gaiety, and with a belief in the validity of the will seeking ultimate satisfactions in their own right.[7] Plato, of course, was completely out of tune with the temper of his time, and he knew it. He was the first freeman of the Western world because he proposed utopia, and a lawful one.

Coming to our own time we might contemplate the figure of Bertrand Russell. He is the author of an essay called "The Free Man's Worship," in a volume titled *Mysticism and Logic*. In this brilliant, and even magnificent, work he wonders what place human values can have in a world inexorably causal and mechanical in which man is doomed to extinction. There is no place for us, and it is best to crush the longing of our hearts and cease deluding ourselves with cosmic utopias. The cold facts of nature are wholly indifferent to our schemes. But Russell's head, though bloody, is unbowed, and like the dying Ludwig van Beethoven he will shake a defiant fist at the shattering lightning, proclaiming his unconquerable resolve to follow the truth, though the truth may slay him. He will not sell out to delusion. It is too great a pose, too earnest and somber, to be lightly dismissed as melodramatic. For after all he is correct in his assumption that mechanism destroys values. Yet, as F. H. Bradley caustically remarks, "where everything is bad, it must be good to know the worst."[8]

In his *Jardin d'Epicure*, Anatole France portrays the doom of all human aspiration, resigning himself to futility and shedding a few restrained tears of pity on the deluded mass of humanity that so fatuously treats the passing show of action as possessing importance enough to warrant a desperate attack on the citadels of fulfillment. Carl Becker furnished a further illustration of the plight of values in the context of a rational, or logically ordered, world. In his genial book *The Heavenly City of the 18th Century Philosophers*, he presents a picture of the rationalistic revulsion from superstition, in both the church and the state. Men were to move God out of the world, and to look on nature as a closed system on the Newtonian model, where some inexorable law barred the intervention of spiritual powers, and so stripped of authority priest and king who claimed to be the mundane representatives of that power. Then, having banished these fancies, they proposed to ameliorate human life, by making men free and equal, by instituting justice and fraternity. And Becker greatly enjoys the spectacle of these liberators who struggle to reconcile a naturalistic determinism with an ethical doctrine of progress. In his celebrated novel *The Magic Mountain*, Thomas Mann presents the vivid figure of Settembrini, rationalist and humanist, caught in this same dilemma. For the rigorous order of nature reduces to subjective prejudice the special recipe for the social utopia to which Settembrini devotes his life.

In sum, the escape from dream and illusion, the realistic drive toward practicable ends, toward limited control and power, has, on the stage of history, tended rather to instate a new dream, a new utopia, in the place of what offered itself initially with so much confidence as the healthy region of practical action. And it is worth making a somewhat systematic point, namely that there is no problem of utopia insofar as discussion is confined to the practical against the impractical. It is only when the status of the practical is itself called into question and a justification sought for its claim to healthy-minded fulfillment that the issue becomes important, and a solution could be proposed. On the level of limited success or failure no one wants to fail, and there is no debate. It is only as the principle of the limited success is examined that one becomes aware of the utopian background of such limited practicality. If to be utopian is to be blind, to blink the facts, to rush for satisfaction regardless of what the truth may be, then the practical life may become only another indulgence, another dogmatic and subjective assertion of values, accidentally distinguished by superficial movement, but to the discerning eye inherently bankrupt and no better than any other dream.

And it seems fair to say that men of action often do appear as the very personification of utopians, insofar as their schemes appear to us as dogmatic and subjective. They are making their dreams come true, but nevertheless *their* dreams are not ours, and consequently cannot win approbation from what we prefer to regard as the truth and the real. This is an everyday consideration wherever men meet to discuss plans, or conflict in their execution. "A hair, perhaps, divides the false and true,"9 and actuality from the illusion.

These examples may serve to bring out the picture of the pessimistic renunciation of life either in the interests of avoiding its fruitless turmoil or because the world is so made as to bar the belief in values. And perhaps it is now possible to claim that the real debate is over value or no value, rather than between utopian values and practical values. Value is a utopian ideal. It is absolute or it is nothing; for if it is not absolute the intellect can always find ways of reducing it to a futile illusion or to a realization in nothing short of death.

III

I said above that an absolute risk must receive an absolute answer, and I have paraded some examples of the pessimistic type of reply to life's demand for fulfillment. But there are positive replies, and they are utopian.

All positive answers to this question go beyond the intellect. It becomes obvious at once that values or hopes are not really that until they are affirmed, and that their affirmation is a matter not of logic but of action. Somewhere in all positive utopias action is involved, and only in the fiat of the deed can the value of the deed be established. Action can never be proved sensible. It can only be the *actuality* of sense. Perhaps it can be put another way: To contemplate action from the passive point of view of logic where nothing happens is simply to miss the place where values occur, and where they become real—namely, in the deed. But in the deed they assert a finality that no amount of reasoning can either bestow or remove. The intellectual fallacy derives from the very attempt to ask the question about the reality of value. There is no possible way of deciding that question by looking about one in the world. For after all the decision rests with the inquirer, and since, by hypothesis, he has never encountered any actual value, he cannot very well know what he is looking for. But if he should claim that he knows what value is, but not whether there is any in fact, one might ask him why he is inquiring. For the inquiry could occupy him only insofar as it was worth his while. His inquiry is itself an assertion of value, and there is no finding it elsewhere. Without our taking a stand, values could not occur to us, but if we do stand, then we have asserted the actuality of value.

Perhaps an illustration will best show this point. In *The Modern Temper*, Joseph Wood Krutch offered one of the pessimistic stories previously described. He says, for example, that there can be no tragedy in the modern world because our world-picture, being mechanistic and deterministic, can no more allow for defeat than for success. Defeat means the failure of an ideal, and there are no Ideals. He has a chapter called "Love, or the Death of Value" where he shows the futility and meaninglessness of such a feeling in a world indifferent to aspirations. He proposes either successful life as uncouth brutality or else a decadent and doomed sophistication, and adduces historical evidence to support this thesis. It was a fine argument, workmanlike, informed, subtle, urbane, and cogent. Later, however, in *Was Europe a Success?*, Krutch asked that question in the interest of bringing out the peculiar merits of European culture. He found those merits in the rich European flowering of individuality, in freedom of speech, of property, and of emotion, and in the resultant aesthetic products. But it is that peculiar achievement of European culture which he sees menaced by the dogmatic encroachments of communism and fascism, and against the destruction of all that he treasures he rebels. He could not do otherwise and be himself, for he is a liberal, a skeptic, and something of an artist. Totalitarian states bring him to bay, and he so far forgets his stoical indifference, or his Epicurean skepticism, as to come very close to a cry. Krutch now affirms, and no skeptic should do that. All his fine arguments go into the discard in a wholly nonlogical assertion of values. But what else can he do? Of course it is nonsense to object to the institutions based on a materialistic interpretation of history where a mechanical or disorderly world makes *all* history meaningless since there is no will or destiny freely unfolding itself in events. But this episode exemplifies the difficulty of maintaining a wholly neutral attitude and of finding values apart from their affirmation. And while decision and action always express some measure of desperation, and so never win to perfection of controlled elegance, they also express the condition of our own existence. Indeed, there seems little use arguing the point that a free man, who, to be free, must be an end and not a means, can find value only in his own autonomy, and hence in his fiat to pursue values. For what is an end in itself can be that only as it freely asserts its unconditioned validity.

On the whole, education stresses the intellect. It deals with assertions for which one must apologize. But for that reason it produces in many men a paralysis of will. The orthodoxy of the time scouts the possibility of any finalities, and hence sterilizes the will and destroys its ardor. There are, of course, reasons for this. We tend to find in the past so much error, ignorance, and greedy lust for power that we have become more alert to the likelihood of error than confident of the possibility of any truth. And so the intellect casts its withering glance on all these rash pretenders to truth and value. We emphasize criticism rather than creation, and tend to frown on any free originality, to patronize it, and to treat it as another well-meant but rather troublesome folly. Our public men are all very clever, but few speak words that are arresting in their clear disclosure of some commitment for which their author will stand, and if necessary go down to defeat. We have ceased to believe in it. Even the revolutionaries don't quite mean it; they have to refresh their resolution by means of somebody's theories, and it is not necessary to fear the tentativeness of such attitudes. They can always be overborne.

In describing the character of Theodore Roosevelt, Henry Adams writes as follows in his *Education:* "Power, when wielded by abnormal energy, is the most serious of facts. Roosevelt, more than any other living man within the range of notoriety, showed the singular primitive quality that mediaeval theologians assigned to God—he was pure act."[10] Yes, such power *is* the most serious of facts because, confronting it, we must take our own resolve and stand for ourselves. It is not that we must stand for this or that, but rather that we must stand for something, make *some* answer whether to agree or to differ, and we must make it freely or else it is not our answer and so not a sign of any personality. If one wants to be a person one must assume the burden of such affirmation. Most of us never quite mean it. And even what looks like emphasis and force from the outside may be in fact a personal technique rather than the heart of quiet resolution. But insofar as one encounters persons capable of such unfaltering assertion, one has met a genius, and life flows the more strongly in us for it. There are, of course, very few such persons. But they are the ones who live and who justify life, and so they call the rest of us back to new courage. This was a quality of Lincoln's, and I like E. A. Robinson's lines from "The Master" very much:

> Was ever master yet so mild as he
> And so untamable?

So mild, and so untamable; a mildness that is possible only *because* the resolution is beyond question, and so calls for no assurances of its power. But untamable persons are dangerous, disturbing. The old bottles cannot hold their new wine. And we so dull the edge of resolution by insisting on a moribund and leering intellectualism. It is safe, but it is decadent. Sometimes we try to compensate for all that by organizing a cheering section of one sort or another, but I find that a person is more likely to drink a cup of coffee with conviction than to give the lone cheer with hearty committal.

This seems a long way from Krutch. But you may recall that having stated the issue between value and no values at all; and having illustrated the negative type of answer from the numerous pessimists, we turned to the way in which positive affirmation might be possible, using the career of Krutch as an example of a man brought to bay, and showing that only in that primitive, absolute, and terrible assertion of will could values be found. If this picture seems a bit rough for the academic scene, it may only go to prove that the academic is utopian. Certainly nothing is more utopian than to pretend that human nature can be understood or met otherwise than in this context of assertion. It is just that free assertion that *is* human nature, and while logic is indispensable and engineering useful, they do not exhaust the personality. For that matter, the pursuit of truth is itself a gesture of will, and usually a very romantic affirmation, rather than a consciously abstract factor in the whole man. Truth is an enterprise, perpetually unfinished, tentative, hypothetical; and it seems blind to the point of perversity that those who try to tell the truth so often overlook the fact that they are *telling* it, and that they can denote no single proposition called true apart from the absolute affirmation of a will that proposes to discipline its ardor to this endless ideal. It is good philosophic technique to pay out plenty of rope until the very heat of denial stares into the face of him that makes it and causes a realization of both his bid for freedom and of its responsibility. *Truths* do not make us free, but the truth is our freedom, for it occurs only in the context of a declaration that has no justification but its own life. We do not die for truths, we argue about them; but for the chance of telling any truths at all we stage revolution and proclaim utopia. Utopia is inevitable; it inheres in the actuality of any person.

The forces that we must meet are not only in individuals but in social groups, in nations, races, churches, or political parties. Insofar as we need pay attention to such groups we must see their thought or theory backed by the will to realize or make actual its programs. It may come to blows;

for a strong insurgency is only the sign of a strong life and as we value ourselves we cannot fail that rendezvous at some disputed barricade. For it is the nature of the will to strike, and it has no reality apart from that implicit readiness to take whatever medicine may be necessary. The will cannot sell out and still remain. And the real place of systematic pessimism in thought is its profound and horrid obscenity. It is death masquerading as life.

It was Hegel's idea that a turning point was reached in the history of cultures when death was seen as the sole condition for an absolute affirmation of life, and the sole evidence of a belief in life.[11] And those are the great ones who have not hesitated to affirm their ideals in that way. By an instinct that outtops logic, all men stand arrested by that spectacle, and pause for a silent moment as they savor the quiet that broods over outer tumult.

Before leaving this endlessly varied theme of the absolute will, it might be useful to point out that basically we do not judge men by moral codes, and that we spontaneously suspect a person who too often refers his deeds for rational approbation. On Shakespeare, Beethoven, Goethe, Michelangelo; on Pericles, Augustus, or Lincoln; on Plato, Newton, or Benjamin Franklin—on such people a moral judgment is an irrelevant impertinence. Others abide our question; they are free. And they are that because they reached out for rich experience with eager hands and were above a niggardly moral economy and the miserly weighing out of personal satisfactions. In his distorted way, Friedrich Nietzsche saw this point and developed his superman. But that monster lived by a theory, and had to keep reminding himself, not that he was alive but that God was dead. And so he is a sapless, humorless, and joyless creature. Zarathustra's ten years of meditation on the mountain bore only this sour fruit. The superman is a dead man, because he lives by the intellect. We need not worry about him. He can be tamed, because he can be argued with. He is not a genius.

IV

The turn from negation to affirmation is unquestionably very terrible to consider. The forces it lets loose seem mad, arbitrary, and uncontrollable. In any case, they are disturbing, and it is only natural to try to put them down. We are likely to become drunk with sight of power and loose wild tongues that deny the law. But one thing is certain: That assertion must occur, and so it is equally certain that it can be met only by a counterthrust equally strong and even more persistent. An absolute assertion can get only an absolute answer if it is to be controlled. The concrete actuality that gives that answer is the state. For the state is the objectification of the conditions of the will to power. In sum, and in conclusion, it seems possible now to stress the point that the utopian character of the will is not due to some intellectually constructed heavenly city at which that will aims. What is more, no such heavenly city would enlist the deeds of the will except as it recommended itself to values already accepted. The will is utopian only because it asserts its own freedom.

Consequently one is now in a position to point out the reason why all intellectual utopias fail to be quite convincing. They fail because, as intellectual constructs, they could at best merely interpret a demand laid down in advance, but being interpretations of an absolute hunger for experience and power they must necessarily prove unsatisfactory. For no infinite appetite can be quenched by particular goods. All that particular utopias can do is to *destroy* the very will to which they owe their own creation. Men are incurably utopian because no specific utopia can bring unquestioning sufficiency. Says Troilus to Cressida,

> This is the monstrousity in love, lady, that the will is infinite and
> the execution confined, that the desire is boundless and the act
> a slave to limit.[12]

The utopian heart of man is thus identical with his necessarily asserted freedom. But it takes a long time and much actual suffering for mankind or any individual to discover that fact. And I do not have any great hope of making the idea persuasive except insofar as anyone who may be listening can find that this is the truth about himself. If one stands off and tries to prove it, it is gone, because it has then become the unconscious and unrecognized urge that directs the proof, but does not fall within the proof. Before intellectual utopias we need not feel reverence; but before this authentic finality of freely asserted personality, everyone must make his obeisance. Few have it in sufficient degree to arrest our attention, but where we do see life flowing strongly, courageously, and with an intensity that goes beyond pleasure and beyond good and evil, we must pause in wonder. History is the unfolding of this search for freedom as manifested in institutions and in art. That, however, is another theme, too large for present purposes.

V

Before going on to a further development of this idea of the state, it might be well to review some of the intellectual utopias with which most persons are familiar. They fall into two groups, utopias of the past and utopias of the future. To be sure, G. W. Leibniz and others have proposed that the present is also perfect in the best of all possible worlds, but while Voltaire's criticism of this idea in *Candide* is thoroughly superficial, it seems fair to say that the present, being the locus of unfulfilled desire, lies outside the sort of utopian scheme in question.

As utopias of the past may be instanced Heaven before creation (or at least before the revolt of the angels), the Garden of Eden, and the golden age of man portrayed in Plato's dialogue *The Statesman*. For the future there stands Heaven, Nirvana, such societies as are found in Plato's *Republic*, the *Utopia* of Sir Thomas More, Edward Bellamy's *Looking Backward*, perhaps the communistic society, and many others.

With regard to utopias of the past there is a striking common property, namely, that they represent the state of affairs prior to some fall from grace. In the Judeo-Christian story of Heaven and of the Garden of Eden, there is no point and no story until the devil appears, whether as the ambitious Lucifer or as the subtle serpent. Without the fall there could have been no sin, no redemption, no death, judgment, or final reward. The persistence of this idea in religion and philosophy, its association with distinguished minds rather than with weak charlatans, and the tendency toward its natural and effortless acceptance by millions of men may well bring one to treat it as something more than a pretty invention or gratuitous conjecture.

For example, Plato, as everyone knows, found in temporal life no adequate explanation of his so-called ideas or universals, and consequently saw no merely natural foundation for logical or ethical principles; yet he observed that as a matter of fact even an uneducated slave boy could somehow out of his own resources solve problems in geometry, being already possessed of innate logical principles. Consequently he regarded earthly life as a fall from a condition of pure spirituality, as a degradation of a purer state of disembodied soul. Again, Plotinus regarded the natural universe with its change, variety, and imperfection as an emanation of a perfect divinity, and like Plato saw the human task as an attempted return to God. Even Aristotle placed God prior to nature, viewing the latter as not quite equal to the divine in perfection. Of course the Christian story follows the same pattern.

In all these views, the imperfection derives from perfection. The fall is due to sin, and in any case brings sin in its wake. Sin seems to destroy perfection, and only for that reason is evil. Were there no assumed perfection, there could be no corruption, no error, and no conscience. In the parable of the prodigal son the return is marked by confession: "Father, I have sinned against Heaven and before thee,"[13] and the poignancy of that surrender turns on the sense of loss. Thus, it is necessary to begin with the ideal in order to discover the failure to realize it in detail. A condition of projecting a future utopia is not only present inadequacy, but the golden age of innocence. In the context of merely finite ends there is only failure, not failure in principle. But just as error is no practical shortcoming, neither is sin. Both stand for the collapse of integrity. A logical error is troublesome, confusing, and clouding only as it infects the whole of one's knowledge and the clarity of a world of experience. Error destroys not a thought, but thought. As the books say, "If George Washington crossed the Rubicon, then the moon is made of green cheese"—that is, the radical incoherence of the antecedent with all that we know of history is so destructive of good sense that all rules are off and anything at all is tolerated. Whirl becomes king. In the same way, sin, deficiency, and desires point to no local and finite imperfection, but rather to some clouding of a postulated and essential wholeness. Criticism, without which neither logical nor volitional shortcomings could be alleged, requires final and absolute standards. And because self-consciousness cannot be achieved at one step, the ideal by which the actual is measured was put into a region of time or of existence prior to the actual. Plato's struggle with this difficulty is one of the masterly pilgrimages of inspired thought. For although he ended by endowing the real with finality, he had begun, as we all know, by placing all ideas and ideals in a heavenly place out of the changing and the temporal. Indeed, the alienation of the ideal from the actual was necessary in order that the problem of their conciliation could occur or be solved, and utopias of the past are the mythological form of a necessary problem and of its equally necessary answer.

There is a further property of these past utopias that should be brought out. Without limitation or deficiency there is no time, no change, no process, and no history. It seems that this has been implicitly recognized in all these stories. Past utopias are static; so too are all utopias of the future, although this latter fact has not been systematically recognized. Because Adam and Eve desired to know good and evil they were cast out of Eden. They craved to become like God, and one cannot blame them for that. The serpent deserves a vote of thanks and not the opprobrium heaped on him. For only as man was tempted and fell could he realize the meaning of his values and begin the desperate struggle to recapture them. In the Persian religion of Zoroaster, there is staged a great contest between light and darkness. In Plotinus the created world alone has variety, movement, direction. Anything we could identify as thought or desire presumes this scene of the unfinished enterprise, this curious antithesis of finite and infinite. And perhaps I may add that the Christian faith has made the incarnation of the divine, its limitation to human form, a central tenet. Perfection is only the imperfect aware of its status. Thus the necessities of actual endeavor require the utopian concept of perfection as well as its dissipation into the actual, that is, into the world of change and appearance. And instinctively we reject utopias of the future just because they cancel and annul one of the necessary conditions of satisfaction, namely, the desperate assertion of a limited and unfinished will. For in that assertion value is literally created, and hence wins its freedom.

Finally, in this situation we may note that a future utopia thus derives from the assumption of a past one. There is no longing for a golden tomorrow where the perfect has not already existed, and hence now exists, since it cannot be destroyed. A gloomy present without the postulated past utopia can see no glowing promise. "And tomorrow, and tomorrow, and tomorrow, there's this little street, and this little house," wails Edna Millay amidst "Ashes of Life." In "Dover Beach," Matthew Arnold, in a world that lies about him with such apparent enticement, can see it only as "a darkling plain, . . . where ignorant armies clash by night."

In sum, utopias proposed as past bear witness to the presence of the idea in the actual, to the necessity of the fall, and to the dependence of history, human or divine, on limitation. They show the craving of men for both a limited personality, knowing good and evil, and the cancellation of that limit in the future. But because that cancellation would only recreate the story of Adam and Eve, it can win only qualified approval. Thus, the present, and that alone, is the locus of both any valid utopia and of its negation in unfulfilled desires. But great men overcome that limit by recognizing it, and so generate nobility out of their bondage. To do that is to be free. The great do not apologize; they are affirmers of finalities.

What has so far emerged is a picture of human nature incurably utopian, not because it is vagrant or irresponsible, not because it prefers dreams to reality, but rather because the hard actuality of any specific deed contains in itself, as a condition of its own persisting force, some assumption of an ideal. Utopias of the past and future are merely the symbols of this necessity. There are no remote finalities, but there are present ones, hidden in the living reality of any actual deed, and compelling just in the measure that the deed drives onward with persistent power. For the bankruptcy of finite deeds can get clear only as they are first desperately undertaken and the illusion of final and static satisfaction thereby disclosed. As a result, one is thrown back on some intrinsic validity of the will itself, not for a certification of its value by some result external and accidental to it. We can only assert value, we cannot *attain* it or *prove* it as an incident to our own selfhood, or to our running experience in this world or another. And it would seem that this self-containment with the fierce fearlessness that it implies is the distinguishing mark of all gallant minds. And when a person has died, and it comes time to pronounce a eulogy, it is just this quality on which we fasten. Particular attainments or failures fall away into insignificance before the spirit that empowered them. This, of course, is wholly impractical and utopian, but it is nevertheless the only consideration that sustains the practical. Utopia is the symbol of *responsibility*, not of vagrancy, and it seems fair to say that where there is no utopian belief there is no trusting anybody. That is the true vagrancy, the true irresponsibility, the true subjectivism of dogmatic dreams.

VI

What is called for, obviously, and what I here only sketch, is an application of this utopian orientation of desire to the state. For insofar as utopia is regarded as having any earthly significance it must involve satisfactory conditions within actual experience. Perhaps I have shown too much concern with the general idea of utopian felicity, and not enough with present proposals. Yet, such a background is not without its good side, since it puts up a few warning signs and offers some counsel about impossible plans.

Theories of the state can be classified into those that describe a status and those that define a process. As an example of the first, consider Plato's *Republic*. Plato was much concerned over the individualism, skepticism, and anarchy of his time and in the first two books of the *Republic* gives as fine a picture as we have of the radical and lawless individualism where might makes right. But he felt that the will did not get what it wanted in such impulsive deeds, and that to be really free it must find a principle of mastery and of restraint beyond the natural man. The true desire of man is justice, he held, because only in justice can one avoid that disorder which frustrates the will and prevents its fulfillment. But Plato's *Republic* describes an essentially static society. It contains neither the rules for bringing it about, nor for modifying it once it has been established. It is out of time, and ahistorical. It does not describe the scene in which men come to themselves, by the trial-and-error process of knowing both good and evil, as a condition of appreciating the good. This static society eliminates anarchy, private assertion, and freedom, since it removes private property and liberty of expression. Plato, as everyone knows, banishes the artists, just as modern communists or fascists allow only the officially approved art. He leaves no room for anarchy, disorder, and injustice. And just as he furnishes no method for instituting utopia, he likewise furnishes none for going beyond it. This too is a mark of all authoritarian states; they can be inaugurated only by arbitrary force, and by the same force overthrown. They do not define the conditions on which the will to power can assert itself,[14] and for that reason they can offer no freedom. In a sense, all static utopias are a sign of decadence, and of abdication. They do not describe the scene of patient progress where minds must be met and convinced. They allow for no tolerance because they have no instruments for converting conflict into agreement. They offer only an absolute choice between complete acquiescence and none, and really between acquiescence and death, or at best exile. For Plato exiled the artists, just as Stalin sent dissenters into Siberia, and Hitler took them into protective arrest or else performed a blood-purge. Finished utopias can do nothing else. They must deny the will, except the subjective will of the autocrat.

The sign of a right is safe dissent and opportunity for winning one's way with ideas. The sign of duty is safe opportunity for offering one's individual best, even though it be at first unacceptable. There is a great illusion

prevalent on this point, namely, that duty can be defined as absolute submission to a previously defined mass will. On the contrary, duty has no
force save as the individual accepts it freely, and executes it in his own
way. There may even be a duty to dissent—a duty to rebel, to differ, and to
propose new schemes; but in no static utopia can such freedom be
acknowledged. It must cancel the very freedom in the interests of which
it was proposed.

What advocates of authoritarianism are afraid of is the absolute anarchy of the individual will. But I venture to point out that the despair of free
government is found in just those persons who do not regard the state as
a procedure calling for patience and sacrifice, but rather as an inherently
arbitrary institution for the protection of one group or another. On that
basis, the class struggle is, for example, only the substitution of one arbitrary advantage for another. There certainly is no color of justice in simply overriding those who define their advantage in their own way. And the
fact that the masses are many and the capitalists few gives absolutely no
moral quality to a preference for the former. It is an arbitrary and subjective choice. But the anarchy of the individual will is not abolished by transferring power. One can extinguish the individual will, but then why talk of
freedom, morality, justice, rights, and the rest? For such concepts mean
nothing at all save as affirmed by persons who are free.

In any authoritarian state, there can be no injustice. This may seem to
be a high recommendation, but it is a condition purchased at the cost of
justice as well. All acts are validated by an abstract good will, and by that
alone. There is only one crime, opposition to the arbitrary. To abolish
injustice is to carry justice down with it. This is not to say that anyone
wants a specific injustice to persist, but it is to say that the conditions that
define justice must permit injustice as well. If one objects to a specific
injustice, the way is open in a free state to effect a remedy. That way will
not be obvious or easy, but only as the way is taken can even the assertion
of injustice be demonstrated. Just so, a judicial process actually defines
justice because it is a *process*, and there is no way of determining that an
injustice has occurred without the labor of trial, any more than an assertion can be called true that has not won its way in the context of controversy and test.

The second type of political order is the liberal state. There is no use in
pretending that such a state is always possible, or that it can ever be fully
attained. But that is the reason why it is both realistic and ideal or utopian.

It may well be that trouble, disorder, poverty, or ignorance may so beset a society that for the moment there can be no way back to order except through autocracy. But it seems fair to say that while one may admit that order is better than disorder, the state of affairs that requires autocracy is deplorable and the mark of moral immaturity. Nobody knows whether in this country we are really safely launched on the utopian ideal of liberalism. If rich men alone were stupid and greedy the answer would be clear; but poor men seem often not a bit better in their own motives, and just as eager to seize power for their own gain, or to vote for those who offer garages and chickens. There are many well-intentioned persons who confuse politics with social welfare, and they are troublesome just because they are generous and high-minded.

The liberal state can do no more than offer an arena for the solution of difficulties and of injustice. It is a school of the will, permitting both private property and free speech, but perpetually seeking to reconcile particular conflicts and local injustice. It allows for relative anarchy and for waste. But it is the only answer to the bid for power that men must make, and the only condition under which they could assert a social or moral will. That the will is social can be discovered only by trial, and everyone must make that trial for himself. There is no vicarious morality.

VII

In sum, utopia suggests itself originally as a conflict between practicality and dream. But the practical will reduces to pessimism, or else must arm itself for action by some picture of the ideal. Those ideal conditions will appear as either past or future and must so appear before the problem can be fully faced. But in the living moment of assertion resides the true absolute. It describes no *fait accompli*, but an endeavor, and a procedure. When that will knows itself, it becomes social, for its freedom can escape subjectivity only as it recognizes its limitation in the will of others. The objectification of that freedom is the liberal state, where by patience and labor the free will gives open testimony of its disinterestedness and impartiality. There it finds both its rights and its duties. That seems to be the direction of the utopian urge that no one who is free can escape.

NOTES

1. Shakespeare, *Macbeth*, Act 1, scene vii.

2. Miller states, in "The Absolute Authority of Criticism" (Part 1, above), that dogmas do not conflict. But the problem with dogma is better stated as a matter in which the conflict between opposing dogmas is so absolute that there is no ground for the creative form of conflict that is the ongoing process of mutual revision. The conflict between dogmas, then, is a cold standoff. Such a conflict, if it precipitates change, would result in a violent wholesale revision.

3. *The Sociology of Religion* (1922. Trans. Ephraim Fischoff, Boston: Beacon, 1966).

4. Theognis was an ancient Greek elegiac poet of the 6th century BCE.

5. Spengler is best known for his pessimist view of history as illustrated in his work *The Decline of the West* (1922. Trans. Charles Francis Atkinson, New York: Knopf, 1976).

6. *Aureum mediocritas* (the golden mean) was recommended by Horace in his *Odes* 2, 10.

7. See *Lectures on the History of Philosophy* (1805–1806. Trans. E. S. Haldane, Lincoln: University of Nebraska Press, 1995).

8. See the Preface to *Appearance and Reality* (1893. Oxford, UK: Clarendon Press, 1968).

9. Drawn from Omar Khayyam's poem "The Rubaiyat" (1878. Trans. Edward Fitzgerald, Harmondworth, UK: Penguin, 1989).

10. Adams makes this remark near the beginning of Chapter 28 of *The Education of Henry Adams* (1918. New York: Oxford University Press, 1999).

11. See Hegel's *Lectures on the Philosophy of Religion* (1840. Trans. R. F. Brown, P. C. Hodgson, and J. M. Stuart, Berkeley: University of California Press, 1984–1987), Part 3, section 2, where he addresses the death of God.

12. Shakespeare, *Troilus and Cressida*, Act 3, scene ii.

13. Luke 15:18.

14. Although the term is Friedrich Nietzsche's, Miller uses *will to power* in light of William Ernest Hocking's interpretation. With respect to power, Hocking thought along the same lines as Nietzsche and refused to define *power* as a property or possession of a being. Yet for Hocking will to power is more human, or personal, in the sense that "to be in control of forces and to know himself in control is a right status for him, a status in which he feels himself in the line of his destiny" (*Man and the State*, New Haven, CT: Yale University Press, 1926, p. 309). To be powerless is "to fail to be human." It is a person's fundamental will "to be in conscious knowing control of such energies as the universe has, and to work with them in reshaping that universe" (p. 309). For Nietzsche, however, will to power is a metaphysical principle articulating an empirical reality composed of matter and forces. In *Beyond Good and Evil*, Nietzsche wrote: "Suppose, finally, we succeeded in explaining our entire instinctive life as the development and ramification of one basic form of the will—namely, the will to power, as my proposition has it; suppose all organic functions could be traced back to this will to power and one could also find in it the solution of the problem of procreation and nourishment—it is one problem—then one would have gained the right to determine all efficient force univocally as—will to power" (1886. Trans. Walter Kaufmann, New York: Vintage, 1989, p. 48).

The Scholar as Man of the World

This essay is Miller's best statement on the interrelated topics of education, philosophy, and community. Hearkening back to Ralph Waldo Emerson's "The American Scholar," this piece is an illuminating, and indeed moving, presentation of Miller's philosophy of education offered near the close of his own teaching career. More than that, "The Scholar as Man of the World" is one of the finer accounts of his conception of philosophical practice.

In the context of Part 3, these pages are most important for what they suggest regarding the integration of philosophy, history, and community. Basic themes touched on here include spontaneity, discipline, responsibility, historical understanding, and critical reflection. All are indicative of what it means to be educated and thus to "idealize the actual." Once the actual is idealized—that is, reflectively apprehended in its historical, symbolic, and ethical dimensions—one is confronted by and comes into partial possession of a world. For Miller, a world is not a brute fact or a haphazard collection of objects about which one has no say. Rather, *world* connotes related orders, revealed in action and reflection, that are themselves coextensive with human action and thought. Comparisons to Martin Heidegger and John Dewey are appropriate, especially insofar as these comparisons enforce Miller's sense of the perpetually incomplete nature of this world—that is, its obscure history, its unruly present, and its indeterminate future. There is no other context in which human thought and action transpire; humankind, as José Ortega y Gasset remarked, has only history.

Education, as Miller conceives of it, places a world before the scholar. This world is not an object of contemplation (at least not exclusively) but an opportunity for efficacious action. The responsible, reflective, and engaged attitude of which Miller writes is equally indispensable if one is to participate in a community. For unless the actual conditions of one's existence are idealized—that is, brought before one's mind as historical, reflective, and systematic concepts—one cannot be an individual, much less a member of a community. Rather one is left isolated, adrift amidst other isolated selves, and, thus, reduced to a mode of experience incapable of reflective thought and moral responsibility.

Scholarship is integral to citizenship. Because of this, the character and scope of scholarly activity must be construed broadly. Reflection and historical understanding are the conditions for being with other persons in "the meeting of minds" in a town council meeting as much as in a classroom. It is a corollary of these conditions that reflection is requisite for persons to truly discover themselves. Scholarship is far from a specialized task or a pursuit of arcana; it is certainly not limited to what is done by academics and researchers. Scholarship is the search for the conditions of local control and self-control. As Emerson proposed, scholarship is the means for establishing the true person, the thoughtful person—"Man thinking."

Prepared at the invitation of the Phi Beta Kappa Society of Hobart College, this paper was delivered on May 26, 1952 (Miller Papers 2:3), on the college's day of commencement. It was subsequently published in a slightly different version in The Paradox of Cause and Other Essays *(pp. 174–92). The "American Scholar" (1837) appears in various editions of Emerson's work, including* Essays and Letters, *edited by Joel Porte (New York: Library of America, 1983). (The quotation from Emerson appears at page 63 of Porte's edition.) Ortega y Gasset's statement is from his essay "History as a System" (1941. In* History as a System and Other Essays Toward a Philosophy of History, *Helene Weyl, trans., New York: Norton, 1961). Miller's phrase regarding "the meeting of minds" comes from an untitled and unpublished essay from 1957 (Miller Papers 4:1). On these themes, see "Memory and Morals" in* The Philosophy of History *(pp. 91–94).*

Education makes us men of the world. It sets before us an ordered totality so that knowledge and action, which are finite and particular, may have a setting in an infinity. In this way it idealizes the immediate situation. The educated man is a man of the world because in a literal sense he perceives and inhabits a world. He stands in a totality illuminated by his thought, and he endeavors to make his thought the vehicle of an endless perspective. To acquire such orientation is the chief motive for advanced study. The search for it explains the excitement and also the desperation of controlled inquiry.

All men possess some perspective, all live in some world, more or less orderly or confused, more or less dark and incoherent, but never wholly formless or inarticulate. But in the scholar the articulate world has become a deliberate quest and an acknowledged need. Such a world cannot be altogether inherited, but must be won afresh by every student, if only that he may the more surely possess it as his own. The scholar must have the courage and the persistence to repossess his heritage and, if possible, to go beyond it.

I propose that we now consider this adventure in some of its data, and in its general implications for the life of a free society. For it is not altogether easy to feel oneself a scholar in the contemporary world. Perhaps it has never been easy, because deliberate study, particularly when formal, must to some extent alienate the inquiring mind from standard habits and values. Study brings into question the very stability that surrounds it and makes it possible. The questioning mind is always to some extent set apart because it sets itself apart. The fraternity of scholarship is based on respect for this risky independence and for all who accept its burdens and obligations.

In this process the student is himself liable to be disturbed in his composure and simple integrity. He may not always receive an answer to his questions, and no answer may be known to teachers, or even discoverable in books. He is on his own, and that is certain to be at times uncomfortable, even though it be also fascinating and glorious. Questions may seem strange even to one's scholarly associates because the motives of questions may be obscure or novel, not well understood by the student himself. Yet in this willingness to stand on one's own ground, cost what it may, is a principal reason for the attraction the scholar exerts on others. There is a boldness about it that wins some acknowledgment and sometimes the vague envy of more acquiescent minds. There can be no scholarship where learning is wholly a matter of instruction, as if all the questions had been anticipated and all the answers worked out in advance. Training conveys no sense of magic, creates nothing new, brings no revision of outlook, and earns no prestige.

In a democracy we need especially to guard against the temper that can so readily reduce all men to mediocrity of spirit. In the end, the free society must be based on respect, and not on equality of consumer's goods. Equal spirits are mysterious to each other and for that reason enticing and authoritative.[1] There can be no urge to community where there is no division, nor where the meaning of the division is not found in the attraction of self-contained inquiry. The society of scholars is necessary in all free association and in it we are redeemed from seeking each other out only for benefits or for practical advantage.

I

Turning from these large considerations let us observe some of the simpler phenomena of educational growth, and the difficulties that attend them. I would like, if I could, to bring these reflections to the conclusion that all education must idealize the actual. That seems to me to be what is open to us to do in our time. We are not likely to feel that we can actualize the ideal. We are not sure what the ideal may be, nor, in any abstract formulation of it, is there likely to be agreement. But we may, I suggest, find in the process of growth some intimations of the form of our world and of the human spirit. For at the close of college studies one needs to capture that morale which gives authenticity to what has been done and assurance to its sequel.

The origins of education are simple because they are natural and spontaneous. This freshness can wither, but, in the end, it must be recaptured. Indeed, its loss is unavoidable and its return dubious. But it is a quality that may not be forsaken unless education is to result in drabness and in the paralysis of energies.

To the child, experience opens as an absorbing immediacy. There it seeks and finds a present mastery. Failures and frustrations more than balance out in the day's transactions and each day awakens innocent ambitions. Walking, speaking, and manipulating, all bring delightful conquests over circumstances, and a gratified sparkle to the eye of the complacent and conscienceless hero. He lords it over the immediate foreground and is content with his ability to bring it under control. In a systematic sense he has no world at all, and no soul that stands opposed to his environment.

It would, however, be a mistake to overlook the artificiality of the circumstances within which this spontaneity operates. For the child all is natural and unforced, but for the parent its activities are known to require a carefully guarded setting. The most natural development is also the most artificial. The child finds great scope in a crib, a pen, or a room. A sandbox of generous proportions offers a scene of enormous possibilities to the imagination and to practical exploits. Yet all this has been provided, and that fact seems sufficient to refute extreme claims for back-to-nature theories of education. What is called "progressive education" translates these opportunities to the school, soliciting natural impulses in the mastery of objects and social situations. It is often thought wise to allow all correction to spring from the direct failures of these lively engagements, so that all external, and perhaps all arbitrary, rebuff may be avoided.

There can probably be no disqualifying doubt that this cult of the spontaneous has marked a prime advance in educational practice. There used to be too much rote learning, and too much birching. Old cuts of school-rooms in books on the history of education show the schoolmaster armed with stick and rod. It seems likely that, as the fund of knowledge has grown larger, and as this accumulation has been clearly seen to be the deposit of our own free efforts, the propriety, and even the need, of fur-nishing to every child the flavor of naturally acquired knowledge has become inarguable. To do otherwise would be to falsify the heritage into which he must eventually enter, and which he must administer in the same spirit that produced it. "Every oracle," says Ralph Waldo Emerson, "must be interpreted by the same spirit that gave it forth."[2]

But spontaneity must come to an end, at least in this original and uncritical form.[3] Perpetual security is beyond our power to provide, how-ever well disposed some might feel themselves to be, and however ready to contain the natural man. A program for such containment is offered by Aldous Huxley in *Brave New World*. It may strike one as curious that adults who must manage the risky enterprises of an open society should be content, and even eager, to permit these protected origins to education and to extend them into adolescence and beyond. Against this progres-sivism one might bring the charge of a fostered sense of unreality that will be bound to cause trouble, as restrictions and obligations curb uncriti-cized impulses. There may even ensue psychical conflicts as the more arbitrary and theoretical factors of nature and society make themselves felt and can be no longer ignored or evaded. In recognizing this limitation on the spontaneous we need not, however, forget that it is an inevitable first stage. The scholar, too, must possess some immunity to the invasion of practical demands if he is to find time to read a book and to allow him-self to become arrested in the muddles of thoughtfulness. Education entails this surplus of means if there is to be time for stories and theoret-ical inquiry, for ceremony, and for choice among activities.

That there exists a surplus of means is a property of the environment that gradually dawns on the growing child. This revelation is of great importance, for it discloses that one is the beneficiary of a type of control with which one is not yet familiar. There comes at last the perception that one's innocent waywardness is itself the sign and evidence of a more deliberate order than spontaneity could itself generate or maintain. Our first world does not exceed our consciousness, and it comes into new existence with every healthy morning. Our second world embraces and includes the days, because it is the necessary condition of their recurrence. The first suggestions of the impersonal are borne on the perception of this powerful control that harbors leisure and permits adventure. There is the inception of wonder that goes beyond curiosity, and the summons to a control that exceeds psychological impulsiveness.

The revelation of this new order appears most sharply as constraint. This factor in education has seemed to many as undesirable or even as arbitrary and tyrannous. But I believe that this is not so. Constraint in its simplest but also in its systematic meaning is the price of the spontaneous. It appears as the need of routine, as drill, and as habit. It has the flavor of things needing to be done whether one wishes to do them or not. Chores must be performed, some facts or practices learned by heart, even when one's heart is not in them. Property must be kept in order. All this must be attended to, however alien it may appear to direct interest. Such authority may loom as punishment, the actual enforcement of the priority of environment over impulse. In these disclosures and encounters there occur the first truly systematic compulsions. And, of course it is at this point that educators themselves are likely to fall out with each other, suspecting a shiftless anarchy on the one side or a dogmatic arbitrariness on the other.

I would not propose to defend the propriety of constraint by treating it as if it might be avoided, but for good reasons must be imposed. To defend it on such grounds suggests an ulterior motive, such, for example, as that it builds character, or is good for the soul, or that it must be accepted eventually, so why not now. Such a line of interpretation would seem to me ill-advised. It assumes a managerial wisdom, perhaps even an ultimate wisdom, on the part of adults about which they themselves may differ, and which the child may itself come to challenge and perhaps repudiate.

I would rather propose to understand restraint as "existential learning" and as the occasion of control over an actual but limited and precarious order. The defect of spontaneity, and its consequences when made absolute, lies in its inability to identify and control its own conditions. It is this obliviousness that we feel, perhaps vaguely, to be the shortcoming of some versions of progressive education. In the encouragement of subjectivity it leaves the established world a mystery, never quite revealed in its necessity and authority, and so in the end, not in its majesty and infinity. Spontaneity is robbed of its own sweetness and of its residual power when it becomes the sole source of control. It eventuates not in equanimity, but in an opacity to the demanding issues in which the conquests of the mind and spirit find their objectification.

Existential learning derives from the mastery of the insistent foreground. It is of that immediacy that we must take charge in principle. It is, indeed, the sole region of control and power. We control only local situations, and not the universe as a whole. But such control has its own enticements. We are not satisfied with spontaneity for a reason that seems to me at once simple and profound. It is that we do not there encounter a systematic antagonist, or any systematic demand. A systematic demand threatens us with an equally systematic frustration, with some loss of power unless it be acknowledged and met in its inexorable presence. Whatever any man may say about that inexorable presence is the portrait of his philosophy, and so of the outlines of his mind and of his world. But by acknowledging it, and only so, can one become a man of the world. We need to ally ourselves with the antagonist if experience is not to remain merely playful and subjective and so, in the end, trivial and without dignity. If experience and education are to become means of asserting *our* power they must identify themselves with *objective* power. And to be clearly identified, every power must loom as a threat when ignored.

It is for this reason that the child is not altogether disconcerted when demands are made on it. In such conformity it discovers a control no less desirable than the fruits of its own natural impulsiveness. Even punishment, when it clearly represents the unapologetic attempt to maintain local control, and is so perceived, breeds no lasting resentment. On the contrary, it suggests rather the security without which activity has no limits and no guard. And so education moves into the control of the conditions of security. Existential knowledge, born of restraint, furnishes the sole avenue to such actual, if limited, power as we possess, or can come to possess.

There can be no greater deception in education than that of leading anyone to believe that he can get what he wants, or that by doing what he wants he can acquire the power of knowledge. All pretension to knowledge rests in the end on the claim that one has grappled with a systematic and objective antagonist. If one wrestles it must be with an angel, in order to win his secrets. In our time knowledge has lost some of its dignity by being presented as nothing more than a tool or means for meeting an environment to which we are to become adjusted. Such a view breaks our alliance with the compulsory. It leaves nature and society alien to our wills as we seek for a subjectivity that we know to be doomed. In the child's experience of order, and of his need for it, there appear in simple form both an unarguable demand and an alliance with it.

II

These seem to me the initial and true sources of an education that can authorize scholarship. The scholar is not indulging his caprice in ways more elaborate or subtle than those of the engrossed child. Nor is he attempting by his great wit to steal a march on less gifted or less fortunate men in order to seize the means of private satisfaction. He is not the altruist, doing good in the world, transferring to others the subjective satisfactions more properly enjoyed by them than by himself. He is rather the person who has made an alliance with the imperative and actual foreground, accepting its discipline and giving expression to its implications.

Natural science and mathematics illustrate the organization of present and actual situations. They are extensions of immediacy.[4] Without yardsticks, clocks, balances, and similar instruments the order of nature remains undiscovered. It is said that meteorology as weather prediction depended on Torricelli's discovery of the barometer. The inquirer into nature's ways begins with these modest, but eloquent and powerful, artifacts. All controlled statements are made in terms of their order. It is so also with mathematics, originally a question of counting or of keeping a tally with stones or pebbles, from which we derive the word *calculate*. Here we find an articulate finitude. This, I venture to say, is also what one means by an *infinity*. It is what one means by a *world*. The function of scholarship is the discovery and maintenance of such modes of the infinite forms of finite actuality.

Natural science has been scolded at times because it is said to deal with the dead world from which man is excluded. Certainly there are no purposes in test tubes. But there is something very like purpose in measurement when it is viewed as the specification of the local and actual for the sake of clarity and control. The constitutional aspects of objects do not, it is true, serve a particular purpose, but a knowledge of them sets the stage for the execution and formulation of *all* purposes as they may happen to occur. The impersonality of science should not be taken to mean its irrelevance to the local, the particular, or the actual. It consists rather in its comprehensive view of the general condition of all purposes.

In dealing with nature we must, accordingly, beware of proving too much. If nature were only an impersonal object we might leave it alone and go our ways. If it were only matter we might turn to the cultivation of our spirits. The trouble with such arguments is that they overlook the fact that we are in league with our circumstances, and that they can be described only in terms of our own exertions. It is the need of local control that generates our interest in the farthest star cluster and the most recondite constituent of the atom. All these are the implications of an articulate immediacy, nor have they any other bearing on an educational program. The neglect of nature is no triumph of the spirit, but is equivalent to the claim that there is no educational worth in counting one's pennies or in doing the household chores. Of course, one cannot altogether overlook natural scholars who sometimes give the impression that they are either the servants of psychological impulses or else the contemplators of a region divorced from our self-maintenance. I believe that they are neither, but that they cultivate the formal order that invests the immediate and projects it into an articulate infinity. They are men of the world. They have a world.

These suggestions indicate the relation between scholarship and our own energies. It would be strange if what begins in childhood as vigorous activity were to eventuate in placidity and contemplation. The truth seems to be that all scholarship has been created by extremely active men, even when they have recommended the meditative or withdrawn life. We are very apt to be deceived by this substitution of a result for a process. It is true that Plato felt that one did well to become the "spectator of all time and all existence,"[5] but it seems hardly plausible to infer from this that one could write a Platonic dialogue if one were to neglect Socrates or Alcibiades, or the turbulent politics of Athens in decay. Aristotle's life of reason concerned with external objects and their timeless forms must somehow be made consistent with his having written a great many books, so intricate and fundamental that Western scholarship still employs his classifications and categories. John Dewey has built a splendid case for the modern world on the claim that until recently scholarship was drowsy with the contemplative ideal.[6] I doubt that Plato was particularly dreamy himself, or that nobody felt the need of power prior to Francis Bacon. What there is of truth in Dewey's claim seems to be rather that the enormous energies necessary to discover and express the order of experience can in the end find no adequate cause until they confess their concern with the particular. It used to be supposed, and it still is in many quarters, that the particular is irrational and that it is to be redeemed only in some inarticulate totality. When that view is taken, the description of discipline as something that is identical with the maintenance of circumstances must, of course, be rejected. What I am here suggesting is that we do not lose a world, but gain one, as we identify our own power with the power of circumstance in its orderly form. The scholar can do nothing about an abstract infinity. There is nothing to be said about it and nothing to be done about it. It provokes no energies and vouches for the propriety of no actual control. The scholar does not dwell in the night in which all cows are black, as G. W. F. Hegel observed.[7]

Perhaps Emerson could serve as an example of a man whose thought expresses the conflict between present actuality and an ideal somewhat remote and contemplative. He says that he stands in the sun and expands like the corn and the melons. Benign, open to every influence, uncontentious, he laid himself open to the illuminations of nature and of history. Yet on the other side he was an independent man, urging us to trust our emotions and to do the day's work. Himself a reformer of sorts, he voiced the issues of the day and paid a personal price for his insurgency and integrity. Although his scale is weighted on the side of the receptive, it trembles downward at times under the heaviness of place, time, and circumstances, and the need of action. It seems safe to say that he was a man of the world. "There is one mind common to all individual men," he wrote in his essay on history.[8] And there were the lines:

> There is no great and no small
> To the soul that maketh all,
> And where it cometh all things are,
> And it cometh everywhere.[9]

Our increasing concern with the local and particular may seem to have invaded such security and assurance. At the same time the very achievements of responsible control have tended to give progressive embodiment to our ideals. We have to an unprecedented extent domesticated an orderly world in pursuing the implications of the closer environment. Whatever one may feel about this it can hardly bring an accusation of vagrancy against the scholar. He is a responsible person though he concern himself with such quite human achievements as grammar and logic.

III

These are the thoughts that have often occurred to me at commencement. For it is a grievous thing to see the young student depart without those convictions on which his morale depends. He must see himself authenticated, not so much by others as by his own conviction that he has at least descried the outlines of an endless order in his own studies, and that the society of which he is a member expects from him a temper that accords with the pursuit of these disinterested perspectives. The scholar is not a furtive appropriator of superior means, but a free man in the perception of a world that is the form of his endeavors. And who shall say in his fidelity to circumstance no serenity may at last be found? Any actual serenity that is not illusion and abdication occurs in the enjoyment of the strength that can steadily sustain an ordered outlook.

Responsibility in the actual means that time must be taken seriously as a dimension of our own reality. But what we do there has the curious quality of generating a fatality merely because we have acted. There are Eastern philosophies that have made much of this fatal entanglement. In the celebrated *Bhagavad Gita* there is posed the problem of how a man can act without taking sides, for in taking sides we are implying that the truth and the good are to be found one way rather than another. To act is to see oneself as limited, and as a trustee for value, especially when the act is warlike, and so destructive of life and of antagonistic values. This is the entanglement with the finite that lures us into the dimension of time. The Eastern doctrine proposes that one would do ill to take that dimension quite seriously. It urges that time and history can bring no actual completion to the intellect, nor to the desires of men. In that dimension we must remain incomplete. Consequently, we should seek a fulfillment apart from all "name and form," apart, that is, from the articulate. No actual moment is ever the auspicious one for the acceptance of circumstance. All circumstance must be treated as if it lacked power to reveal the ideal or could become the occasion for insight and freedom.

However attractive, and it always attracts distressed minds, this disqualification of the articulate and of the temporal has never dominated Western thought. We have always found some value and truth in concern with circumstance. Knowing that inquiry is limitless, we persist in it. Although every proof rests on hypothesis, we go on with our syllogisms and experiments. Every institution generates problems out of its very excellences. We have not disavowed consequences in principle. On the contrary, we have tended to feel that our thought can be tested for truth or error only as consequences are identified and observed. We have established societies, and now at last free societies, that deliberately propose to make change possible in an endless reinterpretation of the conditions of freedom. We see the ahistoric as the static, and so, in terms of practice, as the despotic. For only despotism can bring the career of experience to an end.

There is growth and education only insofar as our words and deeds have consequences. In a play or novel the agent's own action turns back upon him, to his illumination and instruction. What one *is* has no way of being revealed other than through the outcome of what one does. To learn we must bring something to pass, speak a sentence that leads to confusion or to clarity, do an act that enlarges or confounds our powers. But if that be the meaning of education, then history is the record of that learning in its constitutional aspects. Psychology too is concerned with learning, but with skills and habits rather than with that revision of outlook which concerns history.

As a coercive and, hence, as a disciplinary region of experience, history has the peculiar quality of depending entirely on our own willingness to act. It is not an area passively perceived, and no one, so far as I know, has been satisfied to leave us out of the picture entirely. It is a great power, and a region of fate, that we deliberately espouse as the inclusive school of experience.

I submit that the scholar must espouse it, just as firmly as he allies himself with nature in the physical sciences. Indeed, science itself has a history, a record not only of accumulation, but of basic revisions in controlling concepts and procedures. None of that could have come to pass were men to resign themselves from the actual. To disavow time is to reject learning. It is to reject criticism, whether in comedy or tragedy, or in logic, or in the constitutional law of the state.

The importance of consequence to criticism has been stressed by the school of moralists called *utilitarians,* and also by the pragmatists. The utilitarians were earnest men, social reformers, who had tired of formal ethics. They proposed that the moral value of an act be determined by its results. Good intentions they considered insufficient, not only because that left the act quite private, but because no open way of judging it seemed possible. What is here proposed, however, is not utilitarianism but rather the need of commitment to those formal processes that generate consequences. History is such a process. It is the story of the consequences of our commitments. For that reason it is a region of ultimate risk. It is this property of history that gives it both fascination and terror. It is fascinating because it necessitates abandonment. It is terrifying because it entails the treatment of some actual program as the absolute necessity of the moment. On the whole I would say that men are modest, and more given to mistrusting themselves than to pretensions to perfection. But in history they say, like Martin Luther, that we can "do no other."[10] Or they say that we must "do the right as God gives us to see the right."[11] I think that the force of these statements needs no elaboration. They indicate what is meant by our inability to escape history. We cannot escape commanding our circumstances. It seems to mean that. We cannot escape attempting to clothe finitude in the forms of criticism whether in physics or in politics.

IV

All this may seem a long way from the spontaneous child and its slow discovery of the controlled environment that guards his fresh impulsiveness. It is indeed a long way, and yet, I hope, a continuous and unbroken way. All that we can do in education, insofar as our aim is scholarship, is to enlarge that environment. It is our rude antagonist, but it is also our ally. As nature and as history it appears as fate. One gets a clue to these fateful dimensions when one finds what one tries systematically to elude or circumvent. But the scholar has learned that it is only a fateful power that is also his own. He learns that he must immerse in the destructive element and that he will drown if he tries to climb out of that vast sea.[12]

You may perhaps think that all this is a bit grandiose, a lot of high-flying. Well, a child is surely down to earth, and I have been doing no more than sketch what some child encounters in his search for knowledge and command. I fear we are stuck with this story, or another one very much like it. For my part, I cannot bear easily seeing young men leave college enervated in their morale or treating the areas of order as if they were incidental to the meaning of their own prospects of power and discipline. Education should be practical, one is told, and with this one must agree. But what can it be that relates scholarship to the will of man if not its literal embodiment of his thoughtful destiny? I do not feel that science and history have detracted from the authority of the spirit. Quite the other way, it seems to me that there the spirit finds its sole articulate reality and the will its sole manageable commitment. The scholar can deal only in the fateful, but he overcomes fate by identifying himself with its laws. There seems to me quite enough romance in this to satisfy anyone. What more is there than to stand in the presence of that order, at once disciplinary and infinite, through which any world can be defined?

The perception that the immediate is the locus of law is suggested by Paul in the Epistle to the Romans.[15] There Paul, with his characteristic intensity, wishes to avoid a life that is forever under the law and never in itself the generator of law. That is a bold idea indeed. But to Paul this self-generated law finds its actuality in charity. In that spirit, he believed, one can act out of oneself and without offense. But charity needs an object. It is not a boost to morale to deny that some object can be the worthy recipient of disinterested regard. We dare not postpone sufficiency and we dare not postpone the law. Otherwise we will "take the cash and let the credit go, nor heed the rumble of a distant drum."[14] I am proposing that the scholar has made his alliance with fate, and that in so doing he restores to discipline the original spontaneity that first appeared as childish impulsiveness. To bring these two ends together has been the object of these remarks. But that this is possible requires the career of education, and even the temporary separation of impulse from discipline. They are united not in desire, but in will. The will is the force that commits us to all the modes of systematic order. That is the reason the will is free. It does not give us what we want, but it holds us to those endeavors that permit the emergence of law. It is our alliance with law and so with the fateful powers.

V

At this point it may be suitable to say a word about the role of philosophy. As I see it, philosophy is the deliberate endeavor to discover the loci of systematic conflict.[15] It is the essay in maintaining a world that is threatened with dissolution under its own internal stresses. It belongs in education—though you may think me now partisan and unreliable—because nobody understands the appeal of order in principle until it is threatened in principle. There is no doubt about the excitement that students feel when they are first brought to face not an error of fact but an incoherence in the form of the facts, and so in the report that we make of the facts. Let me illustrate this from some of the preceding ideas.

The philosophy of history is a comparative novelty. In the main our knowledge has had an ahistoric ideal. This appeared originally as theology and later as natural science. Time was not of the essence, and all events in time were treated as illustrations of uniformities in which yesterday and today were indistinguishable. Whether at Hobart or at Williams salt is sodium chloride. Whether at Pisa or at Poona the laws of the pendulum are the same. These uniformities have stood as the desideratum of inquiry. Accordingly it is odd to find serious men treating events in time as if they had some order of their own. And, of course, there are views of history that reduce it to physics or to psychology, when the full truth is known. But there actually exists historical knowledge in which such an ultimate truth is not now the control of history-writing. There one finds cropping up the quite scandalous tendency to treat events as unique, and not, accordingly, to be reduced to a formula. Is there, then, any knowledge of the unique? To say so appears to fly in the face of all logic and orderly procedure.

If you have ever been involved in such a conflict you will know what philosophy is about. There are many examples, and different persons find their world coming apart in different places. Some wonder whether the language of biology and psychology should be translated into the language of physics, or vice versa. Others find trouble in the opposition of determinism and freedom, or in the primacy of the empirical or rational procedures. These are familiar occasions for the onset of philosophy.

Education cannot include philosophy until the student already possesses and values formalized modes of knowledge. It is in terms of such assumed organizations that the philosophic problem arises. One may say that philosophy deals in *organization words*, not in *denotation words*. In an older style these are called *categories*; in a newer style, *presuppositions* or *postulates* or *operational rules*.

The present purpose, however, concerns education, and philosophy, if at all, only insofar as it too would help to make us men of the world. To be brief and direct on this relationship, I will say that nobody can evade the confusions that lurk in thought precisely where thought is at its most systematic. No articulate world is without these systematic discontinuities. I will give an example that is of the utmost simplicity.

The original order of experience was in terms of value-control.[16] The answer to the question "Why does it thunder?" is given in terms of the purposes of Zeus or Thor. Such views of order are not superstitious but quite empirical and realistic. This is so because original control is suggested by what one does. One throws a stone directing it at a target. The explanation of that change occurs through purpose, the only sort of control directly apprehended. But it soon developed that objects to be controlled had to have a "nature." One threw a stone, not a piece of wood, or a round stone rather than a flat one. Part, at least, of the event needed to be explained in terms of the properties of the object. Without dependable sequences in nature, purpose can neither formulate nor execute itself. But, in consequence, the region of objects, including in the end the human body, takes on the properties of the objective order and enjoins purposive explanation of any event whatsoever. Nature, discovered as the condition of action, now devours its parent. In consequence thought is in conflict with itself. It is in conflict not with the facts, but with its own incoherent modes of interpreting the facts, or, rather, of arriving at them.

Such differences also break out between men, as well as within the individual. When that happens there is likely to be animosity or even warfare. Nor should one be surprised at that. Nobody who intends to be reasonable can lightly abandon the methods by which he himself maintains a measure of control and integrity. And if he acts out his beliefs, establishing schools and societies on their basis, he has laid down a challenge that his declared enemies can hardly ignore.

It is because we are rational that our worlds lack coherence. There is reason in physics and reason in history, but how they relate may be obscure. And so, when the physicist steps into history—and there are recent examples—he may exhibit what many consider unreason. There is reason in psychology and logic, but how psychology could generate the coercions of inference may not be obvious. Yet every man has a stake in all these modes of orderly statement, in all these modes of enlargement and control.

Violence, when it goes beyond the flare-up of a passing passion, is occasioned by these radical conflicts over the controls of our reason, and so of our commitments.

These conflicts are the fatalities of thought and it is the philosophical task to lend itself to these fatalities in order to understand them, and so to reconcile them. The pathos of our deeper antagonisms lies in this fact, that they are always the signs of what we must respect, namely, some essay at a rational world. Philosophy is the reason that seeks to comprehend the loci of the breakdown of reason.

Wherever there is conflict there is already some self-control, whether within oneself or between persons. Philosophy is the attempt to control one's own systematic thought, and to exert control over others insofar as they are in control over themselves. There are other types of control. There are force control, economic control, psychological control, and the control of prestige in its various forms. But all these are irrelevant to philosophy, which can operate only in a mind urged by its own incoherence to reestablish control over itself. In this way it is part of education because it is a factor in the establishment of a world. Just as the child must identify itself with those coercive circumstances that enforce habit, discipline, and formal inquiry, so the more mature individual must identify himself with the menacing powers of division in the very constitution of his thought. In all cases one must immerse oneself in the destructive element. In all cases one's own powers are found in alliance with one or another form of fatality. We must grasp the nettle and not evade circumstance or hope for any insight or power apart from the systematic implications of local control. And those, I believe, will always indicate the presence of an infinity, that is, a world.

VI

In conclusion, I may say that my object has been simple. It was to reconcile spontaneity and discipline as the two elements in education. Any ordered totality, being articulate, can be sustained only by our efforts. It is indeed equivalent to what one could mean by one's mind. Its maintenance and extension are equivalent to what one could mean by one's will.

NOTES

1. When Miller refers to other persons as "mysterious," it is good to be reminded that he does so with a touch of irony. The other person is a mystery only if one attempts to understand a person on strictly empirical terms—that is, base empiricism cannot capture will, intent, or personhood. The other person is not a set of data but rather an immediate presence and has to be addressed as such. As Miller states, "A

self meeting another self must meet another such world. And it meets that world not as any object in its own world, or of its own" (Miller Papers, 17:24). See also "Knowing Other Minds" (in *In Defense of the Psychological*, pp. 163–72), for a discussion of the status of other minds.

2. Miller slightly misquotes Emerson's *Nature* (1836. In *Essays and Lectures*, Joel Porte, ed., New York: Library of America, 1983.) The passage from chapter 4, "Language," reads: " 'Every scripture is to be interpreted by the same spirit which gave it forth,'—is the fundamental law of criticism" (p. 25).

3. Miller's relationship with romanticism is complex but, as this passage makes clear, he believes that it is critical to rein in some tendencies of the romantic spirit. Spontaneity is basic to Miller's concept of the person and of action. However, spontaneity is incomplete and, on a more developed understanding, not only arises in the context of constraint but also generates forms of constraint. That is, a spontaneous expression or idea, if it is interesting, will come to be repeated, adopted by others, and then regularized in art or science. This formalized expression or idea will then be a form of constraint (as order) that becomes the basis for another new or spontaneous act. See "Order and Disorder" (*The Philosophy of History*, pp. 127–29).

4. See "The Midworld" (Part 2, above).

5. The phrase appears in the sixth book of Plato, *The Republic*, 486a4–10.

6. See, in particular, Dewey's *Experience and Nature* (1925. New York: Dover, 1958).

7. Preface to *The Phenomenology of Spirit* (1807. Trans. A. V. Miller, New York: Oxford University Press, 1977).

8. The quotation is from the first line of Emerson's essay "History" (1841. In *Essays and Lectures*, Joel Porte, ed., New York: Library of America, 1983).

9. This stanza of poetry serves as the epigram to Emerson's "History" (1841. In *Essays and Lectures*, Joel Porte, ed., New York: Library of America, 1983).

10. The conclusion of Luther's famous statement before the Diet of Worms (1521), in which he refused to recant what were considered by the Roman Catholic Church to be heretical statements in his written works, was "On this I take my stand. I can do no other."

11. This expression is perhaps best known as it was used near the conclusion of Lincoln's Second Inaugural Address of 1865 (in *Speeches and Writings, 1859–1865*, Don E. Fehrenbacher, ed., New York: Library of America, 1989): "With malice toward none; with charity for all; with firmness in the right as God gives us to see the right; let us strive on to finish the work we are in . . ." (p. 687).

12. Miller often referred to the passage from Joseph Conrad's *Lord Jim* in which Stein says to Marlow: "In the destructive immerse" (New York: Dell, 1981, p. 138).

13. Romans 2:12–16.

14. Drawn from Omar Khayyam's poem "The Rubaiyat" (1878. Trans. Edward Fitzgerald, Harmondworth, UK: Penguin, 1989).

15. See "Idealism and Freedom" (Part 3, above).

16. See "The Symbol" (Miller Papers 4:13) for a discussion of three other critical modes of control—meaning-control, purpose-control, and information-control.

Madness

While normality admits of psychological and psychoanalytic description, Miller is inclined to address norms from the standpoint of the will expressed by individuals and communities. Madness is a matter of moral significance—not in the sense that it is right or wrong, but that madness is the collapse of those distinctions allowing one to think in terms of right and wrong. One's self and one's world, including one's community, are in play in the maintenance of sanity.

Like Michel Foucault, Miller sees madness and normality as a dialectical pair, each defining and being defined by the other; the story of insanity is necessarily the story of sanity. Unlike Foucault, who approaches both madness and sanity from the outside in the form of sociological observation, Miller is more concerned with "the integrity of the actual person"—that is, the perspective of the first-person singular and the first-person plural. Miller addresses madness in terms of those forms of order that persons and communities affirm, act out, and maintain. These forms of order, in turn, imply agreements regarding and often the need to insist on the recognition of certain norms, principles, and facts.

Madness is as much a condition as it is a product of community. Thus, when he suggests that the "cure" of madness will in some important respect involve "a confrontation with reality," Miller's statement has to be interpreted in terms of the historical career of the midworld. For the distinction between the sane and the mad is not made solely by reference to facts. The difference is determined by an assessment of one's hold on and commitment to basic distinctions and the symbolic instruments, practices, and institutions that establish and maintain critical distinctions (e.g., fact versus fiction, sanity versus insanity). The personal drama to maintain composure that one finds in all persons (and most poignantly in those persons who struggle to be sane) entails a simultaneous public effort to maintain the shared distinctions that articulate the sane psyche.

Written as a letter to Alburey Castell in 1953 (Miller Papers 20:7), this composition was originally published in a slightly different version in In Defense of the Psychological *(pp. 134–38). The reference to Foucault pertains most directly to his work in* Histoire de la Folie à l'Age Classique *(Paris: Plon, 1961), a portion of which appeared in English as* Madness and Civilization *(trans. Richard Howard, New York: Vintage, 1988). See also Miller's essay "Grades of Organic Activity: The Locus of the Abnormal" in* In Defense of the Psychological *(pp. 16–21).*

T he study of the form of appearance is what I take psychology to be. Nature is not just appearance but appearance in the form of the impersonal.

Classical empiricism has no order at all, that is, no structure, "necessary connection," or criticism. It is neither psychology nor physics, neither subjective nor impersonal, neither appearance nor reality. Such distinctions do not occur in the materials of complete passivity. There one finds neither the normal nor the abnormal—no conflict, no error. David Hume and John Stuart Mill seem to me to have no place for the negative and so none for affirmation either.

I wonder whether one could define psychology without the abnormal.[1] It seems to me that there has always been difficulty over the psychological or nonpsychological status of sense-qualities. The psychological should be disclosed as a property of experience, yet it cannot be disclosed as any item within experience. Nor can it be disclosed as a contrast between experience and something else, leastwise something else that could be known. So, where to look? It would need to be disclosure without content, hence formal. It would need to show the psychological through some sort of collapse, as all formalities are shown.

That collapse is madness. It is not error, since both truth and error can be, and have been, viewed as variations of appearance, as differences in what happens, and so as without authority. Nor is the collapse found in ignorance, since ignorance presumes a systematic limit, and so an ordered infinity that goes beyond data. But it seems that in madness one encounters the loss of the distinction between subject and object, and between appearance and reality—one lives violently, or passively, or in fantasy. One loses nature and self together. Madness is the actuality that shows that order and control cannot be treated as mere ideas or ideals. It is always fugitive, in small ways or large ways. In that sense it is volitional. It is the point at which volition appears in principle as the resolve to maintain particulars, or as the loss of that resolve.

Nor is the madman an empiricist. He has ceased finding out. Sanity is a "normal" condition and presumes some conflicts have been overcome. In the absence of the abnormal there can be no norm. What discloses one discloses the other.

Sometimes the objection to the abnormal rests on determinism rather than on empiricism, on an order that is flawless throughout, unconfused and universal. In nature there is no error, no ignorance, and no conflict. But, then, can nature be found without conflict? And I think that nature needs to be lost in particular ways, that is, through personal confusions that displace the formal order of the actual. As a student, I was impressed by Plato and Immanuel Kant; yet such forms seemed in the end arbitrary if made "necessary," and only the phenomenal if left factual, as in Kant.

Universals have to appear in detail, and their neglect must threaten details. They do that when they become a burden. Mad people are troubled and burdened, and not necessarily over creature comforts. They are maladjusted to environment in principle, not to particulars in the manner of general psychology. The madman is smart enough. Hamlet said that he could tell a hawk from a handsaw provided the wind was southerly.[2] In abnormal psychology, the stimulus-response operations break down. That is why one cannot "get at" the sufferer. That is what makes it all so baffling and uncanny. It is no joke to say that one then sees a ghost. One does indeed. The madman shows the perversion of idealism. He proves, though, that stimuli have a meaning because the naive view of stimulus no longer operates with him.

Along such lines I would think one could show that "proper" psychologists would indeed speak of the abnormal. Without the collapse and confusion of madness, there is no clue to propriety. Here, the way we think becomes central. Only this way shows the function of criticism in maintaining, not nature, but the distinction between self and nature. Kant showed how to maintain nature, but not how to lose it. The loss must also be part of experience before experience can be self-controlling. This loss occurs as madness, not as error.

Logic, perhaps, deals with the confusion that loses essences, that is, definitions; abnormal psychology deals with the confusions that lose existence, that is, the basis of the distinction between appearance and reality. The psychiatrists are always talking about a sense of "reality," but I fear they mean only common sense. This suggests that the order of essences is enforced only in actuality, that is, in the maintenance of criticism, and so of the difference between privacy and publicity.

In madness, the loss of nature is not intellectual or theoretical or a matter of speculation. There is here a contrast with skepticism, where nature cannot be reached but is kept as a desideratum, just as the self is kept as an actual control. But in madness one seems to have a condition wholly psychic, yet not skeptical. There is in madness no known failure from its own point of view. The abnormal is the loss of criteria. It is the nonfunctioning of very intimately held criteria because of their irreconcilability. It is not the absence of norms. It is not vagrant. It is the disclosure that action requires norms, and that as action grows deliberate and egoistic the need of coherent norms becomes imperative. Action, as critical deeds, must be controlled; the norms or forms do that controlling. But when these norms are themselves confused, then will collapses.

In common sense there are norms, but they are not self-conscious, that is, not affirmed egoistically as will. Norms become our own at the point where they must be asserted as the formal meaning of action. But this cannot be done until action is threatened in principle.

This emphasis on action is also an emphasis on the finite and actual. Neither the opportunist nor the acquiescent formalist becomes mad. It is the person who must give validity to the moment, yet must also have an organized moment. Thus, madness is the systematic frustration of the individual, that is, of the person as an agent, and so as ordered finitude. The idea of ordered finitude is exhibited in its collapse.

One can see, then, why all monisms take a dim view of pathology. Whether theological or naturalistic, they cannot admit that the individual is the locus of order, or, at least, a factor in all universality. But in madness one makes no mistakes, nor is it to be seen as ordinary willful sin. It is the deeper essay at personal reality. But this personal reality shows also that nature is a function of the integrity of the actual person.

Madness induces fantasy, but without it sobriety is itself without ability to save itself from the charge of dream and phenomenalism. The touchstone is no longer idea but actuality and existence, that is, the self-controlling. Madness, inducing helplessness, is the sign of the condition of freedom where freedom becomes not *what* one wants, but *that* one is actual.

I think that the exploitation of collapse is the nerve of the development.

Sex is surely related to the absoluteness of the actual and finite. People get the idea that sex is a lark. But it turns out to be a restriction. There is a long record of man's aversion to finitude. There is a finitude without form and prospect; there is another sort that shines with prospect and maintains it. Along that line one uncovers humanism.

The mad are "sick" in no usual sense. There is no local disease here, but a constitutional threat. One cannot even say that something is amiss. It is more than that. More knowledge would not cure it because it does not occur in the absence of knowledge. More knowledge is incidental; but here one seems to deal with the condition of knowledge and of getting more of it. Strictly speaking, one does not know how to cure it. Its cure is always an assertion of the point of view of the therapist, not an assertion of fact, or of what is so in nature. There is a curious use of violence in cures, as in shock-therapy, and also a curious use of personal regard, of interest and delicacy and the restoration of confidence. In any case, there is this confrontation with reality, not with ideas, arguments, facts, or essences. None of that is any good. But the method of cure should be a clue to the nature of the malady.

I think that philosophers have not known what to make of madness, and that there is a big opportunity here for new orientations.

NOTES

1. As an idealist, it might be assumed that Miller is against empirical psychology. While he does have a principled opposition to empirical psychology having a monopoly on the description of human being, Miller is committed to the relevance and necessity of psychology. In the preface to *In Defense of the Psychological* he writes: "I hold that all illness of mind is a departure from rationality. It follows that no one will understand illness who does not understand mind in its rational ideal. Self-control, that is freedom, is the essence of psychology, or else psychology disappears" (p. 7). But freedom, too, would disappear without psychology. Like the dove that Kant famously remarked could not fly without the resistance of the air, freedom cannot take shape without the stuff of psychology.

2. Shakespeare, *Hamlet*, Act 2, scene ii.

What Does Art Do?

Miller's approach to the fine arts is intellectual, historical, and social in character. Worthy of lengthy consideration from the standpoint of aesthetics, his remarks about the role of art and the artist are also of interest in elaborating his sense of community. For if, as Miller insists, art is concerned with the *objective* in the form not of facts but of consciousness, then the work of the artist is critical to the formation, maintenance, and revision of any community. Community implies a commonality (if fraught with division) of consciousness and art is a primary means of asserting and criticizing the terms defining a community.

"Take away art," Miller writes in *The Midworld*, "and one is as impoverished about man as one would be about nature if one destroyed all yardsticks." In art we find a means of expression and reflection that is basic to self-understanding. One can go a step further and say that art is important to politics in that good art animates reflection on the status of a community, its terms of agreement and disagreement. Art, like historical study and philosophy, is part of the process of "idealizing the actual" of which Miller writes in "The Scholar as Man of the World." It is a means by which we highlight and offer up for revision the various symbolic objects and practices that constitute our actuality.

This letter, dated May 18, 1949 (Miller Papers 49:1), originally appeared in a slightly different form in The Paradox of Cause and Other Essays *(pp. 161–68). The quotation from* The Midworld *appears on page 189. On the semiotic status of artifacts, see "The Symbol" (Miller Papers 4:13), "Functioning Objects, Facts, and Artifacts" in Part 2, above, and an unpublished letter draft dating from 1973 (Miller Papers 18:7). On the matter of aesthetics and the status of the work of art, see "A Meditation on a Painting" (*The Paradox of Cause and Other Essays, *pp. 169–73), "Art and Wax Figures" of 1956 (Miller Papers 4:20), and "Communication in Beauty" of 1933 (Miller Papers 9:10).*

What makes painter-artists interesting? By common standards they seem a rather low lot. But at the same time they do have passion or intensity. Something about the visual world fascinates them. In some way what is seen becomes sharply focused, but what permits this concentration is obscure. All intensity is in the interest of some general purpose. What is it that is brought to a focus?

A physician also brings facts to a focus. So does a scientist reading a gauge of some sort. The weather map is such a concentration of data. And so it goes.

It seems, further, that painting-art may deal with any visual materials, ships, cabbages, and kings. All one has for sure is this focus-quality. But a focus seems to need a whole world of some sort in order to become a point of concentration. A *symptom* stands out, is declarative and eloquent of a disease, and may have wide implications in physiology, chemistry, diet, habits, psychology, and so forth. That seems to be the sort of situation that allows a *focus* to occur, and to be sought.

So, one may ask, "what is the painter looking for?" It seems he must be looking for something. There are those who say that one paints just what one sees. But that isn't plausible. A biologist draws what he sees, an amoeba, but it seems not—for that reason—to be *art*. A surveyor's sketch is just what is seen, but, again, not art.

So, when one paints, one seems to need to assume that the seeing is directed in some way. It is in that connection that a *focus* is established, apropos of the concern that directs seeing.

I

In general, it appears that all visual experience requires direction. There appears to be no seeing-in-general, but only seeing directed by some concern, such as that of the physician, the mariner, or the surveyor. That is good psychology. One sees a person looking intently, and one may think, "I wonder what he sees in that tree, rock, building, or person."

To say that the gazer finds something interesting is tautologous. Of course he does. But any interest carries one into the question of focus, of relevance to some articulated concern. A hungry man looks at a fowl thinking to eat it, a prospector at a rock thinking to read the presence of gold or lead or uranium. Interest occurs apropos of some larger concern, and it is that concern which controls the seeing and allows another to say what is being seen.

The painter must see something that makes him want to paint, just as the hungry man sees what makes him want to eat. Somehow, the *only* thing the painter sees is whatever it is that makes him want to paint.

If you ask him why he paints, you will probably not get a good answer. Some say it is therapeutic or restful. Others that it shows what is really there, what one really sees. But one really sees food in a fowl just as much as beauty. Anyhow, one finds nothing at all merely by looking where there is no prior concern. The hungry man must eat the fowl, the artist must paint the fowl.

What makes one want to paint some visual experience? To paint, not to eat, or make a weather map? Plainly, there is some deep urgency, and one not necessarily dependent on social position or even on schooling and knowledge of the theoretical world. This seems true about actual painters. Some dunce or mad fellow has to paint. He works, he suffers, he accepts harsh judgments. But he paints. This is striking. We don't wonder that anyone wants to eat the fowl; but why paint the bird?

In all these cases the action taken is incidental to a purpose that in the end is ideal. Even eating is done to sustain *life*, a most imaginative concept. I will assume this principle. The prospector examines a rock to become rich. The physician makes one well. The plumber stops a leak, and allows domestic practice to continue. All that seems to me quite ideal or imaginative. The painter will be doing the same sort of thing.

In all cases there is a focus on the object or situation, no more for the painter than for the others. And it is always a focus with a context. Nobody sees the "object" just as object. That is a sensible statement in metaphysics, but not in any context that leads to one sort of action.

I suggest that the painter is engaged in some attempt to establish the visual as object in principle. The physician is already dealing with the region of objects. So is the draftsman. The painter is like the physicist, trying to set up objects as a region, as an order, getting away from vagueness and confusion.[1] In a sense, the physicist is not trying to tell the truth *about* objects; he gives objective status to his confused experience, setting up nature itself. He is not trying to eradicate error either. He is generalizing conditions for making truths and errors possible.

II

The aesthetic seems, then, somewhat abstractly, to be one of the modes of securing objectivity in principle. That is its "purity." That is the reason why, like physics, it can become a passion.

Objectivity is the other side of selfhood. Only in objectivity is the self real to itself, self-maintaining. This, again, is a general but well-known rule.[2]

Another step and assumption: No mode of objectivity occurs in isolation. It occurs because there are other modes of objectivity. Physics illustrates mathematics, and physics nourishes mathematics. Psychology needs logic and vice versa. It needs history and vice versa. I say this so as to exclude any attempt to leave painting-art in a vacuum, independent of all other modes of objectivity and vice versa. Whatever sort of objectivity the painter seeks will be a function of other sorts that he assumes. So with all pure enterprises.

Objectivity depends on artifacts, on language. Without signs and symbols nature is indistinguishable from the stream of consciousness.

The concern of all passion is the creation of artifacts. Plato saw this in speaking of the generation of beauty.[3] Passion is the demand for objectivity in principle, and is itself wholly inward. The wholly outward is the dialectical opposite of the wholly inward. Passion is the generative source of the nonsubjective, the insistence on having a world.

I think that the difficulty of treating the artist as one who creates a *world* derives from the apparent fact that art—in this case painting—has neither a form nor a content of its own. We can say of mathematics that it deals in the order of quantity, of physics that it explores the order or the form of matter and energy. In this way mathematics and physics project a world—orderly, intelligible, and infinite. But there seems no analogous contribution to nature made by art. It seems to add no new essence, no new mode of intellectual order. Physics and math, although highly intellectual, theoretical, or ideal, define a region that is not subjective. There one does not think as one pleases, but all is under law and restraint. To suggest a simple example: In claiming that every event has a cause one offers a test for illusion. If one believes the doorbell rang and finds no one on the porch, one reasons that one must have been mistaken in supposing that the bell sounded. The bell does not ring without a cause, and there was none. I say this in order to illustrate the claim that science projects a world, and likewise provides a test for appearance and subjectivity.

But nature seems to get along very well without painter-artists. No property of that nonpsychological region is determined by a painter. We do not set our watches or run up weather-flags or determine the location of the magnetic pole by means of any work in an art gallery. Painters have usually been poorly educated in such matters. Paintings propose no errors in our conception of nature. Physics does.

Of course, painters may discover color qualities of objects that have escaped notice. But that is no great matter. A gardener discovers colors in fruits, vegetables, and flowers that likewise escape the casual observer. Anyone who deals with objects in some special way must learn the qualitative signs that control his operations. The discovery by some painter that snow, closely attended to, exhibited many tints and shades was given such exultant publicity as to leave one inert with amazement.

But even if we owed to painters our knowledge of the visual properties of natural objects (and, in the main, we do not), it would not be through painting that the region of objects had been established. Painting is not a test for any matter of fact, and so not for any illusion. Painting seems not to establish the region of objects in principle.

If not, then it is merely subjective, as much without relation to nature as to the order of personality. The mission of all passionate pursuits is to escape from privacy and to establish objective and public reality. Passion is self-defining and nature-defining. Passion is not for "self-expression"; it is for self-establishment where the relinquishment of the passion is a collapse into nonentity. Passion is the energy that moves from nonentity into reality of both self and nature. All reform and all scientific knowledge illustrate this unwillingness of the creative mind to fall back into oblivion. Nor is this petty egotism. It is not petty to sustain those endeavors that are disciplinary and perhaps even fatal. For it is in this discipline that one becomes impersonal, objective, and effective.

III

The mystery of the painting is that it adds no new defining essence to nature or even to personality. But this suggests that painting, and all art, has another function to perform. It is the function of memorializing or embodying such essences of nature and personality as are defined in the *nonaesthetic forms* of man and nature.

Art has no story of its own to tell, whether about man or nature. It tells no tales that are aesthetic. What it does is embody in symbols other modes of order. For example, the Lincoln Memorial adds no new fact to the known life, career, or character of Abraham Lincoln. It does not tell what words he spoke, and some of these words are, in fact, inscribed on the wall of the chamber, appearing merely as words. But the memorial notes that the man Lincoln lived. It is a present evidence of his own contribution to the formal order of the state. Without the symbol, whether it be this memorial, or Robert Lowell's poem,[4] or E. A. Robinson's,[5] there is no evidence that anyone had noted the contribution of Lincoln to our understanding of the essence of man. In those notations Lincoln becomes effective.

Art, in all its aspects, has for content the nonaesthetic forms of reality. Religion, as a defining trait of human nature, its concern with destiny, has always secured actual effectiveness through art. Art is an *existential*, not an *essential* phase of reality. No orderly mode of thought or action escapes the need of aesthetic symbolization. It is not enough to pray; one must show that one knows that one prays, thereby giving objective status to prayer and all its idealized concomitants. It is not enough to have a society; one must be brought to arrest by the statement of that essence in the actual symbol that makes a nation self-conscious. So there is a flag, an anthem, many a poem, story, painting, bust, and edifice. It is not enough to have medical science, or trade, or an orderly house; it is necessary that these essences be asserted as the reality of nature and personality. To do that is the function of art.

As a corollary, it follows that no art is concerned with either appearances or facts. A great deal of aesthetic theory flounders in the morass of appearance. The painter, for example, is said to put down what he "sees," or perhaps what he "feels" or "thinks." All that is entirely formless. What the artist notes, memorializes, and converts into force is the self-consciousness of nonaesthetic modes of order. The rapport of mother and child is not aesthetic, but it is a powerful element in the controlled personality. This the artist shows. A country graveyard is a utility or a sign of religious concern, and so can be treated by a poet, without whom we do not "realize" the graveyard, although he adds no new item of content whatever to its area. Nor does the poet add to its meaning. He does not add, he *proclaims*. That proclamation is the actuality of the graveyard as an item in our self-consciousness. And that is our sole reality as persons.

There is art because without art, including the painting-art, there is no way of asserting and proclaiming the relation of nonaesthetic modes of order to the will. The order of man and nature must be not merely understood or even acted out habitually; it must be identified explicitly, and held before us for contemplation. No essential mode of order attains existence until it is so embodied in the symbol. Then, as a mode of order, it enters into will. Art is the reminder of every attained mode of organization to which man is committed, and through which he defines himself. Consequently it is emotionally moving. Its emotion is not the primary violence of instinct, but the much more profound feeling with which we contemplate the structural and organized truth.

IV

These considerations set the limits of art. Clearly it contributes nothing to our knowledge of essences, whether in nature or in man. It is not physics or psychology. Nor does it contribute directly to history, the process by which man revises his basic forms of order, redefining himself and his world in their fundamental modes of order and control. Nor is it philosophy, the general theory of all criticism. Art is not everything. It is not the same as "culture." But it is necessary as the record of man's realization of such modes of order and control as the nonaesthetic interests have created.

Like all enterprises, art has a history, that is, a career in the fuller grasp of its own meaning. There is no more reason to suppose that every person who tries rhymes or puts paint on walls is aware of the limiting controls of his work than there is in assuming that all efforts at curing disease realize the intent of medical science. The history of art has two dimensions, and faces two questions. One must ask of an artifact: (1) Is it art? and (2) Is it good? A great many things belong to *art* that fall short of fulfilling its intent. An obelisk is a work of art, but a primitive and shady one, just as an incantation is *medicine* but rather incomplete in its grasp of its problem.

At any rate, there is reason to avoid identifying a work of art through such alleged marks as emotion, imagination, proportion, mass, pleasure, or interest. And one should, of course, avoid expressions purporting to claim that the artist sees what is "really" there. He doesn't, and even if he did the result could not possibly be of aesthetic interest. He deals with existence, not with essence. The question "what is art?" can be answered by indicating how the aesthetic symbol gives actuality in will, and force in contemplation to all nonaesthetic modes of order. Art can disclose only what is endowed with a prior discipline and imagination. It asserts and proclaims the modes of imaginative and ordered infinity of the nonaesthetic aspects of experience.

This saves art from triviality and from that quite nasty flavor of the esoteric. Art is not, and never has been, esoteric. It has always been a domestic staple. Francis Bacon had something to say about "elegant learning." The reason for the present chaos in art, and in art criticism, derives from our contemporary positivism, that is, from our current repudiation of nonaesthetic form and authority. Inevitably, the artist flails around in the darkness of his sensations and frustrations and becomes anarchic and incredibly obscure. But where the modern artist has seized on some objective validity, on some mode of social and scientific order, he has steadied down to new modes of eloquence and revelation. But such firm eloquence is rare. Once it was common. As the new world of humanism takes shape we may expect art to proclaim its existence, and so make it a self-conscious force.

NOTES

1. Regions are composed or revealed by categories in an orderly relation among one another. A region is systematically organized data such that the various different categories or orders of experience relate to, support, and integrate with one another (Miller Papers 22:14). See also "Categories as Historical and Existential" (Part 1, above).

2. In "Knowing Other Minds" (in *In Defense of the Psychological*, pp. 163–72) Miller makes the point, contrary to the general tendency of idealism, that objectivity is not found in the resistance of an object of knowledge but in the orderly apprehension of the world that one experiences only in relationship to another person. Objectivity is then not brutal but social in character.

3. See *Phaedrus*.

4. "For the Union Dead" appears in Lowell's *Life Studies; and, For the Union Dead* (New York: Farrar, Straus, and Giroux, 1980).

5. "The Master" appears in Robinson's *Collected Poems* (New York: Brickrow Books Shop, 1921).

Miller Bibliography

BY MILLER

BOOKS
The Paradox of Cause and Other Essays (New York & London: W. W. Norton, 1978).
The Definition of the Thing with Some Notes on Language (New York & London: W. W. Norton, 1980).
The Philosophy of History with Reflections and Aphorisms (New York & London: W. W. Norton, 1981).
The Midworld of Symbols and Functioning Objects (New York & London: W. W. Norton, 1982).
In Defense of the Psychological (New York & London: W. W. Norton, 1983).

ESSAYS
"The Paradox of Cause," *The Journal of Philosophy* 32 (1935): 169–75.
"Accidents Will Happen," *The Journal of Philosophy* 34 (1937): 121–31.
"Motives for Existentialism," *Comment* (Williamstown, MA) 1 (Spring 1948): 3–7.
Review of Walter A. Kaufmann's *Nietzsche: Philosopher, Psychologist, Antichrist,* in *Williams Alumni Review* 43 (1951): 149–50.
"Afterword: The Ahistoric and the Historic," in José Ortega y Gasset, *History as a System and Other Essays: Toward a Philosophy of History*, Helene Weyl, trans. (New York & London: W. W. Norton, 1961), pp. 237–69.
"History and Case History," *The American Scholar* 49 (1980): 241–43.
"For Idealism," *Journal of Speculative Philosophy* 1 (1987): 260–69.
"The Owl," *Transactions of the Charles S. Peirce Society* 24 (1988): 399–407.
"On Choosing Right and Wrong," *Idealistic Studies* 21 (1992): 74–78.

SCHOLARSHIP ON MILLER

BOOKS

Colapietro, Vincent, *The Fateful Shapes of Human Freedom: John William Miller and the Crises of Modernity* (Nashville, TN: Vanderbilt University Press, 2003).

Fell, Joseph P., ed., *The Philosophy of John William Miller* (Lewisburg, PA: Bucknell University Press, 1990).

McGandy, Michael J., *The Active Life: Miller's Metaphysics of Democracy* (Albany: State University of New York Press, 2005).

Tyman, Stephen, *Descrying the Ideal: The Philosophy of John William Miller* (Carbondale: Southern Illinois University Press, 1993).

ESSAYS AND CHAPTERS

Aboulafia, Mitchell, "Review of *The Philosophy of John William Miller*," Joseph P. Fell, ed., *International Studies in Philosophy* 25 (3) (1993): 116–17.

Anderson, Douglas R., "Review of *The Philosophy of John William Miller*," Joseph P. Fell, ed., *Transactions of the Charles S. Peirce Society* 27 (1991): 527–33.

———, "In the Face of Technology: Toward a Recovery of the Human," *Technology in Society* 20 (1998): 297–306.

Bradford, Judith, "Telling the Difference: Feminist Philosophy and Miller's Actualist Semiotics," *Journal of Speculative Philosophy* 11 (1997): 297–314.

Brockway, George P., "John William Miller," *The American Scholar* 49 (1980): 236–40.

———, "John William Miller," in *Masters: Portraits of Great Teachers*, Joseph Epstein, ed. (New York: Basic Books, 1981), pp. 155–64.

———, "Miller on Economics," in *The Philosophy of John William Miller*, Joseph P. Fell, ed. (Lewisburg, PA: Bucknell University Press, 1990), pp. 125–35.

Colapietro, Vincent, "Review of Miller's Five Books," *Journal of Speculative Philosophy* 1 (1987): 239–56.

———, "Reason, Conflict, and Violence: John William Miller's Conception of Philosophy," *Transactions of the Charles S. Peirce Society* 25 (1989): 175–90.

———, "Human Symbols as Functioning Objects: A First Look at John William Miller's Semiotics," in *The Philosophy of John William Miller*, Joseph P. Fell, ed. (Lewisburg, PA: Bucknell University Press, 1990), pp. 70–84.

Corrington, Robert, "John William Miller and the Ontology of the Midworld," *Transactions of the Charles S. Peirce Society* 22 (1986): 165–88.

———, Introduction to "For Idealism," *Journal of Speculative Philosophy* 1 (1987): 257–59.

———, Introduction to "The Owl," *Transactions of the Charles S. Peirce Society* 24 (1988): 395–98.

———, "Finite Idealism: The Midworld and Its History," in *The Philosophy of John William Miller*, Joseph P. Fell, ed. (Lewisburg, PA: Bucknell University Press, 1990), pp. 85–95.

Diefenbeck, James A., "Acts and Necessity in the Philosophy of John William Miller," in *The Philosophy of John William Miller*, Joseph P. Fell, ed. (Lewisburg, PA: Bucknell University Press, 1990), pp. 43–58.

Elias, Robert H., "Literature, History, and What Men Learn," in *The Philosophy of John William Miller*, Joseph P. Fell, ed. (Lewisburg, PA: Bucknell University Press, 1990), pp. 136–52.

Fell, Joseph P., "An American Original," *The American Scholar* 53 (1983–1984): 123–30.

———, "Miller: The Man and His Philosophy," in *The Philosophy of John William Miller*, Joseph P. Fell, ed. (Lewisburg, PA: Bucknell University Press, 1990), pp. 21–31.

———, "John William Miller and Nietzsche's Nihilism," *Eidos: The Bucknell Academic Journal* 10 (1997): 5–21.

Friend, Theodore, "Infinity and Limit: A Teacher's Eye," *Yale Review* 73 (1984): 116–51.

Furtwangler, Albert, "Stories, Histories, and Canoes," *Dalhousie Review* 87 (1988): 178–94.

Gahringer, Robert E., "John William Miller: A Memorial Minute," *The Proceedings and Addresses of the American Philosophical Association* 52 (1979): 518–19.

———, "On Interpreting J. W. Miller," in *The Philosophy of John William Miller*, Joseph P. Fell, ed. (Lewisburg, PA: Bucknell University Press, 1990), pp. 32–42.

Johnstone, Henry W., Jr., "The Fatality of Thought," in *The Philosophy of John William Miller*, Joseph P. Fell, ed. (Lewisburg, PA, Bucknell University Press, 1990), pp. 59–69.

McGandy, Michael J., "John William Miller's Metaphysics of Democracy," *Transactions of the Charles S. Peirce Society* 31 (1995): 598–630.

———, "The Midworld: Clarifications and Developments," *Transactions of the Charles S. Peirce Society* 34 (1998): 225–64.

Stahl, Gary H., "Making the Moral World," in *The Philosophy of John William Miller*, Joseph P. Fell, ed. (Lewisburg, PA: Bucknell University Press, 1990), pp. 111–24.

———, "John William Miller and the Midworld of Action," in *Human Transactions: The Emergence of Meaning in Time* (Philadelphia: Temple University Press, 1995.), pp. 69–84.

Strout, Cushing, "When the Truth is in the Telling," in *The Philosophy of John William Miller*, Joseph P. Fell, ed. (Lewisburg, PA: Bucknell University Press, 1990), pp. 153–64.

Tyman, Stephen, "Review of *The Philosophy of History*," *History and Theory* 23 (1984): 132–40.

———, "The Problem of Evil in Proto-Ethical Idealism: John William Miller's Ethics in Historical Context," in *The Philosophy of John William Miller*, Joseph P. Fell, ed. (Lewisburg, PA: Bucknell University Press, 1990), pp. 96–110.

———, "The Concept of the Act in the Naturalistic Idealism of John William Miller," *Journal of Speculative Philosophy* 10 (1996): 161–71.

PRESENTED PAPERS

Anderson, Douglas R., "Miller's American Scholar: Acting in the Midworld," presented to the American Philosophical Association, Central Division, Kansas City, MO, May 1994.

———, "Some Addenda to Colapietro's *Fateful Shapes*," presented at the Pennsylvania State University, University Park, September 2003.

Colapietro, Vincent, "Confronting the Actuality of History," presented at the Pennsylvania State University, University Park, September 2003.

Fell, Joseph P., "John William Miller and Nietzsche's Nihilism," Roy Wood Sellars Lecture, presented at Bucknell University, October 1996.

Johnstone, Henry W., "Some Observations on J. W. Miller," presented to the American Philosophical Association, Central Division, Kansas City, MO, May 1994.

Smith, John E., "Reflections on Vincent Colapietro's *Fateful Shapes of Human Freedom: John William Miller and the Crises of Modernity*," presented at the Pennsylvania State University, University Park, September 2003.

About the Editors

Joseph P. Fell is J. H. Harris Professor of Philosophy, emeritus, at Bucknell University. He is the author of *Emotion in the Thought of Sartre* (1965) and *Heidegger and Sartre: An Essay on Being and Place* (1979), and the editor of *The Philosophy of John William Miller* (1990).

Vincent Colapietro is professor of philosophy at Pennsylvania State University. He is the author of *Peirce's Approach to the Self: A Semiotic Perspective on Human Subjectivity* (1989) and *Fateful Shapes of Human Freedom: John William Miller and the Crises of Modernity* (1993).

Michael J. McGandy, Ph.D., is the author of *The Active Life: Miller's Metaphysics of Democracy* (2005), as well as journal articles on Miller's philosophy. He is an independent scholar.

On the Cover

"In the caves of the Pyrenees there are drawings of a herd of deer. A friend of mine, a lawyer, who saw them, gave me a quiet but stirring account of his visit. What was it that he saw? Deer? A pretty picture? That would not have prompted his words or his manner. Nor was he commenting on the degree of intelligence of Neanderthal man. It was, rather, that in those caves something was revealed. Here was a voice, an utterance, an announcement, not of any matter of fact, but of the presence of men and objects. Those drawings were a voice.

"Out of the silence a voice, out of the darkness a light. In the story of chaos from which the world emerged it was the generation of particulars—earth, sky, vegetation—that brought content and form. I think my friend felt that he was a spectator of the creation. On what other basis could one find anything awesome in those drawings? The maker, the poet, saw himself in telling what he saw. He is not represented there, but presented."

—*In Defense of the Psychological*, pp. 103–4

Miller's history of philosophy begins well before Thales, in primitive spiritualism. In Ice-Age cave paintings he finds early signs and symbols of the human act of articulating a world. Miller sees it as intellectually and morally necessary to challenge all forms of dogmatism, skepticism, and nihilism that discount this constitutive efficacy of human agency and the democratic environment that seeks to maintain it. The philosophical task begins with recognizing history as the ongoing work of these world-articulating acts and of their responsible revision—the work of all post-primitive generations—by criticism.

Index